S0-EMD-085

1994

CALIFORNIA ENVIRONMENTAL COMPLIANCE HANDBOOK

Published by

California Chamber of Commerce

By
James T. Dufour, J.D., C.I.H., R.E.A.

 recycled paper

 PRINTED WITH SOY INK

Published by
California Chamber of Commerce
P.O. Box 1736
Sacramento, CA 95812-1736

Copyright © 1993 by the California Chamber of Commerce

All rights reserved. Not to be reproduced in any form without written permission from the publisher.

ISBN 1-878630-47-4

5   4   3   2   1

The information compiled in this handbook is being provided by the California Chamber of Commerce as a service to the business community. Although every effort has been made to ensure the accuracy and sufficiency of this information, the California Chamber of Commerce and the author, contributors and reviewers of this publication cannot be responsible for any errors and omissions, nor any agency's interpretations, applications and changes of regulations described herein.

This publication is designed to provide accurate and authoritative information in a highly summarized manner with regard to the subject matter covered. It is sold with the understanding that the publisher and others associated with this publication are not engaged in rendering legal, technical or other professional service. If legal and other expert assistance is required, the services of competent professionals should be sought.

This publication is available from:

California Chamber of Commerce
P.O. Box 1736
Sacramento, CA 95812-1736
(916) 444-6670

Sections of *Barclays Official California Code of Regulations* contained in this publication are reprinted under limited license from Barclays Law Publishers. Copyright © 1993 by Barclays Law Publishers. All rights reserved.

All organization charts and directories have been updated. In addition, look for significant changes in the following chapters:

Chapter 4

Hazardous Materials and Community Right-to-Know
New section on lubricating oil exemption for convenience stores, small auto parts stores and even small auto service outlets; reduces recordkeeping.

Chapter 6

Wastewater Management
New stormwater runoff regulation. The State Water Resources Control Board implements federal regulations for stormwater pollution program with statewide general permit. Board mandates stormwater pollution prevention plan and "Notices of Intent" for industrial facilities and construction sites.

Chapter 7

Underground and Aboveground Tank Storage of Hazardous Substances
Increased underground and aboveground tank storage of hazardous substances facility fee.

Chapter 8

Hazardous Waste Management
- Hazardous Waste Treatment Permitting Reform Act of 1992 (AB 1772) sets forth an April 1, 1993 deadline which establishes tier permitting for on-site treatment of any amount of hazardous waste.
- New compliance requirements for each tier of treatment. Consequences of non-compliance are quite serious: penalties and back fees.
- Amended hazardous waste management - 1992 Hazardous Waste Source Reduction for Generators statute (SB 14) amended to include generators of more than 5,000 kilograms per year (about 11,000 pounds).

Chapter 11

Proposition 65
Current list of chemicals subject to Proposition 65, the Safe Drinking Water and Toxics Enforcement Act.

Chapter 12

Regulated Products, Activities, Professions and Business Practices
- New regulations established by the Clean Air Act to minimize emissions of chlorofluorocarbons (CFCs) and other so-called ozone-depleting substances.
- Chart of ozone-depleting substances and phaseout deadlines; instructions for labeling.
- Alternative substances to replace CFCs for refrigerant manufacturers, distributors, paint manufacturers and other businesses.
- Phaseout of methyl bromide affects agricultural industry in California. Repair service and disposal of appliances also is affected.

Environmental Library

California Environmental Compliance Handbook

Overall guide to California's unique and far-reaching environmental programs. Gives an overview of more than 20 of the most significant environmental programs, along with the essential steps to take for compliance. Provides a thumbnail sketch of numerous additional, but less frequently encountered federal, state and local regulations that have an impact on business and local public facilities. Planning a new facility? The guide summarizes the regulations and environmental permits you will need. In charge of environmental regulations for an existing facility or products? The guide is your checklist and roadmap through California's maze of environmental regulations.

Proposition 65 Compliance

This complex and confusing initiative imposes many requirements on businesses that use or distribute chemicals and products which contain ingredients known to the state to cause cancer or reproductive toxicity. More than 300 substances are subject to the law. The proposition provides for government prosecutions, as well as "bounty hunter" rewards for informants and citizen plaintiffs. The handbook is your best explanation of the law and how to comply.

Community Right-to-Know (Handling Hazardous Materials)

For firms that store, sell or use any of thousands of common materials or chemicals that are regulated by local governments under the concept of community right-to-know. Step-by-step instructions explain how to: determine if your firm handles hazardous materials, qualify for business plan exemptions, immediately report releases and how to develop a business plan in five easy steps.

Hazardous Waste Management

For any business that uses or handles chemicals. Tells how to determine if your business generates hazardous waste, what permits are needed, how to manage hazardous waste, how to ship and dispose of waste and how to determine where permits can be required for certain hazardous waste activities. This handbook explains how to comply with this complicated and stringently enforced area of environmental law.

Environmental Organizer

This compliance tool organizes your many environmental compliance programs and recordkeeping to demonstrate compliance. Divider sections in the *Environmental Organizer* provide thumbnail descriptions of each environmental program and how to comply, with references to the companion handbooks for details.

California Regwatch

A monthly newsletter to alert you to new environmental and Cal/OSHA regulations. It's your early warning system with concise news about proposed and enacted regulations. One-year subscription free with purchase of *Environmental Library*. Free to California Chamber members. Cannot be purchased.

Cal/OSHA Kit

Cal/OSHA Handbook

The *Cal/OSHA Handbook* is written for businesspeople who aren't safety experts. It tells how to find the regulations which apply to your firm. Then it gives step-by-step instructions to satisfy the regulations that apply to every firm, and also the most costly rules that apply to most industries. Know what to do when the inspector arrives, your rights, when to appeal a citation and how to do it.

SB 198 Handbook

SB 198 requires every employer to have a formal, written injury and illness prevention program. The *SB 198 Handbook* was written with the premise that most employers can comply on a do-it-yourself basis. It contains legal requirements, sample plans to follow for various industries, fill-in-the-blank forms and step-by-step instructions.

Hazard Communication Handbook

Hazard communication standards apply to every firm where employees may be exposed to chemicals. Generally, if you receive an MSDS (Material Safety Data Sheet) from a supplier for a product used in your facility, then you need a hazard communication program. The *Hazard Communication Handbook* gives clear guidelines on how to write your own program.

Cal/OSHA Organizer

The *Organizer* is a guide for the safety novice to comply with Cal/OSHA. Follow the steps in the *Organizer* and compile the necessary compliance documentation. It refers to sections in the three companion handbooks where you'll get clear, detailed instructions on what you need to do, and cookbook-like steps on how to do it. Then file your safety programs and records right in the *Organizer.*

Cal/OSHA Tools

Cal/OSHA: Beyond the Basics

This new book covers the hottest and newest Cal/OSHA regulations: bloodborne pathogens • process safety management • lead • HAZWOPER • asbestos • confined spaces • cadmium • formaldehyde • respiratory protection. Includes overview of the latest trends and developments and what they really mean to employers. A step-by-step guide on how to comply with many new regulations, complete with sample plans and procedures. Get a preview of draft regulations with a major impact on your business: tuberculosis • ergonomics • smoking in the workplace • Federal OSHA reform • SB 198 changes.

SB 198 Software

The California Chamber's *SB 198 Software* is made to be used with our *SB 198 Handbook.* It helps you write your SB 198 program and much more. The software is an ongoing recordkeeping system that will save you tremendous amounts of time. Organizes your records of training, accidents and injuries. Allows you to "batch" in updates instead of making single, time-consuming entries. Reminds you to do inspections and training. (IBM PC-AT compatible — *not* XT; 3.5" or 5.25" diskette)

SB 198 Video Safety Set

Two-tape set makes it easy for you to initially train employees and managers about your injury/illness prevention program then review important information annually. One video lets your employees know safety is their responsibility and very important to your company. It offers commonsense instruction about safe work procedures (12 minutes). The second video tells your supervisors and managers how other companies are making their safety programs work and emphasizes the importance of training, hazard identification and inspections (16 minutes). Employee training video also available in Spanish.

Hazard Communication Training

Comply with Cal/OSHA's second most-cited regulation — hazard communication. This standard requires that the employer have a written hazard communication plan, identify and label all chemicals and train employees by communicating information on Material Safety Data Sheets (MSDSs). This video emphasizes proper procedures to store and handle chemicals, reading an MSDS, and maintaining a workplace free from chemical hazards (13 minutes).

Safety Training Video Series

A complete video safety training program at an incredibly low price. You get 12 separate training sessions, each with a quality 8-17 minute video. A quiz at the end of each video keeps employees involved, increases retention and documents your training for Cal/OSHA. Videos will open discussion to unique safety issues at your company. The helpful leader's guide makes your role as safety instructor easy. The program comes on two cassettes, each with six training sessions:

Cassette #1, *Safety for All Employers,* covers the most important safety topics common to every business: reporting to work • back injury prevention • office safety • fire prevention • ergonomics • bloodborne pathogens.

Cassette #2, *Safety for Industrial Employers,* is for the more industrial workplaces with machinery and chemicals: personal protective equipment • electrical safety • flammables/combustibles • machine guarding — lockout/tagout • material handling equipment • the environment.

James T. Dufour, author and editor of the California Chamber's Environmental Compliance Library, as well as the workplace safety and Cal/OSHA compliance guides, is an environmental attorney, certified industrial hygienist and registered environmental assessor. His business interests include a Sacramento-based environmental, agricultural and government relations law practice, Dufour & Associates, and a consulting firm: Dufour Environmental and Resource Management. The firm provides services to businesses and association clients in Cal/OSHA compliance and citation appeals, as well as virtually all other areas of environmental and hazardous materials laws and regulations.

Dufour has more than 20 years of experience in government and chemical industry regulatory compliance and consulting in the areas of environmental, OSHA, labor law and government relations. He has served as the California Chamber's special counsel for occupational safety and health and hazardous materials. Dufour holds a B.S. and M.S. in public health from the University of Michigan and a J.D. in labor and administrative law from the University of Tennessee.

Have a Question?

Call the California Chamber of Commerce, (916) 444-6670. The California Chamber is here to help your business succeed and operate efficiently.

Is there any charge for answering my question?

No. The **HELPLINE** is one of several free services for companies that are members of the California Chamber.

What if my company is not currently a member of the California Chamber?

Call us anyway. Tell us you just bought a book and you have a question. We appreciate your business, so we'll be happy to answer your question so you can see why thousands of businesses — large and small — all across California invest in membership with the California Chamber.

When you join the California Chamber, you will receive the toll-free 800 telephone number and a brochure introducing you to the **HELPLINE** staff.

HELPLINE assistance provides an explanation and clarification of laws and regulations confronting business (not legal advice for specific situations).

Thank you for this opportunity to be of service.

California Chamber of Commerce
P.O. Box 1736
Sacramento, CA 95812-1736
(916) 444-6670

How to Use
the Environmental Compliance Handbook —
What Requirements Apply to My Facility

One of the most difficult tasks facing a facility owner or operator and the person designated as responsible for complying with environmental laws and regulations is understanding how such requirements are organized, which government agency enforces them, and how to locate applicable laws and regulations. The new California Environmental Protection Agency (Cal/EPA), will strive for better coordination and possibly some streamlining of state requirements, but many observers believe it will remain a problem for facilities in the state to determine what are the environmental requirements with which they must comply.

This *California Environmental Compliance Handbook* will answer this question for all types of facilities, whether public or private, large or small, existing or new. The *Handbook* also attempts to provide the information in the most easy-to-understand format possible while presenting sufficient information to be of help to readers.

There are thousands of pages of laws and regulations that prescribe environmental requirements. This *Handbook* will explain the basic requirements and offer compliance advice in about 200 pages. Some regulatory programs covered will apply to nearly all facilities, others may cover only certain facilities. Readers are urged to use the following four approaches to determine what general area applies to their facility and where to find the information in the *Handbook*. To further help the reader determine what applies to his/her facility, each substantive chapter begins with a summary of what subjects the chapter covers and how they apply.

Approaches to Determining What Requirements Apply to a Facility

◆   **Approach One: Subject.** Review the list of topics presented in Figure 1-1. Refer to the chapters identified.

◆   **Approach Two: Existing Facilities.** Review existing facility checklist in Figure 1-2 to identify requirements that apply to an operating facility. Refer to the chapters identified.

◆   **Approach Three: New or Planned Facilities.** Review the checklist in Figure 1-3 to identify requirements that the new facility needs to consider, possibly as a condition of occupancy. Refer to the chapters identified.

◆   **Approach Four: Product Regulations.** Review the checklist in Figure 1-4 to identify product and activity regulations or limitations on how the environmental impact of a product may be described. Refer to the chapters identified.

These approaches are discussed in more detail below and will provide readers with a quick way to find the information they need in the *Handbook*.

Each chapter of the *Handbook* discusses one subject. Chapter 2 describes the organization of California's environmental programs. Chapter 3 addresses new facilities. Chapters 4 through 10 each describe one regulatory program. Chapters 11 and 12 cover additional regulatory programs governing public warnings and product and activity regulations. Chapters are divided into sections that describe in more detail what is required and what a facility must do to comply. The *Handbook* provides thorough references to the official codes and regulation reporters for all laws and regulations covered. Chapter 1 identifies requirements that are *not* covered within the scope of this guide and the reason the area was excluded. Chapter 1 also describes how to obtain copies of relevant laws and regulations. Each chapter's appendices are designed to further help readers to identify important references and other information, but are not a complete copy of the relevant material, given the summary nature of this *Handbook*.

Warning: Due to the limited scope of this *Handbook,* it cannot cover in detail every aspect of the laws and regulations it describes, nor can it provide complete copies of laws and regulations. Furthermore, be-cause laws and regulations are subject to change, information in the *Handbook* may need to be verified for the most current requirements. Readers are urged to review the most current laws and regulations, and consult with competent environmental counsel and agency officials in making compliance decisions.

Determining Which Environmental Requirements Apply

Bars on the edge of the appropriate pages will help readers determine which environmental require-ments apply to their operations and therefore which chapters of this *Handbook* to review. Figures 1-1, 1-2, 1-3 and 1-4 outline alternative methods of approaching the information in this handbook. Once the reader has identified the subject of interest, the bar on the page will refer the reader to the relevant chapter. Introductory information in each chapter will further help the reader get started.

The approaches are geared for different types of readers as follows:

◆ **Approach One: By Subject (Figure 1-1).**

This method is designed for the reader who has a sufficient understanding of environmental regulatory programs to be able to identify by name the programs of interest. This approach is similar to using a table of contents to locate relevant information.

◆ **Approach Two: By Reviewing Existing Facility Operations (Figure 1-2).**

This method is designed for the reader who understands the operation of his/her facility but does not have sufficient knowledge of environmental program organization to identify hose that apply to the facility. This approach is similar to using an index to locate relevant information.

◆ **Approach Three: By Reviewing New or Planned Facilities (Figure 1-3).**

This method will help managers who are planning new facilities or operations to identify applicable environmental requirements.

Figure 1-1
Environmental Requirements: By Subject
(Bars are in same location as bars on applicable chapters.)

Hazardous materials handling/community right-to-know, reporting of releases.	Chapter 4
Air pollution or emissions from stationary sources, air permits required, toxic or hazardous air contaminants emitted: requirements and reports.	Chapter 5
Wastewater discharges to surface water, land and sewer systems. Waste discharges into regulated facilities: surface impoundments, injection wells. Stormwater runoff. Proposition 65 regulated discharges.	Chapter 6
Tank storage of hazardous substances, underground and above ground.	Chapter 7
Hazardous waste management, including hazardous waste determinations, generator requirements for storage and waste minimization. Hazardous waste transportation and disposal requirements. Permit requirements for on-site storage and treatment.	Chapter 8
Medical waste management, including infectious wastes, biological cultures, biohazardous wastes.	Chapter 9
Solid waste management and recycling, including generator requirements and community and disposal facility requirements.	Chapter 10
Proposition 65, warnings and notifications for chemicals known to the state to cause cancer or reproductive toxicity and asbestos-containing building materials.	Chapter 11
Products and activities subject to specific California environmental requirements, including pesticides, fertilizers and products for which environmental claims and advertising are regulated. Ozone-depleting chemical labeling also is covered.	Chapter 12

◆ **Approach Four: By Reviewing a List of Regulated Products and Activities. (Figure 1-4).**

This method relates to the information in Chapters 11 and 12. These two chapters organize the major regulatory programs that mandate hazard warnings for products or facilities or which regulate certain types of products, businesses or professions within the scope of environmental law.

Finding the Responsible Agency and Relevant Law/Regulation

The remaining objective of this *Handbook* is to help those responsible for environmental compliance management to identify agencies responsible for implementing and enforcing regulatory programs and to locate the relevant laws and regulations in each area. Each chapter will guide the reader through the regulatory requirement and refer to applicable laws and regulations. In most cases, users of this *Guide* are urged to obtain a copy of the statutes and regulatory information that apply to the facility. Details on laws and regulations, aside from fundamental provisions and key examples, are outside the scope and space limitations of the *Handbook*.

Chapter 2 identifies the agencies responsible for each regulatory area and the statutes and regulations that apply.

List of Lists to Identify Regulated Chemicals

To help regulated facilities identify how certain environmental programs apply, the state Secretary of Environmental Affairs Office — now incorporated into the California Environmental Protection Agency — published a chemical "List of Lists" that alphabetically lists chemicals and indicates the regulatory program to which each is subject. This list appears in Exhibit B in its most current version as of the date of publication of this handbook. It indicates the applicability of the following regulatory programs discussed in this guide:

- Acutely hazardous materials (Chapter 4).
- Toxic chemicals subject to EPCRA Section 313 (Chapter 4).
- Toxic air contaminants (Chapter 5).
- Chemicals subject to Air Toxics Hot Spots Emissions inventory (Chapter 5).
- Chemicals subject to Proposition 65: known to cause cancer or reproductive toxicity (Chapters 6 and 11).

Use of the List of Lists may provide an easy guide to identify chemicals subject to some of the regulatory programs discussed in this guide. However, if a facility determines that it handles a "regulated substance," it must further determine the applicable volume thresholds and other aspects of the program to make an authoritative determination of how it is regulated.

Figure 1-2
Environmental Requirements: Review for Existing Facility Operations
(Bars are in same location as bars on applicable chapters.)

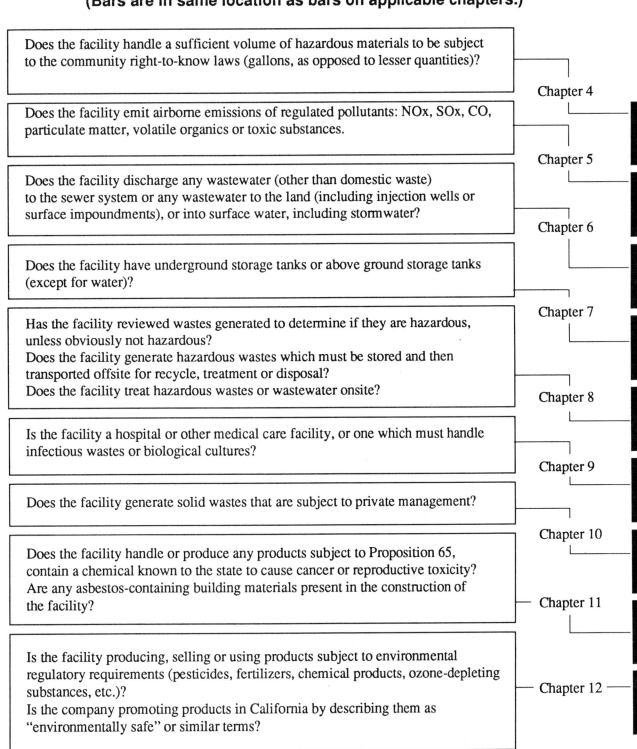

Does the facility handle a sufficient volume of hazardous materials to be subject to the community right-to-know laws (gallons, as opposed to lesser quantities)?

Chapter 4

Does the facility emit airborne emissions of regulated pollutants: NOx, SOx, CO, particulate matter, volatile organics or toxic substances.

Chapter 5

Does the facility discharge any wastewater (other than domestic waste) to the sewer system or any wastewater to the land (including injection wells or surface impoundments), or into surface water, including stormwater?

Chapter 6

Does the facility have underground storage tanks or above ground storage tanks (except for water)?

Chapter 7

Has the facility reviewed wastes generated to determine if they are hazardous, unless obviously not hazardous?
Does the facility generate hazardous wastes which must be stored and then transported offsite for recycle, treatment or disposal?
Does the facility treat hazardous wastes or wastewater onsite?

Chapter 8

Is the facility a hospital or other medical care facility, or one which must handle infectious wastes or biological cultures?

Chapter 9

Does the facility generate solid wastes that are subject to private management?

Chapter 10

Does the facility handle or produce any products subject to Proposition 65, contain a chemical known to the state to cause cancer or reproductive toxicity?
Are any asbestos-containing building materials present in the construction of the facility?

Chapter 11

Is the facility producing, selling or using products subject to environmental regulatory requirements (pesticides, fertilizers, chemical products, ozone-depleting substances, etc.)?
Is the company promoting products in California by describing them as "environmentally safe" or similar terms?

Chapter 12

Laws and Regulations Not Included in the Handbook

Readers should be aware that the subject of environmental law is extremely broad and viewed by many to include virtually all areas of natural resource protection, planning and development. However, this guide is based on a more limited perspective of environmental law: those regulatory provisions that generally apply to facility operators and product manufacturers and distributors. Therefore, the brief discussion of new facility siting presented in Chapter 3 will be the sole reference to the resource protection aspects of environmental law. Readers are urged to consult other sources of information for a broader presentation of environmental law if this is of interest. In addition, this guide does not present information on Cal/OSHA compliance, which focuses on occupational safety and health for workers. For further information on Cal/OSHA requirements and compliance, readers should consult the following California Chamber publications:

- *Cal/OSHA Handbook.*
- *Cal/OSHA: Beyond the Basics.*
- *SB 198: Injury and Illness Prevention Program Handbook.*
- *Hazard Communication Handbook.*
- *Cal/OSHA Organizer.*

These publications are available from:

California Chamber of Commerce
P.O. Box 1736
Sacramento, CA 95812-1736
1-800-331-8877

Figure 1-3
Environmental Requirements: Review of New or Planned Facilities
(Bars are in same location as bars on applicable chapters.)

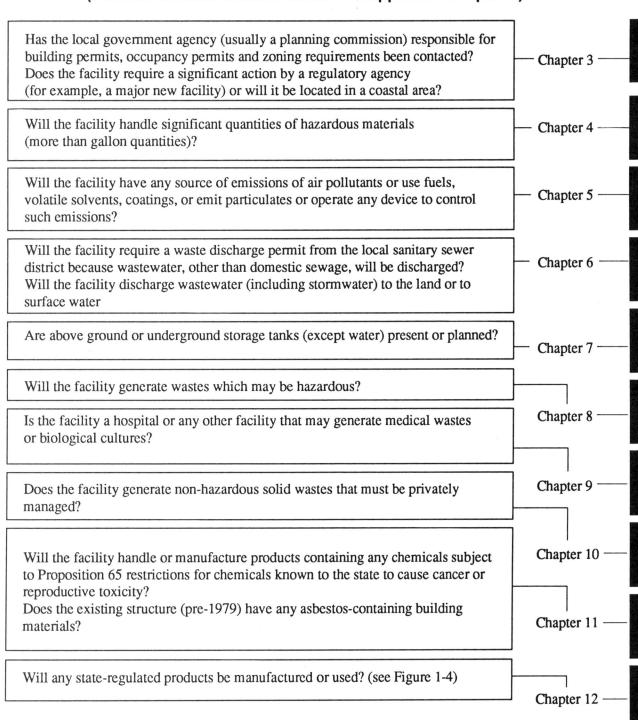

Has the local government agency (usually a planning commission) responsible for building permits, occupancy permits and zoning requirements been contacted? Does the facility require a significant action by a regulatory agency (for example, a major new facility) or will it be located in a coastal area? — Chapter 3

Will the facility handle significant quantities of hazardous materials (more than gallon quantities)? — Chapter 4

Will the facility have any source of emissions of air pollutants or use fuels, volatile solvents, coatings, or emit particulates or operate any device to control such emissions? — Chapter 5

Will the facility require a waste discharge permit from the local sanitary sewer district because wastewater, other than domestic sewage, will be discharged? Will the facility discharge wastewater (including stormwater) to the land or to surface water — Chapter 6

Are above ground or underground storage tanks (except water) present or planned? — Chapter 7

Will the facility generate wastes which may be hazardous?

Is the facility a hospital or any other facility that may generate medical wastes or biological cultures? — Chapter 8

Does the facility generate non-hazardous solid wastes that must be privately managed? — Chapter 9

Will the facility handle or manufacture products containing any chemicals subject to Proposition 65 restrictions for chemicals known to the state to cause cancer or reproductive toxicity? — Chapter 10
Does the existing structure (pre-1979) have any asbestos-containing building materials? — Chapter 11

Will any state-regulated products be manufactured or used? (see Figure 1-4) — Chapter 12

Figure 1-4
Environmental Requirements: Review of Products, Facilities and Activities Subject to Specific Regulations Under California Law
(Bars are in same location as bars on applicable chapters.)

Chemicals or products with ingredients "known to the state to cause cancer or reproductive toxicity" are subject to the warning provision of Proposition 65.

Facilities that are known to contain asbestos-containing building materials are subject to asbestos notices to building occupants.

Chapter 11

Certain types of products and businesses are subject to strict environmental regulations:
- Chemical manufacture and importation.
- Chemical (hazardous substances) distribution.
- Pesticide manufacturing and distribution.
- Manufacture and distribution of fertilizer materials.
- Radiation sources and producing equipment.
- Noise-producing activities and products.
- Products which contain or are manufactured with ozone-depleting substances.

Certain professions are regulated under California environmental laws:
- Registered environmental assessors and environmental health specialists.
- Underground storage tank integrity testers.
- Underground storage tank consultants and contractors.
- Asbestos abatement contractors and consultants.
- Registered geologists.
- Environmental laboratories.

Certain types of business practices are deemed unlawful by California environmental laws:
- Concealing serious dangers in products or business practices — corporate criminal liability.
- Unfair business practices liability.
- Misrepresenting a product as being "environmentally safe."

Chapter 12

Organization of California Environmental Programs

This chapter presents an overview of how California's environmental programs are organized and how to identify and locate applicable laws and regulations.

A facility's environmental manager faces a three-part challenge: identifying the regulatory programs that apply to the operations; determining which federal, state or local agency implements and enforces requirements; and locating applicable laws and regulations. Chapter 1 included several checklists to help the environmental manager identify the broad regulatory areas that apply to a facility. Chapter 2 will discuss the governmental structure for managing environmental regulatory programs and the laws and regulations that apply to each program.

Readers should be aware that, until Governor Pete Wilson reorganized state government in 1991 to create the California Environmental Protection Agency (Cal/EPA) as an environmental superagency, responsibility for administering environmental programs was shared by a myriad of state agencies, as well as regional and local agencies. This chapter will discuss the former organization (which functionally will not change under Cal/EPA as currently conceived) and how these agencies will be organized in the future. It also will describe the roles of state agencies not incorporated into Cal/EPA, local agencies involved in environmental programs and, finally, federal EPA authority, which ranges from oversight of state implementation of federal law to exclusive enforcement authority, depending on the specific environmental program in question.

California Environmental Protection Agency (Cal/EPA)

A government reorganization plan designed by Governor Wilson established Cal/EPA on July 17, 1991. The Governor created Cal/EPA to provide better administration and policy coordination among the governmental agencies and departments responsible for the major environmental programs. These units of government had developed over a period of several decades to address problems in a single environmental media or activity (for example: air, water, solid waste, hazardous waste, etc.). Frequently, areas of jurisdiction overlapped and policies were inconsistent, even when a single subject was addressed by two agencies. Given the problems caused by the former system of independent agencies, the establishment of Cal/EPA holds the promise of improved coordination and more consistent polices.

Cal/EPA was modeled after the U.S. Environmental Protection Agency (EPA), in which a broad array of media-oriented regulatory programs are organized in a single management system. Figure 2-1 depicts the Cal/EPA organization resulting from the reorganization. As the chart indicates, most of the new agency is made up of existing environmental regulatory agencies whose functions and policies are not likely to change significantly in the near future. As of this printing, there are no specific statutory codes, nor a California code of regulations title devoted specifically to Cal/EPA.

Figure 2-1
California Environmental Protection Agency

James M. Strock
Secretary
(916) 445-3846

Office of the Secretary

Richard Green
Undersecretary
(916) 445-3846

Michael A. Kahoe
Assistant Secretary
(916) 324-8124

Charles M. Shulock
Assistant Secretary
Policy Development
(916) 324-8124

James Lee
Communications Director
(916) 324-9670

Integrated Waste Management Board

Michael R. Frost
Chairman
(916) 255-2170

Ralph E. Chandler
Executive Director
(916) 255-2182

Water Resources Control Board

John Caffrey
Chairman
(916) 657-2399

Walter Pettit
Executive Director
(916) 657-0941

Air Resources Board

Jananne Sharpless
Chairwoman
(916) 322-5840

James D. Boyd
Executive Officer
(916) 445-4383

Department of Toxic Substances Control

William Soo Hoo
Director
(916) 323-9723

Department of Pesticide Regulation

James W. Wells
Director
(916) 654-0551

Office of Environmental Health Hazard Assessment

Carol Henry, Ph.D., D.A.B.T.*
Director
(916) 324-7572
*Diplomat American Board of Toxicology

Environmental Agencies Organized Under Cal/EPA

Each agency described in this section has been engaged in environmental enforcement and it is not expected that the scope of responsibility nor general policies will change under Cal/EPA.

◆ Environmental Affairs Agency

This Cabinet-level environmental agency has been primarily involved in policy coordination. However, several specific programs are managed by this agency:

- Registration of environmental assessors [Chapter 12].

- Coordination of hazardous materials data and reports, including publication of the Chemical List of Lists [Chapter 4].

- State recipient of Federal EPA Toxic Chemical Release Reports (Form R) [Chapter 4].

Functions of the Environmental Affairs Agency have been absorbed into the Cal/EPA administration.

◆ Air Resources Board and Air Pollution Control Districts

The Air Resources Board is responsible for implementing federal Clean Air Act requirements in California, the state air pollution control program and oversight of the regional Air Quality Management Districts (AQMDs) and county Air Pollution Control Districts (APCDs). These state, regional and local agencies regulate sources of conventional air pollutants and emissions of specific toxic substances. [Chapter 5].

◆ Water Resources Control Board and Regional Water Quality Control Boards

The State Water Resources Control Board, formerly within the Resources Agency, is one of the major departments of Cal/EPA. Its function is to implement the state Water Quality Control Act and the federal Clean Water Act. The state board is specifically empowered to adopt the California Water Plan in conjunction with regional boards to establish a coordinated program of control, protection, conservation and use of water resources. The state board also promulgates regulations on water quality issues or sources of pollution (for example, underground storage tanks) and oversees the activities of regional water quality control boards.

Regional water quality control boards manage and protect water resources on a regional basis. Facilities that are permitted to discharge wastes, manage waste in regulated facilities or which are involved in pollution cleanup are subject to the jurisdiction of regional boards. [Chapter 6]

◆ Department of Toxic Substances Control (formerly Health and Welfare Agency: Department of Health Services Toxic Substances Control Division)

An important consequence of the reorganization was to shift major units from the Health and Welfare Agency to Cal/EPA. As organized before the creation of Cal/EPA, the office of the Health and Welfare Agency secretary was responsible for implementing Proposition 65 (rulemaking, but not enforcement);

units within the agency's Department of Health Services were responsible for drinking water standards, air toxics and epidemiology and other risk assessment functions; and the Toxic Substances Control Division was responsible for hazardous waste program implementation and enforcement. These functions have been transferred to two departments within Cal/EPA: the Department of Toxic Substances Control and its four regional offices responsible for the state's hazardous waste program; and the Office of Environmental Health Hazard Assessment, which will oversee a number of programs, including Proposition 65, reproductive and cancer hazard assessments, air toxics and epidemiology, hazard identification and risk assessment, hazardous waste toxicology and fish and bay estuary protection (from the Fish and Game Department). No boards are associated with the environmental program management of the former Health and Welfare Agency units transferred to Cal/EPA. Many of the regulated activities described in this *Guide* are managed by the units transferred from the Health Services Department, most importantly hazardous waste regulation and Proposition 65. [Chapters 8 and 11]

◆ Integrated Solid Waste Management Board

The former Solid Waste Management Board was reorganized by the Integrated Solid Waste Management Act of 1989. The act changed the board's name, but more importantly, gave the board authority for an aggressive solid waste reduction program to be implemented by cities and counties under board direction. It has been fully transferred to Cal/EPA.

Government agencies that administer the solid waste program and private firms in this business will be directly regulated by this department of Cal/EPA. Other facilities will be indirectly regulated to the extent that state and local agency policies to reduce solid waste operations and maximize recycling opportunities affect the facilities and product packager's practices. [Chapter 10]

◆ Department of Pesticide Regulation (formerly California Department of Food and Agriculture: Pesticide Registration and Enforcement)

Several environmental management functions involving pesticides have been transferred from the Department of Food and Agriculture to Cal/EPA, most notably pesticide registrations, agricultural worker health and safety, crop and environmental residue testing and food safety. These former Food and Agriculture Department units will comprise the Department of Pesticide Regulation within Cal/EPA. There is no statutory board associated with these activities. Pesticide manufacturers, applicators, growers, processors and consumers will be affected by the regulatory programs of this new Cal/EPA department. [Chapter 12]

State Environmental Agencies Not Incorporated into Cal/EPA

◆ Office of Emergency Services and the Chemical Emergency Response and Planning Commission

The state Office of Emergency Services (OES), responsible for guiding the statewide hazardous material community right-to-know programs directly, is administered by county and city fire and health departments. OES also provides staffing and administrative support for the Chemical Emergency Response and Planning Commission (CEPRC), which was created in response to mandates of the 1986 Federal Emergency Planning and Community Right-to-Know Act. Apparently, it was determined unfeasible to reorganize a portion of OES into Cal/EPA since chemical emergency response activities are closely linked to and dependent upon other OES emergency planning and response activities for earthquakes, floods and other disasters. However, it should be noted that the U.S. EPA is responsible for chemical emergency planning, which makes the current Cal/EPA organization inconsistent with the federal model in this area.

◆ Resources Agency: Department of Fish and Game; Department of Forestry

The various departments within the Resources Agency that administer natural resources programs like the Fish and Game Department and the Department of Forestry have not been incorporated into Cal/EPA.

Similarly, independent state and regional resource protection and planning agencies like the Coastal Commission and other regional planning agencies have not been incorporated into Cal/EPA in the current organization.

◆ California Occupational Safety and Health Administration (Cal/OSHA)

Cal/OSHA is located in the Department of Industrial Relations (DIR) and will not be included within Cal/EPA given Cal/OSHA's focus on workplace safety and the inter-relation of this area of regulation with labor relations and workers' compensation, the other administrative functions of DIR.

◆ Local Agencies with Environmental Responsibilities (County and City Planning, Solid Waste Management, Sanitation, Health and Fire Departments)

As readers will discover, a number of environmental regulatory programs are directly managed by local government. In most cases, there is supervision by state agencies, but a great deal of local autonomy.

Operators of facilities in a community or managers planning to locate a facility should recognize the extent of local government regulatory authority for environmental management. State law in many cases gives local agencies the right to adopt more stringent requirements than the state. Many of these areas will be identified in the applicable chapter of this guide. Facility operators will need to identify the agency responsible for a specific local regulatory area and ask that agency for the local requirements. These agencies are not part of Cal/EPA. Following are examples of the environmental programs typically administered by local agencies.

- **Facility location, building and occupancy permits.** City and county planning departments usually administer zoning compliance and new building construction or facility occupancy permits. Due to the requirement for hazardous materials and other environmental permits, these agencies precondition occupancy permits on satisfaction of environmental requirements. [Chapter 3]

- **Sewer system access and permit requirements.** Local government public works departments or city/county/regional sanitation districts have primary authority for sewer system access and permit requirements. These requirements usually include waste discharge limitations and, for certain types of industries, pretreatment requirements. Sanitation district regulatory programs and enforcement are supervised both by regional water quality control boards and U.S. EPA. [Chapter 6]

● · **Hazardous materials permits and handling requirements.** In response to state and federal laws that delegate to local governmental agencies the primary responsibility for hazardous materials handling requirements and community right-to-know emergency response planning, city and county fire and health departments regulate facilities subject to these laws. In most communities, it will be necessary to ascertain which agency exercises jurisdiction, contact the agency for information, and submit the required reports and permit applications. State law gives these local administering agencies broad authority to impose stricter requirements than the state for hazardous material reporting. In addition, most fire departments exercise independent jurisdiction based on the Uniform Fire Code, as amended by local government, for hazardous materials handling facilities and safety systems. Facilities may discover certain communities have more stringent requirements for hazardous materials handling and storage than other communities and in statewide rules, like Cal/OSHA standards.

● **Underground storage tanks.** Underground storage tanks for fuels and other hazardous materials are subject to requirements established by the local fire or health departments, usually by local ordinance. Although the local requirement must comply with regulations of the State Water Resources Control Board, there is considerable variation in implementation and requirements. Local administering agency programs are supervised by the state water board. [Chapter 7]

● **Hazardous waste and medical waste management.** Local agencies, usually county health departments and sanitation districts, also may regulate hazardous wastes and medical wastes based on delegation of responsibility from Cal/EPA. Such agencies usually charge annual permit fees to support the costs of the program.

◆ Enforcement

Each of the state and local agencies discussed in this chapter may enforce compliance with its requirements by imposing administrative civil penalties on violators and issuing orders to take certain actions. In cases where such sanctions are not effective in obtaining compliance or where violations are particularly serious, the state or local agency can refer cases for prosecution to the attorney general or county district attorneys and city attorneys. They also may immediately initiate a prosecution in a serious case or in matters where state law authorizes such enforcement (for example, Proposition 65).

Federal Environmental Protection Agency

The EPA is involved, to a substantial extent, in California environmental regulatory programs. In most cases, this role is one of supervising or approving state and local programs designed to implement federal laws. However, in some situations, EPA has primary implementation and enforcement authority (no comparable state program), in others, the EPA may independently prosecute violations of federal law, notwithstanding the fact that a state agency is prosecuting the same offense under state law or has taken no action. These cases are called "over filings" and are often unexpected by the offending facilities on the bases that they are adequately regulated by state and local agencies. The areas of EPA's responsibilities in California include the following:

◆ **Primary Authority**

- Hazardous materials - Toxic Chemical Release Reports (EPCRA §313) .... Chapter 4

- Wastewater discharges which threaten underground water sources
(toxic injection wells) .... Chapter 6

- Hazardous waste management facility federal permits .... Chapter 8

- Federally-designated hazardous waste site cleanups .... Chapter 8

- Pesticide registration .... Chapter 12

◆ **Oversight Authority**

- Hazardous materials community right-to-know programs .... Chapter 4

- Compliance with federal Clean Air Act requirements .... Chapter 5

- Wastewater discharge permits to navigable waters .... Chapter 6

- Industrial waste discharges to sewer systems subject to categorical
pretreatment standards and hazardous waste requirements .... Chapter 6

- Underground storage tank compliance with federal regulations .... Chapter 7

- Solid waste landfill facility compliance with federal regulations .... Chapter 10

Understanding the agency with authority for a particular regulatory program is important to finding the laws and regulations which apply.

Sources of Laws and Regulations in Environmental Regulatory Programs

To effectively analyze regulatory requirements and make informed judgments concerning compliance, it will be necessary in many cases to locate and obtain copies of the laws and regulations which apply. The sources of laws and regulations that govern environmental regulation in California are:

◆ **Federal Laws and Regulations**

- Federal laws are codified in the U.S. Code (U.S.C.) and are enacted by Congress. Environmental laws discussed in this *Guide* appear in the following titles of the U.S. Code:

  ✔ Title 7, Section 136, et seq. - Pesticide Law.
  ✔ Title 15, Section 2601, et seq. - Toxic Substances Control Act.
  ✔ Title 33, Section 7251, et seq. - Clean Water Act.
  ✔ Title 42, Section 6901, et seq. - Hazardous and Solid Waste Law.
  ✔ Title 42, Section 6991, et seq. - Underground Storage Tanks.

- ✔ Title 42, Section 300, et seq. - Safe Drinking Water.
- ✔ Title 42, Section 7401, et seq. - Clean Air Act.
- ✔ Title 49, Section 1801, et seq. - Hazardous Materials Transportation.

- Federal regulations are codified in the Code of Federal Regulations (CFR):
  - ✔ Title 40, CFR - EPA Regulations

◆ **State Laws and Regulations**

- State laws are codified in the California Code, where they are organized by subject titles. The following codes are relevant to environmental regulation:

  - ✔ *Health and Safety Code:* Covers hazardous wastes, hazardous materials, medical wastes, stationary sources of air pollution, etc.

  - ✔ *Water Code:* Covers programs of the State Water Resources Control Board.

  - ✔ *Government Code* and *Natural Resources Code*: Covers the program of the Integrated Solid Waste Management Board and resource recovery programs of the Department of Conservation.

  - ✔ *Food and Agriculture Code:* Covers the pesticide registration and enforcement procedures of the California Department of Food and Agriculture.

- State regulations are codified into the California Code of Regulations under 26 titles. The titles relevant to environmental regulation are:

  - ✔ Title 3 - Food and Agriculture.

  - ✔ Title 14 - Natural Resources, Department of Fish and Game, Coastal Commission, Waste Management Board and Department of Conservation.

  - ✔ Title 17 - Public Health, Air Resources Board.

  - ✔ Title 19 - Public Safety (includes OES regulations on hazardous materials).

  - ✔ Title 22 - Division 4, Environmental Health, includes Department of Health Services, Health and Welfare Agency and Proposition 65 regulations.

  - ✔ Title 23 - Waters. Regulations of the State Water Resources Control Board.

  - ✔ Title 26 - Toxics. A reprinting of most of the previous titles as a means of putting environmental regulations into a single convenient title.

How to Obtain Copies of Laws and Regulations

Regulated facilities should be familiar with the source and content of the regulations with which they must comply. Therefore, facilities should obtain copies of relevant laws and regulations. In many cases, the regulatory agency will provide a copy free or for a small charge. This saves the time and potential errors in attempting to obtain these references from less direct sources. However, regulated parties should be aware of these private sources of laws and regulations if they are affected by a variety of requirements and need to monitor developments in this rapidly changing field.

◆ **Source of Federal Laws and Regulations**

● U.S.Code (U.S.C.) available in separate titles from:

U.S. Government Book Store
Superintendent of Documents
450 Golden Gate Avenue
San Francisco, CA 94102
(415) 252-5334

Cost: $1,454, individual volumes are available
Updated: Annually

● Code of Federal Regulations (CFR) available in separate titles/volumes from:

U.S. Government Book Store
Superintendent of Documents
450 Golden Gate Avenue
San Francisco, CA 94102
(415) 252-5334

Cost: $620; each separate volume is about $20 (40 CFR has 13 volumes).
Updated: Annually

● *Current Update* of Federal Regulations (Federal Register) available from:

U.S. Government Book Store
Superintendent of Documents
450 Golden Gate Avenue
San Francisco, CA 94102
(415) 252-5334

Cost: $340
Updated: Every Working Day

◆ Source of State Laws and Regulations

- California Codes (Statutes) available in separate titles/volumes from:

  West Publishing Company
  P.O. Box 64833
  St. Paul, MN 55164-1804
  1-800-328-9352

  Cost: $1,648 (entire set); separate titles available.
  Updated: Annually

- California Code of Regulations (basic code) available in separate titles
  and portions thereof from:

  Barclays Law Publishers
  P.O. Box 3066
  South San Francisco, CA 94083
  (415) 244 - 6611

  Cost: $2,175 - complete set; $2,275 - update service only, separate titles available.
  Updated: Periodically, as Necessary
  See Exhibit A for Barclays order form.

- Current Update of State Regulations *(California Regulatory Notice Register)* available
  from:

  Office of State Printing
  344 N. 7th Street
  Sacramento, CA 95814
  (916) 322-0472

  Cost: $162 **(annual subscription)**
  Updated: Weekly

◆ Source of Local Government Ordinances/Codes

Available upon request from local government agencies. There may be a charge.

The remaining chapters of this *Handbook* describe in more detail the substance of the requirements and what's needed to comply, as well as identifying the relevant laws and regulations.

Facility Siting and Environmental Considerations

Summary and Applicability

This chapter summarizes the basic environmental considerations associated with siting a new facility or making major modifications to an existing facility.

- Government approval issues.
- Zoning and community planning.
- Sanitation (sewer) district requirements.
- Hazardous materials and air pollution permits.
- Environmental impact issues for major facilities or sensitive areas.

It provides the initial insight a manager needs to address site-specific issues during location selection and planning for a new facility.

Selecting a location for a facility is always a serious matter; the decision must weigh important factors such as availability of a skilled workforce, transportation, proximity to suppliers and markets, as well as price for real property and leased space. For a facility subject to any of the environmental regulatory programs described in this *Handbook,* the question of how they are administered will have a dramatic impact on the facility's selection of a community and a location. This chapter presents basic information on facility siting and approval, with emphasis on how environmental regulations interface with this process.

Facility Siting Issues: Government Approval Process

As mentioned above, the facility location usually will be based on practical consideration of economic and human factors. Once a community is selected — or several are chosen for comparative purposes — information on planning a facility start-up in the community must be obtained from the appropriate local authority. This usually means a county agency for unincorporated areas, or a city agency for property within the city limits. The following discussion is based on Sacramento County, which is typical of the various agencies and steps a manager of a proposed facility must consider when obtaining approval to locate and operate in a community.

Zoning and Community General Plans

Zoning is a well-established exercise of the police power of government to both assure the safety, health and comfort of citizens, and plan development in a desired manner in the interest of public welfare. The concept of zoning means that a proposed use of property must conform with the uses established in a zoning plan that has been adopted as an ordinance. Once so devised and approved by the governing body, the zoning ordinance specifies for each zone or district a set of uses by right and a second set of uses by permit. For example, Sacramento County has established the following zoning classifications for commercial and industrial use:

- Permanent Agricultural Zones.

- Agricultural/Residential Zones.

- Interim Agricultural Zones.

- Reserve Land Use Zones:
  ✔ Urban Reserve (UR).
  ✔ Industrial Reserve (IR).

- Recreation Zones.

- Residential Zones.

- Commercial Zones:
  ✔ Business and Professional Zone (BP).
  ✔ Shopping Center Zone (SC).
  ✔ Limited Commercial Zone (LC).
  ✔ General Commercial Zone (GC).
  ✔ Auto Commercial Zone (AC).
  ✔ Travel Commercial Zone (TC).
  ✔ Recreation Zone. (C-O).

- Industrial Zones:
  ✔ Light Industrial (M-1).
  ✔ Heavy Industrial (M-2).
  ✔ Industrial Office Park (MP).

- Combining Land Use Zones.

If the proposed use of property is not consistent with the zoning ordinances, or is designated as a use granted by permit, the applicant for development must apply for a variance or a conditional use permit.

◆ Variances

These usually are used to grant relief in hardship cases where the power is discretionary. A variance balances the governing body's interest in protecting public welfare by strictly enforcing the zoning ordinance versus the individual hardship. As should be apparent, variances will be difficult to obtain unless compelling interests are involved.

◆ Conditional Use Permits

Conditional use permits (CUPs) are used routinely to authorize flexibility in the strict zoning provisions through approval of uses that adjust the use of the property without creating a variance or amending the ordinance. As the name implies, conditional use permits allow the issuing agency to establish conditions the facility must meet before and during its occupancy in order to enjoy the requested use classification. In many cases, the local agency will impose conditions that take the form of environmental protection or public safety measures.

The application process begins with a consultation with the Planning Department (in Sacramento County it is called the Office of Planning and Community Development, elsewhere it may be known by such names as Planning Commission or Building Department). Once the Planning Department determines that a proposed use of property is not "of right" as defined in the zoning or planning ordinance, the property owner or developer must submit an application for approval of the proposed use. Several agencies may have to act on this application before the governing body or its designee department approves it. State law requires applications to be approved or disapproved within one year after an application deemed to be complete is submitted.

A typical conditional use permit includes the following components:

- Purpose of the application.

- Identification of proposed project, location and description.

- List of contacts, including the owner, developer, applicant's representative, architect, etc.

- General plan amendments (current and proposed).

- Rezoning proposals (current zoning and proposed changes).

- Information on commercial developments, including utility availability, parking spaces, etc.

- Information on residential developments.

- Description of proposed structure(s).

- Applicant's certification.

In addition to submitting a complete application, the applicant usually is required to provide scale drawings that indicate present uses of all property within 500 feet of the proposed site and a preliminary site plan. The applicant also must provide a mailing list of property owners around the proposed site for purposes of notice.

Fees based on valuation of the project and an additional fee based on service charges by agency staff are required of the applicant. Once the project is approved, construction may begin. After all required inspections are complete and satisfaction of other conditions is demonstrated, an occupancy permit is granted.

The process of local government review and approval begins when the applicant submits the completed application. The applicant will find that a number of agencies will be consulted during the course of this review and approval will not be forthcoming until all agencies involved are satisfied with permit applications and regulatory requirements. In Sacramento County, for example, an Environmental Impact Section reviews the application to identify applicable state and local environmental requirements and directs the application and/or applicant to the relevant agency. The following agencies usually are involved in granting use permits and occupancy permits.

Local/Regional Agency Regulatory Involvement in Siting Issues

◆ Local Community Sanitation District

The district issues permits which allow commercial or industrial dischargers to hookup and utilize the sewer system, as described in Chapter 6. The application of these agencies usually require engineering descriptions of the proposed operations, process chemicals used, and volume and characteristics of the discharge. Connection or hookup fees, which can be substantial in some locales to offset capital construction costs of the system, and annual fees will be assessed. Permits may include specific conditions on discharges as discussed in Chapter 6.

◆ County Air Pollution Control Districts or Regional Air Quality Management Districts

These districts issue permits called "Authority to Construct" and "Authority to Operate" if the proposed facility or operation will emit any air pollution as regulated by the rules of the local district. Enforcement of the requirement for air district permits has been made part of the local community planning process by AB 3205 [Government Code §65850.2], which requires that all permits required by the local air district must be obtained prior to issuance of an occupancy permit.

◆ Local Administering Agency for Hazardous Materials

The local administering agency for hazardous materials, usually the county or city health or fire department, is involved in the approval of a use permit in that the business plan and hazardous materials inventory required by the state community right-to-know law must be approved prior to issuance of the occupancy permit by planning officials as specified as well by AB 3205. This process usually involves a review of plans with respect to hazardous materials handling and storage areas and hazardous waste management facilities and plans. Particular attention will be given to a facility subject to the business plan requirement which is located within 1,000 feet of a school and may require specific approval for such siting. In addition, if the facility is proposing to handle significant amounts of acutely hazardous materials in excess of 500 pounds, it is likely that a Risk Management Prevention Plan (RMPP) will be required prior to facility occupancy. Acutely hazardous materials and RMPPs are defined in Chapter 4.

◆ Regional Water Quality Control Boards

The regional water quality control boards will need to be involved in any new construction or proposed use of property which impacts state waters, either surface or groundwater. Proposed discharges of wastes or wastewater to the land or to surface waters are required to be submitted to the regional board for consideration of discharge limitations. The board also must be notified of any above ground storage tanks. Underground storage tanks would be subject to permit by the local administering agency for the underground tank program.

Approval of Projects with Potentially Significant Environmental Impacts

If a proposed facility or project poses a significant environmental impact either due to the size or nature of the project or its proposed location, it may be subject to other environmental laws which require a more thorough examination of the proposal's environmental impact.

◆ **California Environmental Quality Act (CEQA) [Public Resources Code §§ 21000, et seq.]**

CEQA applies to projects which are sponsored by, funded by or must receive state or local government approval or permits and the project is determined to have a significant effect on the environment. Guidelines that define the applicability of CEQA to agency practice are in state regulations at Title 14, CCR §15000, et seq. Many agencies are required to incorporate guidelines into their regulations which uniformly identify actions subject to CEQA and those which are not. Procedures for identifying the lead agency where multiple agencies are involved is another important CEQA procedural element. When an agency finds there is no substantial evidence that a project will have a significant environmental effect on the environment, it will issue a "**Negative Declaration.**" [14 CCR §15070.]

If a significant environmental effect is identified, an Environmental Impact Report (EIR) is required. It usually is prepared at the expense of the project proponent by a consultant agreeable to the applicant and the lead agency. An EIR must include the following information necessary to thoroughly evaluate the environmental impact of the proposed project:

- A summary of the proposed action and its consequences.

- Project description, location and other details.

- A catalog of significant environmental effects on the physical environment, ecological systems, population distribution and density, public health and safety, scenic quality and other factors.

- Unavoidable environmental effects.

- Relationships between short term use and long term productivity (certain types of projects).

- Significant irreversible environmental changes.

- Growth inducing impacts.

- Cumulative impacts.

- Economic and social effects.

- Impact on archaeological resources.

- Mitigation measures.

- Alternatives to the project.

The EIR is designed to assist the reviewing agency in its decision-making process and be useful in solicitation of public comment on the proposed project. As a result of the EIR review, public hearings and other procedural steps, the following discretionary actions are available to the lead agency:

- Changing a proposed project.

- Imposing conditions on the approval of the project.

- Adopting plans or ordinances to control a broader class of projects to avoid the adverse changes.

- Choosing an alternative way of meeting the same need.

- Finding that changing or altering the project is not feasible.

- Finding that the unavoidable significant environmental damage is acceptable.

Projects subject to CEQA process are subject to substantial costs and delays in planning to meet the stringent requirements of the act.

◆ California Coastal Act of 1976 [Public Resource Code §§ 30000, et seq.]

This act established the California Coastal Commission and placed special regulatory requirements on property use in coastal areas covered by the act. The act specifies that coastal counties (15) and coastal cities (54) incorporate the protective policies of the act into the planning process of these governmental entities in terms of local coastal programs which are much like the zoning and planning policies discussed above, but more sensitive with respect to coastal resource protection. Once these plans are approved by the Coastal Commission, the local agency is responsible for land use and project approval **except** for the immediate shoreline in which the commission retains permanent permit jurisdiction. The commission also oversees local programs and hears appeals on local land use determinations.

A **coastal permit** is required for projects that modify land or water use in the coastal zone. Applicants for such projects are required to file the permit request with the closest Coastal Commission district office.

◆ Regional Planning and Resource Protection Agencies

There are a number of regional planning and resource protection agencies in California similar in purpose and procedures to the Coastal Commission. They usually are established in sensitive areas to assure that development is balanced with other regional objectives. The following are examples of such agencies that must be factored into any facility location decision within their area of jurisdiction:

- San Francisco Bay Conservation and Development Commission.
- Colorado River Board of California.
- California Tahoe Regional Planning Agency.

There also are a number of "conservancies" established in other sensitive areas which may influence development decisions.

Appendix 3-1
List of Applicable Laws and Regulations
Facility Siting and Environmental Considerations

State Law

● Planning and Zoning	Government Code §§65850-65850.2
● California Environmental Quality Act	Public Resources Code §21000
● California Coastal Commission	Public Resources Code §§30000-31352.5
● San Francisco Bay Conservation and Development Commission	Government Code §§66600, et seq.; Public Resources Code §§29000, et seq.
● Colorado River Basin Board of California	Government Code §§12805; Water Code §§12500, et seq.
● California Tahoe Regional Planning Agency and Tahoe Conservancy	Government Code §§67000, et seq.

State Regulations

● California Environmental Quality Act	14 CCR §§15000-15387
● California Coastal Commission	14 CCR §§13001-13666
● San Francisco Bay Conservation and Development Commission	14 CCR §§10110-11718
● Colorado River Basin Board of California	14 CCR §§12000-12010
● California Tahoe Regional Planning Agency and Tahoe Conservancy	14 CCR §§12052-12120; some rules available from the Agency

Each state agency and local government agency has provisions within its regulations and ordinances that address compliance with the California Environmental Quality Act as well.

Hazardous Materials and Community Right-to-Know

Summary and Applicability

This chapter presents the basic requirements of community right-to-know hazardous material regulation. It applies to any facility that handles any hazardous material (chemicals, chemical-containing products, hazardous wastes, etc.) in a quantity that exceeds reporting thresholds. The most common thresholds that trigger regulation, as described in this chapter, are 500 pounds of solid, 55 gallons of liquid and 200 cubic feet of compressed gas, which are included in state law. Some local agencies that manage community programs impose lesser quantity thresholds. Any facility that handles hazardous materials in quantities greater than the state or local thresholds should be familiar with the contents of this chapter and in compliance with applicable regulatory requirements.

The field of community right-to-know regulation includes the following programs, which will be described in more detail in this chapter:

- ● Reporting of releases or threatened releases of hazardous material.

- ● Preparing and submitting a hazardous materials business plan and inventory.

- ● Registration and regulation of acutely hazardous materials.

- ● Federal EPA-required annual reports of toxic chemical releases by manufacturers.

Further information on these regulatory programs and how to comply with them is presented in this chapter. Facilities that need more detailed information and a copy of the applicable laws and regulations and reporting forms should consult the California Chamber publication *Community Right-to-Know* (see page iii).

Background

Community right-to-know programs to oversee the handling of hazardous materials by local regulatory agencies developed in response to the 1984 Bhopal, India incident. California's 1985 community right-to-know law: Assembly Bill 2185, the Hazardous Materials Release Response Plans and Inventory Law, establishes Chapter 6.95 of the Health and Safety Code which governs hazardous materials handling, reporting requirements and local agency surveillance programs. A succession of state statutes has amended and augmented the program established by AB 2185, most notably AB 3777 in 1986 which established the state acutely hazardous materials regulatory program, and AB 2189 in 1989 which extended hazardous materials regulations to government facilities and partially integrated the federal Community Right-to-Know Act into the California program. In 1986, the Congress enacted as the Superfund Amendments and Reauthorization Act, Title III: The Emergency Planning and Community Right-to-Know Act (EPCRA). Many of the federal requirements administered by EPA have been incorporated into the California program which minimizes duplicative reporting. However, annual reports of release of certain toxic chemicals required of manufacturers by Section 313 of the federal law is a program administered and enforced by federal EPA.

Basic requirements of hazardous materials and community right-to-know for covered facilities include:

- Immediate reporting of releases of hazardous materials.

- Submission and update of a Hazardous Materials Business Plan and inventory as required by the local administering agency.

- Notification of the local administering agency of the handling of specified quantities of acutely hazardous materials and submission of a Risk Management Prevention Program upon request.

- Annual submission by manufacturing facilities of a Toxic Chemical Release Report (Form R) if threshold amounts of certain toxic chemicals are made, processed or used.

- Requirements for hazardous materials storage imposed by local administering agencies and Cal/OSHA standards.

The following discussion more fully explains the organization and provisions of federal, state and local hazardous materials and community right-to-know requirements as they apply to California facilities.

Organization and Administration of Hazardous Materials Programs

The laws and regulations that govern the area of hazardous materials and community right-to-know are briefly summarized below.

◆ State Laws

- AB 2185, Hazardous Materials Release Response Plans and Inventory Law established the basic requirements for the state's community right-to-know program, including immediate reporting of release, business plans for hazardous materials handlers, and the state organization for administration of the program: Office of Emergency services and county health or fire departments and city agencies as the local administering agencies. The statute is codified at Health and Safety Code, Chapter 6.95, §§25500, et seq.

- In 1986, AB 2187 revised certain provisions of the hazardous materials law to afford more time for compliance by establishing January 1, 1988 as the deadline for business plans and specifying that hazardous materials inventories would be based on individual chemicals, not aggregate amounts, and on chemicals at a fixed location for 30 days or more. Also in 1986, AB 3777 established the state's acutely hazardous chemical notification and risk management program. Facilities handling more than threshold planning quantities of EPA-listed extremely hazardous substances are required to register with the local administering agency by January 1, 1988 and submit a Risk Management Prevention Plan (RMPP) upon request. The acutely hazardous materials management program is codified at Health and Safety Code §§25531-25541.

- In 1988, AB 3205 enacted numerous substantial changes in both the basic hazardous materials community right-to-know law and the acutely hazardous materials program. AB 3205 established provisions in the Government Code that link building and occupancy permits to satisfaction of community right-to-know requirements and instituted special provisions for such facilities to be constructed within 1,000 feet of a school. It also provided for Air Pollution Control and Air Quality Management District review of RMPPs and placed special emphasis on proximity of schools, hospitals and health care facilities. It substantially increased the penalty for failure to register the handling of acutely hazardous materials to $25,000 per day.

- AB 2189 further amended the community right-to-know and acutely hazardous materials management law in 1989. It defined public facilities, including state and local government, as well as schools and universities as "businesses" subject to the hazardous materials requirements (which is why this guide refers to "facilities" as subject to these laws and not just businesses). AB 2189 also requires that tenants notify their landlords of hazardous materials handling and a copy of their business plan upon request. Finally, this statute integrated some of the federal Community Right-to-Know Act (EPCRA) reporting requirements into the existing state program.

◆ Federal Law

The **Superfund Amendments and Reauthorization Act of 1986, Title III, Emergency Planning and Community Right-to-Know Act (EPCRA)** [Public Law 99-499, Title III] established the mandatory federal standards for state community right-to-know programs and the toxic chemical release reporting by manufacturers under Section 313. As discussed below, most of the specific requirements of EPCRA have been integrated into the existing California Community Right-to-Know Law. The federal law is administered by EPA and is codified at 42 U.S.C. Section 11001.

◆ Agencies Responsible for Administration

- **State Office of Emergency Services Hazardous Materials Division (OES)** has overall responsibility for administration of the state program and coordination of local agency implementation and federal law compliance. The OES is organized in the Governor's office and is comprised of a headquarters function located in Sacramento and six regional offices. The precommunity right-to-know responsibilities of OES included natural disaster and other emergency response activities. Its mission was greatly expanded by AB 2185 to include coordination of local administering agencies which actually enforce the hazardous materials program and promulgation of regulations to direct implementation of the state program. OES also provides support to the Governor's Chemical Emergency Planning and Response Commission established pursuant to the federal law. Coordination of federal and state hazardous materials programs by OES has contributed to minimizing confusion and duplicative administration and reporting requirements.

  The OES Hazardous Materials Division organization chart appears as Appendix 4-2 and a directory of OES offices as Appendix 4-3.

Regulations developed by OES to implement Chapter 6.95 [§25500, et seq.] of the Health and Safety Code are codified in Title 19 of the California Code of Regulations (CCR) beginning with §2620. Appendix 4-1 presents a summary table of contents of relevant statutory provisions and Title 19 regulations. Specific sections that define a regulated facility's obligations are referenced in this chapter. It should be noted, however, that the state law allows local agencies to adopt provisions stricter than the state program. In such cases, the local rule or ordinance will prevail. The procedure to obtain copies of state regulations is described in Chapter 2.

- **Local Administering Agencies** are the principal enforcement agencies for the state (and federal) community right-to-know program in the local jurisdiction. Health and Safety Code §25501(b) defines administering agency as: "the department, office or other agency of a county or city designated or a fire district designated by a county or city designated. . .[to implement the program]."

Consequently, an array of local government agencies, mainly county health departments, county or city fire departments and other units of government are involved in hazardous materials program administration.

The local agencies are permitted to develop unique forms and program requirements at least as stringent as state requirements, or they may follow the state regulations and use the state's model forms. Regulated facilities must obtain the local agency requirements and forms directly from the agency to meet the minimum requirements of state and federal law. Local agencies are empowered to establish fees (which may be waived for public facilities) to support the costs of the program. Violations of the local program can be prosecuted as administrative violations with relatively small civil penalties (fines) or referred to district and city attorneys for action under state penalty provisions.

- **Governor's Chemical Emergency Planning and Response Commission (CEPRC)** was established in response to the federal EPCRA requirement to implement a state hazardous materials planning program. Given the pre-existence of California's AB 2185 program as overseen by OES, the CEPRC was instituted as a separate unit, but dependent on OES for administrative support. The federal law also specified several additional tiers in its scheme: regional and local planning committees and fire departments as the local community contact for regulated facilities. The federal model did not fit the existing hazardous materials organization in California; for example, many counties have only volunteer fire departments, but all have health departments. Consequently, federal EPCRA implementation has been accomplished by the establishment of local planning committees (with the required representation by government, news media, industry, environmental organization and medical representatives) within each of the OES emergency planning regions and local administering agencies as the local enforcement agency. AB 2189 recognized this "alternative organization" and specified a sharing of information by the local administering agency with other emergency response agencies. It also deemed a regulated facility "in compliance" with federal law if it complied with local agency reporting.

Appendix 4-3 is an organization chart of the CEPRC and the local planning committees. The CEPRC office is located at:

Office of Emergency Services
2800 Meadowview Road
Sacramento, CA 95832
(916) 427-4287

● **U.S. EPA's** role in California hazardous materials programs is principally oversight of the state and CEPRC implementation of the hazardous materials inventory reporting requirements of EPCRA Sections 304, 311 and 312 which, as discussed later in this chapter, have been integrated into the state program. In addition, EPA has direct authority for the remaining reporting requirement: Section 313 Toxic Chemical Release Reports. Therefore, most handlers of hazardous materials address applicable federal and state hazardous materials reporting requirements by complying with the business plan and inventory rules of their local administering agency. If the facility is a manufacturing plant that exceeds the toxic chemical manufacturing, processing or use thresholds, it must comply with EPCRA Section 313 by reporting (on Form R) directly to EPA. There is no state regulatory program that satisfies the requirements of Section 313. Appendix 4-1 provides a list of EPA regulations that implement federal EPCRA.

Regulated Facility Compliance Requirements

Hazardous Material Release or Threatened Release Reporting Requirements

The main premise of the hazardous materials community right-to-know laws is the requirement that releases of hazardous materials be reported to emergency response officials so that an appropriate response may be undertaken immediately. State and federal law differ substantially as to when a release is reportable. State law, AB 2185, requires **immediate** reporting of "any release of hazardous materials," except when there is a reasonable belief that there is no present or potential hazard to human health, the environment or property as adopted by OES regulation 19 CCR §2703. Federal release reporting under EPCRA and previous federal law has been based on releases of reportable quantities or "RQs" within a specified period of time. [40 CFR §§302.4 and 355.40].

◆ What releases are reportable?

Given the strict reporting requirement of state law, regulated facilities must clearly understand their reporting obligations. A "release" is any spilling, leaking, pumping, pouring, emitting, emptying, discharging, injecting, escaping, leaching, dumping or disposing into the environment unless permitted or authorized by a regulatory agency. A threatened release is a condition creating a substantial probability of harm when the probability and potential extent of harm make it reasonably necessary to take immediate action to prevent, reduce or mitigate damages to persons, property or the environment. Hazardous materials include hazardous substances (chemical products subject to the Cal/OSHA Hazard Communication Standard, i.e., require a Material Safety Data Sheet), hazardous wastes and radioactive materials. Based on these definitions, virtually any release of any substance would be reportable. To minimize unnecessary over-reporting, the OES issued a regulatory clarification which states: "The immediate report is not required if the person required to report reasonably believes that the release or threatened release poses no significant present or potential hazard to human health, the environment or property." [19 CCR §2703.]

Local administering agencies are involved in interpreting reporting requirements in that they are the initial recipients of such reports, may interpret state law and regulations, may adopt more stringent rules, and finally, refer cases to local prosecutors for failure to report. Regulated facilities should communicate with local administering agencies if there are any questions about release reporting requirements. In some cases, specific laws provide for a different reporting method than the community right-to-know law; for example, leaks from underground storage tanks or discharges which may threaten state waters. These are not exemptions; they should be regarded as alternative or supplemental reports to those discussed in this chapter.

As discussed above, federal required release reports are more specific, but more complicated. Federal reporting is based on exceeding the reportable quantity, or "RQ," of a chemical listed in 40 CFR §302.4 or §355.40, or a petroleum or petroleum product release that exceeds 42 gallons.

◆ Who is required to make reports?

The state places reporting obligations on the handler of hazardous materials or the facility, and any employee, authorized representative, agent or designees of the handler. Individuals, including facility employees or contractor employees, can be prosecuted for failure to report releases.

◆ How are reports made?

Reports of releases of threatened releases must be made immediately (by telephone) to the local administering agency, to a "911" number established for this purpose, or to the agency's regular telephone number. In addition, the OES also must be notified immediately via (800) 852-7550 or (916) 427-4341. OES will coordinate reports to other agencies. If a federal release (a release in excess of an RQ) occurs, the same procedure should be followed and a verification call to the National Emergency Response Center made: (800) 424-8802.

The following information should be communicated with the initial report of a release or threatened release:

- The exact location of the release or threatened release.

- The name of the reporter.

- The hazardous material involved.

- An estimate of the quantity of material released.

- If known, the potential hazards posed by the hazardous material.

A written follow-up is required on a form specified by OES [19 CCR 2705] if the release is one which would require a report under federal law (exceeds RQs under 40 CFR §302.4 or §355.40). The form must be submitted as soon as practicable, or no later than 30 days to the local administering agency and the CEPRC in Sacramento.

Given the severe state and federal penalties for failure to report releases, it is essential to understand these requirements and any unique local interpretation and assure that all responsible persons at the facility are aware of the obligation to report releases immediately.

Hazardous Materials Business Plans and Inventories

In California, the basic chemical emergency planning document is the "business plan" that originated with AB 2185. The business plan includes an inventory of hazardous materials. Federal EPCRA emergency planning is based on submission of inventory reports (Tier 1 and Tier 2 forms pursuant to 40 CFR 370). In comparison, the California program is more stringent because of the additional business plan requirements and the inventory thresholds, which are 20 times more inclusive (for hazardous materials) than the federal thresholds, or 500 versus 10,000 pounds.

◆ Coordination of Federal and State Requirements

Due to California's more stringent reporting requirements and changes in state and local agency inventory requirements to meet minimum federal information needs, inventory reporting pursuant to state and local administering agency guidelines is deemed to meet federal requirements. [Health and Safety Code §25506(b)]

As a consequence of the integration of state and federal programs accomplished by AB 2189 and regulations issued by OES, once a facility is in compliance with its local administering agency's requirements for business plan and inventory of hazardous materials, it is not required to complete federal forms (Tier 1 or Tier 2), nor submit such information to any other agency.

◆ What Facilities Must Submit a Business Plan?

The state community right-to-know law requires that every facility which handles more than threshold amounts of hazardous materials must submit a business plan. Hazardous materials are defined as:

> "any material that, because of its quantity, concentration, or physical or chemical characteristics, poses a significant present or potential hazard to human health and safety, or to the environment. Hazardous materials include, but are not limited to, hazardous substances, hazardous waste, radioactive materials, and any material which a handler or the administering agency has a reasonable basis for believing that it would be injurious to the health and safety of persons or harmful to the environment if released into the workplace or the environment."

The identification of hazardous substances which would trigger the business plan requirement is more complicated because many thousands of common and some not very hazardous industrial and commercial chemicals and products are included.

Hazardous substances means any substance or chemical product for which any one of the following applies:

- It appears on the list of substances shown in the "Director's List" from the Department of Industrial Relations pursuant to the Hazardous Substances Information and Training Act.

- The substance is listed pursuant to Part 172 of Title 49 of the Code of Federal Regulations, the Department of Transportation Hazardous Materials List.

- The manufacturer or producer is required to prepare a Material Safety Data Sheet (MSDS) for the substance or product under the Hazardous Substances Information and Training Act (California Labor Code, §6360 et seq.) or under any applicable federal law or regulations. The Federal OSHA Hazard Communication Standard (29 Code of Federal Regulations §1910.1200) is an applicable regulation that requires the preparation of an MSDS for any chemical product or substance which exhibits toxic or other hazardous properties. (For further information, see the California Chamber publication: ***Hazard Communication Handbook*** described on page iii.)

- It is a hazardous waste. The definition of hazardous wastes is discussed in Chapter 8 of this guide.

- It is a radioactive material. Radioactive materials are those substances listed as radioactive materials in Appendix B of Chapter 1 of Title 10 of the Code of Federal Regulations under jurisdiction of the Nuclear Regulatory Commission.

Based on the above discussion, any facility in California must identify whether it first handles hazardous materials, and, if so, whether it handles more than the threshold amounts below at any one time. Threshold amounts are defined in state law and regulations as more than:

- 500 pounds of solid materials;
- 55 gallons of liquid; or
- 200 cubic feet of compressed gas.

The majority of administering agencies have adopted these state thresholds; however, more stringent criteria may be used. Facilities must check with the local administering agency to ascertain local requirements. Based on this determination, the facility must submit a business plan unless one of the full or partial exemptions listed below apply.

◆ Exemptions to the Business Plan Requirements

- **Consumer product exemption.** Hazardous materials contained solely in a consumer product and pre-packaged for direct distribution to, and use by, the general public are exempt from the business plan requirements of this regulation unless the administering agency has found, and has provided notice to the facility handling the product, that the handling of certain quantities of the product requires the submission of a business plan due to public health, safety or environmental concerns. [Health and Safety Code §25503.5(c)(1)]

- **Agricultural exemption.** An administering agency shall exempt a business operating a farm for purposes of cultivating the soil or raising or harvesting any agricultural or horticultural commodity from filing certain information required in a business plan, providing all the following requirements are met:

✔ The handler annually provides the inventory of hazardous materials to the county agricultural commissioner before January 1 of each year.

✔ Each building in which hazardous materials subject to this regulation are stored is posted with the following sign, which provides notice to the storage of any pesticides, petroleum fuels, and oils and fertilizers:

> DANGER
>
> **HAZARDOUS MATERIAL STORAGE AREA**
>
> (In this space list the category of hazardous material
> stored within - pesticides, petroleum fuels,
> oils or fertilizers)
>
> **ALL UNAUTHORIZED PERSONS - KEEP OUT**

✔ The county agricultural commissioner forwards the inventory to the administering agency within 30 days after receiving the inventory.

✔ Any business operating a farm that has been exempted still must provide emergency response training for employees. [Health and Safety Code §25503.5(c)(5) and 19 CCR §§2733 and 2734]

● **Lubricating oil exemption.** Convenience stores, small auto parts stores and even small auto service outlets may be exempted from reporting requirements as long as the only "large volume" hazardous materials in their inventory are lubricating oils (e.g., engine, transmission, gearbox and differential oils) and certain volume limits are adhered to. To qualify for the exemption, a "single business facility" must ensure that the total volume of *each type* of lubricating oil handled at the facility does not exceed 55 gallons and the total volumes of *all* types of lubricating oil at the facility does not exceed 275 gallons at any one time. [Health & Safety Code §25503.5(b)(2)(a)]

● **Hazardous materials in transit exemption.** The term "handling," which includes storage, does not apply to the storage of hazardous materials that are in transit or which are temporarily maintained in a fixed facility for less than 30 days during the course of transportation. This exemption does not apply to railroad cards that a business knows or has reason to know will be located at the same railroad facility or business facility for more than 30 days. In the case of a railroad car in which hazardous materials are stored in accordance with the above definition, the business is required to immediately notify the administering agency. [Health and Safety Code §§25501.2 and 25503.7]

● **Medical office exemptions for anesthetic gases.** Oxygen and nitrous oxide present in the office of a physician, dentist, podiatrist, veterinary or pharmacist are exempt from the requirement of a business plan if the gases are stored in quantities of less than 1,000 cubic feet at any one time. [Health and Safety Code §25503.(b)]

- **Pipeline operations partial exemption.** Any business required to file a pipeline operations contingency plan in accordance with the California Pipeline Act of 1981 [Government Code §51510 et seq.] and the regulations of the Department of Transportation, Part 195 of Title 49 of the Code of Federal Regulations, may file a copy of the contingency plan instead of filing an emergency response plan. [Health and Safety Code §25504(d); Appendix B]

- **Other exemptions granted by the administering agency.** The Hazardous Materials Emergency Release Planning and Inventory Law contains provisions for further exemptions upon application by a facility to the administering agency. The handler must demonstrate that the exemption would not pose a significant present or potential hazard to human health or safety or to the environment, and that it would not impair emergency response. The administering agency may, on its own, exempt hazardous materials that meet these same general criteria. [Health and Safety Code §25503.5(c)(2), (3) and (4)]

These exemptions provide relief from all or part of the business plan requirements. Facilities should remember that they must still comply with the release reporting obligation. Furthermore, local administering agencies have the responsibility for determining whether to allow these exemptions in their jurisdictions.

◆ Contents of a Business Plan

The business plan is commonly referred to as a Hazardous Materials Management Plan (HMMP), a name that more clearly describes its purpose and content. A business plan must include the following elements in a format or on forms prescribed by the local administering agency:

- Specific details on the business, including: ownership, street address, Standard Industrial Classification number, principal business activity or description of business and 24-hour emergency telephone numbers for the business.

- An inventory of hazardous materials with specific quantity data, storage or containment descriptions, ingredients of mixtures and physical and health hazard information.

- Site and facility layouts that must be coded to chemical storage areas and other facility safety information.

- Emergency response procedures for a release or threatened release of hazardous materials.

- Procedures for immediate notification of releases to the administering agency.

- Evacuation plans and procedures for the facility.

- A description of training for all employees in evacuation and safety procedures in the event of a release or threatened release of a hazardous material consistent with their responsibilities.

- Identification of local emergency medical assistance appropriate for potential accident scenarios.

The California Chamber's *Community Right-to-Know Handbook* (page iii) includes detailed information and examples of a model business plan to help facilities meet these requirements. However, it should be noted that the business plan is subject to local administering agency jurisdiction and requirements will vary substantially from community to community.

◆ When Business Plans Are Required

Business plans for existing facilities subject to the law were due January 1, 1988 for privately operated facilities and January 1, 1990 for public facilities. Due to delays in enforcement and development of local community programs, voluntary compliance well after the deadline usually is well-received with minimal or no penalties, and a reasonable time allowed to complete the plan.

New facilities or modified facilities will find, beginning on July 1, 1989, that government building and occupancy permitting procedures are being used to enforce the community right-to-know laws.

- Applications for building permits must indicate whether a business plan will be necessary after July 1, 1989. [Government Code §65850.2(a)]

- No city or county shall issue a certificate of occupancy after July 1, 1989 if the community right-to-know requirements and air pollution district permitting requirements have not been met. [Government Code §65850.2(b)]

- No facility may be built within 1,000 feet of a school without meeting community right-to-know requirements and local administering agency approval. [Government Code §65850.2(c)] Health and Safety Code §42301.6 also provides for air pollution districts to issue public notices prior to the approval of such construction.

- Fees may be charged for building permits to recoup government costs to implement these requirements. [Government Code §65850.2(f)]

In addition, landlord-tenant law has been affected by the hazardous materials community right-to-know law which requires, effective January 1, 1990, that: "Owners of leased or rented property must be notified in writing if the tenant must submit a business plan and provide a copy upon request within five days." [Health and Safety Code §25503.6]

◆ When Business Plans Must be Updated

Within 30 days of any one of the following events, a facility that has filed a business plan and inventory must submit an amendment to the inventory form detailing the changes in hazardous materials handling, and other appropriate information:

- A 100 percent or more increase in the quantity of a previously disclosed material.

Chap. 4

- Any handling of a previously undisclosed hazardous material subject to the inventory requirements of this regulation.

- Change of facility address, business name or business ownership.

- Updating as required by the local administering agency.

Acutely Hazardous Materials Requirements

Both the California and federal community right-to-know laws more strenuously regulate materials of higher acute or immediate toxicity identified as acutely hazardous (California) or extremely hazardous (federal). An acutely hazardous material is simply a substance defined by EPA as an extremely hazardous material [Appendix A to 40 CFR 355]. Acutely hazardous materials are included on the List of Lists [Exhibit B at the end of this guide]. The federal requirement for handlers of such substances is primarily notification. The state requires registration and compliance with a rigorous regulatory program enacted by AB 3777 in 1986, including submitting upon request of the local administering agency a Risk Management and Prevention Plan (RMPP).

◆ Federal EPA Requirements

Under EPCRA §304, any facility that handles amounts of an extremely hazardous substance in excess of the threshold planning quantity listed in 40 CFR §355, Appendix A, must notify the Governor's Commission (CEPRC) and the local emergency planning committee. This notification is functionally the same as the initial registration required under state law as described below.

◆ State Acutely Hazardous Materials Requirements

AB 3777 established a new article in the Health and Safety Code called "Hazardous Materials Management," which requires, with certain exceptions, every handler or facility that handles more than the threshold planning quantities of an acutely hazardous material, as defined, to file an acutely hazardous materials registration form with the administering agency and to prepare and submit a Risk Management and Prevention Program upon request by the local administering agency.

Threshold planning quantities are noted in the last column of the list of extremely hazardous substances and are indicated in pounds. Facilities should note that, up to January 1, 1990, state law required reports based on the presence of 500 pounds of solid, 55 gallons of liquid, or 200 cubic feet of compressed gas. This reporting threshold has been changed to require reporting consistent with federal regulations based on the threshold planning quantity. In some cases, registration must be provided at lesser levels than previously, in others at greater quantities. Some of the acutely hazardous materials have threshold planning quantities as low as one pound, others as high as 10,000 pounds.

- **Acutely Hazardous Materials Registration.** The acutely hazardous materials registration form described in Health and Safety Code §25533 must be used to submit the following information to the local administering agency and the CEPRC at 2800 Meadowview Road, Sacramento, CA 95832 to meet both state and federal requirements. The form specifies the following types of information:

    ✔ Information on the submitting facility.

✔ Reference to the facility's business plan.

✔ Process designation.

✔ Identity of acutely hazardous materials handled and their quantity.

✔ A general description of processes and principal equipment.

✔ Acknowledgement.

Facilities subject to this reporting requirement were required to submit the registration form by January 1, 1988.

● **Risk Management and Prevention Program.** AB 3777 instituted the Risk Management and Prevention Program (RMPP) which is an operational and facility-related risk prevention plan which must be prepared and submitted by acutely hazardous materials handlers to local administering agencies upon request. Once approved, the RMPP must be fully implemented within one year.

An RMPP must include all of the following elements:

✔ A description of each accident involving acutely hazardous materials that has occurred at the business or facility within three years of the date of the request for the RMPP.

✔ A report specifying the nature, age and condition of the equipment used to handle acutely hazardous materials.

✔ Design, operating and maintenance controls that minimize the risk of an accident involving acutely hazardous materials.

✔ Detection, monitoring or automatic control systems to minimize potential acutely hazardous materials accident risks.

✔ A schedule for implementing additional steps to reduce the risk of an accident, which may include:
  - Installation of alarm, detection, monitoring or automatic control devices.
  - Equipment modifications, repairs or additions.
  - Changes in the operations, procedures, maintenance schedules or facility design.

The RMPP must be certified as complete by a "qualified person" and the facility operator. A "qualified person" is a technical specialist who must be approved by the administering agency as qualified to perform a competent evaluation of hazardous material risk and the effectiveness of control measures. The Office of Emergency Services has prepared a guidance document on RMPPs, *Guidance for the Preparation of a Risk Management and Prevention Program* (November 1989). It is available free of charge from:

Office of Emergency Services
Attn: Hazardous Materials Division
2800 Meadowview Road
Sacramento, CA 95832
(916) 262-1750

Facilities that handle acutely hazardous materials should obtain a copy of this document to review procedures which administering agencies will use to prioritize facilities for RMPP submission and how to prepare the plans.

- **Exemptions from RMPP Requirements.** Several provisions in the statute allow exemptions from RMPP requirements under certain circumstances:

  ✔ Administering agency discretion based on the likelihood of an acutely hazardous materials incident.

  ✔ Farm or nursery use of a pesticide requires consultation with the Department of Food and Agriculture to determine the necessity of an RMPP.

  ✔ Upon application by an owner or operator, the administering agency may exempt the facility upon a written finding that the exemption would not pose an acutely hazardous materials accident risk.

  It should also be noted, however, that the administering agency may impose stricter reporting requirements because of health, safety and environmental concerns.

- **New Facilities or Modified Facilities.** Legislation enacted in 1988, AB 3205, amends Government Code §65850.2 to require building permits to indicate whether an acutely hazardous materials registration or a Risk Management Prevention Program will be necessary. After July 1, 1989, no final certificates of occupancy may be issued unless the requirements under AB 3777 are satisfied and approved by the local administering agency. Finally, no construction may be approved within 1,000 feet from a school unless the RMPP requirements, if applicable to the facility, are satisfied.

Reports of Releases of Toxic Chemicals by Manufacturing Facilities

A unique federal EPA reporting requirement established by EPCRA Section 313 imposes new toxic chemical release reporting requirements on facilities of manufacturers (SICs 20-39) with more than 10 employees beginning on July 1, 1988 if certain chemicals on a list of more than 300 chemicals and families of chemicals are manufactured, processed or otherwise used in excess of threshold amounts.

The threshold amounts established for manufacturing or processing into another product are:

- 75,000 pounds in 1987;

- 50,000 pounds in 1988; and

- 25,000 pounds in 1989 and subsequent years.

For use in any other way the threshold is:

- 10,000 pounds in 1987 and subsequent years.

Facilities subject to this reporting requirement must submit a Form R annually beginning on July 1, 1988. The Form R requests such information as general business type and location, sources of releases to air, water and off-site facilities for each covered chemical, and an estimate of the amount released. Affected facilities may obtain copies of Form R and other information from one of the following:

Emergency Planning and Community Right-to-Know Document Distribution Center
P.O. Box 12505
Cincinnati, OH 45212

EPA Region 9 San Francisco office
Pesticides and Toxics Branch
(415) 744-1080

The chemicals covered by Section 313 release reporting requirements appear in the list of lists in Exhibit B at the end of this guide. Manufacturers and distributors of covered chemicals and products containing such chemicals over de minimis amounts are required to notify customers of this fact, usually on MSDSs, beginning in 1989.

In California, completed Form Rs are submitted to:

U.S. EPA
P.O. Box 70266
Washington, D.C. 20024-0266
Attn: Toxic Chemical Release Inventory

and

Charles H. Shulock
Assistant to the Secretary
California Environmental Protection Agency
555 Capitol Mall, Suite 235
Sacramento, CA 95814

Penalties for Violations of the Community Right-to-Know Laws

The following table summarizes the criminal, civil and administrative penalties for violations of the federal and state community right-to-know laws.

Offense - State Law	Maximum Penalty
Failure to report a release or threatened release. [Health and Safety Code §25507]	*State:* $25,000 per day and one year imprisonment in county jail. Subsequent offenses punishable by a fine of not less than $2,000 nor more than $50,000 and imprisonment for 16, 20 or 24 years in state prison, or up to one year imprisonment in county jail, or fines and imprisonment.
Failure to submit a business plan* [Health and Safety Code §§25503.5-25505, 25508-25510]	*State:* $2,000 penalty per day, $5,000 per day after reasonable notice. [Health and Safety Code §25514] *Local:* Administrative penalties up to $2,000 per day, established by ordinance, usually much less than state law. [Health and Safety Code §25514.5]
Failure to submit an acutely hazardous registration form or a Risk Management and Prevention Plan.* [Health and Safety Code §25540]	*State:* $2,000 per day. A knowing violation after reasonable notice, up to $25,000 and imprisonment in the county jail for up to one year.

---

* May also constitute a federal violation.

Civil Liability for Response Costs and Damages: Each of the above violations contains a provision stating that if the violation results in or significantly contributes to an emergency, including a fire, to which the county or city is required to respond, the facility or person shall also be assessed the full cost of the county or city emergency response, as well as the cost of cleaning up and disposing of the hazardous materials.

Rewards to Informants: Any person who provides information that materially contributes to the imposition of a civil penalty will be paid a reward by the administering agency equal to 10 percent of the amount of the civil penalty collected. No reward shall exceed $5,000.

Offense - Federal Law	Maximum Penalty
Failure to report inventory of hazardous substances required by EPCRA §313.	Civil and administrative penalties of not more than $10,000 for each violation.
Failure to report inventories of hazardous substances required by EPCRA §312 or comply with state mandated substitute reporting.	Civil and administrative penalties of not more than $25,000 for each violation.
Failure to report a release of hazardous substances and extremely hazardous substances (EPCRA §304).	Civil penalties of up to $25,000 for each violation. Subsequent violation may result in civil penalties of up to $75,000.
	Criminal penalties for knowing and willful violations of a fine up to $25,000 and imprisonment for not more than two years, or both. Subsequent violations are punishable by a fine of up to $50,000 and imprisonment for not more than five years.
Failure to submit a Toxic Chemical Release Report (Form R).	Civil and administrative penalties of not more than $25,000 for each violation.

Note: All the violations above carry the notation that each day constitutes a separate violation so long as the violation continues unabated.

Chap. 4

Chap. 4

Appendix 4-1
List of Applicable Laws and Regulations
Hazardous Materials and Community Right-to-Know

State Laws

- Business Plans and Inventories   Health and Safety Code §§25500-25521 and local ordinances

- Reporting of Releases   Health and Safety Code §§25500-25521 and local ordinances

- Acutely Hazardous Materials Requirements   Health and Safety Code §§25533-25541

Federal Laws

Comprehensive Environmental Response Compensation and Liability Act (CERCLA)
- Federal Reportable Releases: Designation,   42 USC §9602
  Reportable Quantities and Notification

Emergency Planning and Community Right-to-Know
- Notification   42 USC §§11002, et seq.
- Release of Toxic Chemicals   42 USC §§11013 and 11028
  (EPCRA §313 Form Rs)

State Regulations

- Hazardous Material Release Reporting,   19 CCR §§2620-2732, as well as ordinances
  Inventory and Response Plans   adopted by local administering agencies.

- Reporting of Releases   19 CCR §§2701-2705, as well as ordinances
  adopted by local administering agencies.

- Acutely Hazardous Materials   At present, California OES has issued guidelines
  only for delineating the specific structuring and
  applicability of RMPPs to individual facilities.
  Local administering agencies may have policies
  in place governing the handling of acutely
  hazardous materials.

- Hazardous Materials Storage Requirements   8 CCR §§5160-5190 (Cal/OSHA regulations)
  (except hazardous waste, see Chapter 8)   and ordinances adopted by local administering
  agencies, including the Uniform Fire Code.

Federal Regulations

Business Plans and Inventories
- Hazardous Chemical Reporting: 40 CFR 370
  Community Right-to-Know

Reportable Releases
- Reportable Quantities and Notification   40 CFR 302
  Requirements
- Emergency Planning and Notification   40 CFR 355
  (extremely hazardous materials)
- Release of Toxic Chemicals   40 CFR 372
  (EPCRA §313 Form Rs)

Appendix 4-2
Office of Emergency Services, Hazardous Materials Division Organization Chart (September 1991)

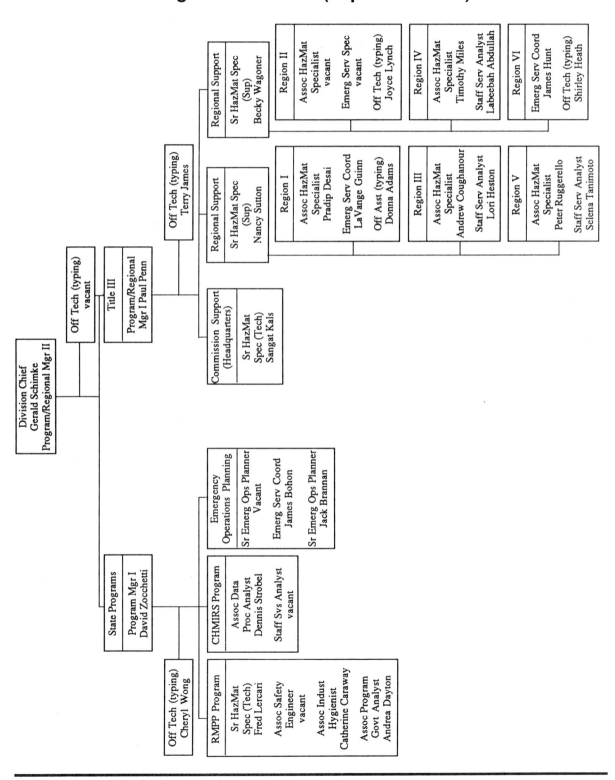

Appendix 4-3
Office of Emergency Services
Mutual Aid Regions

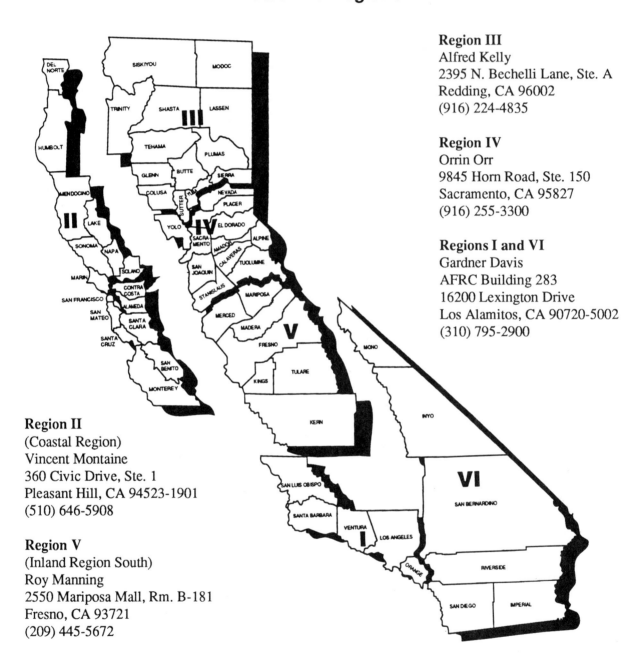

Region III
Alfred Kelly
2395 N. Bechelli Lane, Ste. A
Redding, CA 96002
(916) 224-4835

Region IV
Orrin Orr
9845 Horn Road, Ste. 150
Sacramento, CA 95827
(916) 255-3300

Regions I and VI
Gardner Davis
AFRC Building 283
16200 Lexington Drive
Los Alamitos, CA 90720-5002
(310) 795-2900

Region II
(Coastal Region)
Vincent Montaine
360 Civic Drive, Ste. 1
Pleasant Hill, CA 94523-1901
(510) 646-5908

Region V
(Inland Region South)
Roy Manning
2550 Mariposa Mall, Rm. B-181
Fresno, CA 93721
(209) 445-5672

Local Emergency Planning Committees (LEPCs)
LEPCs have been established within each OES Mutual Aid region. Correspondence and telephone
contacts may be made to the appropriate LEPC through the regional offices listed on this figure.

Stationary Source Air Emissions and Pollution Control

This chapter discusses the regulatory program that governs stationary sources of air pollution. It applies to any facility that emits or has the potential to emit conventional pollutants: oxides of nitrogen and sulfur, carbon monoxide, volatile organic compounds (VOCs) or particulate matter. It also may apply to emission sources of certain toxic chemicals. Facilities that operate equipment or use materials that produce such emissions should be familiar with the information in this chapter. This information, in conjunction with the rules of the local air pollution district, will enable the facility to determine what regulations it faces in obtaining permits for equipment and emissions.

Control of air pollution sources includes permitting and a number of other regulatory programs that will be presented in this chapter.

- District permitting and new source requirements.
- Hazardous substance emissions standards.
- Air toxic emission inventories and assessment.

General information on these regulatory programs is presented in this chapter. Regulated facilities will need to consult local air pollution district rules and officials to determine specific regulatory requirements that apply.

Given the federal Clean Air Act's mandates and the state's clear policy to minimize air pollution problems, California facilities must comply with some of the nation's toughest and most complex controls on both conventional pollutants and emissions of selected toxic substances. This is particularly true in regions of the state where the combination of industrial and other stationary sources and the vehicle traffic associated with urbanization have resulted in decades of significant air pollution and non-compliance with federal ambient air quality standards. This chapter will present the overall federal and state scheme for air pollution control and the organizations which administer the program, the typical air pollution control district regulatory compliance program, and the specialized programs recently developed to address toxic chemical emissions and other concerns.

This chapter does not address vehicular standards as they are not usually within the scope of a facility's environmental program. For more information on the regulatory program established by the federal Clean Air Act to minimize emissions of substances known to deplete the ozone layer of the earth's atmosphere, see the discussion in Chapter 12 under the subhead "Regulation of Ozone-Depleting Substances."

Federal Clean Air Act

The national program for air pollution control was established by the Clean Air Act. Overall administration of the act's requirements is vested in Federal EPA, with the states given direct regulatory activities. States are required to develop state implementation plans (SIPs) which are approved by EPA. The basic objectives of the Clean Air Act are specified in the form of primary and secondary Ambient Air Quality Standards established by EPA. Primary standards are set on the basis of protecting public health and must be met within three years after a state's plan is approved. Secondary standards to protect public welfare (visibility, aesthetics, property and crop protection) must be met within a reasonable time. State regulatory officials set emission standards for specific sources of air pollutants to attain the ambient air quality standard objectives. EPA also establishes some emissions standards for new source performance and emissions of hazardous (toxic) air pollutants. A list of the federal ambient air quality standards and comparable California standards appears in Figure 5-1.

◆ State Implementation Plan

State compliance with federal ambient air quality standards is based on a state implementation plan that designates regions for effective air quality management and contains enforceable provisions to attain compliance with ambient air quality standards and other federal emissions limitations. The state implementation plan incorporates all rules and regulations of the state and regional regulatory agencies involved in air pollution control. Areas of a state that do not meet ambient air quality standards are called "non-attainment areas." State implementation plans for such areas must contain a non-attainment plan that includes further emissions limitations, schedules of compliance and expeditious implementation, all reasonably available control measures, and if ozone or carbon monoxide standards are being exceeded, a motor vehicle inspection and maintenance program.

In addition, any non-attainment plan must contain a permit program for the construction and operation of major new and modified stationary sources. Such sources are required to achieve the most stringent emissions limitation for similar equipment (best available control technology without consideration of cost) plus a determination by the permitting agency that there will be no net increase in emissions in the region. This requires, in some cases, that the operator of a proposed new source achieve or obtain offsets from existing sources in the area in order to build a new facility or operate new equipment.

If a state implementation plan does not demonstrate adequate progress toward achieving compliance with ambient air quality standards in a non-attainment area, EPA may prepare an implementation plan of its own and/or impose construction bans on sources in excess of 100 tons per year of offending pollutants and/or withhold EPA-approved federal funds targeted for the state (for example, sewage treatment and transportation improvement grants).

Prevention of significant deterioration is another objective of the federal Clean Air Act. Areas that exceed ambient air quality standards are not allowed to deteriorate in state implementation plans. Such areas are classified by environmental objectives. EPA allows the less protected areas to experience some increase in air pollution due to industrial and other development, but does not permit them to exceed either primary or secondary standards for air pollutants. Regulatory mechanisms to prevent deterioration include pre-construction review for larger sources of pollutants, emissions limitations for such facilities and best available control technology.

Emissions standards for new sources and hazardous air pollutants (National Emission Standards for Hazardous Air Pollutants - NESHAPs) are established by EPA and must be implemented by the states. Some states, most notably California, exceed federal requirements for new source emissions and therefore reference to the federal standards is not necessary during permitting. EPA has established emissions standards for certain hazardous substances (also called non-conventional pollutants) under

Figure 5-1
Ambient Air Quality Standards*

Pollutant	Averaging Time	California Standards[1] Concentration[3]	National Standards[2] Primary[4]	Secondary[4]
Ozone	1 Hour	0.09 ppm (180 ug/m3)	0.12 ppm (235 ug/m3)	Same as Primary Std.
Carbon Monoxide	8 Hour	9.0 ppm (10 mg/m3)	9.0 ppm (10 mg/m3)	Same as Primary Std.
	1 Hour	20 ppm (23 mg/m3)	35 ppm (40 mg/m3)	
Nitroge Dioxide	Annual Average	—	0.053 ppm (100 ug/m3)	Same as Primary Std.
	1 Hour	0.25 pp (470 ug/m3)	—	
Sulfur Dioxide	Annual Average	—	80 ug/m3 (0.03 ppm)	—
	24 Hour	0.04 ppm[5] (131ug/m3)	365 ug/m3 (0.14 ppm)	—
	3 Hour	—	—	1300 ug/m3 (0.5 ppm)
	1 Hour	0.25 ppm (655 ug/m3)	—	—
Suspended Particulate Matter (PM$_{10}$)	Annual Geometric Mean	30 ug/m3	—	—
	24 Hour	50 ug/m3	150 ug/m3	Same as Primary Std.
	Annual Arithmetic Mean	—	50 ug/m3	
Sulfates	24 Hour	25 ug/m3	—	—
Lead	30 Day Average	1.5 ug/m3	—	—
	Calendar Quarter	—	1.5 ug/m3	Same as Primary Std.
Hydrogen Sulfide	1 Hour	0.03 ppm (42 ug/m3)	—	—
Vinyl Chloride (chloroethene)	24 Hour	0.010 ppm (26 ug/m3)	—	—
Visibility Reducing Particles	8 Hour	In sufficient amount to produce extinction of 0.23 per kilometer due to particles when relative humidity is less than 70 percent.	—	—
Applicable Only in the Lake Tahoe Air Basin				
Carbon Monoxide	8 Hour	6 ppm (7 mg/m3)	—	—
Visibility Reducing Particles	8 Hour	In sufficient amount to produce extinction of 0.07 per kilometer due to particles when relative humidity is less than 70 percent.	—	—

Notes:

1. California standards for ozone, carbon monoxide, sulfur dioxide (1 hour), nitrogen dioxide and particulate matter-PM$_{10}$ are values that are not to be exceeded. The sulfates, lead, hydrogen sulfide, vinyl chloride, and visibility reducing particles standards are not to be equaled or exceeded.

2. National standards, other than ozone and those based on annual averages or annual arithmetic means, are not to be exceeded more than once a year. The ozone standard is attained when the expected number of days per calendar year with maximum hourly average concentrations above the standard is equal to or less than one.

3. Concentration expressed first in units in which it was promulgated. Equivalent units given in parenthesis are based upon a reference temperature of 25 degrees C and a reference pressure of 760 mm of mercury. All measurements of air quality are to be corrected to a reference temperature of 25 degrees C and a reference pressure of 760 mm of mercury (1,013.2 millibar); ppm in this table refers to ppm by volume, or micromoles of pollutant per mole of gas.

4. Terms are defined in text.

5. At locations where the state standards for ozone and/or suspended particulate matter are violated. National standards apply elsewhere.

§112 of the Clean Air Act. A list of substances for which such standards have been promulgated appears in Figure 5-1. Although enforcement authority is delegated to the states and local districts, EPA retains enforcement authority for NESHAP standards concurrently.

◆ Federal EPA Role in Enforcement

As previously discussed, EPA usually carries out its responsibilities under the Clean Air Act through oversight of state implementation plans. However, EPA retains concurrent jurisdiction and may prosecute a facility that violates an emissions standard or permit requirement, notwithstanding state or local district action. These "double jeopardy" enforcement actions are known as "over filings" and result most commonly from the EPA's review of a district's permitting action, granting of a variance or failure to adequately respond to a violation. Citizen suits also are authorized under the Clean Air Act against violating facilities once a 60-day notice is given to EPA, to the state and the alleged violator, and the EPA nor state has diligently prosecuted the case. Citizens also may sue EPA to force any action required by the act for which the agency has discretionary authority.

California's Air Pollution Control Program Organization

The state's implementation of the federal Clean Air Act and organization of the air pollution control program are codified in the Health and Safety Code §§39000-44384. The Air Resources Board is the agency responsible for the statewide program and direct oversight of the local and regional districts. The Air Resources Board has been incorporated as a department within Cal/EPA. This reorganization is not expected to significantly change the policies, procedures and regulations of the state board, nor the districts under its authority.

◆ Air Resources Board

The Air Resources Board (ARB) is composed of nine members appointed by the Governor with the consent of the Senate. Five members are statewide appointees with expertise in certain disciplines related to air pollution issues; four must be appointed from district boards with one each from the Bay Area, South Coast and San Diego boards. One of the board's members is appointed as chairperson, which is a full-time position, whereas other board members are part-time. The ARB is staffed by an executive officer and a considerable staff organized as indicated by Figure 5-2.

The ARB is responsible for developing the State Implementation Plan and assuring that districts are in compliance. The ARB promulgates state regulations found in Title 17 of the California Code of Regulations to further carry out federal and state laws. The state board also is directly responsible for non-stationary sources or vehicular emissions controls, developing test methods, analyzing data on air quality in the state's air basins, and implementing specific statutory programs, including the California Clean Air Act, Toxic Air Contaminant, Atmospheric Acidity Protection and the Airborne Toxic Hot Spots Information and Assessment statutes.

◆ Air Quality Management Districts

State legislation has established air quality management districts for the state's most populated regions: South Coast, Bay Area, Sacramento and San Joaquin Valley. Membership on each of these boards represents local government units incorporated into the district. An air pollution control officer appointed by the board is the enforcement official for the air pollution control law and also may serve as the board's executive officer. Air quality management districts are served by hearing boards made

Figure 5-2
California Air Resources Board

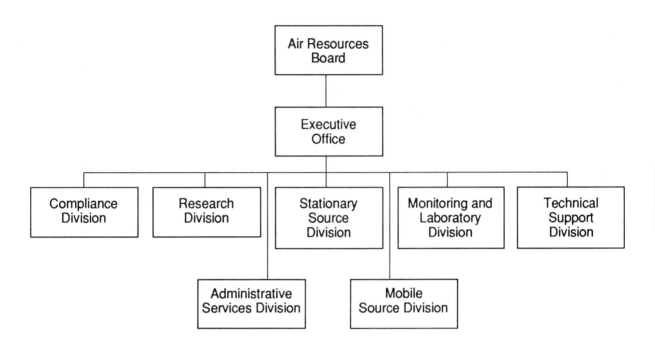

up of five members appointed by the board for the disciplines of law, engineering, medicine and two public members. The hearing boards are empowered to issue abatement orders or modifications, grant variances and conduct permit appeals according to procedures for administrative adjudications and public participation.

◆ County and Unified Air Pollution Control Districts

County and unified air pollution control districts are the additional types of air pollution districts authorized by state law. There are nearly 30 county air pollution control districts, which is a statutory mandate for counties not incorporated in management districts or unified districts (areas of two or more counties) by agreement of county boards of supervisors. These more local districts function in much the same way as the larger management districts, although with considerably smaller staffs and less complex rules.

Appendix 5-2 contains a map of the state's air basins and directory of air pollution control districts.

State Air Pollution Laws and Regulatory Programs

As described above, California's air pollution control programs are designed to meet requirements of the federal Clean Air Act. In addition, the state's air pollution control program is authorized by statute to adopt ambient air quality standards more stringent than federal standards (see Figure 5-1) and implement other specific statutory programs.

- **The Milford-Carrell Act** established the statutory scheme and organization for California's air pollution control program in 1967. It is codified at Health and Safety Code §§39000-44385. The basic regulatory provisions used to implement the state's air pollution control objectives are included in this statute as amended.

- **Permitting Authority.** Health and Safety Code §§42300-42301 require an air pollution control district to issue a permit before any person "builds, erects, alters, replaces, operates, or uses any article, machine, equipment or contrivance that may cause the emission of air contaminations." Air pollution control districts have adopted specific rules for permitting facilities and/or sources within their area of jurisdiction.

- **New Source Review** requirements address federal specifications for control technology, emissions limitations and assure no net increase of pollutant in a non-attainment area. New source review is conducted during the permitting process for a new source or modified source. [Health and Safety Code §§40918, et seq.]

- **Public Health and Nuisance** prohibition allows districts to regulate emissions that cause annoyance to members of the public, endangerment of health or property damage. Agricultural operations are largely exempt, but most other nuisances and sources of potentially toxic emissions may be curtailed under Health and Safety Code §41700. Furthermore, no variances may be granted if the operation of the source would result in a nuisance.

- **Visible Emissions Limitations** based on exceeding opacity as defined by the "Ringelman Chart" (No. 2 in most districts or No. 1 or 20 percent opacity in others) for more than three

Chap. 5

minutes in any hour may be regulated or prohibited by a district. [Health and Safety Code §41701]

● **District Rules Limiting Emissions** are the principal method for reducing emissions from specific types of sources. Such rules are designed to meet the district's ambient air quality objectives for pollutants of concern. These rules are district-specific and usually are organized by the nature of the industry, type of equipment or source. Such rules may require the retrofit of certain control technology, in some cases on a schedule of increments of progress, or limit materials, solvent use, etc. If the district in question is a federal non-attainment area, relevant district rules must be complied with by January 1, 1982.

● **AB 1807, The Tanner Toxic Air Contaminant Identification Act** established in 1983 a new regulatory program to identify and assess the public health risk of selected chemicals and regulate emissions of such chemicals. The Tanner Act established a two-step process. First the Department of Health Services, at the request of the ARB, identifies a substance as a toxic air contaminant and evaluates its health effects. The Scientific Advisory Board on Toxic Air Contaminants, also established by the act, reviews the DHS report and, after a public hearing, the ARB lists the substance as a toxic air contaminant [17 CCR §93000]. Substances identified by EPA under §112 of the Clean Air Act [NESHAPS substances] must be identified as toxic air contaminants in California. In the second phase of the program, the ARB, with participation of air pollution control districts, determines the necessity and content of control measures that are adopted as regulations at 17 CCR §93100, et seq. The statute is codified at Health and Safety Code §§39650-39668. A similar procedure to evaluate whether a pesticide is a toxic air contaminant is included in the act. [Food and Agriculture Code §14021-14027]

● **The Air Toxics "Hot Spots" Information and Assessment Act** introduced a new and far-reaching regulatory program in 1987 that requires covered facilities to submit an emissions inventory of the more than 330 chemicals subject to the statute. The statute further provides for risk assessments of emissions from higher-priority facilities. The risk assessment results, if significant, may lead to further regulatory requirements and/or public notification. The ARB has issued regulations to implement the program and list covered chemicals [17 CCR §93300]. The act is codified as Health and Safety Code §§44300-44384.

● **The California Clean Air Act** of 1988 enacted a wide range of significant changes in California's air pollution prevention regulatory program:

  ✔ ARB may regulate motor vehicle fuel specification and add additional types of vehicles, including motorcycles, off-road vehicles, construction equipment, farm equipment, utility engines, locomotives and marine vessels, to the extent permitted by federal law.

  ✔ ARB may regulate consumer products. Regulations that govern aerosol products have been adopted.

✔ Districts may regulate indirect sources of air pollution, using such means as encouraging ridesharing, van pooling, flexible work hours and other vehicle use by businesses, government and commuters. The South Coast Air Quality Management District has even broader authority in this area.

✔ Mandates that districts have a duty to achieve and maintain federal standards.

✔ ARB must designate air basins as attainment or non-attainment for state standards and identify basins affected by transported pollutants. Non-attainment areas must submit a plan to achieve state standards.

✔ A 5 percent per year reduction of non-attainment pollutants must be achieved.

✔ Based on projections of when non-attainment districts will meet state standards, each is given a classification of air pollution: moderate (end of 1994), serious (end of 1997), or severe (after 1997). Each classification carries additional requirements in its implementation plan to achieve improvement in its status. These measures include more effective permitting requirements, retrofit of control equipment, implementation of the no net increase provision and transportation controls.

The current requirements of these state regulatory programs as they affect regulated stationary sources are discussed below.

Regulated Facility Compliance Requirements

California facilities are subject to federal, state and district air pollution control requirements, but if facilities comply with the requirements of their local district, they generally will be in compliance. However, care should be exercised with technical non-compliance as some instances may violate both federal and state requirements and be separately prosecuted. In addition, variances that exonerate a business from state penalties are not honored by EPA if the variance would constitute a federal violation.

Each facility should identify its air quality management or air pollution control district. Appendix 5-2 includes a list of districts and their location in the state. Once facilities determine the local agency, they need to inquire about any of the regulatory requirements discussed below which may apply.

◆ Air Permits

With certain exceptions, district boards have developed rules that require permits before any person builds, erects, alters, replaces, operates, or uses any article, machine, equipment or other contrivance that may cause the issuance of air contaminants. Statutory exemptions from permitting include:

- any vehicle;

- any structure designed for and used exclusively as a dwelling for not more than four families or any incinerator used exclusively in connection with such a structure;

- barbecue equipment not used for commercial purposes;

- any equipment agricultural operations use to grow crops or raise fowl or animals; and

- repairs or maintenance not involving structural changes to any equipment for which a permit has been granted.

There are significant differences in permitting requirements from district to district. Some districts require permits for virtually any source of air emissions, for example, using a one-gallon can of coating material (South Coast Air Quality Management District). Others exempt operations of a particular size or type from coverage. Any facility that conducts industrial operations involving the emission or potential emission of any air pollutant (organic vapors, particulates, carbon monoxide, nitrogen or sulfur oxides) must review local district rules to determine permit requirements.

Once permit requirements are identified, the facility should submit the district's permit application (authority to construct) or request assistance from the district. Existing facilities should pay particular attention to changes in district permitting rules and permit renewal procedures to avoid being out of compliance. A facility discovered not to have the proper permits may face the following consequences, depending on the importance of the source, the facility's history and efforts to voluntarily comply, and specific factors associated with the non-permitted source:

- The existing source will be permitted with back fees due from date of last permit or first operation.

- Assessment of administrative civil penalties in addition to permit fees.

- Prosecution for criminal or civil penalties (rarely).

- The source will be regarded as a new source subject to new source review requirements. (See the following discussion.)

The latter action, which is a possibility in a non-attainment district that has not accounted for the unpermitted pollutants in its emissions inventory, would result in significant costs to a major source.

Once an authority to construct is issued and the source can operate pursuant to the conditions specified, a permit to operate is issued which is the permit which governs facility operation.

The permit usually must be posted at or near the source, and be renewed annually. The source must operate in compliance with the permit conditions and maintain records of such compliance. Fees are assessed when a facility applies for an authority to construct and as an annual permit fee once the source is permitted. Renewal is usually routine, although the district may change permit conditions or otherwise modify requirements upon renewal.

◆ New Source Review

New sources, in addition to being subject to permitting as discussed above, also must be reviewed by district staff for compliance with the district's new source review rules, which address both non-attainment issues and prevention of significant deterioration. The most significant consequences for a

Chap. 5

source subject to new source review is whether Best Available Control Technology (BACT) will be required and, based on the resulting emissions, whether the facility must obtain offsets so it may operate within the district's emissions inventory.

Each of these issues is determined by individual district rules which may require BACT for all new sources or only those that emit 150 or 250 pounds per day, depending on the pollutant in question. (Federal law requires BACT at 100 tons per year, or 550 pounds per day.) For example, the Sacramento Air Quality Management District requires BACT for new sources that exceed the following thresholds [Regulation 2, Rule 301.1]:

Pollutant	pounds/day
Reactive organic compounds	0
Nitrogen oxides	0
Sulfur oxides	0
PM10	0
Carbon monoxide	550
Lead	3.3
Asbestos	0.04
Beryllium	0.0022
Mercury	0.55
Vinyl Chloride	5.5
Fluorides	1 6
Sulfuric acid mist	38
Hydrogen sulfide	55
Total reduced sulfur compounds	55
Reduced sulfur compounds	55

Offset requirements are necessary when a controlled new source exceeds a threshold amount deemed necessary by the district to offset increases introduced by new or modified sources and result in a net improvement of air quality. Offsets apply to pollutants for which the district exceeds air quality standards. The offset limits vary from district to district and by pollutant. The following thresholds from Sacramento Air Quality Management District are typical for a non-attainment area [Regulation 2, Rule 302.1]:

Pollutant	pounds/day
Reactive organic compounds	150
Nitrogen oxides	150
Sulfur oxides	150
PM10 (particulate matter)	80
Carbon monoxide	550

Again, certain district-specific exemptions apply. Offsets are obtained from the facility itself or from other sources in the district that have or can be induced into reducing emissions of the pollutant in question. Based on the location of the source and other factors, districts have developed in their rules "offset ratios" that determine what portion of the offsets available may be applied to the new source. Offsets "owned" by facilities that have reduced emissions may be banked and used, traded or sold according to district emissions banking rules.

Chap. 5

◆ District Emissions Limitations and Prohibitions, and New Source Performance Standards

Each district's rules contain specific provisions that set emissions limitations, prohibitions and new source performance standards for a variety of industrial and commercial processes and operations. Any facility that engages in a regulated activity will be required to comply with the rules, which are applicable to new or existing sources as the facility's permit is renewed. Each district's rules should be checked for applicability to individual facilities as it is outside of the scope of this guide to cover these literally hundreds of rules in any detail.

◆ Federal, State and Local Hazardous Substance Emissions Standards

Facilities that handle any of the substances regulated by federal, state and local hazardous substance or toxic air contaminant standards in a manner which may result in emissions must review the standards to identify applicable requirements. These standards apply to both new and existing sources. The following table lists those substances for which such standards have been developed.

- Federal NESHAPS Standards:

    ✔ asbestos;
    ✔ benzene;
    ✔ beryllium;
    ✔ coke oven emissions;
    ✔ inorganic arsenic;
    ✔ mercury;
    ✔ radionuclides;
    ✔ radon;
    ✔ uranium mines;
    ✔ vinyl chloride.

- State Toxic Air Contaminant Standards

    ✔ benzene from retail service stations [17 CCR §93101];
    ✔ hexavalent chromium from decorative and hard chrome plating, and chromic acid and anodizing facilities [17 CCR §93102];
    ✔ hexavalent chromium from cooling towers [17 CCR §93103];
    ✔ dioxins from medical waste incinerators [17 CCR §93104];
    ✔ asbestos [17 CCR §93106]; and
    ✔ ethylene oxide [17 CCR §93108].

Local districts are required to implement federal and state hazardous substance standards by adopting local rules and enforcing the rules for facilities in their jurisdiction. Facilities should comply with federal requirements irrespective of local enforcement, because EPA retains concurrent enforcement authority in this area.

- For planning purposes, facilities also should be aware of future hazardous substance requirements. EPA has identified more than 100 substances as hazardous air pollutants and 1990 amendments to the Clean Air Act require that these substances be acted upon by rulemaking according to a fixed timetable. In addition, the state Air Resources Board has listed a number of substances as toxic air contaminants for which standards remain to be developed:

✔ cadmium and cadmium compounds;
✔ carbon tetrachloride;
✔ chlorinated dioxins and dibenzofurans;
✔ chloroform;
✔ ethylene dibromide;
✔ ethylene dichloride;
✔ inorganic arsenic;
✔ methylene chloride;
✔ nickel and nickel compounds;
✔ perchloroethylene;
✔ trichloroethylene.

Acetaldehyde, benzo(a)pyrene, 1,3 butadiene, diesel exhaust, formaldehyde, lead and styrene are currently in the pre-listing review process.

Facilities also should be aware that emissions of any toxic or hazardous air contaminant may be regulated by the local district under its independent authority to establish standards and permit systems and set nuisance emissions regulations that are stricter than state standards [*Western Oil and Gas Association v. Monterey Bay Unified Air Pollution Control District* (49 Cal.3d 408, 1989)]. Consequently, there is no pre-emptive effect of state or federal standards or programs with respect to district regulation of sources of emissions.

◆ **Air Toxic Hot Spots Information and Assessment Act - Emission Inventories and Risk Assessments**

This state statute requires emission inventories where a facility emits or has the potential of emitting 10 or more tons of total air pollutants (organic gases, particulates, carbon monoxide, oxides of nitrogen and sulfur) and manufactures, formulates or releases any of the substances listed as being subject to the act. In addition, the statute allows local districts to include any facility listed on its current toxics use or emissions inventory in the program, which grants broad discretion to include virtually any facility. The act further requires the ARB to devise a timetable for statewide inclusion of facilities with less than 10 tons of emissions in the toxics emissions program.

In practice, the submission of an emissions inventory is in response to a request by the district because the district, through its permit process, identifies the volume of emissions from permitted sources and determines Hot Spots Act applicability. As of this printing, most of the permitted facilities subject to the act based on volume of total air pollutants have been notified of the requirement by local districts. Most of the remaining activity will involve facilities in districts with less comprehensive permitting programs and those facilities that emit less than 10 tons and are being included based on district discretion.

Facilities that are permitted by the district for any reason should review the list of covered chemicals in order to anticipate future requirements. The district also will be able to advise a facility of its progress in implementing the program. Once a facility is notified that it is subject to the act, the following steps will proceed:

- **Request to submit a toxic emissions inventory plan.** This notice from the district triggers the requirement that the subject facility submit, through the specified forms and supporting documentation, a detailed description of its toxic substance emitting equipment (stacks, fugitive, air cleaning devices and processes) and a technical discussion of how emissions of each toxic substance emittent will be quantified by either estimation or measurement. Some of the listed substances do not have to be quantified. Preparation of the emissions inventory plan requires a thorough understanding of the applicable regulations [17 CCR §93300] and the specific materials, processes and controls of the facility. Once notified, the facility is given 120 days to submit its plan to the district. Extensions may be granted if progress toward compliance is shown.

- **Submission of a toxic emissions inventory.** Once the emissions plan is reviewed and approved by the district, the facility is required to complete its Toxics Emissions Inventory within 180 days. The plan must include any monitoring data, calculations, and all other information which supports the emissions measurements or estimates. Extensions may be granted upon a showing of progress toward compliance.

- **Request to prepare a risk assessment.** Based on review of the toxics emissions inventory submitted, the district is required to assign a high, medium or low priority to the facility. Guidelines issued by the California Air Pollution Control Officers Association (CAPCOA) are used by many districts in establishing the priorities, however, there is no specific method required in the act or the Title 17 regulations. CAPCOA also has published guidelines for performing toxic air emission risk assessments. A facility ranked as a high-priority facility will be requested to complete a risk assessment within 150 days of the request. A 30-day extension is provided for in the act.

  A risk assessment is a detailed quantitative calculation of the dispersion of toxic emissions from the facility and the resultant impact on the local population. Computer models are usually used to predict both dispersion and potential health effects to individuals and the population as a whole. The completed risk assessment must be submitted by the district for Cal/EPA review.

- **Regulatory phase.** Once the risk assessment is finalized, the district will determine whether there is a significant risk due to the toxic emissions from the facility. If so, the district will require the operator to provide notice to the affected population and/or require additional control measures to abate emissions deemed to pose a significant risk. Public hearings are also provided for in the statute.

  A system of fees has been established by districts to finance the costs of the program. The fees are associated with each step in the regulatory process. Therefore, a facility which moves through the process to the risk assessment phase can anticipate substantial fees in addition to the extremely expensive costs of compliance. Cost of an emissions inventory through risk assessment involving a single toxic substance has been estimated at more than $20,000.

Summary: Air Emissions and Pollution Control Compliance

Facilities that are subject to the state's air pollution control program are urged to contact their local air pollution control district or air quality management district to determine the specific compliance requirements that apply. Given the extent of district authority, consulting local program administrators is essential for air program compliance.

◆ Air Permits

With certain exceptions, sources of air emissions of conventional pollutants (oxides of nitrogen and sulfur, carbon monoxide, volatile organic compounds and particulates, and other substances) must be granted permits by the local district. Permit requirements and procedures differ from district to district, but the general approach of authority to construct and permit to operate approvals is consistent. Permits must be posted and renewed annually.

◆ New Source Review

New or modified sources must undergo a process called new source review before receiving a permit if they emit certain pollutants and exceed the threshold established by local district rules. Based on the specifics of the district rules and the status of the district's compliance with air quality standards, stringent requirements may be imposed on proposed new sources, including best available control technology (BACT) and/or offsets to assure that there is no net increase in emissions due to the new source. New source review also assures compliance with federal new source performance standards and applicable hazardous substance standards.

◆ Hazardous Substance Emissions Standards

Facilities that emit any of the substances subject to national emission standards for hazardous air pollutants (NESHAP) or state toxic air contaminant standards must comply with the specific requirements of these standards. Facilities that emit substances on yet unregulated federal and state hazardous air pollutant lists need to monitor development in order to plan for future compliance requirements

◆ Air Toxic Hot Spots Emissions Inventories and Risk Assessments

The state Air Toxic Hot Spots Information and Assessment Act requires that emission inventories be prepared by larger emitters of conventional pollutants (based on their permitted emissions) that potentially emit toxic substances subject to the act. These inventories are required within 180 days after a plan is submitted at the request of the district. Once the emissions inventory is submitted, the district will advise the facility of whether a risk assessment is necessary based on the priorities established by the district. If a risk assessment is required, it must be prepared and reviewed by Cal/EPA and, depending on the results, lead to additional control measures or other regulatory actions.

Penalties for Violations of the Air Pollution Control Laws

Like other environmental regulatory programs, air pollution control programs assess stringent penalties that increase in severity with the magnitude or length of the violation. It is essential for regulated facilities to review the information in this chapter and achieve compliance voluntarily at the earliest feasible time to minimize penalties and other adverse consequences.

- **Civil penalties** in various amounts up to $25,000 per day (knowing violations) may be assessed in an action brought by the attorney general or by a local district attorney. [Health and Safety Code §§42401, et seq.] Various factors affect the amount of the penalty, including:

  ✔ Extent of harm caused by the violation.
  ✔ Nature and persistence of the violation.
  ✔ Length of time over which the violation occurs.
  ✔ Frequency of past violations.
  ✔ Record of maintenance.
  ✔ Unproven or innovative nature of the control equipment.
  ✔ Any action taken by the defendant to mitigate the violation.
  ✔ Financial burden to the defendant.

- **Administrative civil penalties** of up to $500 per day may be pursued by the district.

- **Criminal sanctions** can be sought in a prosecution that may result in fines and jail sentences up to one year, depending on whether the violation involved strict liability, negligence or knowing, or resulted in actual injury.

- **Injunctions** may be obtained to require immediate action to abate violations, when orders of abatement are not sufficiently expeditious or effective. [Health and Safety Code §41513]

- **Orders of abatement** may be issued by a district board or district hearing board to compel compliance with district rules or for any other air pollution violation. These orders may be unconditional or conditional, in which case they may serve the purpose of a variance. Orders of abatement are enforceable through an injunction obtainable by a showing that an effective order was issued and violations continue.

- **Variances** may be granted by the district board or hearing board to any source and for any matter out of compliance, except nuisance emissions, and obtaining a permit. A variance in effect allows a source to operate out of compliance without incurring a penalty. Variances are issued when a hearing board finds all of the following:

  ✔ That the petitioner is or will be in violation of Health and Safety Code §41701 or of a rule, regulation or order of the district;

  ✔ That due to conditions beyond the reasonable control of the petitioner, requiring compliance would result in either an arbitrary or unreasonable taking of property, or the practical closing and elimination of a lawful business;

  ✔ That the closing or taking would be without a corresponding benefit in reducing air contaminants;

  ✔ That the applicant has given consideration to curtailing operations of the source in lieu of obtaining a variance;

Chap. 5

✔ That during the period the variance is in effect, the applicant will reduce excess emissions to the maximum extent feasible; and

✔ That during the period the variance is in effect, the applicant will monitor or otherwise quantify emission levels from the source, if requested to do so by the district, and report those emission levels to the district pursuant to a schedule established by the district.

Interim and emergency variances also may be granted more expeditiously to address special problems.

● **Permit denials and suspensions** are also within the discretion of the district. These actions may be appealed before the hearing board by the permit holder or applicant.

● **Federal violations** prosecuted by EPA may result in civil penalties of up to $25,000 per day and criminal enforcement if the violator fails to abate upon notice [42 U.S.C. 7413(b)].

Appendix 5-1
List of Applicable Laws and Regulations
Stationary Source Air Emissions and Pollution Control

State Laws

Authority, Permits and New Source Requirements

● Air Resources Board Powers, Duties and Requirements	Health and Safety Code §§39608-39650
● Local Air Pollution Control District or Local Air Quality Management District Powers, Duties and Requirements	Health and Safety Code §§40150-43020
● New Source Requirements	Health and Safety Code §40918-40926
● Permitting Requirements and Fees	Health and Safety Code §§40501.2-40719

Toxic Air Contaminants

● Identification of Toxic Air Contaminants	Health and Safety Code §§ 39660.5-39664
● Control of Toxic Air Contaminants	Health and Safety Code §§ 39668-39912

Air Toxics Hot Spots

● Facilities Subject to Rules and Emission Inventories	Health and Safety Code §§44300-44346
● Risk Assessment	Health and Safety Code §44360-44384

Federal Laws

● Clean Air Act	42 USC §§7401-7642

State Regulations

Authority, Permits and New Source Requirements

● Air Resources Board Powers, Duties and Requirements	17 CCR §§60000-60053
● Local Air Pollution Control District or Local Air Quality Management District Powers, Duties and Requirements	17 CCR §§80100-90623
● New Source Requirements	Local district rules
● Permitting Requirements and Fees	17 CCR §§60030-60053; 90600-90623, as well as local district regulations.

Toxic Air Contaminants

● Identification of Toxic Air Contaminants - Identification Procedures	17 CCR §§91200-91220; 94100-94145
● Control of Toxic Air Contaminants	17 CCR §§93100-93103

Air Toxics Hot Spots

● Facilities Subject to Rules and Emissions Inventories	17 CCR §§90700-90704; 93300-93324, as well as local district rules

Federal Regulations

● Air Programs	40 CFR 50-99

Chap. 5

Appendix 5-2
Local Air Pollution Control District Directory

Amador County Air Pollution Control District .... (209) 223-3697
108 Court Street, Jackson, CA 95641

Bay Area Air Quality Management District .... (415) 771-6000
939 Ellis Street, San Francisco, CA 94109
(Counties include: Alameda, Contra Costa, Marin, San Francisco, San Mateo,
Santa Clara, Solano and Sonoma)

Butte County Air Pollution Control District.. (916) 891-2882
9287 Midway, Suite 1A, Durham, CA 95938

Calaveras County Air Pollution Control District .... (209) 754-6399
Government Center, San Andreas, CA 95249

Colusa County Air Pollution Control District .... (916) 458-5891
100 Sunrise Boulevard, Suite F, Colusa, CA 95932

El Dorado County Air Pollution Control District .... (916) 621-5897
360 Fair Lane, Placerville, CA 95667

Feather River Air Quality Management District .... (916) 741-6484
142 Garden Way, Yuba City, CA 95991
(Counties include Sutter and Yuba)

Glenn County Air Pollution Control District.. (916) 934-6500
720 N. Colusa Street, P.O. Box 351, Willows, CA 95988

Great Basin Unified Air Pollution Control District .... (619) 872-8211
157 Short Street, Suite 6, Bishop, CA 93514
(Counties include: Mono, Inyo and Alpine)

Imperial County Air Pollution Control District .... (619) 339-4314
150 S. 9th Street, El Centro, CA 92243

Kern County Air Pollution Control District .... (805) 861-3682
2700 M Street, Suite 275, Bakersfield, CA 93301

Lake County Air Quality Management District .... (707) 263-7000
833 Lakeport Boulevard, Lakeport, CA 95453

Lassen County Air Pollution Control District .... (916) 257-8311
175 Russell Avenue, Susanville, CA 96130   Ext. 110

Mariposa County Air Pollution Control District .... (209) 966-0200
P.O. Box 5, Mariposa, CA 95338

Mendocino County Air Quality Management District .... (707) 463-4354
Courthouse, Ukiah, CA 95482

Modoc County Air Pollution Control District .... (916) 233-6401
202 W. 4th Street, Alturas, CA 96101

Mojave Desert Air Quality Management District .... (619) 245-1661
15428 Civic Drive, Suite 200, Victorville, CA 92392

Monterey Bay Unified Air Pollution Control District .... (408) 647-9411
24580 Silver Cloud Court, Monterey, CA 93940
(Counties include: Monterey, San Benito and Santa Cruz)

North Coast Unified Air Quality Management District .... (707) 443-3093
2389 Myrtle Avenue, Eureka, CA 95501
(Counties include: Humboldt, Del Norte and Trinity)

Northern Sierra Air Quality Management District .... (916) 274-9360
P.O. Box 2509, Grass Valley, CA 95945
(Counties include: Plumas, Sierra and Nevada)

Northern Sonoma County Air Pollution Control District .... (707) 433-5911
109 North Street, Healdsburg, CA 95448

Placer County Air Pollution Control District .... (916) 889-7130
11464 B Avenue, Auburn, CA 95603

Sacramento Metropolitan Air Quality Management District .... (916) 386-6650
8411 Jackson Road, Sacramento, CA 95826

San Diego County Air Pollution Control District... (619) 694-3307
9150 Chesapeake Drive, San Diego, CA 92123

San Joaquin Valley Unified Air Pollution Control District .... (209) 497-1000
1999 Tuolumne Street, Suite 200, Fresno, CA 93721
(Counties include: Fresno, Kings, Madera, Merced, San Joaquin, Stanislaus
and Tulare)

San Luis Obispo Air Pollution Control District .... (805) 781-5912
2156 Sierra Way, Suite B, San Luis Obispo, CA 93401

Santa Barbara County Air Pollution Control District .... (805) 961-8800
26 Castilian Drive, Building 23, Goleta, CA 93117

Shasta County Air Quality Management District .... (916) 225-5674
    1826 Butte Street, Redding, CA 96001

Siskiyou County Air Pollution Control District .... (916) 842-8029
    525 S. Foothill Drive, Yreka, CA 96097

South Coast Air Quality Management District .... (714) 396-2000
    21865 E. Copley Drive, Diamond Bar, CA 91765-4182
    (Counties include: Los Angeles, Orange, San Bernardino and Riverside)

Tehama County Air Pollution Control District .... (916) 527-3717
    1750 Walnut Street (P.O. Box 38), Red Bluff, CA 96080

Tuolumne County Air Pollution Control District .... (209) 533-5693
    2 South Green Street, Sonora, CA 95370

Ventura County Air Pollution Control District .... (805) 645-1400
    702 County Square Drive, Ventura, CA 93003

Yolo-Solano County Air Pollution Control District .... (916) 757-3650
    1947 Galileo Court, Suite 103, Davis, CA 95616

Chap. 5

Appendix 5-3
California Air Basins

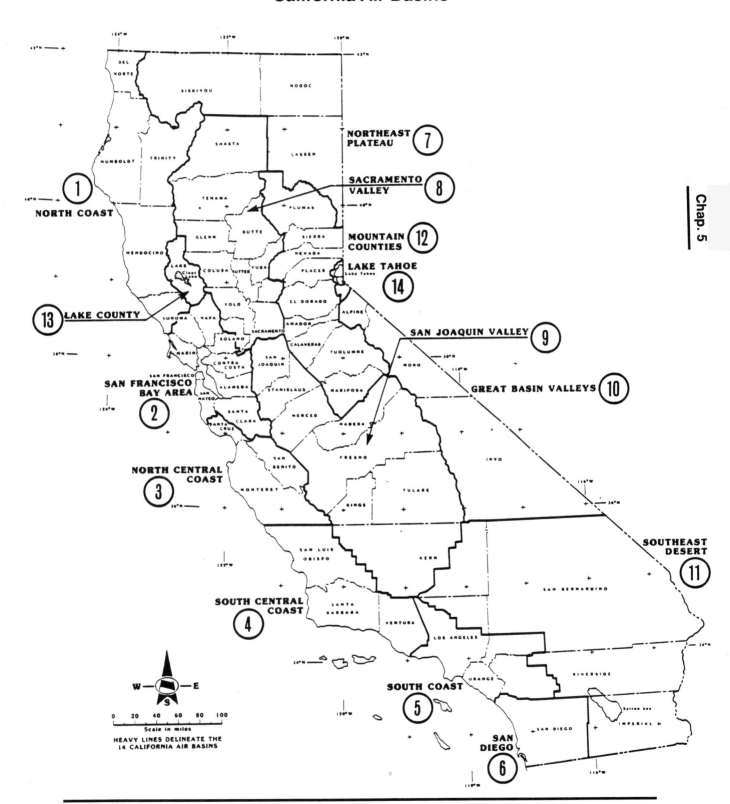

Wastewater Management: Discharges to the Land, State Waters and Sewer Systems

Summary and Applicability

This chapter describes the regulatory programs associated with facilities which, as a part of their operations, discharge wastes, usually waste process water, to the land, surface water or community sewer systems. These wastes are not those considered hazardous wastes, which will be covered in Chapter 8. Nonetheless, as this chapter will indicate, discharge of non-hazardous waste is subject to extensive regulation.

The regulatory programs presented in this chapter include:

- Waste discharge reporting and permitting requirements.
- Regulation of surface impoundments and injection wells.
- Proposition 65 chemical discharge prohibition.
- Stormwater runoff permitting and controls.
- Regulation of discharges to community sewer systems.

A summary of these regulatory requirements appears at the end of this chapter.

Use this chapter to identify the requirements that apply to your facility. Once it is determined that a facility is subject to regulation as a discharger, it is essential to obtain and review the regulations or other requirements of the agency this chapter identifies as having jurisdiction over the activity.

Implementation of the federal Clean Water Act and state Water Quality Act has been a high priority and complicated process in California given the importance of water as a limited and precious resource to the state's population and economy. The state's laws, in many respects, exceed federal requirements because the federal Clean Water Act was not intended by Congress to replace state water law, but to supplement it. In some areas, federal law establishes minimum requirements and federal EPA maintains concurrent enforcement jurisdiction to assure compliance by the state program and facilities subject to federal laws and regulations. However, the regulatory scheme is primarily a creation of state law.

Organization of Water Quality Regulation Programs

◆ Federal EPA

EPA is responsible for administration of the federal Clean Water Act [33 U.S.C. 251], which addresses water pollution issues through a system of permitting designed to control, and eventually eliminate, water pollution. The principal federal regulatory mechanism is the National Pollution Discharge Elimination System (NPDES) permit. All point source discharges of pollution (broadly defined to include virtually anything that affects the natural environment) to navigable water are required to be permitted. This requirement applies to industrial facilities; public facilities, including publicly-owned treatment works (POTWs) or sewage treatment plans; and, most recently, sources of stormwater runoff.

The issuance of an NPDES permit imposes discharge limitations on the permitted facilities which are then periodically required to meet increasingly stringent limitations until federal clean water objectives are attained. The Clean Water Act provides for complete delegation of authority to states for NPDES permitting once the EPA administrator approves the state program. In California, this authority has been delegated to the State Water Resources Control Board and its regional water quality control boards. The federal system of increasingly more stringent discharge limitations is, for the most part, irrelevant in California due to more stringent water quality standards developed under state law.

POTWs are required to regulate their industrial users to maintain the treatment facility's permit. Federal standards for pretreatment requirements for industrial users' discharges to POTWs are based on industrial categories. These stringent standards are required to be enforced by local sanitation districts; if not, the regional or state board may take action and, in some cases, EPA may enforce the requirements directly against industrial dischargers, called "over filing," and also take necessary action against the sanitation district.

◆ State Water Pollution Control Program

The current era of state water quality and pollution control began with the Porter-Cologne Water Quality Control Act of 1969. Porter-Cologne established a comprehensive program for both regulating water quality and controlling sources of pollution. The organizations responsible for implementing the state program include the State Water Resources Control Board and regional water quality control boards.

The State Water Resources Control Board (SWRCB) performs the rulemaking and appeals function of the state water resources control program. This responsibility includes water policy issues, including water rights and allocations, and other resource-related matters outside of the scope of this handbook. Consequently, the SWRCB has been part of the Resources Agency. However, given its important role in this area of water quality and pollution control, it has been reorganized into the new Cal/EPA as a department.

The SWRCB is composed of five full-time positions: four members and a chairperson appointed by the Governor and confirmed by the Senate. Appointees are selected from the following disciplines: attorney qualified in the field of water supply and water rights, a civil engineer similarly qualified, a professional engineer qualified in the field of sanitary engineering and water quality, a person qualified in the field of water quality and a public member. One of the four members with special qualifications must be qualified in the field of irrigated agriculture. The board's members must be selected from different regions, but represent the state as a whole. Appendix 6-2 is the Organizational Chart of the SWRCB.

- **Powers and responsibilities of the state board:** the state board directs and coordinates the activities of the regional boards. It performs this function through its policies and approval of water quality control plans adopted by the regional boards; supervising regional boards in implementing federal Clean Water Act provisions, such as permitting; conducting research;

Chap. 6

approving the budgets of regional boards; promulgating regulations; and reviewing actions taken by regional boards or appealed to the board by aggrieved parties.

- **Regional water quality control boards** were established by the state Legislature in nine regions:

  ✔ North Coast
  ✔ San Francisco Bay
  ✔ Central Coast
  ✔ Central Valley
  ✔ Lahontan (Sierra Nevada and Lake Tahoe)
  ✔ Los Angeles
  ✔ Colorado River Basin
  ✔ Santa Ana
  ✔ San Diego

Appendix 6-3 includes a diagram of the areas of the state covered by each of these regions. Each regional board is composed of nine part-time members appointed by the Governor and confirmed by the Senate. They must be selected from individuals with specific expertise in: water supply, conservation and production; irrigated agriculture; industrial water use; municipal government; county government; non-governmental association with recreation, fish or wildlife; competence in other water quality problems (two members); and a public member. Members must reside or conduct business within the region and efforts must be made to represent all areas of the region in making appointments. Most of the business of a regional board is conducted by its staff under an executive officer.

Powers and responsibilities of regional boards include developing the Water Quality Plan or Basin Plan for the region to meet statutory and state board requirements and provisions of the federal Clean Water Act. This master policy is used to review permit applications, waste discharge requirements and other issues as they relate to sources of water pollution or uses of water resources

Basic Provisions of State Water Quality Control Law

- **Regional Water Quality Control or Basin Plans** are developed by regional water quality control boards to establish and protect "beneficial uses" of water. Beneficial uses include domestic, municipal, agricultural, industrial, power generation, recreation, navigation, aesthetic enjoyment, fish habitat, wildlife preservation and other aquatic resources or preserves. Waste disposal is not recognized as a beneficial use, but a factor that must be assimilated into the basin plan in a manner which does not degrade beneficial uses.

- **Water quality objectives** are established to protect beneficial uses. Water quality objectives are enforceable narrative or quantitative standards for constituents or characteristics that will assure reasonable protection of beneficial uses. Water quality objectives recognize that the quality of basin water may be changed, to some extent, without unreasonably affecting beneficial uses in order to allow industrial and other commercial uses, as well as human

Chap. 6

habitation. Within limits, there is a complex balancing of interests when water quality objectives are established, considering the following factors, among others:

✔ The past, present and probable future beneficial uses of water.

✔ The environmental characteristics of the hydrogeologic unit under consideration, including the quality of water available to that unit.

✔ Water quality conditions that could reasonably be achieved through coordinated control of all factors that affect water quality in the area.

✔ Economic considerations.

✔ The need for developing housing within the region.

◆ Federal Act Compliance

● The **beneficial uses** adopted by the regional boards and the water quality objectives established to protect them meet, and in fact exceed, the requirements of the Clean Water Act. The federal act requires similar designation of "existing uses," which include many of the same beneficial uses as state law protects. The federal act requires the states to adopt criteria for pollutants that would not degrade the designated uses of the water and prohibits states from allowing waters to be used to transport or assimilate wastes. The federal act also requires states to establish a policy of non-degradation which protects waters from deterioration and preserves waters with existing high quality. The state board has adopted Order No. W086-17, which incorporates the federal non-degradation policy into state requirements.

● **Implementation of water quality objectives** is accomplished through planning activities, surveillance and enforcement, and by regulating discharges through permitting. The latter method most directly affects the facilities that discharge or plan to discharge directly or indirectly (through POTWs) to state waters. Regional boards are authorized to regulate discharges of wastes that may affect the quality of state waters. Waters that may be affected include both surface and ground waters, a broader concept than the federal act. Discharges also are broadly construed to mean point and non-point including, for example, agricultural runoff in irrigation canals.

● **Waste** is broadly interpreted to include "sewage, as well as any other waste substance associated with human habitations, or of human or animal origin, or from any producing, manufacturing or processing operation of whatever nature, including waste placed within disposal containers" [Water Code §13050(d)]. Given this extremely broad definition, wastes include:

✔ Drainage from mines.

✔ Debris from logging.

✔ Agricultural drainage.

✔   Wastes disposed of in a landfill.

✔   Cooling water from power plants.

✔   Changes in receiving waters caused by extraction of sand or gravel from a stream.

✔   Construction waste disposed of in a manner affecting state waters.

Based on the increasingly stringent interpretation of the term waste, it must be concluded that any wastewater or liquid that does not meet regional water quality objectives (which may be better than drinking water quality) or solid substances which adversely affect receiving water quality will be regulated. Such discharges are regulated regardless of whether they are made directly into state waters or into land that may affect groundwater.

◆   Regulatory Procedures

● **A reporting requirement** is imposed on any person who discharges or proposes to discharge a waste, other than to a sewer system, or changes the character of a current discharge to the regional board. The report must contain information necessary for the board to evaluate the discharge. In some cases, the board may waive reports of future discharges once it determines that waste discharge requirements are not necessary. [Water Code §13260.]

Once the report of discharge or proposed discharge is made, no further action may be taken by the discharger until: issuance of waste discharge requirements, expiration of 120 days or regional board waiver.

● **Issuance of waste discharge requirements** usually occurs once a discharge report is filed. The other alternative would be to waive discharge requirements for insignificant discharges, such as swimming pool draining, well testing or construction dewatering. However, if the discharge is to surface waters, which requires an NPDES permit, no waiver is permitted. Another alternative would be to prohibit the discharge if sufficiently protective discharge requirements cannot be devised or met by the discharger. Issuance of waste discharge requirements is essentially a permitting process that provides for conditions the discharger must meet. The conditions are based on the water quality objectives and the assimilative capacity of the receiving waters. The discharge limitations usually are a combination of quantitative and narrative specifications. Issuance of waste discharge requirements must be noticed for public comment and approved at a hearing of the regional board.

● **NPDES permits** required by the federal Clean Water Act are issued in California in a manner consistent with establishing waste discharge requirements [Water Code §§13370 -13389]. Therefore, if the discharge is from a point source into surface waters, the waste discharge requirements must consider all necessary aspects of federal and state requirements.

Programs to Address Specific Water-Related Problems

Given the importance of water resources to California and the myriad situations posing a threat to both surface and ground water supplies, a number of special regulatory programs have been developed to assure necessary protection of state waters.

◆ Groundwater Protection

As indicated previously in this chapter, waste discharge notices and regulatory action in response are required for discharges to the land to assure groundwater quality protection. This general method of regulation has been supplemented in several cases by specific regulatory programs.

- **"Subchapter 15" regulations** apply to all waste disposal to land, including hazardous and non-hazardous materials, into landfills and surface impoundments [23 CCR §§2510-2601]. These regulations specify construction, monitoring and closure requirements for such facilities that are imposed as conditions on permits to discharge wastes into the facility. Regional boards have concurrent regulatory authority over solid waste landfills with the Integrated Solid Waste Management Board and, in the case of hazardous waste facilities, with the Department of Toxic Substances Control and EPA. Regulation of solid waste disposal is discussed in Chapter 10. However, the issuance of waste discharge requirements by the regional board is essential to any waste disposal facility's operations. Hazardous waste disposal facilities are discussed in Chapter 8.

- **Toxic Pit Cleanup Act of 1984** (TPCA) [Health and Safety Code §§25208, et seq.] regulates surface impoundments that existed before Subchapter 15 regulations were established and which do not meet the current requirements, such as double containment, leachate collection and monitoring. Operation of a surface impoundment which does not meet Subchapter 15 requirements for the disposal or treatment of hazardous wastes or liquids containing hazardous substances is prohibited. Closed impoundments (toxic pits) that pose a threat to drinking water supplies must be investigated (these studies are called hydrogeologic assessment reports or HARs), and cleaned up pursuant to the requirements of the act. Regional boards have been granted authority for administering the act.

- **Underground and above ground storage tanks** are another area where specific regulatory programs have been authorized by federal and state law, and administered by the state and regional water boards. These programs are discussed in Chapter 7.

- **Toxic or underground injection wells.** Any disposal of wastes into a well shaft or dry well that poses a significant threat to groundwater would be subject to all the provisions for regulating discharges of waste as previously described. In addition to Water Code authority for regional boards to act, the state Legislature enacted the Toxic Injection Well Act of 1984 [Health and Safety Code §§25159, et seq.], which defines injection wells (in effect, holes in the ground deeper than their circumference) and prohibits use of this type of facility for disposal of hazardous waste unless permitted by the Department of Toxic Substances Control. In addition, such wells are covered by prohibitions in the federal Safe Drinking Water Act which proscribe wastewater disposal practices that pose a threat to groundwater [40 CFR §145].

◆ The Safe Drinking Water and Toxics Enforcement Act (Proposition 65)

Proposition 65 prohibits the discharge to a potential source of drinking water of a chemical known to the state to cause cancer or reproductive harm [list at 22 CCR §12000(b) and (c)]. Some 300 chemicals are listed and any detectable amount triggers applicability of the statute unless the discharger can demonstrate that the discharge results in no significant risk. It is anticipated that eventually a Proposition 65 evaluation will be made as part of the waste discharge regulatory system. At the present time, however, the state and regional boards have not developed a regulatory policy that effectively integrates Proposition 65 into existing programs.

◆ Stormwater Runoff Regulation

Beginning in 1992, stormwater runoff will be comprehensively regulated by federal and state permits. The 1987 amendments to the federal Clean Water Act required EPA to establish a regulatory system to manage stormwater discharges. The resulting regulation [40 CFR §122-124] was published in November 1990 and was to have been in effect in November 1991. However, this timetable has been relaxed, primarily to allow states to adopt programs to implement the federal requirements. The State Water Resources Control Board has adopted by resolution a stormwater pollution program that implements the federal regulations. This action, which has the effect of a regulation, defines facilities subject to permitting. At a minimum, these facilities include those specified in the federal regulation:

- Industrial facilities.
- Manufacturing facilities.
- Mining facilities.
- Hazardous waste treatment, storage or disposal facilities.
- Landfills, land application sites and open dumps.
- Recycling facilities.
- Steam electric power generating facilities.
- Transportation facilities.
- Sewage or wastewater treatment works.
- Construction activity that results in a land disturbance of five acres or more.
- Other facilities at which polluting materials are exposed to stormwater.

Although federal regulations allow three permitting options (individual permits, group permits and general permits), the board issues only general permits for industrial activity discharges. This permit structure is a statewide general permit that applies to all industrial stormwater discharge categories except construction. A separate statewide general permit has been issued for construction where more than 5 acres are disturbed. The permit applications are called "Notices of Intent" to be permitted, given the developing nature of the federal and state programs. Notices of Intent were required by March 1, 1992.

The state general permit mandates that dischargers develop and implement a stormwater pollution prevention plans by October 1, 1992 and eliminate illicit discharges of stormwater to sewer systems. In addition, covered facilities must monitor discharges of stormwater for physical characteristics and chemical pollutants during the 1992-93 wet season and submit data by July 1, 1993.

Facilities that may be subject to stormwater runoff regulation should contact the state or regional water boards for more information.

Chap. 6

Industrial Use of Community Sewer Systems

The most common method for facilities to dispose of wastewater is by discharge to a community sewer system. Facilities using this wastewater management practice are called industrial users and are subject to the regulatory requirements of the municipal, county or regional sanitation district that serves the user. As discussed previously, publicly owned treatment works (POTWs) are themselves subject to waste discharge requirements and responsible for implementing federal rules governing industrial categorical pre-treatment standards. The purpose of these standards is to assure that discharges into the sewer system will not adversely affect treatment plant operations or compromise the waste discharge requirements of the POTW, and will result in a sewage sludge which is sufficiently inert that disposal or beneficial reuse will be feasible.

◆ General Sanitation District Requirements for Industrial Users

Industrial and commercial users of sewer systems are required by the district to apply for and obtain a permit and pay the associated fees. The facility must comply with the basic requirements, effluent standards and prohibitions applicable to industrial users. These requirements vary from district to district, so the user must study its district's specific rules. The following general prohibitions and requirements are typical:

No person shall discharge or deposit, or allow to be discharged or deposited into any opening leading to the wastewater system, any discharges which contain the following:

- Oils and grease.
- Explosive mixtures.
- Noxious material.
- Improperly shredded organic garbage.
- Radioactive waste.
- Solid or viscous wastes.
- Chemical toilet waste.
- Excessive discharge rates.
- Toxic substances.
- Unpolluted water.
- Colored material.
- Corrosive waste.

The following specific chemical and physical property discharge limits are typical of limitations imposed on users of the wastewater system:

Constituent	Discharge Limits - mg/l or ppm
Arsenic	1.0
Cadmium	0.8
Total Chromium	2.5
Copper	2.0
Lead	0.6
Mercury	0.01

Nickel 2.0
Silver 0.5
Zinc 5.0
Cyanide (total) 2.5
Selenium 0.1
Phenols 1.0
Total Identifiable Chlorinated Hydrocarbons 0.05
Boron 1.0
Fluoride 3.0

Restrictions also usually include the following prohibitions on discharges:

● Having a temperature higher than 150 degrees Fahrenheit (65 degrees Celsius).

● Containing more than 25 mg/l of oil and grease or petroleum or mineral origin, or 175 mg/l of oil and grease of animal or vegetable origin.

● Having a pH of less than six or greater than 11.5.

● Containing suspended solids greater than 500 mg/l.

● Having a standard five-day biochemical oxygen demand more than 600 mg/l.

● Containing a dissolved sulfide and/or sulfite content higher than 1.0 mg/l.

● Containing a TDS (total dissolved solids) content that exceeds 1,000 mg/l or the potable water supply TDS by more than 250 mg/l, whichever is greater.

● Containing a chloride content that exceeds 200 mg/l or the potable water supply by more than 50 mg/l, whichever is greater."

The district's engineer may impose further requirements depending on the discharger's operations and the district's evaluation. In addition, the district may require periodic monitoring and testing of wastewater. In some cases, the district may perform the testing or conduct supplementary testing.

◆ Compliance With Federal Categorical Pretreatment Standards

Facilities in industries for which EPA has adopted categorical pretreatment standards [40 CFR §400, et seq.] must comply with the federal pretreatment requirements. These standards are designed to protect treatment plant operations and the quality of its effluent. In some cases, however, the sanitation districts have not aggressively enforced the requirements. Nonetheless, EPA may enforce these standards and impose federal penalties on violators. It is essential that the industrial user identify the federal standard applicable and assure that it is in compliance. The following is a table of the current industrial categories with established pretreatment standards. It should be noted that each category contains may subcategories.

Chap. 6

Table of Categorical Treatment Standards

40 CFR Part

400 [Reserved]

401 General provisions

402 [Reserved]

403 General pretreatment regulations for existing and new sources of pollution

405 Dairy products processing point source category

406 Grain mills point source category

407 Canned and preserved fruits and vegetables processing point source category

408 Canned and preserved seafood processing point source category

409 Sugar processing point source category

410 Textile mills point source category

411 Cement manufacturing point source category

412 Feedlots point source category

413 Electroplating point source category

414 Organic chemicals, plastics and synthetic fibers

415 Inorganic chemicals manufacturing point source category

416 [Reserved]

417 Soap and detergent manufacturing point source category

418 Fertilizer manufacturing point source category

419 Petroleum refining point source category

420 Iron and steel manufacturing point source category

421 Nonferrous metals manufacturing point source category

422 Phosphate manufacturing point source category

423 Steam electric power generating point source category

424 Ferroalloy manufacturing point source category

425 Leather tanning and finishing point source category

426 Glass manufacturing point source category

427 Asbestos manufacturing point source category

428 Rubber manufacturing point source category

429 Timber products processing point source category

430 Pulp, paper and paperboard point source category

431 The builders' paper and board mills point source category

432 Meat products point source category

433 Metal finishing point source category

434 Coal mining point source category;
    BPT, BAT, BCT limitations and new source performance standards

435 Oil and gas extraction point source category

436 Mineral mining and processing point source category

439 Pharmaceutical manufacturing point source category

440 Ore mining and dressing point source category

443 Effluent limitations guidelines for existing sources and standards of performance and pre-treatment standards for new sources for the paving and roofing materials (tars and asphalt) point source category

446 Paint formulating point source category

447 Ink formulating point source category

454　Gum and wood chemicals manufacturing point source category
455　Pesticide chemicals
457　Explosives manufacturing point source category
458　Carbon black manufacturing point source category
459　Photographic point source category
460　Hospital point source category
461　Battery manufacturing point source category
463　Plastics molding and forming point source category
464　Metal molding and casting point source category
465　Coil coating point source category
466　Porcelain enameling point source category
467　Aluminum forming point source category
468　Copper forming point source category
469　Electrical and electronic components point source category
471　Nonferrous metals forming and metal powders point source category

◆ Compliance With Hazardous Waste Prohibitions

The federal hazardous waste law or Resource Conservation and Recovery Act (RCRA) contains provisions that exempt sewer system discharges from many of the regulatory requirements of the hazardous waste regulations. This potential gap in hazardous waste controls has been addressed by a new regulation that applies to industrial users of sewer systems. This regulation [40 CFR §403] immediately prohibits discharge of certain hazardous wastes (ignitable, oils, toxic or transported pollutants) that technically may already be prohibited by the sanitation district. However, the federal regulation also requires, beginning February 23, 1991, a notification to the sanitation district, Department of Toxic Substances Control and EPA if the industrial user is discharging any waste which, if otherwise disposed of, would be characterized as a hazardous waste (see Chapter 8). This type of hazardous waste discharge would already be a violation of California law and, therefore, not a widespread practice, although there has not been a focused regulatory program to determine whether such practices are occurring and to what extent. The new federal regulation, which also addresses this aspect of the sanitation districts' regulatory program for industrial dischargers, will promote a more stringent enforcement program.

Summary: Facility Compliance with Water Pollution Control Program

The following information summarizes the regulatory requirements discussed in this chapter:

 To comply with the various provisions of the water pollution control program, a facility must review its operations and determine how it handles its wastes, wastewater and stormwater runoff. Any hazardous wastes will be discussed in Chapter 8; solid wastes shipped to off-site facilities are discussed in Chapter 10.

◆ Waste Discharge Notification

If the facility discharges wastes (any liquid resulting from operations, processes or solid material to the ground or to surface water) that may adversely affect water quality or characteristics, it is subject to waste discharge notification to the regional water quality control board unless it has received a waive or is meeting current waste discharge requirements for the activity.

◆ **Waste Discharge Requirements**

Once the regional board has been notified of the discharge and does not waive discharge requirements, it will either issue waste discharge requirements and permit the discharge or prohibit the discharge. Facilities subject to waste discharge requirements must meet the limitations established by the board and report any discrepancies.

◆ **National Pollution Discharge Elimination System Permits**

National Pollution Discharge Elimination System (NPDES) permits are required (as a matter of both federal and state law) if the discharge is to surface waters. Consequently, if waste discharge requirements are issued to govern surface water discharges, it satisfies the requirements of both federal and state law.

◆ **Specifically Regulated Wastewater Management Systems**

The following types of treatment, storage or disposal systems for any type of waste management are strictly regulated by the Water Code and other applicable statutes and regulations:

- **Surface impoundments or discharges onto land.** Discharges of wastes into surface impoundments are subject to the waste discharge reporting and requirements as described above. In addition, Subchapter 15 regulations specifically address the requirements for use of the land for waste management facilities [23 CCR §§2510-2601]. Surface impoundments operated in the past to manage liquids containing hazardous wastes are regulated by the Toxic Pits Cleanup Act [TPCA at Health and Safety Code §§25208, et seq.]. This act effectively prohibits use of impoundments unless they meet the Subchapter 15 requirements and the discharger establishes a program to investigate and close previously operated impoundments.

- **Injection wells (or dry wells)** for disposal of wastewater are subject to the waste discharge reporting and requirement provisions of the regional board. However, with certain exceptions (mainly petroleum wells), use of injection wells for disposal of wastewater and hazardous waste is prohibited due to the significant potential of groundwater contamination resulting from these activities. The federal Safe Drinking Water Act prohibits injection well discharges that may threaten sources of drinking water [40 CFR §145] and the Toxic Injection Well Control Act [Health and Safety Code §§25159, et seq.] prohibits the use of injection wells for hazardous waste disposal unless permitted by the Department of Health Services.

- **Proposition 65 discharge prohibitions.** The Safe Drinking Water and Toxics Enforcement Act [Health and Safety Code §25249.5] prohibits discharges of any chemical known to cause cancer or reproductive toxicity to potential sources of drinking water. Any significant discharge of such chemicals as waste or constituents of waste would be regulated under the waste discharge reports and requirements discussed above. State enforcement policies for other discharges as trace but detectable amounts of listed chemicals have not been finalized and remain to be implemented. Facilities or dischargers responsible for such discharges containing Proposition 65 chemicals should carefully evaluate the regulatory significance of their activities.

Chap. 6

- **Stormwater and other non-point source discharges.** Stormwater discharges of industrial, manufacturing, construction and other facilities are subject to a new permitting program by March 1, 1992 and pollution control program by October 1, 1992. A resolution of the State Water Resources Control Board established this regulatory program. Facilities that may be subject to stormwater permitting should inquire about the need to submit a "notice of intent."

- **Community sewer district discharges.** Facilities termed "industrial users" that discharge their wastewater into sewer systems operated by community sanitation districts are required to be permitted by the district as an industrial or commercial discharger. The characteristics of the discharges are evaluated by district engineers based on information provided by the user applicant prior to permitting. Industrial users are required to meet all generally applicable requirements and prohibitions, discharge limits for specific constituents and any additional requirements imposed by the district.

  Industrial users also are required by federal EPA and the sanitation district to comply with the categorical pretreatment standards applicable to the facility (if any). Finally, discharge of any hazardous wastes into the sewer system is prohibited by district rules, the state hazardous waste laws, and further subject to new federal regulations that require notifications of the sanitation district, the state Department of Toxic Substances Control and EPA if a hazardous waste is disposed into a sewer system. Hazardous waste in this context means that if the waste were disposed of in any other manner, it would be characterized as a hazardous waste. [See Chapter 8.]

Penalties for Violations of the Water Pollution Control Program

Stringent penalty and enforcement provisions have been included in the state and federal water pollution control statutes to punish violators and to apply sufficient sanctions to bring facilities into compliance. Most penalties in this environmental program are levied as administrative civil penalties and are not usually severe relative to other environmental violations, if compliance is achieved promptly.

◆ Enforcement Provisions of the Porter-Cologne Act

- **Cease and desist orders** may be issued by a regional board whenever it finds a discharge or threatened discharge of waste is occurring in violation of state law, waste discharge requirement or prohibition. The cease and desist order requires the violator to comply immediately, comply on a schedule set by the board or take appropriate remedial or corrective actions. These orders become effective upon notice and hearing by the regional board.

- **Cleanup and abatement orders** are used to address problems caused by unregulated discharges, such as spills or leaks, and require the recipient to clean up wastes, abate the effects of the waste discharge or take other remedial actions. Cleanup and abatement orders may be issued to the discharger who is in violation of waste discharge requirements or other order or prohibitions, and to any person who causes or permits waste to be discharged and which causes or threatens to cause pollution or nuisance [Water Code §13304]. This provision means that a person other than the discharger can be held responsible for and ordered to abate the effects of an unauthorized discharge, for example: property owners whose tenants have caused the discharge and, in some cases, owners and operators who have acquired their interest after the discharge has occurred. In these latter cases, cleanup and abatement orders have been issued on the theory of a continuing discharge.

Cleanup and abatement orders may be enforced by the attorney general's office, if the recipient does not comply, through a petition to the superior court for an injunction requiring compliance. In an emergency, the regional board may expend state funds to prevent injury to waters, pollution or nuisance, and recoup costs in a civil action against the discharger.

◆ Civil Liability for Violations of Porter-Cologne Act

- **Administrative civil liability** may be imposed by the regional board against violators of any provisions of the Water Code or waste discharge limitations. The extent of liability imposed depends on whether a hazardous substance was involved (up to $1,000 for non-hazardous; $5,000 for hazardous substances), an NPDES permit was violated (up to $5,000 for non-hazardous; $25,000 per day for hazardous), or whether other situations are in question (statutory provisions also allow civil liability of up to $10 per gallon, as well).

  The penalty imposed by the regional board must consider a number of factors:

  ✔ Nature, circumstances, extent and gravity of the violation.
  ✔ Whether discharge can be cleaned up or abated.
  ✔ Degree of toxicity of the discharge.
  ✔ Ability of the violator to pay.
  ✔ Effect on the violator's ability to stay in business.
  ✔ Voluntary cleanup efforts undertaken.
  ✔ History of violations.
  ✔ Degree of culpability of the violator.
  ✔ Economic savings.
  ✔ Other matters as justice may require.

- **Civil liability** imposed by the superior court upon petition by the attorney general for the same offenses, but with penalties in slightly higher amounts. This proceeding would likely be pursued by the state in the event that compliance cannot be obtained by the regional board and the matter must be referred to the attorney general for enforcement.

- **Criminal sanctions** also are available, although rarely utilized, to further punish violations of the Water Code. In such cases, the violator would be prosecuted for a misdemeanor, with a possibility of imprisonment for up to one year and imposition of civil penalties.

Chap. 6

Appendix 6-1
List of Applicable Laws and Regulations
Wastewater Management, Discharges to the Land,
State Waters and Sewer Systems

State Laws:

- Wastewater Discharges of Waste to Land   Water Code §§13370-13389
  and State Waters
- Water Quality Programs   Water Code §§13000, et seq.
- Water Quality Regulatory Procedures   Water Code §§13370-13389
- Toxic Pit Cleanup Act (TPCA)   Health and Safety Code §§25208-25208.2
  (surface impoundments)
- Toxic or Underground Injection Wells   Health and Safety Code §§ 25159-25159.25
- Safe Drinking Water and Toxics   Health and Safety Code §§ 24249.5-24249.13
  Enforcement Act (Proposition 65)
  Discharge Prohibitions

Federal Laws

- Federal Clean Water Act - the National   42 USC §§1251-1389
  Pollution Discharge Elimination System
  (NPDES). Includes provisions on stormwater
  runoff regulations, discharges to sewer
  systems and pretreatment requirements.

State Regulations

- Wastewater Discharges of Waste to Land   23 CCR §§2200-2260, as well as local
  and State Waters   sanitation district regulations
- Waste Discharges from Non-Point Sources   23 CCR §§2205-2234
- Waste Discharges from Point Sources   23 CCR §§2235-2235.4
- Enforcement Procedures   23 CCR §§2240-2245
- Waste Classification and Management   23 CCR §§2520-2533
- Surface Impoundments and Other   23 CCR §§2510-2601
  Discharge to Land
- Safe Drinking Water and Toxics   22 CCR §§ 12401, et seq.
  Enforcement Act (Proposition 65)
  Discharge Prohibitions
- Discharges to Sewer Systems   Local sanitation district regulations

Federal Regulations

- Water Programs and Enforcement   40 CFR §§100-149
- Wastewater Discharges of Waste to Land   40 CFR §§122
  and Waters (Federal Permits)
- Stormwater Runoff Regulations   40 CFR §§122-124
- Pretreatment Requirements   40 CFR §§400-424

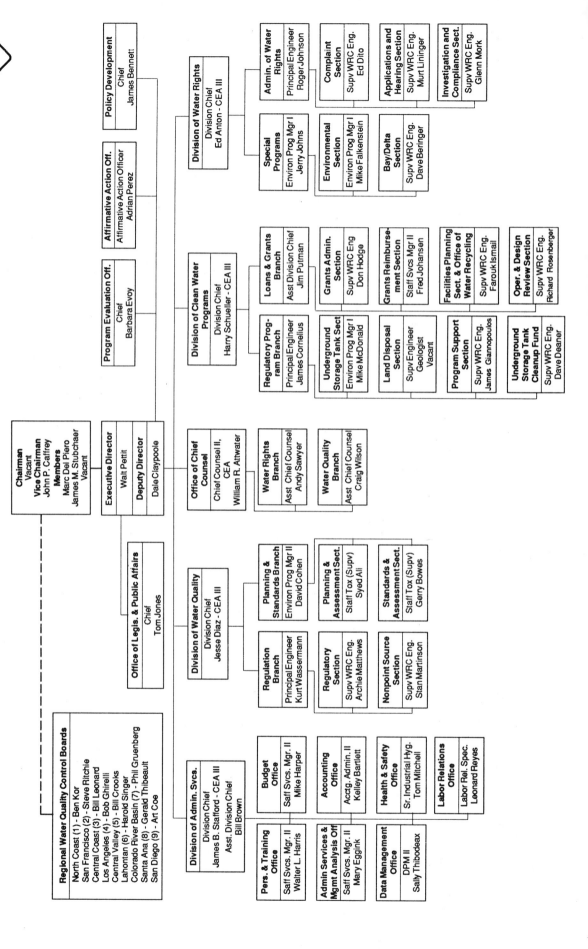

Appendix 6-2
State of California
State Water Resources Control Board

Appendix 6-3
California Regional Water Quality Control Boards

Central Valley Region (5)
3443 Routier Road
Sacramento, CA 95827-3098
(916) 255-3000

Fresno Branch Office
3614 East Ashlan Avenue
Fresno, CA 93726
(209) 445-5116

Redding Branch Office
415 Knollcrest Drive, Ste. 100
Redding, CA 96002
(916) 224-4845

Lahontan Region (6)
2092 Lake Tahoe Blvd.
South Lake Tahoe, CA 96150
(916) 544-3481

Victorville Branch Office
Civic Plaza
15428 Civic Drive, Ste. 100
Victorville, CA 92392
(619) 241-6583

Colorado River Basin Region (7)
73-720 Fred Waring Drive, Ste. 100
Palm Desert, CA 92260
(619) 346-7491

Santa Ana Region (8)
2010 Iowa Avenue, Ste. 100
Riverside, CA 92507-2409
(714) 782-4130

San Diego Region (9)
9771 Clairemont Mesa Blvd., Ste. B
San Diego, CA 92124
(619) 265-5114

Chap. 6

North Coast Region (1)
5550 Skylane Blvd., Ste. A
Santa Rosa, CA 95403
(707) 576-2220

San Francisco Bay Region (2)
2101 Webster Street, Ste. 500
Oakland, CA 94612
(510) 286-1255

Central Coast Region (3)
81 Higuera Street, Ste. 200
San Luis Obispo, CA 93401-5427
(805) 549-3147

Los Angeles Region (4)
101 Centre Plaza Drive
Monterey Park, CA 91754-2156
(213) 266-7500

**State Water Resources
Control Board**
P.O. Box 100
Sacramento, CA 95812-0100
(916) 657-2390

Underground and Aboveground Tank Storage of Hazardous Substances

Summary and Applicability

This chapter presents the state's program to regulate underground and aboveground storage tanks. These types of installations have a history of releases that have had serious environmental consequences. Facilities are subject to the regulatory programs discussed in this chapter if they own or operate either or both of the following types of tank storage.

- Any type of underground storage tank (with the exception of residential heating oil storage tanks) which contains a hazardous substance, including fuels, lubricants, solvents and other chemicals.

- An aboveground storage tank larger than 660 gallons or total capacity in above ground tanks exceeds 1,320 gallons, *if* the tankage contains a substance comprised of 5 percent or greater petroleum fraction. This latter qualification means fuels, oils, solvents, etc., even if dilute concentration.

If either or both of these structures are present at a facility, it is subject to the state regulatory program described in this chapter. This program includes the following elements:

- Underground storage tanks
  ✔ Permitting by the local administering agency.
  ✔ Specific regulatory and control measures, like leak detection and monitoring, inspections and release reporting.
  ✔ Financial responsibility and closure requirements.

- Aboveground storage tanks
  ✔ Filing of a storage statement with the State Water Resources Control Board.
  ✔ Depending on the size of the tank and the industry in which it is used, preparation of a Spill Prevention Control and Counter-Measures Plan.
  ✔ Meet financial responsibility and other current regulatory requirements, and those which may be imposed by the regional water board.

This chapter briefly describes these regulatory requirements for storage tanks. However, any facility subject to these requirements should contact the local underground tank agency (Appendix 7-2) or the State Water Resources Control Board or regional board (Appendices 6-2 and 6-3) for more information.

Background

To combat the serious threat to groundwater resources posed by underground fuel and solvent tanks realized in the early 1980s, first California, then federal EPA established a rigorous regulatory and remediation program. Similar concerns for the hazards posed to both surface and groundwater and public safety from aboveground storage tanks also resulted in federal and state regulatory programs to assure environmental protection and safety for such facilities. This chapter will describe the regulatory agency organizations and the laws and regulations that apply to tank storage of hazardous materials.

Underground Storage Tank Regulatory Program

The California statute that established the state's underground storage tank regulatory program was the Sher bill enacted in 1983. [Health and Safety Code §§25280-25299.1.] This law instituted a local administering agency regulatory program based on the statute and regulations issued by the State Water Resources Control Board. County programs are required to be operated pursuant to state board regulations. Appendix 7-2 is a list of the local agencies responsible for underground storage tanks in their respective communities.

Subsequent adoption of federal regulations on underground storage tanks by EPA in late 1988 has required changes in the state program to obtain federal approval [40 CFR §280]. Once regulations fully implementing federal regulations are promulgated, the state will apply for federal approval of its program as provided for in the EPA rule. Major differences between EPA's regulations and the state program are in the areas of financial responsibility assurances for cleanups, some details of technical installation requirements, compliance deadlines, exemptions for some types of tanks under state law, and consistency of local-to-local implementation. These differences are expected to be resolved as the state program seeks federal approval.

Underground Tank Regulatory Requirements

The state underground tank law applies to underground storage of hazardous substances in tanks (including tanks and the piping systems that are substantially or totally beneath the ground). Hazardous substances are broadly defined to include both flammable and combustible liquid fuels, any hazardous substance defined as a listed hazardous waste, hazardous material or on the Director's List of Hazardous Substances pursuant to Labor Code §6382 (most common chemicals and fuels).

Regulatory requirements applicable to underground storage tanks include:

- **Permitting** [Health and Safety Code §25284]. A permit must be obtained by the owner or operator of a tank from the local agency on a form prescribed by the agency which requires information on the tank(s) location and description, hazardous substance(s) stored, monitoring system, person responsible and an emergency contact. The required fee must be submitted. The permit is issued if the local agency determines the tank complies with the statute and applicable regulations. Permits usually are effective for five years.

- **Fees for Petroleum Tanks** [Health and Safety Code §25299]. Every permittee of an underground tank containing petroleum products must pay a fee per gallon stored to the State Board of Equalization to finance tank cleanups through the Underground Storage Cleanup Fund. Storage of other types of substances is not subject to this fee.

- **Regulatory Requirements Applicable to Underground Tanks** [Health and Safety Code §25292] The specific requirements for underground tanks are based on when the tank was installed and the specifics of the local agency's ordinance. If the tank was installed after January 1, 1984, it must have double-containment and a primary containment leakage monitoring system. Tanks installed before this date must be equipped with a monitoring system capable of detecting leaks and a visual method of inspection unless the local agency has adopted more stringent requirements. All such tanks must be replaced or upgraded to meet secondary containment by December 22, 1998.

- **Monitoring Requirements** [Health and Safety Code §25293]. The statute mandates that the monitoring requirements of the regulations and local agency be met by the permittee. The monitoring alternatives are set forth in the regulations as eight different methods or methods in combination ranging from tank testing and gauging to leak detection and soil or water monitoring [23 CCR §2641].

- **Inspections** [Health and Safety Code §25288]. The local agency is required by statute to inspect each underground tank system at least every three years and to determine compliance status in a written report. The agency also may require the permittee to employ a professional engineer for a special inspection related to the structural requirements for the tank installation.

- **Unauthorized Releases** [Health and Safety Code §25294]. Unauthorized releases from an underground tank that is not contained within the secondary containment system and cleaned up within eight hours must be verbally reported to the local agency within 24 hours of detection and a written report submitted within five days. The regulations at 23 CCR §2650 further describe reporting requirements. In certain cases, repairs are allowed; otherwise the tank must be removed or closed [23 CCR §2660].

- **Closure Requirements** [Health and Safety Code §25298]. The operator or owner of the underground tank may not remove the tank unless the closure requirements of the regulations [23 CCR §2670] and the requirements of the local agency are satisfied. Under certain conditions, temporary closures are allowed. Permanent closures must comply with applicable procedures and "demonstrate to the satisfaction of the local agency that no unauthorized release has occurred" or that the site has been remediated. The local agency and regional water board must approve closure when there has been a tank leak that must be remediated.

- **Financial responsibility** [Health and Safety Code §25292 et seq. and 40 CFR §280]. Financial responsibility for damages caused by tank leaks rests on the owner or operator of the underground tank. Both the federal underground tank regulations and the state statute provide for financial responsibility. The state law specifies that owner/operator liability is limited to $10,000 in the case of petroleum tanks. However, such owners and operators may be required to expend funds as ordered by local agency or regional water boards with the expectation of reimbursement from the state Underground Storage Tank Fund. Regulations that more fully describe this procedure have been promulgated by the State Water Resources Control Board [23 CCR §2810]. Other types of tanks are not covered and, therefore, owners will be required to make financial responsibility demonstrations based on the federal regulations (up to $1 million per tank) or state requirements to implement the federal rule.

Chap. 7

Any person who acquires an underground storage tank through a property or business acquisition will be considered the owner of the tank and responsible for compliance by the local agency regardless of whether the person knew about or operated the tank. The owner may be able to recover its costs from the previous owner or operator of the tank, depending on the terms of the transaction and other equitable factors. The state Underground Tank Cleanup Fund may reimburse costs incurred after January 1, 1998 for a petroleum fuel tank cleanup. In other cases, there is not a clear statutory scheme for "innocent party" recoveries.

Summary of Requirements for Underground Storage Tanks

If the facility owns or operates any underground storage tank of any size that stores hazardous substances, including fuels, lubricants, waste lubricants, solvents, liquids chemicals or solutions of chemicals, it must comply with the following requirements:

- Contact the local agency in Appendix 7-2 about permitting requirements and whether any exemptions apply.

- Assure that regulatory requirements for design and containment (based on date of installation) are satisfied, as well as local agency requirements.

- Devise a monitoring and recordkeeping system that meets the local agency's requirements.

- Submit the permit application and fee required to the local agency. Implement applicable requirements.

- If a petroleum storage underground tank, notify the Board of Equalization and pay the required mil tax on volume of fuel stored.

- Address the financial responsibility requirements as defined in the state and federal regulations.

- Plan for closure or upgrade of tanks that do not meet double containment criteria by December 22, 1998, if a tank fails in the interim or if a removal or closure is elected.

Aboveground Storage Tanks

In 1989, the state Legislature acted to address the environmental and safety concerns about aboveground storage tanks and to better coordinate federal Clean Water Act provisions on aboveground storage tanks with state requirements. The Aboveground Petroleum Storage Act [Health and Safety Code §25270] requires owners or operators of aboveground petroleum storage tanks to file a storage statement with the State Water Resources Control Board if tank storage exceeds 10,000 gallons and holds a substance containing at least 5 percent of crude oil or its fractions In addition, if the tank or tanks are subject to federal requirements at 40 CFR §112 (which potentially expands the storage statement to any tank over 660 gallons or aggregate storage of 1,320 gallons), they must be registered.

The statement must include the location of the tank facility, person responsible, a description of the tankage (size, age and contents) of each 10,000-gallon or greater tank and the applicable fee, ranging from $50 for a tankage less than 100,000 gallons, to $1,000 if over 100 million gallons. The funds collected are deposited in the Environmental Protection Trust Fund for administering the program, funding various regulatory and research projects, and cleanups. The regional water quality board is responsible for inspections and other regulatory requirements.

This new state law and regulatory program is somewhat duplicative of existing federal law. Aboveground storage tanks containing petroleum products have been subject to regulation under federal EPA regulations "Oil Pollution Prevention" [40 CFR §112] under the Clean Water Act. The federal regulation applies to tanks larger than 660 gallons (individual size) or 1,320 gallons (aggregate capacity) that "reasonably could be expected to discharge oil into or upon navigable waters or adjoining shorelines." The federal regulations required such facilities to prepare and implement a Spill Prevention Control and Countermeasures Plan (SPCC) within six months of the effective date of the regulation or by late 1976. SPCCs must be approved by a professional engineer and maintained by the facility, but submission and review by EPA is not required unless a spill of more than 1,000 gallons occurs or two spill events of harmful quantities occur in any 12-month period [40 CFR §110]. The state program will further expand the development of SPCC plans in California.

Regulatory Requirements for Aboveground Petroleum Storage Tanks

In California, owners and operators of aboveground storage tanks must consider both state requirements and federal regulations that apply.

◆ State Aboveground Petroleum Tank Requirements

Regulations have not been issued, but the state law is self-implementing in that it imposes clear requirements on owners and operators of aboveground tanks as defined in the above discussion:

Chap. 7

- File a storage statement with the State Water Resources Control Board (P.O. Box 100, Sacramento, CA 95801) by July 1, 1990 and every two years thereafter, including the name and address of the facility and a contact person. This requirement applies to any tank over 660 gallons or aggregate storage over 1,320 gallons of petroleum-containing material (5 percent or greater petroleum fraction).

- File a more detailed storage statement with the state water board for each petroleum storage tank that exceeds 10,000 gallons including: location, size in gallons, age in years and content (type of petroleum product).

- Pay the required fee with the notification according to the following schedule:

Total Tank Facility Storage Capacity (Gallons)	Facility Fee
less than 10,000	$ 100
10,000 - 100,000	200
100,001 - 1,000,000	400
1,000,001 - 10,000,000	1,600
10,000,001 - 100,000,000	8,000
100,000,001 or more	30,000

- Implement spill prevention measures based on the type of activity and size of tank (see below).

- Farms, nurseries, logging and construction sites, if total tank capacity is less than 100,000 gallons and individual tanks are less than 20,000 gallons:

    ✔ Daily visual inspections;
    ✔ Consent to regional board inspections; and
    ✔ Install secondary containment if the regional board determines it is necessary to protect state workers.

- All other tank facilities with petroleum storage in excess of 10,000 gallons:

    ✔ Prepare and implement by January 1, 1991 a Spill Prevention Control and Counter-measures (SPCC) Plan. [**Note:** These plans may have been required for such facilities by the federal regulations since 1976.]

    ✔ When the regional board determines a discharge could adversely affect surface water or sensitive ecosystems, establish a monitoring system based on visual observation or approved alternative systems to control drainage valves.

    ✔ When it is determined a discharge may adversely affect groundwater, storage contents are lighter than 16 degrees API and not subject to other federal, state or local requirements, the facility must install a tank bottom or release monitoring system approved by the regional board.

- All other tank storage facilities with capacity greater than 660 gallons of aggregate storage are subject to the above state requirements **if** the facility would be required by the federal regulations [40 CFR §112] to implement an SPCC Plan. The registration requirement probably will be used to help regional boards and EPA to identify facilities subject to the federal requirements.

- **Reporting of Releases.** Owners and operators of aboveground storage tanks must immediately report the spill or release of 42 gallons or more to the city and county where the facility is located. [**Note:** The reporting requirements for releases in Chapter 4 should be followed.]

◆ Federal Requirements for Aboveground Storage Tanks: Spill Prevention Control and Counter-Measure (SPCC) Plans

Whether federal requirements apply for aboveground storage tanks is based on the size of the petroleum storage tanks (over 660-gallon individual/1,320-gallon aggregate capacity) and the "reasonable expectation of discharges if harmful quantities to navigable waters." Once this is determined, an SPCC must be prepared and implemented in accordance with the federal regulations [40 CFR §112.3 and §112.7]. The basic content includes:

- An analysis of past spill incidents.

- A discussion of failure points, predictions of volumes and fate of released product.

- Appropriate containment or equipment to divert spillage from sensitive areas.

- If appropriate, a demonstration that containment and alternative controls are impractical, including an oil spill contingency plan and a written commitment of resources.

- A discussion of compliance with facility-specific requirements for drain valves, drainage systems, treatment systems and procedures for operations, maintenance and testing.

- Inspections and a recordkeeping system.

- Security for the facility and critical operating points.

- Personnel training.

Guidelines ("suggested procedure") for preparing SPCCs are available in the *American Petroleum Institute Bulletin* D16, February 1976, available from:

American Petroleum Institute
1220 L Street, N.W.
Washington, D.C. 20005

The requirements for preparing an SPCC would apply to both federal and state regulatory programs.

Spills in excess of 1,000 gallons must be reported to the EPA administrator, which may result in the agency taking action to review and possible order changes.

Summary of Requirements for Aboveground Storage Tanks

The facilities that own or operate aboveground petroleum product (at least 5 percent) storage tanks which are larger than 660 gallons individual, or 1,320 gallons aggregate storage capacity must comply with **both** the state and federal aboveground storage tank programs.

- All aboveground tanks, as defined above, must be registered with the State Water Resources Control Board in the form of a "storage statement" filed first by July 1, 1990 and every two years thereafter.

- Aboveground tanks in excess of 10,000-gallon capacity must provide additional information about the tanks (location, size, age and content).

- A fee based on the capacity of the tankage at a facility must accompany the storage statement for all tanks over 10,000 gallons.

Chap. 7

- A Spill Prevention Control and Countermeasures (SPCC) Plan must be prepared and implemented for all tank facilities in excess of 10,000-gallon capacity, or where federal regulations may require one. Exemptions exist **under state law** for farms, nurseries, logging and construction if individual tanks are less than 20,000 gallons and total facility capacity is less than 100,000 gallons. The SPCC must meet federal requirements.

- The facility must respond to additional regional board requirements if the board determines that a discharge from the facility may adversely affect surface water, sensitive ecosystems or groundwater.

- Releases of 42 gallons or more must be reported according to state hazardous materials release reporting requirements (Chapter 4). If the release exceeds 1,000 gallons from a facility subject to the SPCC requirements, EPA must be notified.

Penalties for Violations of Tank Storage Regulatory Programs

Strict penalties may be imposed for violation of the laws and regulations that establish regulatory programs for underground and aboveground storage tanks. Most penalties will be levied as administrative civil penalties designed to achieve compliance by cooperative facilities. More severe sanctions may be imposed if necessary to force compliance.*

State Underground Storage Tank Law Violations

- Operating without a permit. .... Civil liability of not less than $500, nor more
- Violation of permit conditions.   than $5,000 for each day of violation.
- Failure to properly close a tank.
- Failure to make necessary tests, reports, or making false statements.

- Violation of financial responsibility .... Civil penalties of up to $10,000 per day per requirements for a petroleum tank (mil tax) or tank. Local agencies must request superior court violation of corrective action requirements enforcement. State and regional boards may in the event of an unauthorized release. impose this penalty administratively.

- Intentional failure to comply .... Civil enforcement by local prosecutor or the with requirements of the underground attorney general: up to $5,000 for most storage statute. violations of the undergound tank law; not less
- Providing false information in report. than $5,000 or more than $10,000 for providing
- Failure to report releases. false information or not reporting releases. Criminal enforcement as a misdemeanor (up to one year imprisonment) also is available.

*All penalties stated are the maximum provided for in the statutes.

Federal Underground Storage Tank Regulation Violations

Any offense .... Civil liability of up to $5,000 per day.

State Aboveground Storage Tank Law Violations

- Failure to file a storage statement. .... Civil liability of up to $5,000 per day.
- Failure to comply with additional .... Civil liability of up to $5,000 per day for the
  provisions, including reporting a spill.   first offense, $10,000 for subsequent violations
  imposed by the state or regional board or the
  attorney general.

Federal Aboveground Storage Tank SPCC

Any violation of §112 of the Clean Water Act. .... Civil penalty of up to $5,000 per day.

Chap. 7

Appendix 7-1
List of Applicable Laws and Regulations
Underground and Aboveground Tank Storage
of Hazardous Substances

State Laws:

Underground Storage Tank Regulatory Program	Health and Safety Code §§25280-25299.1
Permitting and Fees	Health and Safety Code §§25284 and 25299
Regulatory and Monitoring Requirements	Health and Safety Code §§25292-25293
Inspections	Health and Safety Code §25288
Unauthorized Releases	Health and Safety Code §25294
Closure Requirements	Health and Safety Code §25298
Financial Responsibility	Health and Safety Code §25299.30-25299.34
Aboveground Storage Tank Regulatory Program	Health and Safety Code §§25270-25270.13
Permitting and Fees	Health and Safety Code §25270
Regulatory and Monitoring Requirements	Health and Safety Code §§25270.4 and 25270.7
Inspections	Health and Safety Code §25270.5
Unauthorized Releases	Health and Safety Code §§25270.8-25270.9
Financial Responsibility	Health and Safety Code §25270.9

Federal Laws

Clean Water Act (Oil Spill Prevention)	3 USC 1251
RCRA (Underground tank provisions)	42 USC 6991

State Regulations

Underground Storage Tank Regulatory Program	23 CCR §§2610-2873
Monitoring Requirements	23 CCR §§2630-2648
Unauthorized Releases	23 CCR §§2650-2652
Allowable Repairs	23 CCR §§2660-2663
Closure Requirements	23 CCR §§2670-2672
Petroleum Underground Storage Tank Cleanup Fund	23 CCR §§2810-2873

[See also: Local agency ordinances and requirements.]

Federal Regulations

Aboveground Storage Tank Regulatory Program	40 CFR §112
Spill Prevention Control and Countermeasures (SPCC Plans)	40 CFR §112.3 and 112.7
Underground Storage Tank Regulation	40 CFR §280

Chap. 7

Appendix 7-2
State Water Resources Control Board
Underground Tank Program
Administrating Public Agency

Alameda County

Alameda County Department of Environmental Health,
    Hazardous Materials Division .... (510) 271-4320
Berkeley: HHS - Community Health Protection .... (510) 644-6510
Fremont: Building Inspection Division - Public Works .... (510) 791-4300
Hayward Fire Department .... (510) 293-8695
Newark Fire Department .... (510) 793-1400
Pleasanton Fire Department .... (510) 484-8114
San Leandro Fire Department .... (510) 577-3318
Union City Fire Department .... (510) 471-3232

Alpine County
Alpine County Health Department .... (916) 694-2146

Amador County
Environmental Health .... (209) 223-6407

Butte County
Environmental Health .... (916) 538-7281

Calaveras County
Environmental Health .... (209) 754-6399

Colusa County
Environmental Health .... (916) 458-7717

Contra Costa County
Occupational Health .... (510) 646-2286

Del Norte County
Agricultural Commissioners Office .... (707) 464-7235

El Dorado County
Division of Waste Management .... (916) 621-5300

Fresno County
Environmental Health Systems .... (209) 445-3271

Glenn County
Glenn County Air Pollution Control District .... (916) 934-6500

Humboldt County
Environmental Health .... (707) 445-6215

Imperial County
Planning & Building Inspection Department .... (619) 339-4236

Inyo County
Environmental Health .... (619) 878-0238

Kern County
Environmental Health .... (805) 861-3636
Bakersfield City Fire Department (Hazardous Materials Division) .... (805) 326-3979

Kings County
Division of Environmental Services .... (209) 584-1411

Lake County
Lake County Health Department .... (707) 263-2241

Lassen County
Lassen County Department of Agriculture .... (916) 257-8311

Los Angeles County
Waste Management Department of Public Works .... (818) 458-3539
Burbank Fire Department .... (818) 953-8771
Glendale Fire Department .... (808) 539-4715
Long Beach Fire Department .... (310) 590-2560
Los Angeles City Fire Department .... (213) 485-7543
Pasadena Fire Department .... (818) 405-4115
Santa Monica: Department of General Services .... (310) 458-8228
Torrance: Fire Prevention Division .... (310) 618-2973
Vernon: Environmental Health .... (213) 583-8811

Madera County
Environmental Health .... (209) 675-7823

Marin County
Waste Management Division .... (415) 499-6647
San Rafael Fire Department .... (415) 485-3308

Mariposa County
Mariposa County Health Division .... (209) 966-3689

Mendocino County
Environmental Health .... (707) 463-4466

Merced County
Environmental Health .... (209) 385-7391

Modoc County .... (916) 233-6413

Mono County
Mono County Health Department .... (619) 932-7484

Monterey County
Environmental Health .... (408) 755-4511
Monterey Fire Department .... (408) 646-3908
Scotts Valley Fire Department .... (408) 438-0211

Napa County
Environmental Management .... (707) 253-4471

Nevada County
Nevada County Environmental Health Department .... (916) 265-1452

Orange County
Environmental Health .... (714) 667-3773
Anaheim: Fire Prevention Division, Underground Tank Section .... (714) 254-4050
Fullerton: Fire Department, Underground Storage Tank Section .... (714) 738-3160
Orange Fire Department .... (714) 744-0400
Santa Ana Fire Department .... (714) 647-5700

Placer County
Division of Environmental Health .... (916) 889-7335
Roseville Fire Department .... (916) 781-0185

Plumas County
Environmental Health Section .... (916) 283-6355

Riverside County
Hazardous Materials .... (714) 358-5055
Indio Fire Department .... (619) 347-0756

Sacramento County
Sacramento County Environmental Health Management Division .... (916) 386-6160
Sacramento City Fire Department .... (916) 449-8011

San Benito County
Health Department .... (408) 637-5367
Hollister Fire Department .... (408) 636-4325

Chap. 7

San Bernardino County
Environmental Health Services .... (714) 387-3080

San Diego County
Division of Environmental Health, HMMD Division .... (619) 338-2222

San Francisco County
Department of Public Health (Hazardous Materials Division) .... (415) 554-2775

San Joaquin County
San Joaquin Environmental Health Division .... (209) 468-3420

San Luis Obispo County
Environmental Health .... (805) 781-5544
San Luis Obispo: City Fire Department .... (805) 781-7380

San Mateo County
Environmental Health .... (415) 363-4305
Belmont: South County Fire Department .... (415) 593-8016
San Carlos: South County Fire Authority .... (415) 593-8011

Santa Barbara County
Department of Health Care Services .... (805) 681-4749

Santa Cruz County
Scotts Valley Fire Department .... (408) 438-0211
Watsonville Fire Department .... (408) 728-6060

Santa Clara County
Department of Public Health, Hazardous Materials .... (408) 299-6930
Campbell Fire Department .... (408) 378-4010
Cupertino: Central Fire Protection District .... (408) 378-4015
Gilroy Fire Department .... (408) 848-0370
Los Gatos: Central Fire District .... (408) 378-4015
Milpitas: Office of the Fire Marshal .... (408) 942-2381
Morgan Hill Fire Department .... (408) 776-7351
Mountain View Fire Department .... (415) 903-6365
Palo Alto Fire Department .... (415) 329-2184
San Jose Fire Prevention Department .... (408) 277-4659
Santa Clara Fire Department (Hazardous Materials Division) .... (408) 984-3084
Sunnyvale Department of Public Safety .... (408) 730-7212

Shasta County
Environmental Health .... (916) 225-5787

Sierra County
Health Department .... (916) 993-6700

Siskiyou County
Health Department .... (916) 842-8230

Solano County
Environmental Health Services .... (707) 421-6770
Vallejo Fire Prevention Department .... (707) 648-4565

Sonoma County
Sonoma County Department of Public Health .... (707) 525-6560
Healdsburg Fire Department .... (707) 431-3360
Santa Rosa Fire Department .... (707) 524-5311
Sonoma Fire Department .... (707) 996-2102

Stanislaus County
Environmental Resources, Solid Waste .... (209) 525-4160

Sutter County
Department of Agriculture .... (916) 741-7500

Tehama County
Department of Agriculture .... (916) 527-4504

Trinity County
Trinity County Department of Health .... (916) 623-1358

Tulare County
Environmental Health .... (209) 733-6013

Tuolumne County
Environmental Health .... (209) 533-5990

Ventura County
Environmental Health Department (Underground Tank Section) .... (805) 654-3519
Ventura Fire Department .... (805) 389-9710

Yolo County
Environmental Health .... (916) 666-8646

Yuba County
Office of Emergency Services .... (916) 741-6254

Chap. 7

Hazardous Waste Management

Summary and Applicability

This chapter covers the information needed to initiate an understanding of the hazardous waste laws and regulations as they apply to a facility in California. Facilities and persons subject to the strict requirements of the state's hazardous waste control program are those that generate wastes considered hazardous as described in this chapter. Hazardous wastes include such items as spent chemicals and solvents, and chemical products that are unusable or stored in damaged containers. However, a much larger volume of relatively ordinary wastes or recyclable materials also are regulated under the hazardous waste laws, including, but not limited to:

- Waste lubricating oils.
- Empty containers, aerosol cans and filters.
- Process water being discharged to a sewer system in many cases.
- Soil contaminated with chemicals, fuels, oils and other substances.

Simply stated, if a facility generates any waste material that is not obviously non- hazardous, like waste paper, refuse and food wastes, it should review the contents of this chapter, which includes the following topics:

- Hazardous waste laws and regulations, and organization of the state program.
- How to determine if hazardous wastes are being generated.
- How to properly store and manage hazardous wastes on-site.
- Personnel training and emergency response requirements.
- Off-site shipment and disposal of hazardous waste for treatment or disposal; and recordkeeping requirements.
- Hazardous waste source reduction.
- On-site hazardous waste treatment tiered permitting.
- Requirements for hazardous waste service facilities.
- Hazardous waste liability and cleanups.
- Hazardous waste compliance overview.
- Penalties for violations.

Given the complexity of the requirements and severity of penalties for non-compliance, facilities subject to the hazardous waste laws must carefully review the requirements that may apply. Readers should use this chapter to identify whether and to what extent they are covered by the hazardous waste laws. Further information, including the relevant regulations, should be obtained as necessary. The California Chamber publication *Hazardous Waste Management* provides more detailed information on hazardous waste requirements and how to comply.

Federal and State Hazardous Waste Statutes

California's hazardous waste laws and regulations are among the most stringent and complicated in the nation. The state's hazardous waste regulations begin with the requirements of the federal Resource Conservation and Recovery Act (RCRA) and add unique and more onerous state requirements.

◆ Federal Statutes

- **Resource Conservation and Recovery Act** (RCRA, 42 USC, §§6901-6987) was enacted in 1974 as the first step in regulating the potential health and environmental problems associated with solid hazardous and non-hazardous waste disposal. RCRA and the regulations developed by EPA to implement it provide the general framework of the national hazardous waste management system, including the determination of whether hazardous wastes are being generated, techniques for tracking wastes to eventual disposal and the design and permitting of hazardous waste management facilities. RCRA amendments enacted in 1984 began the process of eliminating land disposal as the principal hazardous waste disposal method.

- **Comprehensive Environmental Response, Compensation and Liability Act** (CERCLA, 42 USC, §§6901-6957), also known as Superfund, was enacted in 1980 to ensure that a source of funds ($1.7 billion) was available to clean up abandoned hazardous waste dumps, compensate victims, address releases of hazardous materials and establish liability standards for responsible parties.

- **Superfund Amendments and Reauthorization Act** (SARA) amended CERCLA in 1986 to increase the Superfund to $8.5 billion, modify contaminated site cleanup criteria, and revise settlement procedures. As discussed in other chapters, it also provides a regulatory program for leaking underground storage tank cleanups, and a broad, new emergency planning and community right-to-know program (EPCRA).

To the extent applicable to California businesses that generate wastes, these federal measures will be discussed in the *Handbook* along with the California requirements.

◆ State Statutes

- **Hazardous Waste Control Law** (HWCL, Health and Safety Code §§25100-25249) is the basic hazardous waste control law in California. It established one of the first comprehensive hazardous waste management programs in the nation in 1972, and has been amended many times to address current needs, including bringing the state law and program into conformance with the various federal laws discussed above. The HWCL implements the RCRA cradle-to-grave waste management system in California. It specifies that generators have the primary duty to determine whether their wastes are hazardous and to assure safe handling and disposal. It is more stringent than federal law with regard to regulation of small quantity generators, transportation, permitting and penalties for violations. The HWCL also exceeds federal requirements by mandating recycling of certain wastes and stricter regulation of hazardous waste facilities. Amendments to HWCL have introduced land disposal restrictions comparable, but more stringent than federal law, and mandatory hazardous waste source reduction planning for larger generators.

- **Carpenter-Presley-Tanner Hazardous Substance Account Act** (HSAA, Health and Safety Code §§25340-25392) was enacted in 1981 to address similar concerns as federal CERCLA: establish release response authority, compensate injured parties, and establish a "state superfund" to pay the 10 percent state share of any federal cleanups in the state. Hazardous waste generation, disposal and management facilities are taxed under the HSAA to finance the state's hazardous waste regulatory program.

Organization of the State's Hazardous Waste Regulatory Program

The Hazardous Waste Control Law established the Toxic Substances Control Division of the Department of Health Services as the agency with primary responsibility for implementing and enforcing the state's hazardous waste laws. This agency is now a department within Cal/EPA: the Department of Toxic Substances Control (DTSC), with regional offices in Sacramento, Emeryville, Los Angeles and Fresno. The DTSC shares enforcement and implementation responsibility with other state and local government agencies, including the State Water Resources Control Board and regional water quality control boards, and county governments. These relationships may be formalized by a *memorandum of understanding* or specified by statute. Other state and local agencies also may be involved in hazardous waste regulation enforcement, particularly in permitting and prosecuting violations. Appendix 8-2 is a directory of DTSC offices. In addition to DTSC, many county health departments have an active role in hazardous waste regulatory activities.

Hazardous Waste Compliance Requirements for Generators

The following are the basic compliance elements of the hazardous waste regulations that apply to generators of hazardous wastes.

A generator is defined as a person or business whose acts or processes produce a hazardous waste or who, in some other manner, causes a hazardous substance or waste to become subject to the California Hazardous Waste Control Law.

Generators are subject to specific requirements of the hazardous waste laws, including:

- Responsibility to characterize wastes. It is the obligation of the generator to determine whether the waste it generates is hazardous based on its chemical composition and the criteria in Title 22, California Code of Regulations.

- Storage time limits and proper management of hazardous wastes on-site in accordance with the applicable regulations.

- To comply with personnel training and emergency response requirements.

- Assure proper shipment and off-site disposal or management of hazardous waste.

- Maintain required records.

- Prepare a hazardous waste source reduction plan.

Chap. 8

Each of these requirements as they apply to a generator of hazardous wastes is discussed in the following subchapters.

How to Determine if Hazardous Wastes are Being Generated

To begin the process of determining if hazardous wastes are being generated, the facility must first decide what materials are usable products in the operation and what are wastes. The products are subject to labeling and other requirements of the Cal/OSHA Hazard Communication Standard [8 CCR §5194] and hazardous materials storage rules. The wastes are subject to the hazardous waste law (for example, rags, if reused by a rag service company, are dirty products and, therefore, not hazardous wastes). The generator is required to characterize any waste generated and intended to be disposed or recycled to determine whether it is hazardous. This usually requires characterization to identify whether a listed hazardous waste is present or if the waste exhibits hazardous characteristics: corrosivity, reactivity, ignitability or toxicity.

◆ Listed Hazardous Wastes

A waste is considered hazardous if it appears on the lists of hazardous wastes included in federal RCRA regulations as incorporated into Title 22 state regulations. Wastes have been placed on these lists because they are known to exhibit certain toxicological properties with respect to human health or the environment, are hazardous or dangerous from some other standpoint, or tend to be difficult to store or dispose of effectively. These listed wastes may be from any type of operation and have non-specific sources. Other listed wastes are from specific sources, generated in the course of certain manufacturing or processing operations. If a facility generates a waste that appears on these lists, it must be presumed that it is a hazardous waste.

The list of hazardous wastes appears at 22 CCR §66261.30-.33. This section of Title 22 adopts federal hazardous wastes for purposes of the state's hazardous waste regulations. The appendices after §66261.126 provide additional information on the waste materials listed as hazardous wastes. Appendix 8-3 is the common name list of hazardous wastes.

◆ Criteria for Hazardous Waste Characterization

If the waste being reviewed is not on the list of hazardous wastes, it still may be considered hazardous by virtue of hazardous characteristics. These four characteristics, the reference to Title 22, and their definitions are:

- **Ignitability** [22 CCR §66261.21]. A waste is ignitable if it is easily combustible or flammable or, if ignited, burns so vigorously that it creates a hazard. This category includes:

    ✔ Liquid with a flashpoint less than or equal to 140° F.

    ✔ A non-liquid capable of causing fire by means of friction, absorption of moisture, or spontaneous chemical changes and which, when ignited, burns so vigorously and persistently that it creates a hazard.

✔   A flammable compressed gas.

✔   An oxidizer.

Examples of ignitable wastes are: paint wastes, certain degreasers, thinners and solvents (petroleum distillates), stripping agents, epoxy resins, adhesives, rubber cements and glues, and some waste inks.

● **Corrosivity** [22 CCR §66261.22]. A waste is corrosive if it dissolves metals and other materials, or burns the skin or eyes on contact. Aqueous wastes with a pH equal to or less than two, or equal to or greater than 12.5 are corrosive.

Examples of corrosive wastes are alkaline degreasers, spent metal treating and plating solutions, corrosive cleaning solutions, rust removers, waste acids and bleach compounds (peroxides and chlorine compounds).

● **Reactivity** [22 CCR §66261.23]. A waste is reactive if it is unstable and undergoes rapid or violent chemical reactions, such as catching fire, exploding or giving off fumes when exposed to, or mixed with, water, air or other materials.

Examples of reactive wastes are chromic acids used in plating; copper stripping and aluminum anodizing; cyanide compounds from electroplating, metal treating and ore leaching processes; permanganate and manganese wastes from dry cell batteries; paint, ink and dye manufacturing; bleaches and hypochlorites from water treatment processes, and swimming pool and sanitizing operations.

● **Toxic** [22 CCR §66261.24]. Whether a waste is hazardous by virtue of the toxicity characteristic is based on a succession of technically complex tests that are outside the scope of this guide to explain in any detail. Readers should consult the California Chamber's *Hazardous Waste Handbook* or the Title 22 regulations directly for more information. Following is a brief explanation of this process.

✔   **First,** the waste must be analyzed by a state-certified laboratory to determine if it contains any toxic metals or organic substances listed on Table 1 at 22 CCR §66261.24(a)(i) in excess of regulatory levels using a testing method called Toxicity Characteristic Leaching Procedure (TCLP). The contaminants and regulatory levels of concern are shown in the table on the following page.

Chap. 8

Contaminant	Regulatory Level (mg/l or ppm)	Contaminant	Regulatory Level (mg/l or ppm)
Arsenic	5.0	Hexachlorobenzene	0.13
Barium	100.0	Hexachlorobutadiene	0.5
Benzene	0.5	Hexachloroethane	3.0
Cadmium	1.0	Lead	5.0
Carbon tetrachloride	0.5	Lindane	0.4
Chlordane	0.03	Mercury	0.2
Chlorobenzene	100.0	Methoxychlor	10.0
Chloroform	6.0	Methyl ethyl ketone	200.0
Chromium	5.0	Nitrobenzene	2.0
o-Cresol	200.0	Pentachlorophenol	100.0
m-Cresol	200.0	Pyridine	5.0
p-Cresol	200.0	Selenium	1.0
Cresol	200.0	Silver	5.0
2,4-D	10.0	Tetrachloroethylene	0.7
1,4-Dichlorobenzene	7.5	Toxaphene	0.5
1,2-Dichlorethane	0.5	Trichloroethylene	0.5
1,1-Dichloroethylene	0.7	2,4,5-Trichlorophenol	400.0
2,4-Dinitrotoluene	0.13	2,4,6-Trichlorophenol	2.0
Endrin	0.02	2,4,5-TP (Silvex)	1.0
Heptachlor (and its epoxide)	0.008	Vinyl chloride	0.2

If any of these regulatory levels are exceeded, the waste is hazardous.

✔ **Second,** the waste must be analyzed by a state-certified laboratory to determine whether it exceeds any of the regulatory levels established for inorganic or organic chemicals in Table II or Table III of 22 CCR 66261.24(a)(2). The test methods used are based on regulatory levels established for Soluble Threshold Limit Concentration (STLC) or Total Threshold Limit Concentration (TTLC).

The tables of STLC and TTLC contaminants and regulatory levels appear on the following page.

Notes to Table:
1. STLC and TTLC values are calculated on the concentrations of the elements, not the compounds.
2. If the soluble chromium, as determined by TCLP, is less than 5 mg/l, and the soluble chromium equals or exceeds 560 mg/l and the waste is not otherwise identified as a RCRA hazardous waste, then the waste is a non-RCRA hazardous waste.
3. In the case of asbestos and elemental metals, the specified concentration limits apply only if the substances are in a friable, powdered or finely divided state.
4. Excluding barium sulfate.

If any of the regulatory levels are exceeded, the waste is hazardous.

Regulatory Levels

Metals[1,3]	STLC mg/l (ppm)	TTLC Wet-Weight mg/kg (ppm)
Antimony and/or antimony compounds	15	500
Arsenic and/or arsenic compounds	5.0	500
Asbestos (all forms)		1.0 (as %)
Barium and/or barium compounds (excluding barite)	100	10,000[4]
Beryllium and/or beryllium compounds	0.75	75
Cadmium and/or cadmium compounds	1.0	100
Chromium (VI) compounds	5	500
Chromium and/or chromium (III) compounds[2]	5	2,500
Cobalt and/or cobalt compounds	80	8,000
Copper and/or copper compounds	25	2,500
Fluoride salts	180	18,000
Lead and/or lead compounds	5.0	1,000
Mercury and/or mercury compounds	0.2	20
Molybdenum and/or molybdenum compounds	350	3,500
Nickel and/or nickel compounds	20	2,000
Selenium and/or selenium compounds	1.0	100
Silver and/or silver compounds	5	500
Thallium and/or thallium compounds	7.0	700
Vanadium and/or vanadium compounds	24	2,400
Zinc and/or zinc compounds	250	5,000

Organic Compounds:

	STLC mg/l (ppm)	TTLC Wet-Weight mg/kg (ppm)
Aldrin	0.14	1.4
Chlordane	0.25	2.5
DDT, DDE, DDD	0.1	1.0
2,4-Dichlorophenoxyacetic acid	10	100
Dieldrin	0.8	8.0
Dioxin (2,3,7,8-TCDD)	0.001	0.01
Endrin	0.02	0.2
Heptachlor	0.47	4.7
Kepone	2.1	21
Lead compounds, organic	—	13
Lindane	0.4	4.0
Methoxychlor	10	100
Mirex	2.1	21
Pentachlorophenol	1.7	17
Polychlorinated biphenyls (PCBs)	5.0	50
Toxaphene	0.5	5
Trichloroethylene	204	2,040
2,4,5-Trichlorophenoxypropionic acid	1.0	10

✔   **Third**, it must be determined whether the waste contains carcinogenic substances, listed below, in a single or combined concentration of 0.001% by weight by testing or other information available.

2-Acetylaminofluorene (2-AAF)	4-Dimethylaminoazobenzene (DAB)
Acrylonitrile	Ethyleneimine (EL)
4- Aminodiphenyl	a-Naphtylamine (1-NA)
Benzidine and its salts	B-Naphtylamine (2-NA)
bis (Chloromethyl) ether	4-Nitrobiphenyl (4-NBP)
Methyl chloromethyl ether	N-Nitrosodimethylamine (DMN)
1,2-Dibromo-3-chloropropane (DBCP)	B-Propiolactone (BPL)
3,3-Dichlorobenzidine and its salts (DCB)	Vinyl chloride (VCM)

If this level is exceeded for any one or a combination of these substances, the waste is hazardous.

✔   **Fourth,** and last, objective biological tests (or data from such tests) must be evaluated to determine whether the test material is more toxic than any of the criteria listed below:

■   An acute oral LD_{50} less than 5,000 milligrams per kilogram ($LD_{50} < 5,000$ mg/kg);

■   An acute dermal LD_{50} less than 4,300 milligrams per kilogram ($LD_{50} < 4,300$ mg/kg);

■   An acute inhalation LC_{50} less than 10,000 parts per million as a gas or vapor ($LC_{50} < 10,000$ ppm); and

■   An acute aquatic 96-hour LC_{50} less than 500 milligrams per liter (96-hour LC_{50} < 500 mg/l).

■   *Or* it can cause illness or death if inhaled, swallowed or absorbed through the skin.

If any of these tests result in greater toxicity than the threshold listed, the material is a hazardous waste.

Examples of wastes meeting the toxic criteria are pesticides, some organic and inorganic chemicals, ethylene glycol anti-freeze solution, and many other spent chemicals and discarded products.

Based on these criteria, any waste not on the list of hazardous wastes can be characterized to determine whether it is hazardous. In addition, a listed hazardous waste that is dilute, inactivated or less hazardous due to processing in the operation, may be "delisted" through application of these criteria.

◆   **Determining Whether Any Extremely Hazardous Wastes Are Generated**

In California, extremely hazardous wastes may not be handled or disposed of **unless covered by an extremely hazardous waste permit** issued by the Department of Toxic Substances Control (DTSC)

and are subject to other regulatory requirements more onerous than those for ordinary hazardous wastes. Care must exercised both in determining whether a facility generates an extremely hazardous waste and in its handling. (Note that once diluted or otherwise inactivated, many potential extremely hazardous wastes can be "delisted" by applying the criteria below.)

Extremely hazardous waste is any hazardous waste that could cause death or severe illness in humans. Extremely hazardous wastes are designated with an asterisk in the list of hazardous wastes in Appendix 8-3 [22 CCR §66261.126, Appendix X]. Extremely hazardous wastes also may be identified by the following criteria found in 22 CCR §66261.110.

A material or waste is **extremely hazardous** when it possesses any of the following characteristics:

- An acute oral LD_{50} less than or equal to 50 mg/kg.

- An acute dermal LD_{50} less than or equal to 43 mg/kg.

- An acute inhalation LC_{50} less than or equal to 100 parts per million as a gas or vapor.

- Contains any of the cancer-causing substances listed in 22 CCR §66261.24(a)(7) in a single or combined concentration that equals or exceeds 0.1 percent by weight.

- Has been shown through experience or testing to pose an **extreme hazard** to public health.

- Is water reactive.

For more information on extremely hazardous waste handling requirements, generators should consult the California Chamber's *Hazardous Waste Handbook* or DTSC.

Exceptions to the Requirement of Determining Whether the Wastes Generated are Hazardous

Given the extensive and complicated requirements for hazardous waste characterization if the generator does not know whether its wastes are hazardous, there are some exemptions to the determination requirement. These exceptions are narrow and the rules must be followed carefully:

- **Empty containers.** Completely empty containers are not generally considered hazardous wastes. The hazardous waste regulations are based on listed hazardous wastes in sufficient quantities to result in hazardous characteristics being present. Empty containers rarely have such properties. This question arises only with larger quantity containers that have substantial liquid residue. A regulation has delineated procedures that must be followed if the generator wants to avoid characterizing its empty containers [22 CCR §66261.7]:

    ✔ The containers must be empty, which means as much of the contents removed as possible so that none will pour out in any orientation.

    ✔ If the empty containers are less than five gallons, they may be disposed of as a non-hazardous solid waste or scrapped for metal recovery.

Chap. 8

✔ If the empty containers are greater than five gallons, they must be handled in the following manner:

- Returned to the vendor for re-use.
- Sent to a drum recycler for reconditioning.
- Used or recycled on-site.

✔ All these actions must occur within one year of the container being emptied.

- **Waste oil filters.**
  ✔ **Used, metal canister oil filters** can be managed as non-hazardous waste as long as they are thoroughly drained of "free flowing" oil (oil exiting drop-by-drop is not considered "free flowing"); the filters are accumulated, stored and transferred in a closed, rainproof container; and the filters are transferred for recycling. [22 CCR §66266.13.]

  ✔ However, **paper cartridge waste oil filters,** on the other hand, pose a potential problem because the new regulations exempting oil filters from handling as a hazardous waste apply *only* to the canister, metal filters. The exemption (according to Cal/EPA) was granted by EPA using the "recyclable metal" provision of EPA's hazardous waste exemptions. As of now, the paper filters would need to be characterized, even after all oil was removed.

- **Solvents and degreasers.** Parts cleaning solvents and degreasers should be recycled by a service firm. Waste solvents must never be mixed with waste oil.

- **Spent antifreeze.** Although no regulation specifically addresses antifreeze, it should be considered a hazardous waste (toxicity criteria) unless it is reused on-site.

- **Scrap metal.** These materials are excluded from the definition of hazardous waste, unless finely divided.

- **Materials reused on-site or transferred to a second site owned by the same person.** These materials are considered to be "excluded recyclable materials" if they are reclaimed or used to make products. Regulations which govern this activity must be carefully followed. [22 CCR §66261.6.]

- **Specifically regulated materials.** Readers should be aware that special rules apply to the recycle of certain materials, including: waste fuels, petroleum refinery wastes, spent sulfuric acid, spent lead acid storage batteries, agricultural recyclable materials, and waste elemental mercury. Readers should consult the California Chamber's *Hazardous Waste Management Handbook* or the Department of Toxic Substances Control for more information as it is outside of the scope of this guide to present sufficient information to comply.

- **Waste lubricating oil.** Facilities that produce waste oil in their operations should be aware that waste oil is a hazardous waste by definition. However, provisions of Health and Safety

Code §25250 allow for expeditious transportation and recycling as long as all the applicable requirements are followed. Generators need to know that waste oil stored on-site must be treated exactly the same as other hazardous wastes. Furthermore, uses of waste oil other than recycling it; for example, as fuel, road oil, weed control etc., are strictly prohibited.

Storage Time Limits and Proper Management of Hazardous Wastes While On-Site

Facilities must handle the hazardous wastes they generate in a specified manner. This includes limits on the time which wastes can be stored before storage facility permits are required. The generator must also handle wastes on-site in conformance with the containment and storage provisions of the Title 22 regulations, specifically 22 CCR §66262.34 Accumulation Time.

◆ Accumulating Versus Storing Hazardous Wastes

The hazardous waste regulations are very strict about how long hazardous wastes can be accumulated and the length of time before the facility must be specially permitted and designed as a storage facility. Given the onerous design requirements and other difficulties in obtaining a storage permit, a typical facility would not want to engage in hazardous waste storage. Fortunately, the federal and state hazardous waste laws make an important distinction between the situation where a generator needs to "accumulate" waste until it can be economically transported and the situation where larger volumes of wastes are to be stored for a longer period.

In California, a facility that generates less than 100 kilograms (220 pounds) per month is allowed to accumulate up to 100 kilograms of hazardous waste for an indefinite period of time, but once the 100 kilogram quantity is reached, it may be stored for only 90 days before a storage permit and other requirements go into effect. If extremely hazardous wastes are being generated, the facility may accumulate one kilogram (2.2 pounds) before triggering the 90-day limitation on storage. However, if the facility generates more than 100 kilograms of hazardous waste or more than one kilogram of extremely hazardous wastes in any calendar month, the 90-day time period begins when any amount of hazardous waste first begins to accumulate.

Note, however, if the facility stores more than 5,000 gallons or 45,000 pounds of hazardous waste in a tank at any time, it is required to have a storage permit.

◆ Exception to the 90-Day Storage Limitation

One exception to the 90-day rule is the "satellite rule" [Health and Safety Code §25123.3(d) and 22 CCR §66262.34(e)], which allows longer accumulation of a small amount of hazardous waste for up to one year as long as certain conditions are met:

- a maximum of 55 gallons are stored;

- the waste is stored at the initial point of generation (or reasonably close) and under control of operator(s) whose process generated the hazardous waste;

- the container must be labeled as hazardous waste with the initial date of accumulation indicated; and

Chap. 8

- within three days of reaching the 55-gallon or one-year limit, a new and current accumulation start date must be indicated and the wastes held no longer than 90 days more at the location where hazardous wastes are normally stored.

  Note: If the 55-gallon limit was exceeded, the waste must be transported off-site within one year of the initial accumulation start date.

Many facilities find that use of the "satellite rule" provisions affords increased flexibility to arrange for more conveniently scheduled and cost-effective hazardous waste pickups.

Proper Handling of Accumulating and Stored Waste

The regulatory provision setting forth accumulation times for the generator [22 CCR §66262.34] includes references to other sections of Title 22 that specify the on-site waste management practices which apply to the generator.

Accumulating waste and wastes being stored must be stored in compliance with regulations beginning at 22 CCR §66265.10, which require that:

- Wastes be placed in containers that are in good condition. The container used for storage does not need to meet the Department of Transportation's (DOT) shipping container specifications, but they must be structurally sound and free of leaks. However, prior to shipping, the waste must be placed in a DOT-approved container. [§66265.171.]

- The waste must be compatible with the container. [§66265.172.]

- The container must be kept closed during storage except when adding or removing contents. [§66265.173.]

- The hazardous waste generator must inspect the container storage area weekly for leaking containers and deterioration of the containment system. [§66265.15.]

- Ignitable and reactive wastes must be stored 50 feet from the facility property line. [§66265.175.]

- The container storage area must be designed and operated to contain any leaks or spills. [§66265.176.]

- The waste must be stored in a secure enclosure with applicable signs, such as "No Smoking," "Caution," "Fire Hazard," etc. [§66265.14.]

- Incompatibles must be kept separated by barriers such as walls, berms, etc. [§66265.17(b).]

- Containers must be clearly labeled with the following information:

  ✔ The date on which each period of accumulation begins on each container.

✔ The words "HAZARDOUS WASTE" on each container, and the chemical name (or another descriptive name), whether the waste is a solid or a liquid, identification of the hazardous properties of the waste (for example, flammable, corrosive, toxic, etc.), and the name and address of the generator. [§66262.34.]

● A sign also must be placed on the facility in which hazardous waste is stored. These signs must include the following information:

"WARNING: Hazardous waste storage area — Authorized personnel only." [§66265.14.]

Requirements for Personnel Training and Emergency Response

◆ Personnel Training

Persons involved in hazardous waste management must be adequately trained [22 CCR §66265.16]. The training program must consist of classroom or on-the-job instruction that teaches employees to perform their duties in compliance with all applicable regulations. The program must be directed by a person trained in hazardous waste management and it must contain information relevant to the employee's position and responsibilities, including contingency plan implementation and in-house waste management policies. New employees must be trained within six months and may not manage hazardous wastes in unsupervised positions until they have been trained. All personnel must participate in an annual refresher training. The training program must be designed to ensure that employees can respond effectively to emergencies by familiarizing them with emergency procedures, safety equipment and hazardous waste management practices.

The regulation further requires the facility to maintain the following records to document its training program:

● The job title for each employee position related to hazardous waste management and the name of the employee filling the job.

● A written job description for each job listed, including the required skill, education or other qualifications and duties of employees assigned to each position.

● A written description of the type and amount of training (introductory and continuing) that will be given to each person filling the listed positions.

● Documentation that the required training has been completed by each employee trained.

● Employee records must be maintained until closure of the facility. (Records for former employees must be preserved for three years after the employee has left.)

It is important to identify employees with hazardous waste management responsibility and assure that they meet the above requirements.

◆ Contingency/Emergency Response Plan

A hazardous waste contingency plan must be prepared by the generator to minimize hazards to human

Chap. 8

health or the environment from fires, explosions or other accidents involving the hazardous waste. This plan can dovetail the community right-to-know business plan (Chapter 4) and the Cal/OSHA Hazardous Waste Operations and Emergency Response Standard [8 CCR §5192], but must contain all required elements specified in 22 CCR §66265.51, et seq.

The facility must name an emergency coordinator familiar with the facility who has the authority to commit resources needed to carry out the contingency plan. This coordinator also must be prepared to follow designated emergency procedures, including notifying the state Office of Emergency Services in the event of a release. Emergency response facilities and organizations (hospitals, fire departments and others) must be notified in writing of their role in the event of a site emergency.

Off-Site Shipment of Hazardous Waste for Treatment or Disposal and Recordkeeping

◆ Obtaining an EPA Identification Number

Any generator of hazardous waste must have an EPA Identification Number [22 CCR §66262.12]. This number is necessary to complete the hazardous waste manifest needed to transport hazardous wastes off-site for treatment or disposal. The EPA Identification Number with the manifest also is the means used to track hazardous wastes from cradle-to-grave as required by the laws in this area. Furthermore, it provides an accounting method for both enforcement purposes and to help the state Board of Equalization assess the hazardous waste fees and taxes, which are based in large measure on the volume of hazardous wastes generated and disposed.

The EPA Identification Number may be obtained by completing EPA Form 8700-12 (revised 1/90) - Notification of Hazardous Waste Activity - and either mailing the form to EPA at:

CSC(T-1-2)
U.S. Environmental Protection Agency, Region IX
215 Fremont Street
San Francisco, CA 94105

or calling the agency in the event of an emergency at (415) 974-7473. Identification numbers can be issued by telephone, if necessary. Depending on the amount of wastes being generated, treated or disposed of, or if the facility applying for the number is a storage, treatment or disposal facility, it will be required to pay the state Board of Equalization fees that are used to support the operations of the Department of Toxic Substances Control (DTSC) and contribute to the state cleanup fund. Therefore, all but the smallest generators must register with the Board of Equalization once the EPA Identification Number is obtained. State law also requires a notice to DTSC that hazardous wastes are being generated, so a copy of the 8700-12 form should be sent to DTSC. [Health and Safety Code §25158.] The DTSC may be contacted for further information or copies of forms at (916) 324-1781.

Every two years, a generator will be requested to submit a report called the Biennial Generator's Report in which it must describe its hazardous wastes, amounts generated and efforts to minimize the wastes.

◆ Proper Shipment and Off-Site Waste Management and Disposal

To prepare hazardous wastes for shipment, generators must package and label the waste in accordance with 22 CCR §66262.30, et seq. The Department of Transportation (DOT) requires specific packaging, a shipping name recognized by DOT, or a "not otherwise specified" designation and a hazard class label based on the shipping name or properties of the waste. The waste must be packaged in accordance with the applicable DOT regulations on packaging found in 49 CFR, Parts 173, 178 and 179; label, placard and mark each package in accordance with the applicable DOT regulations on hazardous materials under 49 CFR, Part 172; and mark each container to be transported with the appropriate label. In addition, a hazardous waste manifest (see below) must accompany the shipment to verify its safe arrival at the designated destination. These requirements usually are meticulously complied with by the service firms, which are subject to strict regulations and loss of license if violations occur.

◆ Hazardous Waste Manifest

Completing a hazardous waste manifest facilitates the cradle-to-grave tracking of hazardous wastes that the regulatory agencies need to monitor the generation and eventual disposal of such wastes. Generators that ship their hazardous wastes off-site are required to complete a "Uniform Hazardous Waste Manifest" [22 CCR §66262.20] that identifies the nature and amount of waste that is being transported off-site, the generator, the transporter and the waste's destination. The manifest also is needed to meet DOT requirements for papers to accompany shipments of hazardous materials.

The hazardous waste manifest is important to the generator to protect itself from future liability. Once the shipment of hazardous waste arrives at its intended destination, an "acknowledgement copy" is returned to the generator. This document must be preserved as a legal record that the generator complied with the law, that no mishap occurred during the transportation, and that the wastes arrived at their specified destination. Due to the importance of the hazardous waste manifest, the requirements for its proper completion are very strict and non-compliance may result in the inability to ship the wastes, as well as fines and other penalties.

The EPA and DOT developed the "Uniform Hazardous Waste Manifest," which is the form to be used by generators for shipping their hazardous wastes off-site. For California facilities, only the revised Uniform Manifest (EPA Form 8700-22/DTSC 8022 A) obtained from the DTSC should be used because certain state-specific items relate only to California facilities. Note that California changes its manifesting procedures and form from time-to-time so that only current manifests may be used. Given that generators are responsible for their wastes from cradle to grave, it is essential to investigate why an acknowledgement copy has not been received within 35 days. If this copy is late, the generator must file an Exception Report with DTSC within 45 days.

Exemptions from the full manifesting requirements cover hazardous waste haulers who collect "milk run" volumes of certain hazardous wastes. For example:

- Drycleaning wastes that contain only perchloroethylene as a hazardous component.

- Waste oils that have been removed from vehicles or equipment powered by internal combustion engines.

Chap. 8

- Recyclable metal part cleaning solvents.

These exemptions are designed to promote recycling. The simplified procedures allow the hauler to prepare an alternative manifest. Under this system, the transporter is able to pick up small amounts from a number of businesses, thereby reducing costs to each. There also are limited exemptions for transporting hazardous wastes by unlicensed private parties without manifests if only five gallons or 50 pounds are transported to a permitted facility.

◆ Recordkeeping Requirements

Hazardous waste documentation, including manifests, tax returns, biennial generator reports, EPA number application (Notice of Hazardous Waste Activity), and hazardous waste profiles, or characterization records must be kept for three years. Further, the EPA Identification Number must be updated as "new" waste streams are added or old ones deleted within 30 days by notifying the EPA and DTSC in writing. [22 CCR §66262.20, et seq.]

◆ Selecting a Hazardous Waste Transporter and Hazardous Waste Management Facility

More than with any other party in the cradle-to-grave management system, generators of hazardous waste bear the burden of verifying that the other parties are following the law. The generator has the most to lose if a transporter or treatment, storage and/or disposal facility (TSDF) intentionally or unintentionally fails to manage the waste properly and legally. The generator is ultimately responsible for their waste and liable for any damage it may cause, almost irrespective of any negligence or misconduct of others. Given this potential liability, it is essential that a generator adequately understand the responsibilities of transporters and treatment or disposal facilities before selecting those that will handle its waste. Requesting verification of permits and compliance with regulatory requirements is essential in selecting a service firm.

Mandatory Hazardous Waste Source Reduction for Generators

A 1990 statute requiring the establishment of a hazardous waste source reduction program [Health and Safety Code §25244.12, et seq.] applied to generators of over 12,000 kilograms per year (about 30,000 pounds, or 60 drums). A 1992 statute amends this requirement by making it applicable to generators of more than 5,000 kilograms per year (about 11,000 pounds) beginning on September 1, 1993 based on 1992 waste generation. Each facility that generates hazardous waste should carefully account for its hazardous waste generation and determine whether a source reduction plan must be prepared. Most recyclable materials, like waste lubricating oil and wastewater which is hazardous waste prior to treatment, are not counted in the facility's hazardous waste generation.

If applicable, the requirements of the hazardous waste source reduction program are:

- A description of waste streams and quantities generated.

- An evaluation of feasible source reduction strategies.

- The rationale for rejecting any source reduction alternatives.

- An evaluation of the effects of methods chosen.

- A timetable for making reasonable and measurable progress towards source reduction.

- Certification by the generator and a registered professional (environmental assessor or registered engineer).

The initial plan must be prepared by September 1, 1991 (September 1, 1993 for generators between 5,000 and 12,000 kilograms), and every four years thereafter. A $1,000 per day fine may be assessed for failure to comply within 30 days of a request by the Department of Toxic Substances Control (DTSC) or a county health department for a copy of the hazardous waste source reduction plan. The statute requires DTSC to identify and prioritize categories of waste generators to which feasible waste reduction methods apply and through study and, eventually, enforcement, assure that waste reduction is being attained.

This concludes the basic requirements for a generator of hazardous wastes. The following information briefly describes additional hazardous waste activities subject to further regulatory requirements, including permits.

On-Site Hazardous Waste Treatment Permits

In California, any treatment of hazardous waste requires a permit from the Department of Toxic Substances Control. This requirement is substantially different and more stringent than the permitting requirements of federal EPA and many other states. This is due to the fact that, in California, more wastes are considered hazardous (like waste lubricating oil) and the state law and regulations do not exempt hazardous waste treatment from permitting if it is associated with wastewater pre-treatment prior to discharge to a community sewer system or discharge to surface water pursuant to an NPDES permit.

Given that so many operations are affected by this permitting requirement and the state has latitude because many types of waste treatment are not subject to federal Resource Conservation and Recovery Act (RCRA) permitting, it has been able to develop a "streamlined" permitting process called "tiered permitting." This new form of regulation was enacted by AB 1772, the Hazardous Waste Treatment Permitting Reform Act of 1992. Its provisions simplify the permit application or notification and agency review process and establishes tiers of regulatory requirements based on level of treatment activity. However, it does not provide relief from the regulatory requirements and fees associated with any treatment of hazardous waste.

The applicability of this law is triggered by any hazardous waste treatment that is not subject to federal EPA treatment permitting, and which employs treatment technologies like:

- precipitation and crystallization;
- ion exchange;
- evaporation;
- absorption;
- chemical stabilizing;

- physical processes;
- phase separation by filtration, centrifugation or gravity settling, but excluding critical fluid extraction;
- distillation;
- neutralization of corrosive hazardous wastes;
- pH adjustment of non-corrosive hazardous wastes;
- separation based on difference in physical properties, such as size, magnetism and density;
- reverse osmosis; and
- biological process conducted in tanks or containers and utilizing naturally occurring microorganisms.

The list of currently approved treatment technologies is in the former permit-by-rule regulation (general superseded by AB 1772) at 22 CCR §67450.11.

Any facility treating any amount of hazardous wastes (including pre-treatment of wastewater prior to sewer discharge) must comply with the notification requirement by April 1, 1993 and meet the regulatory requirements applicable for its permit tier.

AB 1772 establishes the following four tiers for on-site treatment permitting:

- *Conditionally Exempt - Small Quantity Treatment (CESQT)*. This tier covers any approved treatment method within the limit of 500 pounds or 55 gallons of hazardous waste treated in any calendar month.

- *Conditionally Exempt - Specified Waste Stream (SESW)*. This tier covers certain types of treatment and certain industries. Included in this tier are the following activities:
  ✔ Polymerizing resins.
  ✔ Rinsing empty containers.
  ✔ Magnetic gravity separation or screening with some limits.
  ✔ Drying certain wastes.
  ✔ Neutralization of demineralizer regenerants.
  ✔ Neutralization of food processing wastes.
  ✔ Silver recovery from photo processing up to 500 gallons per month.
  ✔ Wastewater treatment (neutralization and toxics removal) by state-certified testing laboratories and educational institution labs.

- *Conditionally Authorized (CA)*. This tier covers many of the approved treatment processes, but imposes limits on either the concentration of toxic organic or metallic hazardous waste constituents in the waste being treated or the total volume per month or at any one time, or both.

- *Permit By Rule (PBR)*. This tier includes all of the approved treatment activities which do not qualify for regulation in one of the lesser regulated tiers.

Each facility covered by the on-site treatment permitting program (including facilities that use the services of a transportable treatment unit brought on-site by a service firm) must submit a Facility Specific Notification and a Unit Specific Notification for the appropriate tier for each treatment unit the facility operates by April 1, 1993. A fee must accompany the notification in the amount of $100 for conditionally exempt tiers and $1,140 for conditionally authorized and permit-by-rule tiers. The facility pays only one fee for each tier in which it is permitted, irrespective of the number of units in each tier.

Once the notifications are submitted, the facility must comply with the regulatory requirements applicable to the tier or tiers in which its treatment units are permitted. Briefly summarized, these regulatory requirements include:

- Compliance with all hazardous waste generator requirements (all tiers).
- Proper treatment residual management (all tiers).
- Written operating instructions (all tiers).
- Maintenance of an operating log (all tiers).
- Proper closure of the treatment unit (all tiers).
- Annual waste minimization statement (CA & PBR).
- Modified disclosure of environmental violations and convictions (CA & PBR).
- Conduct an environmental assessment by January 1, 1995 (CA & PBR).
- Financial assurance for closure by January 1, 1994 (CA & PBR).
- Financial assurance for liability for damage claims by January 1, 1994 (PBR).
- Closure plan and cost estimate (PBR).
- Corrective action requirements (PBR).
- Tank and container certification of integrity and secondary containment (PBR).

Facilities that are treating hazardous wastes on-site should review the permitting and regulatory requirements and contact DTSC regional or headquarter offices as indicated in Appendix 8-2 to verify coverage and to obtain needed information and notification forms.

Given that there are severe penalties for treating hazardous wastes without a permit and that the facility may be liable for facility fees for such treatment activities in the past if it does not comply with AB 1772, prompt compliance is essential.

Hazardous Waste Treatment Storage and Disposal Facilities

Facilities in the hazardous waste service business or those which are large enough that on-site storage of large quantities of wastes in tanks or in containers over 5,000 gallon capacity or in excess of 90 days is necessary, are subject to extensive and vigorously enforced regulatory requirements.

◆ Definition of Treatment, Storage and Disposal Facility

Health and Safety Code §25201 prohibits an operator of a storage facility, treatment facility, waste transfer station, resource recovery facility or waste disposal site from accepting, treating, storing or disposing of a hazardous waste unless the operator holds a hazardous waste facility permit from the Department of Toxic Substances Control and/or EPA.

- A disposal facility is a facility where waste is intentionally placed and which the waste will remain after closure. [22 CCR §66044.]

- A storage facility is a facility that meets any of the following requirements:

✔ Hazardous wastes are contained for greater than 90 days at an on-site location.

✔ A tank that contains more than 5,000 gallons or 45,000 pounds of hazardous wastes for any period of time.

✔ A storage location for hazardous wastes at an off-site facility that is not a transfer facility.

✔ A transfer facility where hazardous wastes are held for more than 96 hours.

A hazardous waste *treatment facility* is subject to permitting requirements unless it is directly connected to an industrial production process that prevents the release of hazardous waste into the environment.

Federal law contains specific exemptions from permitting for various types of treatment facilities, for example: wastewater treatment systems subject to NPDES permitting. However, California HWCL's board language encompasses many types of treatment, including wastewater treatment. Some on-site and transportable hazardous waste treatment facilities are subject to permit by rule as discussed previously, many others are subject to full permitting.

◆ **Requirements for a Hazardous Waste Facility Permit**

Permits are obtained from DTSC and are reviewed by EPA. The permit application has two sections, Part A and Part B. Part A covers basic facility information and was used to expeditiously permit facilities in operation before November 10, 1980. Currently, both parts must be satisfied. Part B contains more exhaustive management plans and emergency response program documentation, and a showing of financial responsibility. In addition, a closure and post-closure plan, cost estimate and financial guarantees must be provided and approved. [22 CCR §66270-66271.19.]

In view of these stringent requirements, facilities must carefully analyze whether it is advisable for their waste management program to include permitted hazardous waste facilities. In the case of storage and disposal, unless the facility has a special need, it should ensure that its wastes are removed within 90 days and that wastes are not disposed of on-site. As far as treatment is concerned, on-site treatment may be technically and economically advantageous to shipping wastes off-site. Facilities planning to treat hazardous wastes on-site should be familiar with the requirements of operating a hazardous waste facility and meeting permit conditions, and apply this information to their hazardous waste management decisions.

Further discussion of these requirements are outside of the scope of this handbook, given their complexity and the detailed information and understanding needed for compliance. Such facilities are encouraged to consult with regulatory officials, and technical and legal counsel.

Hazardous Waste Liability and Cleanups

This area of hazardous waste laws has received the greatest attention and is responsible for the extremely stringent regulatory requirements for facilities that currently handle hazardous wastes, as well as liability for and procedures which govern cleanup of past hazardous waste facilities and disposal sites. The existence of abandoned waste disposal and storage sites and the need for public financing for their cleanup has produced federal Comprehensive Environmental Response, Compensation and

Liability Act (CERCLA) and the California Hazardous Substance Account Act (HSAA). These laws not only established a funding mechanism for cleanup or response activities at federal and state priority sites, but also the legal premise of hazardous waste generator "strict, joint and several" liability for its hazardous wastes along with other parties connected with the generator's waste or the property. It is outside of the scope of this chapter to pursue in any detail this important body of law. Furthermore, it does not directly relate to current regulatory compliance, which is the main purpose of this handbook, but to past failures.

The following information is provided as a brief highlight of laws in this area. Readers affected by hazardous waste liability will need to consult the applicable laws and regulations and experts in the field.

- For hazardous waste site cleanup liability which authorizes state recovery of costs, the statute defines as a "responsible party" or "liable person" any person who would be defined as such pursuant to federal CERCLA. [Health and Safety Code §25323.5.]

- However, contrary to federal law, which has been interpreted by the courts as specifying strict, joint and several liability for any party with a connection to the wastes disposed or the property, state law provides for an apportionment of liability among potentially responsible parties. An arbitration mechanism is provided to apportion liability. [Health and Safety Code §§25356.2-25356.10.]

- Innocent parties injured or economically damaged by hazardous waste disposals or other incidents may pursue claims against the state's Hazardous Substances Account. [Health and Safety Code §§25372-25381.]

- Written notices of releases of hazardous substances or to property by owners upon sale to potential buyers, and by lessees or renters to owners is required. [Health and Safety Code §25359.7.]

- Prior to residential development of property onto which a significant disposal of hazardous wastes or within 2,000 feet of a significant disposal of hazardous wastes, defined as "hazardous waste and border zone property", the Department of Toxic Substances Control must be notified and approve the development. [Health and Safety Code §25221.]

- DTSC is authorized to assess fees for oversight of hazardous waste site cleanups performed voluntarily by responsible parties. These fees are based on the size of the site and the department's involvement. [Health and Safety Code §25343.]

- Severe sanctions, including punitive damages of three times the cleanup costs, are available if a responsible party fails to respond as required to an order for site remediation. [Health and Safety Code §25359.]

- The innocent purchaser provision in federal law which allows a purchaser or lender to avoid liability if due diligence is exercised during the transaction, has not been directly adopted into statute in California. Health and Safety Code §25359(b) prohibits punitive damages (discussed above) against such persons and, arguably, Health and Safety Code §25323.5

adopts the federal innocent purchaser defense by reference. However, other state laws, for example, the Water Code, should be considered whenever reviewing a current property owner's potential environmental liability.

As this information indicates, the state's scheme of hazardous waste liability is modeled after federal law. However, the enforcement and cost recovery provisions probably are stricter, providing severe sanctions to force responsible parties to remedy contaminated sites.

Hazardous Waste Compliance Overview

Facilities that generate wastes must carefully review their wastes from the perspective of the hazardous waste regulations to assure meticulous compliance because, as the next section indicates, hazardous waste violations carry significant penalties. The following information will facilitate verification of compliance with the applicable regulations:

◆ Hazardous Waste Determination

- Are wastes generated (except for obviously non-hazardous refuse) checked to determine whether or not they are hazardous? Waste lubricating oil is hazardous by definition. Listed hazardous wastes are identified [22 CCR §66261.126] or the waste may exhibit hazardous characteristics:

    ✔ Ignitable.
    ✔ Corrosive.
    ✔ Reactive.
    ✔ Toxic.

    Note: This question must be answered for all waste streams.

- If the waste is empty containers, are the following procedures being followed? (Otherwise, they may be a hazardous waste.)

    ✔ Containers are completely empty?
    ✔ If five gallons or less and disposed of as non-hazardous within one year?
    ✔ If more than five gallons, are they provided to a recycler within one year?

- Are there any containers of hazardous substances (products) which are leaking, deteriorated, or not legibly labeled? If not immediately repackaged, these materials will be deemed hazardous wastes.

- Are any extremely hazardous wastes being generated, as defined? [22 CCR §66261.110.] If so, special rules apply.

◆ On-Site Management of Hazardous Wastes

- Hazardous wastes must not be stored for more than 90 days before off-site shipment from date of first accumulation unless the satellite rule (below) does not apply.

- If the satellite rule is used for storage time extension for small volume wastes, is the facility storing no more than 55 gallons at the point of generation for up to one year?

● Are the hazardous waste storage containers in good condition (no cracks, breaks or leaks)?

● Are the containers properly closed and appropriately labeled with the name of the company, accumulation start date, and the nature and hazard of the contents?

● Are the containers compatible with the waste contents?

● Are weekly documented inspection conducted of the containers and the entire storage area?

● Is the hazardous waste storage area secured with a fence and locked gate (or is the property secure), and are appropriate warning signs posted as required?

● Incompatible hazardous wastes are stored separate from each other (e.g., acids from petroleum-based wastes)?

● If ignitable and/or reactive wastes, are they stored at least 50 feet from the property line setback?

● Is the storage area double-contained or bermed and covered to avoid concern over rainwater management, or does it drain to a wastewater treatment system?

◆ Contingency Plan and Training

● Is a hazardous waste contingency plan written and in place?

● Are personnel who handle hazardous wastes properly trained before they work with them?

◆ Off-Site Shipment

● Does the facility have an EPA Identification Number for the wastes being generated?

● Are hazardous waste haulers that are used screened to ensure they are currently licensed by the Department of Toxic Substances Control?

● Are destination facilities (for treatment or disposal) appropriate for the wastes being shipped and are they in compliance with applicable requirements?

◆ Manifests and Recordkeeping

● Are hazardous waste shipments manifested properly?

● Are procedures for manifest management being followed?

✔ Original matched to acknowledged copy with any discrepancies noted?
✔ DTSC notified if acknowledged copy of manifest is not received within 45 days?
✔ Manifests and other hazardous waste records maintained for at least three years?
✔ Are biennial generator's reports being completed?

◆ **Mandatory Hazardous Waste Reduction**

● Does the facility generate over 5,000 kilograms of non-exempt hazardous waste per year?

● If yes, has a hazardous waste source reduction program been prepared (due September 1, 1991 for facilities which generate more than 12,000 kilograms and on September 1, 1993 for those which generate more than 5,000 kilograms) and is it available on-site?

◆ **On-Site Hazardous Waste Treatment Permit**

● Does the facility treat hazardous waste? Examples include: a system that separates oil and water, separates sludge from water, neutralizes wastewater which has a pH of less than two or greater than 12.5; or evaporates, incinerates or otherwise reduces the volume of hazard of a waste, which would be characterized as hazardous.

● If yes, the facility is subject to permitting as a hazardous waste treatment facility, under the AB 1772 tiered permitting statute.

● If subject to tiered permitting, the facility should file the "Facility and Unit Notifications" by April 1, 1993 and comply with the applicable regulatory requirements for its tier(s).

Note: No facility may accept wastes from off-site for treatment, storage or disposal, and no facility may treat or dispose of wastes on-site without a permit from DTSC or EPA.

Penalties for Violations

Violations of the HWCL can result in three different types of enforcement actions:

● Administrative sanctions, entailing citations and fines.
● Civil actions resulting in court orders and penalties.
● Criminal prosecutions seeking fines and imprisonment.

◆ **Administrative Sanctions**

For violations of the HWCL or any regulation, misrepresentation or omission of a significant fact in information provided to the Department of Toxic Substances Control (DTSC), non-payment of tax or fees, and other violations, the DTSC is empowered to suspend or revoke a hazardous waste registration or permit. The director may issue an order that requires corrective action to be taken by the facility operator. Failure to comply with a corrective order may result in a fine of up to $25,000 per day. If imminent substantial danger is found, the DTSC itself may take corrective actions. The facility operator is liable for three times the costs of the corrective action, as well as any civil fines that may be imposed. Offenders will be provided a hearing and an opportunity for an administrative appeal.

◆ **Civil Actions**

Civil actions may be brought at the request of DTSC, by city or district attorneys where the violation occurred, or by the Attorney General. Such actions may be instituted for an injunction to stop an activity out of compliance with the HWCL and to seek civil penalties. Civil monetary penalties under the HWCL are summarized in the following table:

Chap. 8

Violation	Penalty*
● False statement	Up to $25,000
● Violation of the HWCL or its regulations	Up to $25,000
● Unlawful disposal	Up to $25,000

*In most cases, the penalty is calculated on a per day of violation basis.

◆ Criminal Prosecution

Facilities handling hazardous wastes should pay particular attention to the potential of criminal liability associated with hazardous waste law violations. In California, criminal penalties are much more severe for HWCL violations than other regulatory crimes. A conviction under the HWCL can occur without a showing of intent or negligence leading to the violation. For crimes relating to the mismanagement of hazardous waste, knowing or negligence in the case of disposal is the requisite state of mind, not a showing of criminal intent. The following table summarizes the potential crime violations, state of mind and associated penalties, which are codified in Health and Safety Code §§25189-25192.

Criminal Penalties

Violation	State of Mind	Penalty[1]
1. Disposal at, or transportation to an unpermitted site.	Knowing or reasonably should have known.	Up to 1 year in jail or up to 36 months in prison AND court must impose fine of $5,000 to $100,000.[2]
2. False statement in preparing a compliance document.	Knowing	*First offense:* $2,000 to $25,000 per day and/or 1 year in jail. *Subsequent offense:* $2,000 to $50,000 per day and/or up to 24 months in prison.[3]
3. Produces, receives, stores or submits for transportation in violation of Health and Safety Code §§25160 (manifest), 25161 (regulations) or 25163.	Knowing	*First offense:* $2,000 to $25,000 per day and/or 1 year in jail. *Subsequent offense:* $2,000 to $50,000 per day and/or up to 24 months in prison.[3]
4. Possession of altered compliance documents.	Knowing	*First offense:* $2,000 to $25,000 per day and/or 1 year in jail. *Subsequent offense:* $2,000 to $50,000 per day and/or up to 24 months in prison.[3]
5. Transportation in non-compliance with regulations.	Knowing	*First offense:* $2,000 to $25,000 per day and/or 1 year in jail. *Subsequent offense:* $2,000 to $50,000 per day and/or up to 24 months in prison.[3]

Chap. 8

6.	Withholding requested information regarding a "real and substantial danger."	Knowing	*First offense:* $2,000 to $25,000 per day and/or 1 year in jail. *Subsequent offense:* $2,000 to $50,000 per day and/or up to 24 months in prison.[3]
7.	Transports in violation of Health and Safety Code §§25160 (use of manifest) or 25168.3 (inspection certificate).	Knowing	Not less than $2,000, nor more than $25,000 and up to 6 months in jail.
8.	Treats or stores hazardous waste at unpermitted facility.	Knowing	Not less than $5,000 nor more than $100,000 and 1 year in jail or 3 years in prison.
9.	Any other violation of the HWCL.	Knowing	*First offense:* misdemeanor, up to $1,000 fine and 6 months in jail.

Notes to Table

1. All monetary penalties arise on a per day basis.
2. If the violation causes great bodily harm or caused a substantial probability that death could result, the fine can be increased to up to $250,000 per day.
3. Minimum fine must be imposed upon conviction for a knowing violation.

◆ Rewards for Informants

The Hazardous Waste Control Law (HWCL) provides for payment of rewards of 10 percent of the civil penalty up to $5,000 for informants who provide information that "materially contributes to the imposition of the penalty." Government employees who discover violations in the course of their employment and employees of the penalized facility who caused the violation, or whose regular responsibilities included investigating the violation are not eligible for rewards. [Health and Safety Code §25191.5.]

As mentioned at the beginning of this section, facilities should take action to avoid liability for the types of penalties described above. Enforcement activities are expected to increase as county and local officials assume enforcement authority and become better staffed and trained to enforce hazardous waste laws. The HWCL provides for reimbursement for local prosecutors in the form of a share of penalties collected. Criminal and civil penalties, less rewards, are apportioned in the following manner:

- 50 percent to the Hazardous Waste Control Account.
- 25 percent to the DTSC.
- 25 percent to the local prosecutional agency.

The following appendices describe DTSC, the principal hazardous waste enforcement agency in California, and highlight the applicable laws and regulations.

Appendix 8-1
Laws and Regulations on Hazardous Waste Management

State Laws

- Hazardous Waste Control Law (HWCL)   Health and Safety Code §§25100-25249
- Hazardous Substance Account Act (HSAA)   Health and Safety Code §§25340-25392
- Hazardous Waste Treatment Permitting Reform   Health and Safety Code §25201
  Act (AB 1772)

Federal Laws

- Resource Conservation and Recovery Act   42 USC 6901-6987
  (RCRA)
- Comprehensive Environmental Response,   42 USC 6901-6957
  Compensation and Liability Act (CERCLA)
  and the Superfund Amendments and
  Reauthorization Act (SARA)

State Regulations

- Identification and Listing of Hazardous Waste   22 CCR §§66261-66261.126
- Requirements for Generators, Generally   22 CCR §§66262.10-66262.70
- Requirements for Generators, Contingency   22 CCR §§66264.50-66264.56
  Plan
- Requirements for Generators, Personnel   22 CCR §66265.16
  Training
- Requirements for Transporters   22 CCR §66263
- Hazardous Waste Permitted Facility   22 CCR §§66264-66265
  Requirements, Generally
- Recyclable Materials   22 CCR §66266
- Land Disposal Prohibitions   22 CCR §66268
- Hazardous Waste Facilities - Permitting   22 CCR §66270
  Procedures
- Enforcement Procedures and Reporting   22 CCR §66272-67382
  Procedures
- Extremely Hazardous Waste Requirements   22 CCR §67430
- Hazardous Waste Treatment - Permit by Rule   22 CCR §67450

Federal Regulations

- Hazardous Waste Identification, Generator   40 CFR 261
  Requirements
- Standards Applicable to Transporters   40 CFR 263
- Permitted Facility Requirements   40 CFR 264-267
- Hazardous Waste Response, Liability and   40 CFR 300-311
  Remediation

Chap. 8

Appendix 8-2
Cal/EPA Department of Toxic Substances Control

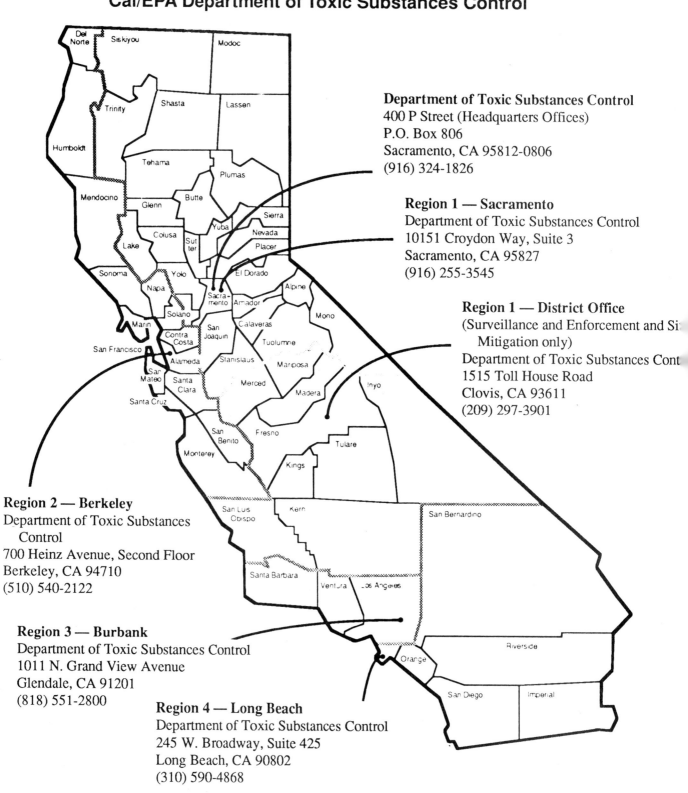

Department of Toxic Substances Control
400 P Street (Headquarters Offices)
P.O. Box 806
Sacramento, CA 95812-0806
(916) 324-1826

Region 1 — Sacramento
Department of Toxic Substances Control
10151 Croydon Way, Suite 3
Sacramento, CA 95827
(916) 255-3545

Region 1 — District Office
(Surveillance and Enforcement and Si
  Mitigation only)
Department of Toxic Substances Cont
1515 Toll House Road
Clovis, CA 93611
(209) 297-3901

Region 2 — Berkeley
Department of Toxic Substances
  Control
700 Heinz Avenue, Second Floor
Berkeley, CA 94710
(510) 540-2122

Region 3 — Burbank
Department of Toxic Substances Control
1011 N. Grand View Avenue
Glendale, CA 91201
(818) 551-2800

Region 4 — Long Beach
Department of Toxic Substances Control
245 W. Broadway, Suite 425
Long Beach, CA 90802
(310) 590-4868

Chap. 8

Appendix 8-3
Environmental Health Standards — Hazardous Wastes
California Code of Regulations, Title 22, §66261.126

indicated in the list as follows:(X) toxic, (C) corrosive, (I) ignitable and (R) reactive. A chemical denoted with an asterisk is presumed to be an extremely hazardous waste unless it does not exhibit any of the criteria set forth in section 66261.110 and section 66261.113. Trademark chemical names are indicated by all capital letters.

1. Acetaldehyde (X,I)
2. Acetic acid (X,C,I)
3. Acetone, Propanone (I)
4. Acetone cyanohydrin (X)
5. Acetonitrile (X,I)
6. * 2–Acetylaminofluorene, 2–AAF (X)
7. Acetyl benzoyl peroxide (X,I,R)
8. * Acetyl chloride (X,C,R)
9. Acetyl peroxide (X,I,R)
10. Acridine (X)
11. * Acrolein, Aqualin (X,I)
12. * Acrylonitrile (X,I)
13. * Adiponitrile (X)
14. * Aldrin; 1,2,3,4,10,10–Hexachloro–1,4,4a,5,8,8a–hexahydro–1,4,5,8–endo–exodimethanonaphthalene (X)
15. * Alkyl aluminum chloride (C,I,R)
16. * Alkyl aluminum compounds (C,I,R)
17. Allyl alcohol, 2–Propen–1–ol (X,I)
18. Allyl bromide, 3–Bromopropene (X,I)
19. Allyl chloride, 3–Chloropropene (X,I)
20. Allyl chlorocarbonate, Allyl chloroformate (X,I)
21. * Allyl trichlorosilane (X,C,I,R)
22. Aluminum (powder) (I)
23A. Aluminum chloride (X,C)
23B. * Aluminum chloride (anhydrous) (X,C,R)
24. Aluminum fluoride (X,C)
25. Aluminum nitrate (X,I)
26. * Aluminum phosphide, PHOSTOXIN (X,I,R)
27. * 4–Aminodiphenyl, 4–ADP (X)
28. * 2–Aminopyridine (X)
29. * Ammonium arsenate (X)
30. * Ammonium bifluoride (X,C)
31. Ammonium chromate (X,I)
32. Ammonium dichromate, Ammonium bichromate (X,C,I)
33. Ammonium fluoride (X,C)
34. Ammonium hydroxide (X,C)
35. Ammonium molybdate (X)
36. Ammonium nitrate (I,R)
37. Ammonium perchlorate (I,R)
38. Ammonium permanganate (X,I,R)
39. Ammonium persulfate (I,R)
40. Ammonium picrate (I,R)
41. Ammonium sulfide (X,C,I,R)
42. n–Amyl acetate, 1–Acetoxypentane (and isomers) (X,I)
43. n–Amylamine, 1–Aminopentane (and isomers) (X,I)
44. n–Amyl chloride, 1–Chloropentane (and isomers) (X,I)
45. n–Amylene, 1–Pentene (and isomers) (X,I)
46. n–Amyl mercaptan, 1–Pentanethiol (and isomers) (X,I)
47. n–Amyl nitrite, n–Pentyl nitrite (and isomers) (X,I)
48. * Amyl trichlorosilane (and isomers) (X,C,R)
49. Aniline, Aminobenzene (X)
50. Anisoyl chloride (X,C)
51. Anthracene (X)
52. Antimony (X)
53. Antimony compounds (X)
54. * Antimony pentachloride (X,C,R)
55. * Antimony pentafluoride (X,C,R)
56. Antimony pentasulfide (X,I)
57. Antimony potassium tartrate (X)
58. Antimony sulfate, Antimony trisulfate (X,I)
59. Antimony trichloride, Antimony chloride (X,C)
60. Antimony trifluoride, Antimony fluoride (X,C)
61. Antimony trioxide, Antimony oxide (X)
62. Antimony trisulfide, Antimony sulfide (X,I,R)
63. * Arsenic (X)
64. * Arsenic acid and salts (X)
65. * Arsenic compounds (X)
66. * Arsenic pentaselenide (X)
67. * Arsenic pentoxide, Arsenic oxide (X)
68. * Arsenic sulfide, Arsenic disulfide (X)
69. * Arsenic tribromide, Arsenic bromide (X)
70. * Arsenic trichloride, Arsenic chloride (X)
71. * Arsenic triiodide, Arsenic iodide (X)
72. * Arsenic trioxide, Arsenious oxide (X)
73. * Arsenious acid and salts (X)
74. * Arsines (X)
75. Asbestos (including chrysotile, amosite, crocidolite, tremolite, anthophyllite, and actinolite) (X)
76. * AZODRIN, 3–Hydroxy–N–cis–crotonamide (X)
77. Barium (X,I)
78. Barium azide (I,R)
79. Barium bromide (X)
80. Barium carbonate (X)
81. Barium chlorate (X,C,I,R)
82. Barium chloride (X)
83. Barium chromate (X)
84. Barium citrate (X)
85. Barium compounds (soluble) (X)
86. * Barium cyanide (X)
87. Barium fluoride (X)
88. Barium fluosilicate (X)
89. Barium hydroxide (X)
90. Barium iodide (X)
91. Barium manganate (X)
92. Barium nitrate (X,I)
93. Barium oxide, Barium monoxide (X)
94. Barium perchlorate (X,I,R)
95. Barium permanganate (X,I,R)
96. Barium peroxide (X,I,R)
97. Barium phosphate (X)
98. Barium stearate (X)
99. Barium sulfide (X)
100. Barium sulfite (X)
101. Benzene (X,I)
102. * Benzene hexachloride, BHC; 1,2,3,4,5,6–Hexachloro-cyclohexane (X)
103. * Benzenephosphorous dichloride (I,R)
104. Benzenesulfonic acid (X)
105. * Benzidine and salts (X)
106. * Benzotrifluoride, Trifluoromethylbenzene (X,I)
107. * Benzoyl chloride (X,C,R)
108. Benzoyl peroxide, Dibenzoyl peroxide (X,I,R)
109. Benzyl bromide, alpha–Bromotoluene (X,C)
110. Benzyl chloride, alpha–Chlorotoluene (X)
111. * Benzyl chlorocarbonate, Benzyl chloroformate (X,C,R)
112. * Beryllium (X,I)
113. * Beryllium chloride (X)
114. * Beryllium compounds (X)
115. * Beryllium copper (X)
116. * Beryllium fluoride (X)
117. * Beryllium hydride (X,C,I,R)
118. * Beryllium hydroxide (X)
119. * Beryllium oxide (X)
120. * BIDRIN, Dicrotophos, 3–(Dimethylamino)–1–methyl–3–oxo–1–propenyldimethyl phosphate (X)
121. * bis (Chloromethyl) ether, Dichloromethylether, BCME (X)
122. Bismuth (X,I)
123. * bis (Methylmercuric) sulfate, CEREWET, Ceresan liquid (X)
124. Bismuth chromate (X)
125. * BOMYL, Dimethyl 3–hydroxyglutaconate dimethyl phosphate (X)
126. * Boranes (X,I,R)
127. * Bordeaux arsenites (X)
128. * Boron trichloride, Trichloroborane (X,C,R)
129. * Boron trifluoride (X,C,R)
130. Bromic acid (X)
131. * Bromine (X,C,I)
132. * Bromine pentafluoride (X,C,I,R)
133. * Bromine trifluoride (X,C,I,R)
134. * Brucine, Dimethoxystrychnine (X)
135. 1,2,4–Butanetriol trinitrate (R)
136. n–Butyl acetate, 1–Acetoxybutane (and isomers) (X)
137. n–Butyl alcohol, 1–Butanol (and isomers) (X)
138. n–Butyl amine, 1–Aminobutane (and isomers) (X)
139. n–Butyl formate (and isomers) (X)

Chap. 8

Register 91, No. 22, 5-31-91

140.   tert–Butyl hydroperoxide (and isomers) (X,I)
141.   * n–Butyllithium (and isomers) (X,C,I,R)
142.   n–Butyl mercaptan, 1–Butanethiol (and isomers) (X,I)
143.   tert–Butyl peroxyacetate, tert–Butyl peracetate (I,R)
144.   tert–Butyl peroxybenzoate, tert–Butyl perbenzoate (I,R)
145.   tert–Butyl peroxypivalate (I,R)
146.   * n–Butyltrichlorosilane (C,I,R)
147.   para–tert–Butyl toluene (X)
148.   n–Butyraldehyde, n–Butanal (and isomers) (X,I)
149.   * Cacodylic acid, Dimethylarsinic acid (X)
150.   * Cadmium (powder) (X,I)
151.   Cadmium chloride (X)
152.   * Cadmium compounds (X)
153.   * Cadmium cyanide (X)
154.   Cadmium fluoride (X)
155.   Cadmium nitrate (X,I,R)
156.   Cadmium oxide (X)
157.   Cadmium phosphate (X)
158.   Cadmium sulfate (X)
159.   * Calcium (I,R)
160.   * Calcium arsenate, PENSAL (X)
161.   * Calcium arsenite (X)
162.   * Calcium carbide (C,I,R)
163.   Calcium chlorate (I,R)
164.   Calcium chlorite (I)
165.   Calcium fluoride (X)
166.   * Calcium hydride (C,I,R)
167.   Calcium hydroxide, Hydrated lime (C)
168.   * Calcium hypochlorite, Calcium oxychloride (dry) (X,C,I,R)
169.   Calcium molybdate (X)
170.   Calcium nitrate, Lime nitrate, Nitrocalcite (I,R)
171.   Calcium oxide, Lime (C)
172.   Calcium permanganate (X,I)
173.   Calcium peroxide, Calcium dioxide (C,I)
174.   * Calcium phosphide (X,I,R)
175.   Calcium resinate (I)
176.   Caprylyl peroxide, Octyl peroxide (I)
177.   * Carbanolate, BANOL, 2–Chloro–4,5–dimethylphenyl
      methylcarbamate (X)
178.   Carbon disulfide, Carbon bisulfide (X,I)
179.   Carbon tetrachloride, Tetrachloromethane (X)
180.   * Carbophenothion, TRITHION, S[[(4–Chlorophenyl)
      thio]methyl] O,O–diethyl phosphorodithioate (X)
181.   Chloral hydrate, Trichloroacetaldehyde (hydrated) (X)
182.   * Chlordane; 1,2,4,5,6,7,8,8–Octachloro–4,7–methano–
      3a,4,7,7a–tetra– hydro– indane; (X)
183.   * Chlorfenvinphos, Compound 4072, 2–Chloro–1–(2,4–
      dichlorophenyl) vinyl diethyl phosphate (X)
184.   * Chlorine (X,C,I,R)
185.   * Chlorine dioxide (X,C,I,R)
186.   * Chlorine pentafluoride (X,C,I,R)
187.   * Chlorine trifluoride (X,C,I,R)
188.   * Chloroacetaldehyde (X,C)
189.   * alpha–Chloroacetophenone, Phenyl chloromethyl ketone (X)
190.   * Chloroacetyl chloride (X,C,R)
191.   Chlorobenzene (X,I)
192.   para–Chlorobenzoyl peroxide (I,R)
193.   * ortho–Chlorobenzylidene malononitrile, OCMB (X)
194.   Chloroform, Trichloromethane (X)
195.   * Chloropicrin, Chlorpicrin, Trichloronitromethane (X)
196.   * Chlorosulfonic acid (X,C,I,R)
197.   Chloro–ortho–toluidine, 2–Amino–4–chlorotoluene (X)
198.   Chromic acid, Chromium trioxide, Chromic anhydride (X,C,I)
199.   Chromic chloride, Chromium trichloride (X)
200.   Chromic fluoride, Chromium trifluoride (X)
201.   Chromic hydroxide, Chromium hydroxide (X)
202.   Chromic oxide, Chromium oxide (X)
203.   Chromic sulfate, Chromium sulfate (X)
204.   Chromium compounds (X,C,I)
205.   * Chromyl chloride, Chlorochromic anhydride (X,C,I,R)
206.   Cobalt (powder) (X,I)
207.   Cobalt compounds (X)
208.   Cobaltous bromide, Cobalt bromide (X)
209.   Cobaltous chloride, Cobalt chloride (X)
210.   Cobaltous nitrate, Cobalt nitrate (X,I)
211.   Cobaltous resinate, Cobalt resinate (X,I)

212.   Cobaltous sulfate, Cobalt sulfate (X)
213.   Cocculus, Fishberry, Picrotoxin (X)
215.   * Copper acetoarsenite, Paris green (X)
216.   Copper acetylide (I,R)
217.   * Copper arsenate, Cupric arsenate (X)
218.   * Copper arsenite, Cupric arsenite (X)
219.   Copper chloride, Cupric chloride (X)
220.   Copper chlorotetrazole (I,R)
221.   Copper compounds (X)
222.   * Copper cyanide, Cupric cyanide (X)
223.   Copper nitrate, Cupric nitrate (X,I,R)
224.   Copper sulfate, Cupric sulfate, Blue vitriol (X)
225.   * Coroxon; ortho,ortho–Diethyl–ortho–(3–chloro–4–
      methylcoumarin–7–yl) phosphate (X)
226.   * Coumafuryl, FUMARIN, 3–[1–(2–Furanyl)–3–oxobutyl]
      1–4–hydroxy–2H–1–benzopyran–2–one (X)
227.   * Coumatetralyl, BAYER 25634, RACUMIN 57,
      4–Hydroxy–3–(1,2,3,4–tetrahydro–1–naphthalenyl)–
      2H–1–benzopyran–2–one (X)
228.   * Crimidine, CASTRIX, 2–Chloro–4–dimethylamino–6–
      methyl–pyrimidine (X)
229.   * Crotonaldehyde, 2–Butenal (X)
230.   Cumene, Isopropyl benzene (X,I)
231.   Cumene hydroperoxide; alpha,alpha–Dimethylbenzyl
      hydro–peroxide (X,I)
232.   Cupriethylene diamine (X)
233.   * Cyanide salts (X)
234.   Cyanoacetic acid, Malonic nitrile (X)
235.   * Cyanogen (X,I,R)
236.   Cyanogen bromide, Bromine cyanide (X)
237.   Cyanuric triazide (I,R)
238.   Cycloheptane (X,I)
239.   Cyclohexane (X,I)
240.   Cyclohexanone peroxide (I)
241.   * Cyclohexenyltrichlorosilane (X,C,R)
242.   * Cycloheximide, ACTIDIONE (X)
243.   * Cyclohexyltrichlorosilane (X,C,R)
244.   Cyclopentane (X,I)
245.   Cyclopentanol (I)
246.   Cyclopentene (X,I)
247.   DDT; 1,1,1–Trichloro–2,2–bis(chlorophenyl) ethane (X)
248.   * DDVP, Dichlorvos, VAPONA, Dimethyl dichlorovinyl
      phosphate (X)
249.   * Decaborane (X,I,R)
250.   DECALIN, Decahydronaphthalene (X)
251.   * Demeton, SYSTOX (X)
252.   * Demeton–S–methyl sulfone,
      METAISOSYSTOX–SULFON, S–[2–(ethyl–sulfonyl)
      ethyl] O,O–dimethyl phosphorothioate (X)
253.   Diazodinitrophenol, DDNP, 2–Diazo–4,6–dinitrobenzene–1–
      oxide (I,R)
254.   * Diborane, Diboron hexahydride (I,R)
255.   * 1,2–Dibromo–3–chloropropane, DBCP, Fumazone,
      nemagon (X)
256.   n–Dibutyl ether, Butyl ether (and isomers) (X,I)
257.   Dichlorobenzene (ortho, meta, para) (X)
258.   * 3,3–Dichlorobenzidine and salts, DCB (X)
259.   1,2–Dichloroethylene; 1,2–Dichloroethene (X,I)
260.   Dichloroethyl ether, Dichloroether (X,I)
261.   Dichloroisocyanuric acid, Dichloro–S–triazine–2,4,6–tri–
      one (X,I)
262.   Dichloromethane, Methylene chloride (X)
263.   * 2,4–Dichlorophenoxyacetic acid; 2,4–D (X)
264.   1,2–Dichloropropane, Propylene dichloride (X,I)
265.   1,3–Dichloropropylene; 1,3–Dichloropropene (X,I)
266.   Dicumyl peroxide (I,X)
267.   * Dieldrin; 1,2,3,4,10,10–Hexachloro–6,7–epoxy–1,4,4a,5,6,7,
      8,8a–octahydro–1,4–endo,exo–5,8–dimethanonaphthalene
      (X)
268.   * Diethylaluminum chloride, Aluminum diethyl monochloride,
      DEAC (I,R)
269.   Diethylamine (X,I)
270.   * Diethyl chlorovinyl phosphate, Compound 1836 (X)
271.   * Diethyldichlorosilane (X,C,I,R)
272.   Diethylene glycol dinitrate (I,R)
273.   Diethylene triamine (X)

Register 91, No. 22; 5–31–91

Chap. 8

274. * O,O–Diethyl–S–(isopropylthiomethyl) phosphorodithioate (X)
275. * Diethylzinc, Zinc ethyl (C,I,R)
276. * Difluorophosphoric acid (X,C,R)
277. * Diglycidyl ether, bis(2,3–Epoxypropyl) ether (X)
278. Diisopropylbenzene hydroperoxide (X,I)
279. Diisopropyl peroxydicarbonate, Isopropyl percarbonate (X,C,I,R)
280. * Dimefox, Hanane, Pextox 14, Tetramethylphosphorodiamidic fluoride (X)
281. Dimethylamine, DMA (X,I)
282. * Dimethylaminoazobenzene, Methyl yellow (X)
283. * Dimethyldichlorosilane, Dichlorodimethylsilane (X,C,I,R)
284. 2,5–Dimethylhexane–2,5–Dihydroperoxide (I)
285. * 1,1–Dimethylhydrazine, UDMH (X,I)
286. * Dimethyl sulfate, Methyl sulfate (X)
287. * Dimethyl sulfide, Methyl sulfide (X,I,R)
288. 2,4–Dinitroaniline (X)
289. * Dinitrobenzene (ortho, meta, para) (I,R)
290. Dinitrochlorobenzene, 1–Chloro–2,4–dinitrobenzene (I,R)
291. * 4,6–Dinitro–ortho–cresol, DNPC, SINOX, E
292. * Dinitrophenol(2,3–;2,4–;2,6–isomers) (I,R)
293. 2,4–Dinitrophenylhydrazine (X,I,R)
294. Dinitrotoluene (2,4–;3,4–;3,5–isomers) (X,I,R)
295. * DINOSEB; 2,4–Dinitro–6–sec–butylphenol (X)
296. 1,4–Dioxane; 1,4–Diethylene dioxide (X,I,R)
297. * Dioxathion, DELNAV; S,S–1,4–dioxane–2,3–diyl bis(O,O–diethyl phosphorodithioate) (X)
298. Dipentaerythritol hexanitrate (R)
299. * Diphenyl, Biphenyl, Phenylbenzene (X)
300. Diphenylamine, DPA, N–Phenylaniline (X)
301. * Diphenylamine chloroarsine, Phenarsazine chloride (X)
302. * Diphenyldichlorosilane (X,C,R)
303. Dipicrylamine, Hexanitrodiphenyl amine (I,R)
304. Dipropyl ether (X,I)
305. * Disulfoton, DI–SYSTON; O,O–Diethyl S–[2–(ethylthio) ethyl] phosphorodithioate (X)
306. * Dodecyltrichlorosilane (X,C,R)
307. * DOWCO–139, ZECTRAM, Mexacarbate, 4–(Dimethylamino)–3,5–dimethylphenyl methylcarbamate (X)
309. * DYFONATE, Fonofos, O–Ethyl–S–phenylethyl phosphonodithioate (X)
310. * Endosulfan, THIODAN; 6,7,8,9,10,10–Hexachlor–1,5,5a,6,9, 9a–hexa–hydro–6,9–methano–2,4,3–benzo–dioxathiepin–3–oxide (X)
311. * Endothal, 7–Oxabicyclo[2.2.1]heptane–2,3–dicarboxylic acid (X)
312. * Endothion, EXOTHION, S–[(5–Methoxy–4–oxo–4H–pyran–2–yl)–methyl] O,O–dimethyl phosphorothioate (X)
313. * Endrin; 1,2,3,4,10,10–Hexachloro–6,7–epoxy–1,4,4,4a,5,6,7, 8,8a–octahydro–1,4–endo–endo–5,8–dimethanonaph–thalene (X)
314. Epichlorohydrin, Chloropropylene oxide (X,I)
315. * EPN; O–Ethyl O–para–nitrophenyl phenylphosphonothioate (X)
316. * Ethion, NIALATE; O,O,O',O'–Tetraethyl–S,S–methylenediphos–phorodithioate (X)
317. Ethyl acetate (X,I)
318. Ethyl alcohol, Ethanol (X,I)
319. Ethylamine, Aminoethane (X,I)
320. Ethylbenzene, Phenylethane (X,I)
321. Ethyl butyrate, Ethyl butanoate (I)
322. Ethyl chloride, Chloroethane (X,I)
323. * Ethyl chloroformate, Ethyl chlorocarbonate (X,C,I,R)
324. * Ethyldichloroarsine, Dichloroethylarsine (I,R)
325. * Ethyldichlorosilane (X,C,I,R)
326. * Ethylene cyanohydrin, beta–Hydroxypropionitrile (I,R)
327. Ethylene diamine (X)
328. Ethylene dibromide; 1,2–Dibromoethane (X)
329. Ethylene dichloride; 1,2–Dichloroethane (X,I)
330. * Ethyleneimine, Aziridine, EI (X,I,R)
331. Ethylene oxide, Epoxyethane (X,I,R)
332. Ethyl ether, Diethyl ether (I,R)
333. Ethyl formate (X,I)

334. * Ethyl mercaptan, Ethanethiol (X,I,R)
335. Ethyl nitrate (I,R)
336. Ethyl nitrite (I,R)
337. * Ethylphenyldichlorosilane (X,C,R)
338. Ethyl propionate (I)
339. * Ethyltrichlorosilane (I,R)
340. * Fensulfothion, BAYER 25141, DASANIT, O,O–Diethyl–0–[4–(methyl—sulfinyl)phenyl] phosphorothioate (X)
341. * Ferric arsenate (X)
342. Ferric chloride, Iron (III) chloride (X,C)
343. * Ferrous arsenate, Iron arsenite (X)
344. * Fluoboric acid, Fluoroboric acid (X,C)
345. Fluoride salts (X)
346. * Fluorine (X,C,R)
347. * Fluoroacetanilide, AFL 1082 (X)
348. * Fluoroacetic acid and salts, Compound 1080 (X)
349. * Fluorosulfonic acid, Fluosulfonic acid (X,C,R)
350. Formaldehyde, Methanal (X,I)
351. Formic acid, Methanoic acid (X,C)
352. Fulminate of mercury, Mercuric cyanate (I,R)
353. * FURADAN, NIA 10,242, Carbofuran; 2,3–Dihydro–2,2–dimethyl–7–benzofuranylmethylcarbamate (X)
354. Furan, Furfuran (X,I,R)
355. Gasoline (I)
356. * GB, O–Isopropyl methyl phosphoryl fluoride (X)
357. Glutaraldehyde (X)
358. Glycerolmonolactate trinitrate (R)
359. Glycol dinitrate, Ethylene glycol dinitrate (R)
360. Gold fulminate, Gold cyanate (R)
361. Guanidine nitrate (I,R)
362. Guanyl nitrosaminoguanylidene hydrazine (R)
363. * Guthion; O,O–Dimethyl–S–4–oxo–1,2,3–benzotriazin–3(4H)–ylmethyl phosphorodithioate (X)
364. Hafnium (I,X,R)
365. * Heptachlor; 1,4,5,6,7,8,8–Heptachloro–3a,4,7,7a–tetra–hydro–4,7–methanoindene (X)
366. n–Heptane (and isomers) (X,I)
367. 1–Heptene (and isomers) (X,I)
368. * Hexadecyltrichlorosilane (X,C,R)
369. Hexaethyl tetraphosphate, HETP (X)
370. Hexafluorophosphoric acid (X,C)
371. Hexamethylenediamine; 1,6–Diaminohexane (X)
372. n–Hexane (and isomers) (X,I)
373. 1–Hexene (and isomers) (X,I)
374. n–Hexylamine, 1–Aminohexane (and isomers) (X,I)
375. * Hexyltrichlorosilane (X,C,R)
376. * Hydrazine, Diamine (X,I)
377. Hydrazine azide (I,R)
378. Hydrazoic acid, Hydrogen azide (I,R)
379. * Hydriodic acid, Hydrogen iodide (X,C,R)
380. * Hydrobromic acid, Hydrogen bromide (X,C,R)
381. * Hydrochloric acid, Hydrogen chloride, Muriatic Acid (X,C,R)
382. * Hydrocyanic acid, Hydrogen cyanide (X,I,R)
383. * Hydrofluoric acid, Hydrogen fluoride (X,C,R)
384. Hydrofluosilicic acid, Fluosilicic acid (X,C)
385. Hydrogen peroxide (X,C,I,R)
386. * Hydrogen selenide (X,I)
387. * Hydrogen sulfide (X,I)
388. * Hypochlorite compounds (X,C,I,R)
389. Indium (X)
390. Indium compounds (X)
391. * Iodine monochloride (X,C,R)
392. Isooctane; 2,2,4–Trimethylpentane (X,I)
393. Isooctene (mixture of isomers) (I)
394. Isopentane, 2–Methylbutane (I)
395. Isoprene, 2–Methyl–1,3–butadiene (I)
396. Isopropanol, Isopropyl alcohol, 2–Propanol (X,I)
397. Isopropyl acetate (X,I)
399. Isopropylamine, 2–Aminopropane (X,I)
400. Isopropyl chloride, 2–Chloropropane (I)
401. Isopropyl ether, Diisopropyl ether (I,R)
402. Isopropyl mercaptan, 2–Propanethiol (X,I)
404. * meta–Isopropylphenyl–N–methylcarbamate, Ac 5,727 (X)

Register 91. No. 22; 5–31–91

405A.   *Kepone; 1,1a,3,3a,4,5,5,5a,5b,6-Decachloro-
        octahydro-1,2,4-metheno-2H-cyclobuta (cd)
        pentalen-2-one, Chlorecone (X)
405B.   Lauroyl peroxide, Di-n-dodecyl peroxide (X,C,I,R)
406.   Lead compounds (X)
407.   Lead acetate (X)
408.   *Lead arsenate, Lead orthoarsenate (X)
409.   *Lead arsenite (X)
410.   Lead azide (I,R)
411.   Lead carbonate (X)
412.   Lead chlorite (I,R)
413.   *Lead cyanide (X)
414.   Lead 2,4-dinitroresorcinate (I,R)
415.   Lead mononitroresorcinate (I,R)
416.   Lead nitrate (X,I)
417.   Lead oxide (X)
418.   Lead styphnate, Lead trinitroresorcinate (I,R)
419.   *Lewisite, beta-Chlorovinyldichloroarsine (X)
420.   *Lithium (C,I,R)
421.   *Lithium aluminum hydride, LAH (C,I,R)
422.   *Lithium amide (C,I,R)
423.   *Lithium ferrosilicon (I,R)
424.   *Lithium hydride (C,I,R)
425.   *Lithium hypochlorite (X,C,I,R)
426.   Lithium peroxide (C,I,R)
427.   Lithium silicon (I,R)
428.   *London purple, Mixture of arsenic trioxide, aniline, lime,
        and ferrous oxide (X)
429.   *Magnesium (I,R)
430.   *Magnesium arsenate (X)
431.   *Magnesium arsenite (X)
432.   Magnesium chlorate (I,R)
433.   Magnesium nitrate (I,R)
434.   Magnesium perchlorate (X,I,R)
435.   Magnesium peroxide, Magnesium dioxide (I)
436.   *Maleic anhydride (X)
437.   Manganese (powder) (I)
438.   Manganese acetate (X)
439.   *Manganese arsenate, Manganous arsenate (X)
440.   Manganese bromide, Manganous bromide (X)
441.   Manganese chloride, Manganous chloride (X)
442.   Manganese methylcyclopentadienyl tricarbonyl (X)
443.   Manganese nitrate, Manganous nitrate (X,I)
444.   Mannitol hexanitrate, Nitromannite (R)
445.   *MECARBAM; O,O-Diethyl S-(N-ethoxycarbonyl
        N-methylcarba-moyl-methyl) phosphorodithioate (X)
446.   *Medinoterb acetate, 2-tert-Butyl-5-methyl-4,6-dinitro-
        phenyl acetate (X)
447.   para-Menthane hydroperoxide, Paramenthane hydroperoxide
        (I)
448.   Mercuric acetate, Mercury acetate (X)
449.   Mercuric ammonium chloride, Mercury ammonium chloride
        (X)
450.   Mercuric benzoate, Mercury benzoate (X)
451.   Mercuric bromide, Mercury bromide (X)
452.   *Mercuric chloride, Mercury chloride (X)
453.   *Mercuric cyanide, Mercury cyanide (X)
454.   Mercuric iodide, Mercury iodide (X)
455.   Mercuric nitrate, Mercury nitrate (X,I)
456.   Mercuric oleate, Mercury oleate (X)
457.   Mercuric oxide (red and yellow) (X,I)
458.   Mercuric oxycyanide (I,R)
459.   Mercuric-potassium iodide, Mayer's reagent (X)
460.   Mercuric salicylate, Salicylated mercury (X)
461.   Mercuric subsulfate, Mercuric dioxysulfate (X)
462.   Mercuric sulfate, Mercury sulfate (X)
463.   Mercuric thiocyanide, Mercury thiocyanate (X)
464.   Mercurol, Mercury nucleate (X)
465.   Mercurous bromide (X)
466.   Mercurous gluconate (X)
467.   Mercurous iodide (X)
468.   Mercurous nitrate (I,R)
469.   Mercurous oxide (X)
470.   Mercurous sulfate, Mercury bisulfate (X)
472.   *Mercury (X)
473.   *Mercury compounds (X)

474.   Metal carbonyls (X)
475.   *Metal hydrides (I,R)
476.   Metal powders (X,I)
477A.   *Methomyl, LANNATE, S-Methyl-N-((methyl-carbamoyl)
        oxy) thioacetimidate (X)
477B.   *Methoxychlor; 1,1,1-Trichloro-2, -bis(p-methoxyphenyl)
        ethane, CHEMFLORM, MARLATE (X)
478.   *Methoxyethylmercuric chloride, AGALLOL, ARETAN (X)
479.   Methyl acetate (X,I)
480.   Methyl acetone (Mixture of acetone, methyl acetate, and
        methyl alcohol) (X,I)
481.   Methyl alcohol, Methanol (X,I)
482.   *Methylaluminum sesquibromide (I,R)
483.   *Methylaluminum sesquichloride (I,R)
484.   Methylamine, Aminomethane (X,I)
485.   n-Methylaniline (X)
486.   *Methyl bromide, Bromomethane (X)
487.   2-Methyl-1-butene (I)
488.   3-Methyl-1-butene (I)
489.   Methyl butyl ether (and isomers) (X,I)
490.   Methyl butyrate (and isomers) (X,I)
491.   Methyl chloride, Chloromethane (X,I)
492.   *Methyl chloroformate, Methyl chlorocarbonate (X,I,R)
493.   *Methyl chloromethyl ether, CMME (X,I)
494.   Methylcyclohexane (X,I)
495.   *Methyldichloroarsine (X)
496.   *Methyldichlorosilane (X,I,R)
497.   *4,4-Methylene bis(2-chloroaniline), MOCA (X)
498.   Methyl ethyl ether (X,I)
499.   Methyl ethyl ketone, 2-Butanone (X,I)
500.   Methyl ethyl ketone peroxide (X,I)
501.   Methyl formate (X,I)
502.   *Methyl hydrazine, Monomethyl hydrazine, MMH (X,I)
503.   *Methyl isocyanate (X,I)
504.   Methyl isopropenyl ketone, 3-Methyl-3-butene-2-one (X,I)
505.   *Methylmagnesium bromide (C,I,R)
506.   *Methylmagnesium chloride (C,I,R)
507.   *Methylmagnesium iodide (C,I,R)
508.   Methyl mercaptan, Methanethiol (X,I)
509.   Methyl methacrylate (monomer) (X,I)
510.   *Methyl parathion; O,O-Dimethyl-O-para-nitrophenyl-
        phosphorothioate (X)
511.   Methyl propionate (I)
512.   *Methyltrichlorosilane (X,C,I,R)
513.   Methyl valerate, Methyl pentanoate (and isomers) (I)
514.   Methyl vinyl ketone, 3-Butene-2-one (X,I)
515A.   *Mevinphos, PHOSDRIN, 2-Carbomethoxy-1-methylvinyl
        dimethylphosphate (X)
515B.   *Mirex; 1,1a.2,2,3,3a,4,5,5,5a,5b,6-Dodecachlorooctahydro-
        1,3,4-metheno-1H-cyclobuta (cd) pentalene,
        Dechlorane (X)
516.   *MOCAP, O-Ethyl-S,S-dipropyl phosphorodithioate (X)
517.   Molybdenum (powder) (I)
518.   Molybdenum trioxide, Molybdenum anhydride (X)
519.   Molybdic acid and salts (X)
520.   Monochloroacetic acid, Chloracetic acid, MCA (X,C)
521.   Monochloroacetone, Chloroacetone, 1-Chloro-2-propanone
        (X)
522.   Monofluorophosphoric acid (X,C)
523.   Naphtha (of petroleum or coal tar origin), Petroleum ether,
        Petroleum naphtha (X,I)
524.   Naphthalene (X)
525.   *alpha-Naphthylamine, 1-NA (X)
526.   *beta-Naphthylamine, 2-NA (X)
527.   Neohexane; 2,2-Dimethylbutane (X,I)
528.   Nickel (powder) (X,I)
529.   Nickel acetate (X)
530.   Nickel antimonide (X)
531.   *Nickel arsenate, Nickelous arsenate (X)
532.   *Nickel carbonyl, Nickel tetracarbonyl (X)
533.   Nickel chloride, Nickelous chloride (X)
534.   *Nickel cyanide (X)
535.   Nickel nitrate, Nickelous nitrate (X,I,R)
536.   Nickel selenide (X)
537.   Nickel sulfate (X)
538.   Nicotine, beta-pyridyl-alpha-N-methyl pyrrolidine (X)

539. Nicotine salts (X)
540. Nitric acid (X,C,I)
541. Nitroaniline, Nitraniline (ortho, meta, para) (I,R)
542. * Nitrobenzol, Nitrobenzene (X)
543. * 4–Nitrobiphenyl, 4–NBP (X)
544. Nitro carbo nitrate (I,R)
545. Nitrocellulose, Cellulose nitrate, Guncotton, Pyroxylin, Collodion, Pyroxylin (nitrocellulose) in ether and alcohol (I,R)
546. Nitrochlorobenzene, Chloronitrobenzene (ortho,meta,para) (X)
547. Nitrogen mustard (X,C)
548. Nitrogen tetroxide, Nitrogen dioxide (X,I)
549. Nitroglycerin, Trinitroglycerin (X,I,R)
550. Nitrohydrochloric acid, Aqua regia (X,C,I)
551. * Nitrophenol (ortho, meta, para) (X)
552. * N–Nitrosodimethylamine, Dimethyl nitrosoamine (X)
553. Nitrosoguanidine (R)
554. Nitrostarch, Starch nitrate (I,R)
555. Nitroxylol, Nitroxylene, Dimethylnitrobenzene (2,4–;3,4–; 2,5–isomers) (X)
556. 1–Nonene, 1–Nonylene (and isomers) (X,I)
557. * Nonyltrichlorosilane (I,R)
558. * Octadecyltrichlorosilane (I,R)
559. n–Octane (and isomers) (X,I)
560. 1–Octene, 1–Caprylene (X,I)
561. * Octyltrichlorosilane (I,R)
563. * Oleum, Fuming sulfuric acid (X,C,R)
565. Osmium compounds (X)
566. Oxalic acid (X)
567. * Oxygen difluoride (X,C,R)
568. * Para–oxon, MINTACOL; O,O–Diethyl–O–para–nitrophenyl phosphate (X)
569. * Parathion; O,O–Diethyl–O–para–nitrophenyl phosphorothioate (X)
570A. * Pentaborane (X,I,R)
570B. Pentachlorophenol, PCP, DOWICIDE 7 (X)
571. Pentaerythrite tetranitrate, Pentaerythritol tetranitrate (R)
572. n–Pentane (and isomers) (X,I)
573. 2–Pentanone, Methyl propyl ketone (and isomers) (X,I)
574. Peracetic acid, Peroxyacetic acid (X,C,I,R)
575. Perchloric acid (X,C,I,R)
576. Perchloroethylene, Tetrachloroethylene (X)
577. * Perchloromethyl mercaptan, Trichloromethylsulfenyl chloride (X)
578. Perchloryl fluoride (X,C,I)
580. Phenol, Carbolic acid (X,C)
581. * Phenyldichloroarsine (X)
582. Phenylenediamine, Diaminobenzene (ortho,meta,para) (X)
583. Phenylhydrazine hydrochloride (X)
584. * Phenylphenol, Orthozenol, DOWICIDE I (X)
585. * Phenyltrichlorosilane (I,R)
586. * Phorate, THIMET; O,O–Diethyl–S–[(Ethylthio)methyl] phosphorodithioate (X)
587. * Phosfolan, CYOLAN, 2–(Diethoxyphosphinylimino)–1,3–dithio–lane (X)
588. * Phosgene, Carbonyl chloride (I,R)
589. * Phosphamidon, DIMECRON, 2–Chloro–2–diethyl-carbamoyl–1–methylvinyl dimethyl phosphate (X)
590. * Phosphine, Hydrogen phosphide (X,I)
591. Phosphoric acid (C)
592. Phosphoric anhydride, Phosphorus pentoxide (C,I)
593. Phosphorus (amorphous, red) (X,I,R)
594. * Phosphorus (white or yellow) (X,I,R)
595. * Phosphorus oxybromide, Phosphoryl bromide (X,C,R)
596. * Phosphorus oxychloride, Phosphoryl chloride (X,C,R)
597. * Phosphorus pentachloride, Phosphoric chloride (X,C,I,R)
598. * Phosphorus pentasulfide, Phosphoric sulfide (X,C,I,R)
599. * Phosphorus sesquisulfide, tetraphosphorus trisulfide (X,C,I,R)
600. * Phosphorus tribromide (X,C,R)
601. * Phosphorus trichloride (X,C,R)
602. Picramide, Trinitroaniline (I,R)
603. Picric acid, Trinitrophenol (I,R)
604. Picryl chloride, 2–Chloro–1,3,5–trinitrobenzene (I,R)
605. * Platinum compounds (X)

606. * Polychlorinated biphenyls, PCB, Askarel, aroclor, chlorextol, inerteen, pyranol (X)
607. Polyvinyl nitrate (I,R)
608. Potasan; O,O–Diethyl–0–(4–methylumbelliferone) phosphoro–thioate (X)
609. * Potassium (C,I,R)
610. * Potassium arsenate (X)
611. * Potassium arsenite (X)
612. * Potassium bifluoride, Potassium acid fluoride (X,C)
613. Potassium binoxalate, Potassium acid oxalate (X)
614. Potassium bromate (X,I)
615. * Potassium cyanide (X)
616. Potassium dichloroisocyanurate (X,I)
617. Potassium dichromate, Potassium bichromate (X,C,I)
619. Potassium fluoride (X)
620. * Potassium hydride (C,I,R)
621. Potassium hydroxide, Caustic potash (X,C)
622. Potassium nitrate, Saltpeter (I,R)
623. Potassium nitrite (I,R)
624. Potassium oxalate (X)
625. Potassium perchlorate (X,I,R)
626. Potassium permanganate (X,C,I)
627. Potassium peroxide (C,I,R)
628. Potassium sulfide (X,I)
629. * Propargyl bromide, 3–Bromo–1–propyne (X,I)
630. * beta–Propiolactone, BPL (X)
631. Propionaldehyde, Propanal (X,I)
632. Propionic acid, Propanoic acid (X,C,I)
633. n–Propyl acetate (X,I)
634. n–Propyl alcohol, 1–Propanol (X,I)
635. n–Propylamine (and isomers) (X,I)
636. * Propyleneimine, 2–Methylaziridine (X,I)
637. Propylene oxide (X,I)
638. n–Propyl formate (X,I)
639. n–Propyl mercaptan, 1–Propanethiol (X,I)
640. * n–Propyltrichlorosilane (X,C,I,R)
641. * Prothoate, FOSTION, FAC; O,O–Diethyl–S–carboethoxy-ethyl phosphorodithioate (X)
642. Pyridine (X,I)
643. * Pyrosulfuryl chloride, Disulfuryl chloride (X,C,R)
644. * Quinone; 1,4–Benzoquinone (X)
645. Raney nickel (I)
646. * Schradan, Octamethyl pyrophosphoramide, OMPA (X)
647A. * Selenium (X)
647B. * Selenium compounds (X)
648. * Selenium fluoride (X)
649. * Selenous acid, Selenious acid and salts (X)
650. * Silicon tetrachloride, Silicon chloride (X,C,R)
651. * Silver acetylide (I,R)
652. Silver azide (I,R)
653. Silver compounds (X)
654. Silver nitrate (X)
655. Silver styphnate, Silver trinitroresorcinate (I,R)
656. Silver tetrazene (I,R)
657. * Sodium (C,I,R)
658. Sodium aluminate (C)
659. * Sodium aluminum hydride (C,I,R)
660. * Sodium amide, Sodamide (C,I,R)
661. * Sodium arsenate (X)
662. * Sodium arsenite (X)
663. Sodium azide (I,R)
664. * Sodium bifluoride, Sodium acid fluoride (X,C)
665. Sodium bromate (X,I)
666. * Sodium cacodylate, Sodium dimethylarsenate (X)
667. Sodium carbonate peroxide (I)
668. Sodium chlorate (X,I)
669. Sodium chlorite (X,I)
670. Sodium chromate (X,C)
671. * Sodium cyanide (X)
672. Sodium dichloroisocyanurate (I)
673. Sodium dichromate, Sodium bichromate (X,C,I)
674. Sodium fluoride (X)
675. * Sodium hydride (X,C,I,R)
676. Sodium hydrosulfite, Sodium hyposulfite (I)
677. Sodium hydroxide, Caustic soda, Lye (X,C)
678. * Sodium hypochlorite (X,I,R)

Register 91, No. 22; 5–31–91

679. * Sodium methylate, Sodium methoxide (C,I,R)
680. Sodium molybdate (X)
681. Sodium nitrate, Soda niter (X,I,R)
682. Sodium nitrite (X,I,R)
683. Sodium oxide, Sodium monoxide (X,C)
684. Sodium perchlorate (X,I,R)
685. Sodium permanganate (X,I)
686. * Sodium peroxide (X,I,R)
687. Sodium picramate (X,I,R)
688. * Sodium potassium alloy, NaK, Nack (C,I,R)
689. * Sodium selenate (X)
690. Sodium sulfide, Sodium hydrosulfide (X,I)
691. Sodium thiocyanate, Sodium sulfocyanate (X)
692. Stannic chloride, Tin tetrachloride (X,C)
693. * Strontium arsenate (X)
694. Strontium nitrate (X,I,R)
695. Strontium peroxide, Strontium dioxide (I,R)
696. * Strychnine and salts (X)
697. Styrene, Vinylbenzene (X,I)
698. Succinic acid peroxide (X,I)
699. Sulfide salts (soluble) (X)
700. * Sulfotepp, DITHIONE, BLACAFUM, Tetraethyldithio-
      pyrophosphate, TEDP (X)
701. * Sulfur chloride, Sulfur monochloride (X,C,R)
702. * Sulfur mustard (X,C,R)
703. * Sulfur pentafluoride (X,C)
704. Sulfur trioxide, Sulfuric anhydride (X,C,I)
705. Sulfuric acid, Oil of vitriol, Battery acid (X,C)
706. Sulfurous acid (X,C)
707. * Sulfuryl chloride, Sulfonyl chloride (X,C,R)
708. * Sulfuryl fluoride, Sulfonyl fluoride (X,C,R)
709. * SUPRACIDE, ULTRACIDE,
      S-[(5-Methoxy-2-oxo-1,3,4-thia-diazo13(2H)-yl)
      methyl] -O,O-dimethyl phosphorodithioate (X)
710. * SURECIDE, Cyanophenphos, O-para-Cyanophenyl-
      O-ethyl phenyl phosphonothioate (X)
711. * Tellurium hexafluoride (X,C)
712. * TELODRIN, Isobenzan; 1,3,4,5,6,7,8,8-Octachloro-1,3,3a,4,
      7,7a-hexahydro-4,7-methanoisobenzofuran (X)
713. * TEMIK, Aldicarb, 2-Methyl-2(methylthio)
      propionaldehyde-O-(methylcarbamoyl) oxime (X)
714. * 2,3,7,8-Tetrachlorodibenzo-para-dioxin, TCDD, Dioxin (X)
715. sym-Tetrachloroethane (X)
717. * Tetraethyl lead, TEL (and other organic lead) (X,I)
718. * Tetraethyl pyrophosphate, TEPP (X)
719A. Tetrahydrofuran, THF (X,I)
719B. Tetrahydrophthalic anhydride, Memtetrahydrophthalic an-
      hydride (X)
720. TETRALIN, Tetrahydronaphthalene (X)
721. Tetramethyl lead, TML (X,I)
722. * Tetramethyl succinonitrile (X)
723. * Tetranitromethane (X,I,R)
724. * Tetrasul, ANIMERT V-101, S-para-Chlorophenyl-2,4,5-
      trichlorophenyl sulfide (X)
725. Tetrazene, 4-Amidino-1-(nitrosamino-amidino)-1-
      tetra-zene (I,R)
726. * Thallium (X)
727. * Thallium compounds (X)
728. * Thallous sulfate, Thallium sulfate, RATOX (X)
729. * Thiocarbonylchloride, Thiophosgene (X,C,R)
730. * Thionazin, ZINOPHOS; O,O-Tetramethylthiuram
      monosulfide (X)
731. * Thionyl chloride, Sulfur oxychloride (X,C,R)
732. * Thiophosphoryl chloride (X,C,R)
733. Thorium (powder) (I)
734. Tin compounds (organic) (X)
735. Titanium (powder) (I)
736. Titanium sulfate (X)
737. * Titanium tetrachloride, Titanic chloride (X,C,R)
738. Toluene, Methylbenzene (X,I)
739. * Toluene-2,4-diisocyanate, TDI (I,R)
740A. Toluidine, Aminotoluene (ortho,meta,para) (X)
740B. * Toxaphene, Polychlorocamphene (X)
741. * TRANID, exo-3-Chloro-endo-6-cyano-2-
      norbornanone-O-(methylcarbamoyl) oxime (X)
743. 1,1,2-Trichloroethane (X)

744. Trichloroethylene; Trichlorethene (X)
745. Trichloroisocyanuric acid (X,I)
746. * 2,4,5-Trichlorophenoxyacetic acid; 2,4,5-T (X)
747. * Trichlorosilane, Silicochloroform (X,C,I,R)
748. Trimethylamine, TMA (X,I)
749. Trinitroanisole; 2,4,6-Trinitrophenyl methyl ether (I,R)
750. 1,3,5-Trinitrobenzene, TNB (I,R)
751. 2,4,6-Trinitrobenzoic acid (I,R)
752. Trinitronaphthalene, Naphtite (I,R)
753. 2,4,6-Trinitroresorcinol, Styphnic acid (I,R)
754. 2,4,6-Trinitrotoluene, TNT (X,I,R)
755. * tris(1-Aziridinyl) phosphine oxide, Triethylenephospho-
      ramide, TEPA (X)
756. Tungstic acid and salts (X)
757. Turpentine (X,I)
758. Uranyl nitrate, Uranium nitrate (X,I,R)
759. Urea nitrate (X,I,R)
760. n-Valeraldehyde, n-Pentanal (and isomers) (X,I)
761. Vanadic acid salts (X)
762. Vanadium oxytrichloride (X,C)
763. * Vanadium pentoxide, Vanadic acid anhydride (X)
764. Vanadium tetrachloride (X,C)
765. Vanadium tetraoxide (X)
766. Vanadium trioxide, Vanadium sesquioxide (X)
767. Vanadyl sulfate, Vanadium sulfate (X)
768. Vinyl acetate (I,X)
769. * Vinyl chloride (X,I)
770. Vinyl ethyl ether (I)
771. Vinylidene chloride, VC (X,I)
772. Vinyl isopropyl ether (I)
773. * Vinyltrichlorosilane (X,C,I,R)
774. VX, O-Ethyl methyl phosphoryl N,N-diisopropyl
      thiocholine (X)
775. * WEPSYN 155, WP 155, Triamiphos, para-(5-Amino-3-
      phenyl-1H-1,2,4-triazol-1-yl)-N,N,N',N'-tetramethyl
      phosphonic diamide (X)
776. Xylene, Dimethylbenzene (ortho,meta,para) (X,I)
777. Zinc (powder) (I)
778. Zinc ammonium nitrate (X,I)
779. * Zinc arsenate (X)
780. * Zinc arsenite (X)
781. Zinc chloride (X,C)
782. Zinc compounds (X)
783. * Zinc cyanide (X)
784. Zinc nitrate (X,I,R)
785. Zinc permanganate (X,I)
786. Zinc peroxide, Zinc dioxide (X,I,R)
787. * Zinc phosphide (X,I,R)
788. Zinc sulfate (X)
789. Zirconium (powder) (I)
790. * Zirconium chloride, Zirconium tetrachloride (X,C,R)
791. Zirconium picramate (I)

(b) This subdivision sets forth a list of common names of wastes which are presumed to be hazardous wastes unless it is determined that the waste is not a hazardous waste pursuant to the procedures set forth in section 66262.11. The hazardous characteristics which serve as a basis for listing the common names of wastes are indicated in the list as follows:

(X) toxic, (C) corrosive, (I) ignitable and (R) reactive.

Acetylene sludge (C)
Acid and water (C)
Acid sludge (C)
AFU Floc (X)
Alkaline caustic liquids (C)
Alkaline cleaner (C)
Alkaline corrosive battery fluid (C)
Alkaline corrosive liquids (C)
Asbestos waste (X)
Ashes (X,C)
Bag house wastes (X)
Battery acid (C)
Beryllium waste (X)

Bilge water (X)
Boiler cleaning waste (X,C)
Bunker Oil (X,I)
Catalyst (X,I,C)
Caustic sludge (C)
Caustic wastewater (C)
Cleaning solvents (I)
Corrosion inhibitor (X,C)
Data processing fluid (I)
Drilling fluids (X,C)
Drilling mud (X)
Dyes (X)
Etching acid liquid or solvent (C,I)
Fly ash (X,C)
Fuel waste (X,I)
Insecticides (X)
Laboratory waste (X,C,R,I)
Lime and sulfur sludge (C)
Lime and water (C)
Lime sludge (C)
Lime wastewater (C)
Liquid cement (I)
Mine tailings (X,R)
Obsolete explosives (R)
Oil and water (X)
Oil Ash (X,C)
Paint (or varnish) remover or stripper (I)
Paint thinner (X,I)
Paint waste (or slops) (X,I)
Pickling liquor (C)
Pigments (X)
Plating waste (X,C)
Printing Ink (X)
Retrograde explosives (R)
Sludge acid (C)
Soda ash (C)
Solvents (I)
Spent acid (C)
Spent caustic (C)
Spent (or waste) cyanide solutions (X,C)
Spent mixed acid (C)
Spent plating solution (X,C)
Spent sulfuric acid (C)
Stripping solution (X,I)
Sulfonation oil (I)
Tank bottom sediment (X)
Tanning sludges (X)
Toxic chemical toilet wastes (X)
Unrinsed pesticide containers (X)
Unwanted or waste pesticides —an unusable portion of active ingredi-
    ent or undiluted formulation (X)
Waste epoxides (X,I)
Waste (or slop) oil (X)
Weed Killer (X)

Chap. 8

CHAPTER 9

141

Chap. 9

Medical and Infectious Waste Management

Summary and Applicability

This chapter describes the state's new regulatory program for medical and infectious waste management. The specific regulatory requirements apply to clinical and research laboratories, biotechnology facilities, hospitals, nursing centers, clinics and medical waste transporters and management firms. The requirements vary based on the size of the facility and amounts of waste generated or handled, and the nature of the waste-related activity. However, any operation that generates or otherwise handles medical or infectious wastes should review this chapter and any additional reference material necessary to determine which apply, and steps necessary to comply with the Medical Waste Management Act.

The regulatory requirements, as discussed in this chapter, are based on the nature of activity and size/volume of wastes generated.

- Determining whether medical wastes are being generated.
- Requirements for a small quantity medical waste generator that does not treat its wastes.
- Requirements for small quantity generators that treat wastes on-site.
- Large quantity generator requirements.
- Permitting and requirements for on-site treatment facility.
- Medical waste hauler registration and certification.
- Permit and requirements for off-site medical waste treatment facility.

Given the technical details of these compliance requirements and potential fines of $1,000 to $10,000 for first offenses, covered facilities should carefully review the information in this chapter.

Background

In response to public concern over infectious medical wastes and to assure proper identification, management and eventual treatment and disposal of such wastes, the Medical Waste Management Act of 1990, was enacted by the state Legislature. There is no federal counterpart to this state program. However, readers should be aware that future federal regulatory activity involving medical wastes is probable.

Organization of the State Program

The Medical Waste Management Act authorizes the Department of Health Services (DHS) to issue regulations and to act as the enforcement agency unless DHS grants authority to a local health department or environmental agency to implement the program in the county. The DHS unit responsible for medical waste management appears in Appendix 9-2. County environmental health agencies are listed in Appendix 9-3.

Counties that elect to be the enforcement agency must establish a Medical Waste Management Program that includes the following provisions:

- Issuance of medical waste regulations and permits.

- Review of medical waste management by small quantity generators.

- Oversight of on-site medical waste treatment.

- Inspections of medical waste generators and treatment facilities in response to complaints and emergencies. (*Note:* DHS retains exclusive jurisdiction over permitting and inspections of off-site medical waste treatment facilities.)

- Enforcement activities against violators.

- Preparation and submission of reports to DHS.

A number of technical definitions are critical to determining whether a particular waste or facility is subject to the act.

- **Medical waste** is defined to include:

  ✔ "Biohazardous wastes," which includes various types of laboratory waste; waste containing microbiologic specimens sent for laboratory analysis, human tissue or other surgery specimens potentially contaminated with contagious infectious agents, animal tissues, fluids and carcasses similarly suspected of being contaminated; waste containing fluid blood or blood products; and waste contaminated by quarantined humans or animals with highly communicable diseases.

  ✔ "Sharps waste," which includes hypodermic needles, syringes, blades, broken glass items such as pipettes, and other instruments or materials with acute corners or protuberances capable of cutting or piercing, which are contaminated with biohazardous waste.

  ✔ Other waste produced in research pertaining to the diagnosis, treatment or immunization of human beings or animals, or in the production of biologicals, which are biological products used in medicine.

- **"Medical waste" does not include:** radioactive waste; household waste; waste that is commonly found in medical facilities but is not biohazardous; waste generated from normal agricultural and livestock practices; non-infectious waste containing microbiological cultures used in food processing and biotechnology; human bodily fluids (e.g., saliva, vomit, etc.) and bodily waste unless they contain fluid blood; and hazardous waste.

- **Infectious waste** means a type of microorganism, bacteria, mold, parasite or virus which normally causes, or significantly contributes to the cause of, increased morbidity or mortality of human beings.

Chap. 9

- **Highly communicable diseases** are diseases such as those caused by organisms classified by the federal Centers for Disease Control as Biosafety Level IV organisms, which merit special precautions to protect staff, patients and other persons from infection. Highly communicable diseases do not include diseases such as the common cold, influenza or other diseases not representing a significant danger to non-immuno compromised persons.

It is essential for potentially regulated facilities to determine, based on these definitions, whether their wastes are subject to the Medical Waste Management Act. It is clear the act was not intended to regulate all medical or biohazard waste, only wastes that pose an infectious disease risk.

Regulatory Requirements

The regulatory program covers "medical waste generators," "medical waste haulers" and "medical waste treatment facilities."

- **Medical waste generators** are divided into small (less than 200 pounds of medical waste per month) and large (more than 200 pounds of medical waste per month) quantity generators.

- **Medical waste haulers** are not specifically defined in the statute, but are persons who transport medical wastes.

- **Treatment facilities** are those that treat medical wastes by incineration, steam sterilization or microwave technology, and may include any other process designated by the Department of Health Services as a process or technique employed to eliminate the disease-causing potential of medical waste. Treatment facilities are regulated in accordance with whether they are on-site treatment facilities or off-site treatment facilities. Some treatment facilities had been regulated as hazardous waste treatment facilities under the Title 22 hazardous waste regulations. The Medical Waste Management Act establishes alternative permitting for medical waste treatment facilities.

◆ **Regulation of Medical Waste Generators**

- **Large quantity generators** were required **to register** with the enforcement agency (DHS or county) by April 1, 1991 or before generating medical waste after this date. Shared facilities in the same building, property or adjacent facilities may register as a single generator. The registration must be renewed annually (90 days before it expires) and updated if any material change occurs in the operation. A **medical waste management plan** also must be filed with the enforcement agency on specified forms. The waste management plan must include:

    ✔ The name of the person filing the plan.

    ✔ The business address of the person.

    ✔ The type of business.

    ✔ The types and estimated monthly quantity of medical waste generated.

✔ The type of treatment used on-site, if applicable. For generators with on-site medical waste treatment facilities, including incinerators or steam sterilizers or other treatment facilities as determined by the enforcement agency, the treatment capacity of the on-site treatment facility.

✔ The name and business address of the registered medical waste hauler used by the generator to have untreated medical waste removed for treatment, if applicable.

✔ The name and business address of the registered hazardous waste hauler service provided by the building management to which the building tenants may subscribe or are required by the building management to subscribe, if applicable.

✔ The name and business address of the off-site medical waste treatment facility to which the medical waste is being hauled, if applicable.

✔ An emergency action plan complying with regulations adopted by the department.

✔ A statement certifying that the information provided is complete and accurate.

Treatment and tracking records must be maintained for three years.

Large quantity generators are subject to at least annual inspections by the enforcement agency.

Containment and storage of medical waste must meet the requirements described later in this section that apply to all medical waste generators.

Registration and annual permit fees are established in the statute for DHS as the enforcement agency. A hospital with fewer than 99 beds — $600, up to a hospital with more than 251 beds — $1,400; a clinic — $350; a nursing facility with fewer than 99 beds — $275 up to a nursing facility with more than 200 beds — $400; medical offices, veterinary clinics, clinical laboratories — $200. These fees are subject to change through regulations issued by the department or counties may establish their own fee structure based on recovering costs of the program

● **Some small quantity generators are required to register** by April 1, 1991 as described above for larger quantity generators, if the small quantity generator treats medical wastes on-site using steam sterilization, incubation or microwave technology.

Small quantity generators required to register also must file with the local agency a medical waste management plan that includes the following information on forms specified by the agency:

✔ The name of the person filing the plan.

✔ The business address of the person.

✔ The type of business.

✔ The types and estimated monthly quantity of medical waste generated.

✔ The type of treatment used on-site.

✔ The name and business address of the medical waste treatment facility used by the generator for backup treatment and disposal of waste for which the on-site treatment method is not appropriate due to hazardous or radioactive characteristics, and the name of the registered hazardous waste hauler used by the generator to have untreated medical waste removed for treatment and disposal.

✔ A statement indicating that the generator is hauling the medical waste generated in his or her business under the limited quantity hauling exemption (below) and the name and business address of the treatment and disposal facilities to which the waste is being hauled, if applicable.

✔ The name and business address of the registered medical waste hauler service provided by the building management to which the building tenants may subscribe or are required by the building management to subscribe, if applicable.

✔ A statement certifying that the information provided is complete and accurate.

Records of medical waste treatment and tracking records must be maintained for three years.

Small quantity generators required to register must comply with the containment and storage requirements described later in this chapter.

Small quantity generators required to register are subject to inspections by the enforcement agency every two years.

The registration and inspection fee for small quantity generators is $100 every two years.

● **Small quantity generators** that **do not treat** medical wastes on-site **are not required to register.** Such small quantity generators are required to maintain the following records in their files for two years:

✔ An information document stating how the generator contains stores, treats and disposes of any medical waste generated through any act or process of the generator.

✔ Records of any medical waste transported off-site for treatment and disposal, including the quantity of waste transported, the date transported and the name of the registered hazardous waste hauler or individual hauling the waste.

● **Medical waste haulers** are required to be registered under the act. However, a medical waste hauler that generates less than 20 pounds of medical waste per week, transports less

Chap. 9

than 20 pounds at any one time and maintains the documentation required of small quantity generators (see above) may transport the waste under a **limited quantity hauling exemption.** The exempt hauler must maintain a medical waste tracking document.

Medical waste haulers not exempt must comply with the act's requirements, which include:

✔ Register with the enforcement agency.

✔ Issuance of a registration certificate by the agency.

✔ Transport wastes to treatment facilities or transfer stations.

✔ Transport wastes in leak-resistant and fully enclosed rigid containers in vehicle compartments, separate from other wastes being transported.

✔ Transfer facilities are issued permits by the enforcement agency and inspected annually. The permit fee for transfer facilities is $500.

✔ Persons loading or unloading containers of medical wastes must be provided and required to wear clean protective gloves, coveralls, lab coats or other protective clothing.

In addition, medical waste training documents must be maintained for all wastes removed for treatment or disposal for three years. The generator must receive a copy of this document which includes the following information:

✔ The name, address and telephone number of the hauler.

✔ The type and quantity of medical waste transported.

✔ The name of the generator.

✔ The name, address, telephone number and signature of an authorized representative of the permitted facility receiving the waste.

● **Transportation requirements.** Any hazardous waste hauler or generator transporting medical waste in a vehicle must possess a tracking document while transporting the waste. The tracking document must be shown upon demand to any enforcement agency personnel or an officer of the California Highway Patrol. If the waste is transported by rail, vessel or air, the railroad, vessel operator or airline shall enter on the shipping papers any information about the waste which the enforcement agency may require. Medical waste transported out of state shall be consigned to a medical waste facility in the receiving state. Absent a permitted facility in the receiving state or if medical waste is crossing an international border, the waste must be treated to render it safe before it is transported out of the state.

● **Medical waste treatment facilities** must be permitted. Off-site facilities are permitted and inspected by DHS. On-site treatment facilities are permitted and inspected by the enforcement agency.

All treatment facilities (on- or off-site) were required to register and "be permitted" by April 1, 1991. Those facilities previously subject to operation and permitted as hazardous waste treatment facilities are no longer subject to hazardous waste regulations, but are subject to the Medical Waste Management Act.

The treatment facility registration and permit application must include the following information:

✔   The name of the applicant.

✔   The business address of the applicant.

✔   The type of treatment provided, the treatment capacity of the facility, a characterization of the waste treated at this facility and the estimated average monthly quantity of waste treated at the facility.

✔   A disclosure statement about the ownership and regulatory history of the facility.

✔   Evidence which satisfies the department or local enforcement agency that the operator of the medical waste treatment facility has the ability to comply with the regulations adopted pursuant to the Medical Waste Management Act.

✔   Any other information required by the DHS or the enforcement agency for the administration or enforcement of regulations.

The decision on the permit must be made within 120 days of the application. The permit is effective for five years unless revoked by the DHS or enforcement agency for cause.

Other regulatory requirements include recordkeeping for three years regarding the facility and its capacity, operating records, and tracking documents for wastes received and treated.

The annual permit fees for an off-site treatment facility are $10,000 for an autoclave, $15,000 for an incinerator or other approved technology. DHS may charge the applicant $100 per hour up to $50,000 to process the application or as otherwise provided in the department's regulations. Permit fees and application processing fees for on-site treatment facilities are established by the local enforcement agency.

The statute also specifies certain methods of treatment that are approved for various medical wastes. [Health and Safety Code §25090.]

●   **Containment and storage requirements for medical wastes** apply to all generators, haulers, transfer and treatment facilities.

Chap. 9

Medical and biohazardous waste must be contained at the point of origin in a red biohazard bag, conspicuously labeled as biohazardous waste or bearing the international symbol and word "Biohazard." The bags must be tied to prevent leakage and then placed in rigid, covered containers for storage or transportation. The wastes must not be removed from the bag or disposed of until treatment is complete. Bagged waste may be stored under refrigeration for up to 90 days before treatment or seven days without refrigeration. Small quantity generators may store wastes, if properly containerized, without refrigeration. Rigid containers may be reused if sanitized. Other containers may not be reused. Sharps waste must be placed in a sealed sharps container and enclosed in bags with other wastes.

Accumulation areas used to store medical waste containers must be secure and marked with warnings signs in English:

"CAUTION — BIOHAZARDOUS WASTE STORAGE AREA — UNAUTHORIZED PERSONS KEEP OUT"

and in Spanish:

"CUIDADO — ZONA DE RESIDUOS — BIOLOGICOS PELIGROSAS — PROHIBIDA LA ENTRADA A PERSONAS NO AUTORIZADAS"

Language(s) in addition to English must be used if the generator or enforcement agency determine them to be appropriate. Warning signs shall be readily legible during daylight from a distance of at least 25 feet.

The statute prohibits use of trash chutes and compactors or grinders to process medical waste unless treated or as part of the treatment process.

Summary of Compliance Requirements for Medical Waste Management

The following compliance advice is designed to streamline understanding of the regulatory requirements for medical waste management.

◆ **Determining whether medical wastes are being generated and type of facility.** The facility should review the definitions of medical wastes to determine whether it is subject to the act. It should further identify its status with respect to the regulatory requirements:

● Small quantity generator (less than 200 pounds per month).

● Small quantity generator with on-site treatment.

● Large quantity generator (more than 200 pounds per month).

● Limited quantity hauler (generates less than 20 pounds per month; transports less than 20 pounds at a time).

- Medical waste hauler.

- On-site treatment facility.

- Off-site treatment facility.

◆ **Requirements for a Small Quantity Medical Waste Generator**

- Prepare an information document on how the facility manages medical wastes.

- Keep records of medical wastes transported off-site (tracking documents) for two years.

- Comply with containment and storage requirements.

- Use a registered and certified medical waste hauler.

◆ **Requirements for Small Quantity Medical Waste Generator with On-Site Treatment**

- Register with the enforcement agency by April 1, 1991.

- File a medical waste management plan with the enforcement agency.

- Keep records of medical wastes generated, treated and shipped off-site for three years.

- Allow inspections every two years.

- Pay a $100 fee every two years.

- Comply with the containment and storage requirements.

- Use registered and certified medical waste hauler.

◆ **Requirements for a Large Quantity Medical Waste Generator**

- Register with the enforcement agency by April 1, 1991.

- File a medical waste management plan with the enforcement agency.

- Keep records of medical wastes generated, treated and shipped off-site for three years.

- Allow inspections every year.

- Pay fees of up to $1,400 per year.

- Comply with the containment and storage requirements.

- Use registered and certified medical waste hauler.

◆ **Requirements for a Limited-Quantity Hauler**

● Must be the generator.

● Only 20 pounds per load.

● Must maintain tracking documents.

● Load must be transported to permitted off-site transfer or treatment facility.

◆ **Requirements for Medical Waste Hauler**

● Registration and certification by enforcement agency.

● Wastes must be transported to treatment facility or transfer station.

● Wastes must be properly contained and segregated from other wastes.

● Transfer stations must be specifically permitted and a $500 fee paid.

● Workers who handle medical wastes must be provided safety equipment and protective clothing.

● Medical waste tracking documents must accompany the shipment, be maintained for three years. A copy must be provided to the generator.

◆ **Requirements for an On-Site Medical Waste Treatment Facility**

● Apply for permit by April 1, 1991, including all required information.

● Permit from the enforcement agency.

● Recordkeeping for medical wastes treated for three years.

● Pay application fee and annual permit fees to the local agency.

◆ **Requirement for an Off-Site Medical Waste Treatment Facility**

● Apply to DHS for a permit before April 1, 1991, pay the applicable application fees ($100 per hour up to $50,000).

● Obtain a permit.

● Pay annual permit fees ($10,000 for an autoclave; $15,000 for other technology).

● Keep records of wastes treated for three years.

Chap. 9

- Meet containment and storage requirements.

- Use approved treatment methods.

Penalties and Enforcement of the Medical Waste Management Act

Offense	Penalty (Maximum)
Any violation (infraction) by a small quantity generator or registered hauler.	$1,000 fine imposed by the enforcement agency
Other violations handled as infractions by the enforcement agency and corrected by the violator.	$1,000 fine imposed by the enforcement agency
Any first offense by a person other than a small quantity generator or registered hauler.	Misdemeanor with a fine of not less than $2,000 and up to one year imprisonment in the county jail.
Second violation within three years.	Felony with not less than $5,000 fine, nor more than $25,000, and 1 to 3 years in state prison.
Knowing violation of the treatment or disposal prohibitions.	Felony with not less than $5,000 fine, nor or disposal prohibitions.
False representations in any application or record.	$10,000 per day the violation continues.
Failure to obtain a medical waste treatment permit or comply with any order.	$10,000 per violation or day the violation continues.

Appendix 9-1
List of Applicable Laws and Regulations
Medical and Infectious Waste Management

State Laws

● **Medical Waste Management Act**   Health and Safety Code §§25015-25099.3
   Generator Requirements   Health and Safety Code §§25040-25059
   Medical Waste Management Program   Health and Safety Code §§25019 and 25034-25039.2

   Medical Waste Haulers   Health and Safety Code §§25060-25064
   Medical Waste Treatment Facilities   Health and Safety Code §§25070-25079.3
   Containment and Storage Requirements   Health and Safety Code §§25080-25088

State Regulations

● Permitting of Treatment Facilities   22 CCR §§65601 et seq.

Federal Regulations

None at present time.

Appendix 9-2
Medical Waste Program
California Department of Health Services
Environmental Management Branch

California Department of Health Services
Environmental Management Branch
P.O. Box 942732
601 North 7th Street
Sacramento, CA 94234-7320
(916) 322-2042

The Medical Waste Management Program administers the Medical Waste Management Act, which stipulates how medical waste is to be contained, stored, transported and treated (rendered non-infectious). This office responds to inquiries regarding appropriate handling of medical waste, inspects medical waste generators, permits medical waste treatment facilities and enforces the act in the 24 counties and one city for which the state Department of Health Services is the local enforcement agency. In the remaining 35 counties and three cities, the local health jurisdiction serves as the enforcement agency.

Counties and the city for which this office is the local enforcement agency are:

Alpine	Imperial	Mono	Santa Barbara
Amador	Inyo	Nevada	Sierra
Butte	Lake	Placer	Solano
Calaveras	Los Angeles	Plumas	Sutter
Fresno	Mariposa	San Benito	Yolo
Glenn	Mendocino	San Luis Obispo	City of Berkeley

Appendix 9-2 (continued)
California Department of Health Services
Environmental Management Branch

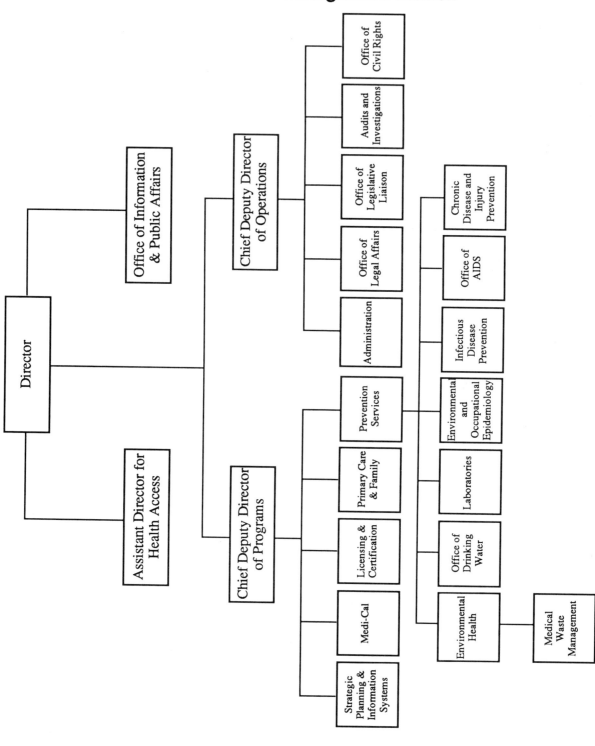

Appendix 9-3
County Environmental Health Agencies

Alameda County
Environmental Health Department .... 80 Swan Way, Room 200 .... (510) 271-4320
Hazardous Materials Division   Oakland, CA 94621

Alpine County
County Health Officer .... P.O. Box 545 .... (916) 694-2146
                                          Markleeville, CA 96120

Amador County
County Health Officer .... 108 Court Street .... (209) 223-6439
                                          Jackson, CA 95642   ext. 407

Butte County
Division of Environmental Health .... 7 County Center Drive .... (916) 538-7281
                                          Oroville, CA 95965

Calaveras County
Environmental Health .... Government Center .... (209) 754-6399
                                          San Andreas, CA 95249

Colusa County
Director of Environmental Health .... 251 East Webster Street .... (916) 458-7717
                                          P.O. Box 610
                                          Colusa, CA 95932

Contra Costa County
Deputy Director of Health Services .... 1111 Ward Street, 3rd Floor .... (510) 646-2521
                                          Martinez, CA 94553

Del Norte County
Environmental Health Services .... 909 Hwy 101 North .... (707) 464-7227
                                          Crescent City, CA 95531

El Dorado County
Environmental Management Dept. .... 2850 Fairlane Court .... (916) 621-5300
                                          Placerville, CA 95667

Fresno County
Environmental Health Systems .... 1221 Fulton Mall .... (209) 445-3391
                                          P.O. Box 11867
                                          Fresno, CA 93775

Glenn County

Environmental Health .... 242 North Villa Avenue .... (916) 934-6588
Willows, CA 95988

Humboldt County

Director of Environmental Health .... 100 H Street, Suite 100 .... (707) 445-6215
Eureka, CA 95501

Imperial County

Division of Environmental Health .... Courthouse, 939 Main Street .... (619) 339-4203
Services   El Centro, CA 92243

Inyo County

Environmental Health .... 168 N. Edwards .... (619) 878-2411
P.O. Box 427
Independence, CA 93526

Kern County

Environmental Health .... 2700 M Street, Suite 300 .... (805) 861-3636
Bakersfield, CA 93301

Kings County

Division of Environmental Health .... 330 Campus Drive .... (209) 584-1411
Hanford, CA 93230

Lake County

Environmental Health .... 922 Bevins Court .... (707) 263-2241
Lakeport, CA 95453

Lassen County

Health Department .... 555 Hospital Lane .... (916) 257-8311
Susanville, CA 96130   ext. 183

Los Angeles County

Hazardous Materials Division .... 5825 Rickenbacker Road .... (213) 890-4045
City of Commerce, CA 90040

Madera County

Environmental Health .... 135 West Yosemite .... (209) 675-7823
Madera, CA 93637

Chap. 9

Marin County
Environmental Health Services .... Marin Civic Center, Room 283 .... (415) 499-6907
Health and Human Services   San Rafael, CA 94903
   Department

Mariposa County
County Health Officer .... P.O. Box 5 .... (209) 966-3689
                               Mariposa, CA 95338

Mendocino County
Environmental Health .... Mendocino County Courthouse .... (707) 463-4466
                               880 N. Bush Street
                               Ukiah, CA 95482

Merced County
Environmental Health .... 385 East 13th Street .... (209) 385-7391
                               Merced, CA 95340

Mono County
Health Department .... P.O. Box 476 .... (619) 932-7485
                               Ridgeport, CA 93517

Modoc County
Health Department .... 131 B Henderson Street .... (916) 233-6311
                               Alturas, CA 96101

Monterey County
Environmental Health .... 1270 Natividad Road, Room 301 .... (408) 755-4505
                               Salinas, CA 93906

Napa County
Environmental Health .... 1195 Third Street, Room 101 .... (707) 253-4471
                               Napa, CA 94559

Nevada County
Department of Environmental Health ... 950 Naidu Avenue .... (916) 265-1452
                               P.O. Box 6100
                               Nevada City, CA 95959

Orange County
Hazardous Materials Program .... 180 South Water Street .... (714) 289-7430
                               Orange, CA 92666

Chap. 9

Placer County

Division of Environmental Health .... 11454 B Avenue .... (916) 889-7335
Auburn, CA 95603

Plumas County

Environmental Health .... Highway 70, Courthouse Annex .....:................ (916) 283-6355
P.O. Box 480
Quincy, CA 95971

Riverside County

Deputy Director of Health.................... 4065 County Circle Drive .... (714) 358-5058
   for Environmental Health   P.O. Box 7600
Riverside, CA 92513-7600

Sacramento County

Environmental Health .... 8475 Jackson Road, Suite 240 .... (916) 386-6108
Sacramento County Health   Sacramento, CA 95826
   Department

San Benito County

County Health Officer .... 439 Fourth Street .... (408) 637-5367
Hollister, CA 95023

San Bernardino County

Environmental Health Services .... 385 North Arrowhead................................... (714) 387-4646
Environmental Management Group   San Bernardino, CA 92415

San Diego County

Division of Environmental Health .... 1255 Imperial Avenue .... (619) 338-2222
   Protection   San Diego, CA 92101

San Francisco City and County

Director of Environmental Health .... 101 Grove Street, Room 217 .... (415) 554-2777
San Francisco, CA 94102

San Joaquin County

Environmental Health .... 445 North San Joaquin Street .... (209) 468-3420
Stockton, CA 95202

San Luis Obispo County

Director of Environmental Health .... 2156 Sierra Way .... (805) 781-5544
P.O. Box 1489
San Luis Obispo, CA 93406

San Mateo County

Director of Environmental Health .... 590 Hamilton Street, 4th Floor .... (415) 363-4305
Redwood City, CA 94063

Santa Barbara County

Environmental Health Services .... 120 Cramona, Suite C .... (805) 681-5200
Goleta, CA 93110   Ext. 385

Santa Clara County

Acting Director .... 2220 Moorpark Avenue, Room 100 .... (408) 299-6060
Environmental Health Services   San Jose, CA 95128

Santa Cruz County

Environmental Health .... 701 Ocean Street, Room 312 .... (408) 454-2022
Santa Cruz, CA 95060

Shasta County

Environmental Health .... 1640 West Street .... (916) 225-5787
Redding, CA 96001

Sierra County

County Health Officer .... P.O. Box 7 .... (916) 993-6700
202 Front Street
Loyalton, CA 96118

Siskiyou County

Environmental Health .... 806 South Main Street .... (916) 842-8230
Yreka, CA 96097

Solano County

Environmental Health .... 601 Texas Street .... (707) 421-6770
Fairfield, CA 94533

Sonoma County

Environmental Health .... 1030 Center Drive, Suite A .... (707) 525-6500
Santa Rosa, CA 95403

Stanislaus County

Department of Environmental .... 1716 Morgan Road .... (209) 525-4154
Resources   Modesto, CA 95358

Sutter County

Environmental Health .... 1445 Circle Drive .... (916) 741-7219
Yuba City, CA 95993

Tehama County

Director of Environmental Health .... 633 Washington Street, Room 36 .... (916) 527-8020
Red Bluff, CA 96080

Trinity County

Environmental Health .... P.O. Box 1257 .... (916) 623-1358
One Industrial Parkway
Weaverville, CA 96093

Tulare County

Environmental Health .... County Civic Center .... (209) 623-1358
Visalia, CA 93291

Tuolumne County

Environmental Health .... 2 South Green Street .... (209) 533-5990
Sonora, CA 95370

Ventura County

Environmental Health Dept. L1730 ...... 800 South Victoria Avenue .... (805) 654-2813
Environmental Resources Agency   Ventura, CA 93009

Yolo County

Environmental Health .... 10 Cottonwood Street.................................. (916) 666-8646
Woodland, CA 95695

Yuba County

Environmental Health .... 938 14th Street.. (916) 741-6251
Marysville, CA 95901

Solid Waste Management and Recycling Programs

Summary and Applicability

This chapter presents an overview of the state's solid waste management and major recycling programs. It is intended as an overview for both those in the solid waste management business and users of solid waste management services. As this area of environmental law is changing rapidly to address new requirements of state law and the economics of limited disposal site capacity and resource conservation, readers are urged to monitor developments if this field is critical to operations.

Included in this chapter is information on the following solid waste programs:

- State solid waste agency — the California Integrated Waste Management Board.
- City and county solid waste source reduction plans.
- Regulatory requirements for solid waste management facilities.
- Recycling and resource conservation recovery programs.

Given that solid waste management and resource recovery facilities are subject to permitting requirements, compliance with applicable regulatory requirements is an essential condition of doing business. Severe penalties also are specified if non-compliance results in an enforcement action.

Background

Solid waste disposal faces increasing challenges, given the limited capacity of landfills as the primary method of disposal, the environmental problem posed by such landfills and the interest in conserving resources. These issues have been aggressively addressed in California by the Integrated Solid Waste Management Act of 1989 and other progressive measures. This chapter presents the regulatory requirements the state's solid waste management programs establish for both operators and users of solid waste management facilities. Included in the discussion will be the federal and state solid waste regulatory scheme, organization of regulatory programs, standards for facilities, other regulatory requirements, and recycling programs (mandatory or voluntary).

Organization of Solid Waste Management Programs

The federal law establishing the national hazardous waste regulatory scheme also initiated the federal solid waste management program: Resource Conservation and Recovery Act (RCRA) of 1976. The federal act's approach was to classify solid waste management facilities and practices, and to direct the states to develop comprehensive state plans. The federal classification criteria provided minimum national performance standards to protect human health and the environment. They are codified at 40 CFR 257 which specifies criteria designed for the protection of eight interests: flood plain, endangered species, surface waters, groundwater, crops from sewage, sludge disposal, disease vector control, burning control and public safety.

The states were required to develop comprehensive state plans for solid waste management subject to an EPA approval process. The 1984 hazardous and solid waste amendments to RCRA expanded the federal role by authorizing federal EPA enforcement of landfill requirements if a state fails to take appropriate action [42 USC 6945(c)(2)]. In California, EPA's role in solid waste management is primarily oversight with direct enforcement authority if the state or local agencies fail to act.

California's formal waste management program actually preceded the federal program by several years with the establishment of the California Waste Management Board in 1972 by the Solid Waste Management and Resource Recovery Act. The state law was amended in 1976 by the Solid Waste Control Act, which required local enforcement agencies in each county to regulate solid waste facilities under supervision of the state board. Under the state scheme, solid waste management planning was primarily a local government function in which counties developed and the state board approved a County Solid Waste Management Plan, or "CoSWMP." The Integrated Waste Management Act of 1989 has completely revamped the local solid waste planning function and will phase out CoSWMPs.

The Integrated Waste Management Act of 1989, AB 939, established the California Integrated Waste Management Board (CIWMB) to replace the Waste Management Board, completely revised the state's solid waste management program and recodified the previous laws, which were part of the Health and Safety Code and Government Code, placing solid waste management into the Public Resources Code [§§40000-49620]. The purpose of this major piece of environmental legislation was to preserve local responsibility in the field of solid waste management, while requiring an ambitious planning program under state board regulation and oversight. The principal focus of the act was to shift the direction of the state's solid waste management program from regulating disposal sites to waste redirection and recycling through planning and program implementation.

The act also modified the part-time Waste Management Board into a full-time, six-member California Integrated Waste Management Board. The members are selected as follows:

- One member who has private sector experience in the solid waste industry. Appointed by the Governor and subject to Senate confirmation.

- One member who has been an official of a non-profit organization promoting recycling and protection of air and water quality. Appointed by the Governor and subject to Senate confirmation.

- Two members appointed by the Governor to represent the public. Subject to Senate confirmation.

- Two public members, one appointed by the Senate Rules Committee, one by the Speaker of the Assembly.

A chairperson is elected from the board's membership, although neither the industry nor the environmental representative may serve as chair.

- **Local enforcement agencies** (LEAs) are designated by a city council, county board of supervisors or by governments participating in a joint exercise of powers agreement and certified by the CIWMB. Certification is based on assessment of staffing, expertise and resources. In the absence of an approved LEA, CIWMB may carry out the duties of the LEA. The principal duties of the LEA are to enforce the requirements of the Integrated Solid Waste Management Act, regulations of the CIWMB and minimum standards for solid waste handling and disposal. LEA activities are supported by fees on waste facilities and haulers.

LEAs must inspect each solid waste facility it has permitted at least once a month. CIWMB must inspect each facility once a year to verify the facility's compliance status and the effectiveness of the LEA's oversight. Violations noted during these inspections must be abated within 90 days or the facility is placed on an inventory of violators and subject to meeting a compliance schedule or loss of the permit to operate.

- **Enforcement mechanisms** available to LEAs include the administrative issuance of cease and desist or cleanup orders if an operator violates its permit, operates a facility without a permit, or if a property owner allows such violations to occur. CIWMB also may issue cease and desist and cleanup orders after notifying the LEA, or upon request of the LEA.

The CIWMB may expend funds in the absence of activity by the party subject to an order if it deems that action is necessary to protect the public health, and recoup the cost from the private party. The Solid Waste Disposal Site Cleanup and Maintenance Account in the Solid Waste Management Fund has been established to collect an annual fee from facility operators to fund corrective actions after the issuance of an order or to prepare and implement closure and post-closure plans. Civil penalties of up to $10,000 per day are also provided for in the statute for intentional and negligent violation of permit terms or standards applicable to facilities.

The powers of the board and the local enforcement agencies are limited by other requirements of state law and agency jurisdiction which were expressly honored in AB 939. For example, land use conditions in terms of zoning and land use planning, as discussed in Chapter 3, remain in effect for solid waste management facilities. Water quality issues continued to be regulated by the Regional Water Quality Control Board as a function of waste discharge requirements which must be obtained by solid waste management facilities.

Solid Waste Management Plan

The act's solid waste management planning scheme is to mandate on a county-by-county basis an enforceable plan to assure solid waste is reduced at the source and diverted from transformation (e.g. incineration or other treatment) and landfill disposal. The goal is a 25 percent reduction in solid waste by 1995 and a 50 percent reduction by 2000. An elaborate study and planning process based on legislatively authorized emergency regulations establishes the waste stream categories, source reduction, recycling alternatives and other components leading to the development of a County Integrated Waste Management Plan. (This plan replaces the existing CoSWMP.)

The schedule for preparing and submitting county plans to the State Integrated Waste Management Board is:

- January 1, 1992: Counties with less than five years of landfill capacity.

Chap. 10

- January 1, 1993: Counties with between five and eight years of landfill capacity.

- January 1, 1994: Counties with more than eight years of landfill capacity.

In addition, each county must develop a Siting Plan which identifies existing and needed capacity for 15 years of solid waste management activities in the county.

Counties were required to establish task forces that may include solid waste industry, environmentalists, general public, special district, and governmental representation by March 1, 1990 to prepare the plan and afford an opportunity for public comment by interested parties prior to completion.

◆ Solid Waste Generation Study

By July 1, 1991, each city and county (for unincorporated areas) were required to prepare a solid waste generation study of wastes generated during a continuous six-month period subsequent to 1987 by source, waste category and waste type as specifically listed below. The amount of wastes calculated include those transformed, disposed and diverted, but does not include solid wastes not disposed of in permitted solid waste disposal facilities (private) and materials not considered waste-like, for example, concrete, fill, etc. This study looked at sources of generation: residential, commercial, industrial and other sources, including governmental activities like public facility maintenance and sewage treatment.

Waste categories and waste types:

- Paper: Corrugated containers, mixed paper, newspaper, high-grade ledger paper and other paper.

- Plastics: High-density polyethylene (HDPE) containers, polyethylene terephthalate (PET) containers, film plastics and other plastics.

- Glass: Refillable glass beverage containers, California Redemption Value glass, other recyclable glass and other nonrecyclable glass.

- Metals: Aluminum cans, bimetal containers, ferrous metals and tin cans, nonferrous metals including aluminum scrap, and white goods.

- Yard waste: Leaves, grass and prunings.

- Other organics: Food waste, tires and rubber products, wood wastes, agricultural crop residues, manure, and textiles and leather.

- Other wastes: Inert solids, including rock, concrete, brick, and soil and fines; household hazardous materials and discarded household hazardous waste materials containers.

- Special wastes: Ash, sewage sludge, industrial sludge, asbestos, auto shredder waste, auto bodies, and other special wastes.

◆   Solid Waste Reduction and Diversion

Based on the distribution of solid wastes within these categories, the counties are required to meet the waste generator reduction and recycling goals of 25 percent by 1995 and 50 percent by 2000. As the act does not specify that the goals must be achieved in each category, it may be assumed that the bulk of the attainment will be via the most easily accomplished methods and waste categories. However, the "integration" concept suggests that goals should be met by a combination of methods. To reinforce this premise, the act calls for "all feasible source reduction" as a primary emphasis. Nonetheless, all of the aspects of waste management will be required to be integrated into each county's plan. The eventual plan must include the following components in its Source Reduction and Recycling Element (SRRE):

- Waste characterization.
- Source reduction.
- Recycling.
- Composting.
- Solid waste facility capacity.
- Education and public information.
- Funding.
- Special waste.
- Household hazardous waste.

It should be noted that on-site composting and recycling at the point of generation constitute "source reduction." Therefore, it can be anticipated that significant efforts to encourage composting as source reduction will occur to achieve a major percentage of the source reduction goals. Regulations govern the process of SRRE preparation and format [14 CCR 18731].

Facilities that generate significant quantities of solid wastes currently disposed into landfills should be concerned about the planning process for each waste stream discussed above. AB 939 contains provisions for economic management, as well as enforcement to direct changes in solid waste management practices.

◆   Fees

Establishing a disposal cost fee system is one method of economic incentives designed to encourage waste reduction and recycling. AB 939 authorized a fee on goods sold in California (except those currently subject to the Beverage Container Recycling and Litter Reduction Act) that normally are disposed of in solid waste landfills or processed in transformation (destructive processing) facilities. In setting the fees, the board is required to look at the relative importance of the disposable goods and their volume, and the economic impact on manufacturers, consumers and other practical considerations.

Counties and cities also may assess user fees to recover costs incurred in solid waste management planning based on the types and amount of wastes. In addition, reasonable fees may be imposed on the importation of waste from outside the county to public or private facilities in the county. The state board may limit exporting solid waste from a county that has not complied with AB 939.

Regulation of Solid Waste Facilities

Solid waste management facilities are regulated by the California Integrated Waste Management Board (CIWMB) and local enforcement agencies (LEAs). The LEA is the permitting agency and may issue a permit to a solid waste management facility as long as it meets CIWMB requirements. The permits also must be consistent with permitting requirements of other agencies, including air pollution district, regional water board, local fire and health departments, and land use authorities. Regulations establish minimum standards concerning design, operation, maintenance an closure of such facilities [14 CCR §§17200-17840]. The standards include the following activities:

- Waste storage and removal.
- Landfills.
- Transfer and processing stations.
- Litter receptacles.
- Agricultural waste management.

Areas of anticipated future regulation include waste-to-agency projects, recycling or composting, and more comprehensive closure requirements.

Local governments exercise independent regulatory control of solid waste management in collection schedules, means of collection and transportation, facility operating schedules, and charges and fees.

Permitting of solid waste facilities conducted by LEAs is governed by regulations of the board [14 CCR §§18200-18217], and is subject to board approval. As mentioned above, this process must respect all other local siting and agency permitting requirements. Furthermore, new facilities or those with significant changes in their operations necessitating permitting must conform with the county's integrated waste management plan, unless a specific exemption is granted by CIWMB.

◆ Closure and Post-Closure Plans.

By January 1, 1989, any person operating or proposing to operate a solid waste landfill on or after January 1, 1988 must certify that an estimate of closure and post-closure costs has been developed, a trust fund or other financial arrangement established and has funds deposited into the account to assure adequate resources for closure and post-closure maintenance for a period of 15 years. Current operators must submit closure plans to the LEA, CIWMB and the regional water quality control board. Current operations and closure plans also must address the problem of landfill gas generation. [14 CCR §17705.]

Regulation of Specific Types of Solid Waste Management Activities

◆ Regulation of Transfer Stations

Regulation of transfer stations is based on whether the facility is a small volume (less than 100 cubic yards per day) or a larger volume station. Small volume facilities must be designed in accordance with accepted practices for such facilities with a plan of operation which must be approved by the LEA. [14 CCR §17401, et seq.]

Large quantity stations must file a Report of Station Information with the LEA, including:

- Plans and specifications.
- An engineering report describing processes employed.
- Description of operations.
- Estimate of design capacity.

Furthermore, operators must meet facility operating standards by providing adequate qualified personnel to operate the station. In addition, supervision of public access maintained roads, and security, as well as many other specific requirements established in the regulations must be satisfied by facility operators.

◆ Waste to Energy Facilities

In addition to LEA and CIWMB permitting, waste to energy facilities must meet requirements specified by local air pollution districts to address toxic air contaminant concerns, and disposal of incinerator ash. To attempt to streamline permitting for such facilities, legislation was enacted in 1974 to authorize the California Energy Commission to issue a single certificate preempting other permit requirements. However, the change, which entails participation by the various "preempted" agencies, has not led to a more efficient process. There is a market for the electricity generated by such facilities as required by federal law, administered by the California Public Utilities Commission.

◆ Waste Tire Facilities

Waste tire facilities are subject to CIWMB regulations on permits and operating requirements. Waste tire facilities are regulated on the basis of their capacity. Minor facilities where 500 or more, but fewer than 5,000 tires, are stored at any one time may be exempt from specific permit requirements (other than as a solid waste facility), but are subject to certain operating requirements. Similar exemptions apply to tire recappers, which store a limited volume of used tires.

Major waste tire facilities where more than 5,000 waste tires are stored are subject to a specific permitting and regulatory program that will include operation plans and closure requirements supported by financial assurances. It will be illegal to transport waste tires to an unpermitted major facility after September 1, 1992 and July 1, 1993 for a minor facility.

A Waste Tire Registration Statement is required on forms provided by the board whenever 500 or more tires accumulate (with certain exceptions).

◆ Regulation of Refuse Collection

As discussed above, regulation of refuse collection is a function of local government; consequently, cost, level of service, operating requirements and how the service is provided are matters of local discretion. In some cases, the municipal or county government may provide the service, in others, special districts have been established to manage solid wastes, The governmental entity may award franchises or contracts to private service firms.

◆ Special Wastes

Certain wastes have properties that are not clearly hazardous or non-hazardous, or if hazardous, may be exempt from the hazardous waste regulations to encourage recycling or because of other considerations. Regulations of some of these special wastes are being reviewed by the state Legislature and regulatory agencies and may change in the future. It is outside of the scope of this handbook to describe in any detail how these specific wastes are currently regulated. The following information should serve to direct the reader to more comprehensive sources of information.

- **Used lubricating oil** has been identified by statute as a hazardous waste in California. Its handling is discussed in Chapter 8.

- **Shredder waste,** or "fluff," is the non-metallic waste left after shredding auto bodies or appliances. This waste stream may contain hazardous constituents and, therefore, may be considered as a hazardous waste unless testing (characterization — see Chapter 8) demonstrates otherwise. [Health and Safety Code §25143.6.]

- **Infectious waste** is subject to the Medical Waste Management Act (Chapter 9). However, medical or infectious waste produced by small quantity generators (less than 200 pounds per month) can be disposed to landfills as non-hazardous solid waste with the exception of anatomical remains and unsterilized cultures of etiologic organisms. Local landfill rules must be followed.

- **Sewage sludge** is classified based on its characteristics as solid waste (Class III landfill), designated waste (Class II landfill), or hazardous waste (Class I hazardous waste disposal facility). Most sewage sludge is being managed as solid waste and disposed of in landfills. The EPA has issued regulations on sewage sludge classification to place the burden of assuring appropriate disposal practices on the generators of the sludge. [40 CFR 257 and 503.]

- **Household hazardous wastes** are subject to the definition of hazardous waste, but the regulations do not apply to residences, therefore, control of disposal is ineffective. In response, to more effectively deal with the problem, voluntary household hazardous waste collection programs have been established by local solid waste management agencies. Public education and collection program guidelines are being developed by CIWMB. [Public Resources Code §47109.]

Recycling and Resource Recovery Programs

As discussed above, one of the most important aspects of the 1989 Integrated Waste Management Act was the inclusion in the mandatory city and county planning process of waste reduction goals that can be achieved only by a combination of source reduction and recycling and composting. To further encourage the process, the state has established several economic incentive programs:

- State Assistance for Recycling Markets Act of 1989, which requires state and local agencies to purchase recycled products of equivalent price and quality as non-recycled products and preference to achieve goals in this area [Public Contract Code §§12150, et seq.].

- Recycling Market Development Commission in the CIWMB [Public Resources Code §42100].

- Recycling Market Development Zones in which recycling opportunities are encouraged through tax incentives, low-interest loans and other incentives. [Public Resources Code §§42140-42158.]

◆ Specific Recycling Programs

- **Used lubricating oils** are required to be recycled and the state has substantially stimulated this practice by making waste oil a hazardous waste for which the generator is responsible [Health and Safety Code §25250.1]. In addition, public education and procurement policies have been established to promote waste oil recycling [Public Resources Code §3465; Public Contract Code §10405.8].

- **Tire recycling** has been substantially promoted by the California Recycling Act [Public Resources Code §§42860-42895]. This law specified that tires that are stored or disposed of should be shredded and segregated from other solid wastes to promote recycling of the materials. The law also provides financial assistance to further this objective. A fee of 25 cents per tire upon disposal is the source of revenues for the program. The law also requires state and local agencies to preferentially purchase products recycled from waste tires, including the mandatory installation of retreaded tires on many state vehicles.

- **Lead-acid storage batteries** are required to be recycled [Public Resources Code §42442] and disposal prohibited. Dealers of new batteries must accept storage batteries from customers in exchange for new batteries. State agency vehicles must be equipped with recycled replacement batteries to the extent feasible.

- **Household sealed batteries** generally are disposed of as solid waste largely exempt from the hazardous waste regulations given their residential source. However, as a matter of state policy, this is undesirable and the CIWMB has been authorized to study the current disposal practices and recycle opportunities for household batteries. [Public Resources Code §42450(e).]

- **Recycled paper products.** Newspaper and commercial publishers are required to use a percentage of recycled newsprint as defined in their operations if the recycled product is available in comparable quantity and price as virgin newsprint. The required percentage increases periodically from 25 percent in 1991 to 50 percent after 2000 [Public Resources Code §16002]. Users of newsprint are required to annually certify the percentage of recycled paper used. The Department of Conservation is responsible for enforcement of this program.

- **State agencies** are required to set a 5 percent preference on the purchase of recycled paper products. Furthermore, goals have been established by the Department of General Services to periodically increase the percentage of recycled paper products purchased by the state from 35 percent in 1992 to 50 percent in 1996. For high grade paper, the percentage goals are 25 percent in 1991 to 40 percent after 2000. Local agencies are required to purchase recycled paper products and must require bidders to provide information on recycled paper products, but no firm quotas have been established.

- **Plastic recycling** is facilitated in California by the requirement for manufacturers or vendors

Chap. 10

of products in the state to mold a label in all rigid plastic bottles and containers with a code indicating the plastic used in its manufacture:

1 = PETE (polyethylene terephthalate)
2 = HDPE (high density polyethylene)
3 = V (vinyl)
4 = LDPE (low density polyethylene)
5 = PP (polypropylene)
6 = PS (polystyrene)
7 = OTHER (includes multi-layer)

- **Trash bag** manufacturers and sellers are required, beginning January 1, 1993, to use at least 10 percent recycled material in 1.0 mil or thicker bags and certify this fact to the CIWMB. The Department of Conservation is authorized to enforce this requirement effective January 1, 1992. The state Department of General Services is required to adopt specifications to direct state preferential purchases of such recycled materials for recycled plastic products by July 1, 1992.

- **Compost,** which is the humus material derived from decomposed organic wastes and sewage sludge, is required to be preferentially purchased by state government when it may be used and costs no more than fertilizer and soil amendments from non-recycled materials. Composted materials that meet the Department of General Services specifications will be required in place of commercial fertilizers wherever possible by the departments of Transportation, Forestry, and Parks and Recreation. [Public Contract Code §12181; Public Resources Code §42240.]

- **Recycled paving materials** must be considered in highway construction projects by the Department of Transportation in consultation with the Department of Conservation. Road construction quality may not be affected and price must be competitive. [Public Resources Code §17000.]

- **Beverage containers.** California's ambitious beverage container recycling law, Beverage Container Recycling and Litter Reduction Act [Public Resources Code §§14500-591], established 80 percent recycling as the goal and instituted financial incentives and convenient recycling opportunities. Beverage containers covered by the act include sealed containers made of aluminum, glass, plastic and non-aluminum metals.

  Redemption payment and refund value on beverage containers are the main economic incentives for the program. Beverage distributors are required to pay 2 cents per container (less a half-cent administrative cost) to the Department of Conservation Beverage Recycling Fund. A refund value of 5 cents for every two containers redeemed and 2 cents for single containers (large containers over 24 ounces are considered as two containers for redemption value) has been set. After January 1, 1993, the redemption value increases to 5 cents per container if the redemption rate is less than 65 percent for the type of container. Manufacturers of beverage containers are required to label the containers with the message "California Redemption Value" or "California Cash Refund."

Operators of beverage recycling centers must be certified and meet certain requirements established by the Department of Conservation. Certificates are issued for five years. The act specifies that at least one recycling center must be established within each "convenience zone" or half-mile radius of a supermarket. Assistance is available from the Department of Conservation to establish recycling centers. In the absence of a recycling center in a convenience zone, dealers must accept containers or pay a $100 per day fee to the department.

Processors that receive beverage containers from recycling containers are paid the refund value plus a 1.75 percent administrative fee and a processing fee by the Department of Conservation. Processors, in turn, pay recycling centers the refund value plus .5 percent for administrative costs plus an additional amount set by the department from the processor's fee, which assures an adequate financial return.

Beverage manufacturers are responsible for paying a processing fee established as necessary by the department on the basis of recycling program costs in comparison to scrap value of reclaimed materials. Its purpose is to assure that containers are recycled by providing adequate financial incentives to processors.

All regulated parties in the Beverage Recycling Program are required to provide reports to the department as required. The department is authorized to impose administrative civil and criminal penalties for violations of the act.

Compliance with Solid Waste Management and Recycling Programs

The facilities and product vendors to which this handbook is directed need to be cognizant of solid waste management programs that affect their operations and products. For many, these programs will result in only indirect regulation in the form of increased costs to dispose of wastes, or inconvenience in meeting local community waste reduction or recycling objectives established in Integrated Solid Waste Management Plans. For facilities or individuals involved in the regulated facility aspects of the program, it is essential that all applicable laws, regulations and regulatory agency procedures be obtained and be well understood to avoid the substantial pitfalls involved in the event of non-compliance; normally loss of permit to operate and assessment of penalties.

As there is no generally applicable regulatory compliance program that affects businesses and other facilities, the presentation of a compliance summary has been omitted from this chapter. For facilities and businesses involved in solid waste management, this chapter is merely a summary of the level of knowledge that such operations must be aware of and in compliance with to succeed in this increasingly regulated field.

Enforcement and Penalties

Enforcement mechanisms available to LEAs include the administrative issuance of cease and desist or cleanup orders if an operator violates its permit, operates without a permit, or if a property owner allows such violations to occur. The California Integrated Waste Management Board (CIWMB) also may issue cease and desist and cleanup orders after notifying the LEA, or upon request of the LEA.

The CIWMB may expend funds in the absence of activity by the party subject to an order if it deems that action necessary to protect the public health and recoup the cost from the private party. The Solid Waste Disposal Site Cleanup and Maintenance Discount in the Solid Waste Management Fund has been established to collect an annual fee from facility operators to fund corrective actions after the issuance of an order or to prepare and implement closure and post-closure plans. Civil penalties of up to $10,000 per day also are provided for in the statute for intentional and negligent violation of permit terms or standards applicable to facilities.

There are, in addition, mounting penalties and other sanctions for violations of the specific solid waste regulatory program discussed in this chapter. For further information on these, readers should consult the state statute referred to in the chapter or Appendix 10-1.

Appendix 10-1
Applicable Laws and Regulations
Solid Waste Management and Recycling Programs

State Laws

- Integrated Solid Waste Management Act   Public Resources Code §§40000-49620

Recycling and Resource Recovery Programs

- California Recycling Act   Public Resources Code §§42860-42895
- Beverage Container Recycling and Litter Reduction Act   Public Resources Code §§14500-14591

Federal Laws

- Resource Conservation and Recovery Act (RCRA)   42 USC 6901, et seq.

State Regulations

- Solid Waste Management Plans   14 CCR §§17100-17165
- Minimum Standards for Solid Waste Handling and Disposal   14 CCR §§17200-17840
- Solid Waste Facility Permits   14 CCR §§17900-18355

Federal Regulations

- Sewage Sludge Disposal   40 CFR 257 and 503
- Solid Waste Disposal Facility Criteria   40 CFR 257 and 258

Appendix 10-2
California Integrated Waste Management Board

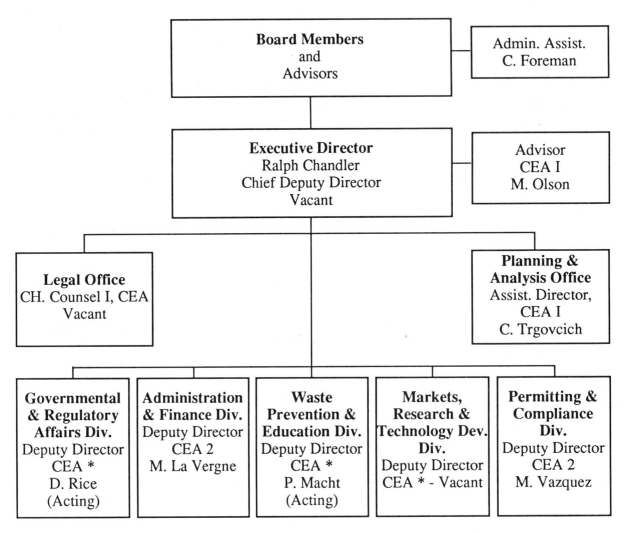

* Pending DPA/SPB approval of CEA allocations

Headquarters and Northern California Regional Office

Northern California .... 8800 Cal-Center Drive, Sacramento, CA 95826 .... (916) 255-2200

Regional Offices

Fullerton .... 1501 E. Orangethorpe Avenue, Suite 150, 92631 .... (714) 449-7072
Redlands .... 1752 Orangetree Lane, 92374 .... (714) 798-5455
Valencia .... 25031 West Avenue Stanford, Suite 50, 91355 .... (805) 294-1360

Proposition 65 and Other Required Warnings

Summary and Applicability

This chapter describes the requirements of a relatively new area of environmental requirements, warnings for products and other activities that result in exposure to certain chemicals subject to the respective law. There are two such laws in California: Proposition 65, the Safe Drinking Water and Toxics Enforcement Act, and the statute requiring warnings to building occupants when asbestos is present. The products, operations and facilities subject to these laws are:

Proposition 65

- Businesses that manufacture and distribute products that contain chemicals subject to the act.
- Businesses whose employees may be exposed to chemicals subject to the act due to its operations.
- Business facilities that may expose persons in the community to chemicals subject to the act in its emissions or other releases.

Asbestos Warnings

- Building owners who have actual knowledge of the presence of asbestos-containing building materials.
- Any person in a contractual relationship (for example, a lease) with such a building owner who has employees or other persons' employees as occupants of the building.

The chemicals subject to Proposition 65 are those "known to the state to cause cancer or reproductive toxicity" and can be identified by a review of the list in Appendix 11-3 at the end of this chapter or by consulting the List of Lists in Exhibit B at the end of this guide.

This chapter will cover the following topics, which explain the laws in this area:

- Basic provisions of Proposition 65 and the regulations that implement it.
- Chemicals subject to the act.
- Regulatory compliance requirements.
- Enforcement procedures and penalties under Proposition 65.
- Requirements for asbestos warnings, contents of notices and penalties.

Given the potential penalties of up to $2,500 per day for each violation (Proposition 65), environmental managers should carefully review their products and operations for compliance with these new and likely to be aggressively enforced laws.

For more information on Proposition 65 specifically and how to comply with this complicated statute, consult the California Chamber publication *Proposition 65 Compliance.*

Proposition 65: The Safe Drinking Water and Toxics Enforcement Act

Proposition 65 [Health and Safety Code §25249.5 et seq.] contains two major provisions that impose regulatory requirements on distribution and manufacture of products and operation of facilities.

- First, it prohibits discharges of any chemical "known to the state to cause cancer or reproductive toxicity" and listed by the state as subject to the act, to a potential source of drinking water, with certain exceptions. This requirement is mentioned in Chapter 6 as it relates to regulation of discharge of water pollutants.

- Second, it requires "clear and reasonable" warnings, with certain exceptions, to be provided prior to an exposure to any of the listed chemicals.

The somewhat vague terms of the act, how to interpret the exceptions to the requirements, and the list of chemicals subject to the act are more fully explained in regulations issued by the state Health and Welfare Agency in Title 22 of the California Code of Regulations beginning at §12000.

The exceptions to the warning requirements (and discharge prohibitions as well) are:

- Government and water purveyors (water districts, even if privately operated) because they do not fall under the "person in the course of doing business" applicability of the act. However, doing business is not limited to profit-making activities, therefore, charities and other not-for-profit organizations are covered.

- Businesses with fewer than 10 employees at the time of the Proposition 65 violation.

- Exposures for which federal law governs warnings in a manner which preempts state authority.

- Exposures that do not pose a significant risk as defined in regulations to implement the act.

- Warnings are not required until 12 months after the chemical is listed; discharges are not prohibited until 20 months after listing.

The unique enforcement provisions of Proposition 65 are what has made it a somewhat notorious environmental and consumer law in that there is no well-organized administrative implementation, only rulemaking authority. As described later in this chapter, most enforcement actions are in the hands of public prosecutors and private citizens.

The state Health and Welfare Agency was designated as lead agency as required by the act. The Proposition 65 implementation unit has been made a part of Cal/EPA under the Office of Environmental Hazard Assessment. A Scientific Advisory Panel was established to assist the lead agency in identifying chemicals known to cause cancer and reproductive toxicity, and to advise it on other technical issues, including:

- Determine chemicals known to the state to cause cancer or reproductive toxicity.

- Identify authoritative organizations that identify carcinogens or reproductive toxicants.

- Identify chemicals subject to state or federal testing requirements.

- Review proposed standards and procedures for determining carcinogenicity and reproductive toxicity of chemicals.

- Review or propose standards, procedures and definitions related to the implementation, administration or interpretation of the act by the lead agency.

The lead agency also may render advisory opinions called "interpretive guidelines" or "safe use determinations" following procedures specified in its regulations. The roles of these units in enforcing the act are described in Appendix 11-2.

Chemicals and Substances Subject to Proposition 65

The act requires the Governor to publish a list of chemicals known to the state to cause cancer or reproductive toxicity and revise and republish the list in light of additional knowledge at least once per year. The first list was published on February 27, 1989, and has been expanded several times a year since. The act requires, at a minimum, the substances identified by reference in Labor Code §6382(b)(1) and substances identified in Labor Code §6382(d). These Labor Code provisions are part of the state's Occupational Carcinogen Act of 1976, designed to identify and regulate chemicals posing a carcinogenic risk in workplaces. The final criteria for listing is the definition in §25249.8(b) of the Safe Drinking Water and Toxics Enforcement Act:

"A chemical is known to the state to cause cancer or reproductive toxicity within the meaning of this chapter if in the opinion of the state's qualified experts it has been clearly shown through scientifically valid testing according to generally accepted principles to cause cancer or reproductive toxicity, or if a body considered to be authoritative by such experts has formally identified it as causing cancer or reproductive toxicity, or if any agency of the state or federal governments has formally required it to be labeled or identified as causing cancer or reproductive toxicity."

More than 300 chemicals and substances have been listed to-date. The list appears in regulations at 22 CCR §12000(b) and (c). Subsection (b) contains chemicals known to the state to cause cancer; subsection (c) those known to cause reproductive toxicity. The list is provided at Appendix 11-3 and in the state's List of Lists (Exhibit B). When making regulatory compliance decisions, managers should take care to consult the most current list.

Regulatory Requirements of Proposition 65

The act forces businesses or other covered entities to carefully examine workplace chemicals and products, emissions from facilities, and consumer products to determine whether any detectable amount of a chemical subject to the act is present and whether a detectable exposure may result from the chemical's use or emission from a facility. If no detectable presence or exposure to a listed chemical is found to exist, it is not subject to the act. However, if a detectable presence of a listed chemical is identified and an exposure is determined to exist, the exposure is subject to Proposition 65.

Chap. 11

The required knowledge and duty to investigate is defined by the act as "knowingly and intentionally exposes," which means the business knows or should have known of the chemical's presence and the exposure resulting from an intended use of the product.

Once subject to the act, the worker exposure, emissions from a facility or exposure to a consumer product must be evaluated to determine whether it exceeds a significant risk level in the case of a cancer-causing chemical or no observable effect level. Alternatively, precautionary warnings may be provided. If the no significant risk option is pursued, the business must be able to defend its determination based on the procedures established in the regulations at 22 CCR §12701, et seq. for cancer-causing substances and §12801, et seq. for reproductive toxicants. The no significant risk levels and no observable effect levels are established by regulation and expressed in a microgram (μg) per day dose level that can be related to the exposed persons either by modeling or actual exposure determinations.

Clear and reasonable warnings are defined in the regulations as a method employed to transmit the warning which is **reasonably calculated, considering the alternative methods available** under the circumstances, to make the warning available to the individual **prior to exposure**. The message must clearly communicate that **the chemical in question** is known to the state to cause cancer, birth defects or other reproductive harm. The message can vary from the specific examples discussed in the following material as long as it meets the general requirements. Individualized separate warnings to each exposed individual are not required [22 CCR §12601(a)].

The regulations define with considerable specificity what are deemed to be clear and reasonable warnings for consumer products, environmental or community exposures, and employees.

Consumer Products Warning Methods and Language

- Product label or package inserts.

- Written warnings about the product at retail outlets on shelves, signs, menus or other places.

- A system of signs, public advertising, or toll-free information services which provide clear and reasonable warnings.

- The model consumer product warning language contained in the regulations is:

    "WARNING: This product contains a chemical known to the State of California to cause cancer."

    or

    "WARNING: This product contains a chemical known to the State of California to cause birth defects or other reproductive harm."

Note: Alcoholic beverages are covered by more specific requirements in the regulations that other consumer products.

Employee Warning Methods and Language

- A label on the product or container as used in the workplace sufficiently prominent to be seen prior to exposure. Product and container labels must provide the same clear and reasonable warning as those for consumer products, as discussed previously.

- A warning sign conspicuously posted and likely to be seen prior to exposure.

- A warning that complies with the Federal OSHA Hazard Communication Standard [29 CFR §1910.1200] or California General Industry Safety Order on Hazard Communication [8 CCR §5194], including Material Safety Data Sheets (MSDSs), training and labeling. For pesticides, the worker safety requirements authorized in Food and Agriculture Code Section 12980 and contained in 3 CCR §6700, et seq. also are deemed to be clear and reasonable warnings.

  The model workplace warning language contained in the regulations is:

  > **"WARNING: This area contains a chemical known to the State of California to cause cancer."**

  > **or**

  > **"WARNING: This area contains a chemical known to the State of California to cause birth defects or other reproductive harm."**

Note: Cal/OSHA will be enforcing Proposition 65 as a component of the state Hazard Communication Standard adopted as an emergency regulation on May 31, 1991 in response to a court order.

Environmental and Community Warning Methods and Language

- A warning sign posted in the affected area.

- A notice including the warning mailed or delivered to each occupant in the affected area and provided at least quarterly.

- A public media announcement targeting the affected area including the warning and made at least quarterly.

  > "WARNING: This area contains a chemical known to the State of California to cause cancer."

  > or

  > "WARNING: This area contains a chemical known to the State of California to cause birth defects or other reproductive harm."

Readers should be aware that more specific regulatory requirements for warning methods and language are in the rulemaking process as of the date of this publication.

The proposed changes likely to be adopted would require identification of the chemical or chemicals subject to the act (up to three on signs) and the particular hazard posed (cancer, reproductive harm or birth defects) and how additional information may be obtained from the person providing the warning.

Compliance with Proposition 65's Warning Requirements

Any business that handles, uses, sells or otherwise is involved with chemicals or products containing chemicals, including foods and beverages, may be subject to Proposition 65. Consequently, given the public enforceability and potentially severe penalties that accompany violations of the act, it is essential to determine Proposition 65 compliance status. The following approach provides an outline to review in addressing the regulatory requirements described above:

- **Determine whether any product, substance or chemical used by the business or in products sold by the business contains a chemical subject to Proposition 65.** Product labels, MSDSs, information from vendors and laboratory tests are means to identify chemical content of a product.

- **Determine whether there is any exposure that would be detectable from the handling or use of the product or chemical as intended to employees, emissions to the community, or to consumers.** The physical properties of the product and chemical, and intended uses are most relevant to this determination.

- If the intended use of a product or chemical results in a detectable exposure, provide warnings as a precautionary matter or conduct a no significant risk determination. The no significant risk determination must follow procedures in the regulations. Precautionary warnings can be used when product sales and other considerations do not contradict precautionary warnings.

- Any warnings provided must be "clear and reasonable" as described in the references above, using the methods stated in the regulation. Alternative methods that meet the "clear and reasonable" test may be used if the means indicated in the regulation are incompatible with the product or other activity. The warnings must be provided to persons exposed in the workplace, community and/or consumers, depending on the product and the intended use.

- Periodically review the list of chemicals to determine whether new substances have been added. Also take note of changes in the regulations which may affect compliance status.

- If subject to the act, review discharges as discussed in Chapter 6 to verify that no prohibited discharges are occurring.

Enforcement and Penalties for Violations of Proposition 65

◆ Enforcement Actions

The attorney general, any district attorney or city attorney may initiate enforcement actions to enjoin violations or threatened violations, and seek penalties against the violator. In addition, any person, usually an environmental organization, may bring an action in the public interest if the above officials are notified and fail to diligently prosecute the violation within 60 days.

A reward or bounty based on 25 percent of the penalty collected is available to a person who brings a successful enforcement action under the proposition. The remainder of the penalties are applied as follows: 50 percent to the state Hazardous Waste Site Cleanup Fund (Hazardous Substance Account) and 25 percent to the Department of Health Services to support local health officials' hazardous waste regulatory activities. A smaller percentage of the latter amount also is available to compensate the local police department or highway patrol if involved in the prosecution. The penalty for a violation of Proposition 65 is up to $2,500 per day for each violation, in addition to any other penalty established by law.

◆ Reporting by Government Employees

Unless an illegal discharge of hazardous waste or threatened illegal discharge is already a matter of general public knowledge, any designated government employee who knows such discharge is likely to cause substantial injury to the public health or safety must report it to the local board of supervisors and local health officer within 72 hours. Local health officers are required to notify local news media without delay. Violations of this government employee reporting requirement are punishable by loss of employment, imprisonment of not less than one year nor more than three years, and the possibility of a fine of up to $25,000. State agencies have established a routine system of "logging in" such reports to minimize risk for failure to report by an employer.

Notification of Presence of Asbestos-Containing Building Materials

Effective July 1, 1989, pursuant to AB 3713 [Health and Safety Code §25915], the owner of any building built before 1979 (when asbestos-containing building materials were largely banned) who knows the building includes asbestos-containing building materials must provide a notice to its employees in the building and any other employer's workers who occupy the building. The statute requires this notice or, alternatively, establishment of an "asbestos management plan" and compliance with the notice requirements as part of the plan. The unique language of this statute defines "owner" as any person in privity of contract or lease with the owner. It excludes residential dwellings.

◆ Requirements of the Notice of Asbestos-Containing Building Materials

The notice of the presence of asbestos-containing building materials must be provided in writing to each employee within 15 days of knowledge of the presence or location of asbestos, and annually thereafter.

The contents of the written notice must include:

- The existence of, conclusions from, and a description or list of the contents of any survey known to the owner conducted to determine the existence and location of asbestos-containing construction materials within the building and information describing when and where the results of the survey are available.

- Specific locations within the building known to the owner, or in a survey where asbestos-containing construction materials are present in any quantity.

- General procedures and handling restrictions necessary to prevent, and, if appropriate, to minimize disturbance, release and exposure to the asbestos. If detailed handling instructions are necessary to ensure employee safety, the notice required shall indicate where those instructions can be found.

- A summary of the results of any bulk sample analysis, or air monitoring, conducted for or by the owner or within the owner's control, including reference to sampling and laboratory procedures utilized, and information describing when and where the specific monitoring data and sampling procedures are available.

- Potential health risks or impacts that may result from exposure to the asbestos in the building as identified in surveys or tests referred to in the statute, or otherwise known to the owner.

- The notice may contain a description and explanation of the health action levels or exposure standards established by the state or federal government. However, if the notice contains this information, it must specifically indicate and describe the following regulatory levels:

    ✔ Proposition 65 no significant risk level (100 fibers/day).
    ✔ School abatement clearance level (0.01 fibers/cc).
    ✔ Action level established by the Cal/OSHA Asbestos Standard (0.1 fibers/cc).

- If the owner has no special knowledge of hazards and preventive measures, the owner shall specifically inform his or her employees in the required notice that he or she lacks knowledge regarding handling instructions necessary to prevent and minimize release of, and exposure to, asbestos and the potential health impacts resulting from exposure to asbestos in the building. The notice must then encourage employees to contact local or state public health agencies.

Alternatively, the owner may elect to prepare an asbestos management plan and comply with the notice requirements by notifying the other owners or any employees of the following:

- The specific locations within the building where asbestos-containing building materials are present in any quantity.

- Potential health risks or impacts that may result from exposure to the asbestos.

- Information to convey that moving, drilling, boring or otherwise disturbing the asbestos-containing building material identified may present a health risk and, consequently, should not be attempted by an employee who is not qualified to handle asbestos-containing building material.

- The existence and availability of the management plan and a description of its contents.

An asbestos management plan must be prepared by a person accredited to prepare asbestos management plans for schools and contain the following information:

- All the information that must be included in the written notice requirement for owners who do not elect to prepare a management plan.

● A description of ongoing operations and maintenance program which shall include, but not be limited to, periodic reinspection and surveillance, and information and training programs for building engineering and maintenance staff.

● Recordkeeping procedures to demonstrate implementation of the plan, which shall be maintained for the life of the building, to which they apply.

◆ Limitations and Exceptions to Notice Requirement, Contractor Provisions

The statute provides some limits and exceptions to the notice and specific requirements for contractors:

● If the asbestos-containing building material is limited to unique and physically defined areas, and are not connected through a common ventilation system — the notice may be provided only to employees in the affected area.

● If the asbestos is limited to areas accessible only to maintenance employees or contractors, with only incidental access by other employees, not replicated throughout the building and the owner knows no fibers are being released, the notice may be provided only to maintenance and construction personnel.

● If the asbestos-containing materials are completely encapsulated and no fibers are being released, the notice provided may be limited to the locations where the asbestos is located **and**

✔ A description of any survey conducted to determine the existence and location of asbestos-containing building materials within the building, and information describing when and where the results of the survey are available.

✔ Information to convey that moving, drilling, boring, or otherwise disturbing the asbestos-containing building material identified may present a health risk and, consequently, should not be attempted by an unqualified employee. The notice shall identify the appropriate person the employee is required to contact if the condition of the asbestos-containing building material deteriorates.

● If a person contracting with an owner receives notice, that contractor shall provide a copy of the notice to employees or contractors working within the building.

◆ Warning Signs Requirement

The statute also provides for specific warnings signs. If any construction, maintenance, or remodeling is conducted in an area of the building area where there is the potential for employees to come into contact or disturb asbestos-containing building materials, the owner responsible for the performance of, or contracting for, any construction, maintenance, or remodeling in the area shall post that area with a clear and conspicuous warning notice:

"CAUTION: ASBESTOS. Cancer and lung disease hazard. Do not disturb without proper training and equipment."

Chap. 11

or

"DANGER: ASBESTOS. Cancer and lung disease hazard. Authorized personnel only. Respirators and protective clothing are required in this area."

◆ Enforcement and Penalties for Violations of the Asbestos Notification Requirement

Any owner who knowingly or intentionally fails to comply with the statute, or who knowingly or intentionally presents any false or misleading information to employees or any other owner after July 1, 1989, is guilty of a misdemeanor punishable by a fine of up to $1,000 or up to one year in the county jail, or both. As there is no administrative agency designated to enforce this statute, cases must be brought by public prosecutors: city attorneys or county district attorneys.

Appendix 11-1
Applicable Laws and Regulations
Proposition 65 and Other Required Warnings

State Laws

- The Safe Drinking Water and Toxics Enforcement Act (Proposition 65) — Health and Safety Code §§25249.5-25249.13

- Chcmicals and Substances Subject to Proposition 65 — Labor Code §6382; Health and Safety Code §25249.8

- Notification of the Presence of Asbestos-Containing Building Materials — Health and Safety Code §25915

State Regulations

- Proposition 65 Generally — 22 CCR §§12000, et seq.

- List of Proposition 65 Chemicals — 22 CCR §§12000(b) and (c)

- Warning Requirements and Methods — 22 CCR §12601 et seq.

- Discharge Prohibition — 22 CCR §12401 et seq.

- No Significant Risk and No Observable Effect Level Determination — 22 CCR §12701 and §12801 et seq.

Appendix 11-2
Office of Environmental Health Hazard Assessment
California Environmental Protection Agency
Progress Report on Implementation of Proposition 65

STATE OF CALIFORNIA—ENVIRONMENTAL PROTECTION AGENCY

PETE WILSON. *Governor*

OFFICE OF ENVIRONMENTAL HEALTH HAZARD ASSESSMENT
714 P STREET. ROOM 460
SACRAMENTO, CA 95814
(916) 445-6900

Dear Interested Party:

Thank you for your recent request for information about the Safe Drinking Water and Toxic Enforcement Act of 1986, also known as Proposition 65. The Act is codified in California Health and Safety Code Section 25249.5, et seq.

The following publications can help you keep informed about the Act:

Regulations pertaining to the Act as well as the list of chemicals known to the State to cause cancer or reproductive toxicity are published in Division 2 of Title 22 beginning with Section 12000 of the California Code of Regulations. Information on purchasing Division 2 of Title 22 and on subscribing to updates to the regulations is available from Barclays Law Publishers, P. O. Box 3066, South San Francisco, CA 94083, (415) 244-6611.

Notices of action on regulations, notices of public interest, agenda of meetings, draft regulations, and updates of the list of chemicals known to the State to cause cancer or reproductive toxicity are published in the California Regulatory Notice Register, which is published weekly. Information on subscribing to the Notice Register is available from the Office of Administrative Law, 555 Capitol Mall, Suite 1290, Sacramento, CA 95814, (916) 323-6225.

A copy of the most recent update of the list of chemicals, dated July 1, 1991, is enclosed.

Sincerely,

STEVEN A. BOOK, Ph.D.
Acting Director

Enclosure

Appendix 11-2 (continued)

Office of Environmental Health Hazard Assessment
California Environmental Protection Agency

The Implementation of Proposition 65

A Progress Report

July 1991

Summary of the Proposition

The Safe Drinking Water and Toxic Enforcement Act of 1986 (Proposition 65) was passed by the voters of California in November, 1986, and became effective January 1, 1987. The Act required the Governor to publish a list of chemicals known to the State to cause cancer or reproductive toxicity no later than March 1, 1987, with updates and revisions no less frequently than annually thereafter. For chemicals so listed, warnings are required 12 months after listing for knowing and intentional exposures, and knowing discharges to the State's drinking water sources are prohibited 20 months after listing.

The Act contains several exemptions: First, no warning is required if exposures to listed carcinogens would result in a risk lower than the level of "no significant risk," (defined as one excess case of cancer per 100,000 individuals exposed over a 70-year lifetime) or if exposures to listed reproductive toxicants are less than one one-thousandth of the no observable effect level (NOEL). Similarly, discharges to the State's drinking water sources are not prohibited if they pose no significant risk or if they do not exceed one one-thousandth of the NOEL. Second, the Act is not applicable to businesses employing fewer than ten employees. Third, the Act is not applicable to government agencies. Fourth, the Act is not applicable to drinking water utilities.

Enforcement is via the attorney general, district attorneys, certain city attorneys, and private citizens.

The burden of proof is affected by the Proposition. The plaintiff is required to show that an exposure or a discharge occurred and then the burden shifts to the defendant to show that such action did not result in exposures or discharges greater than those allowed by the Act.

Lead Agency

In January, 1987, the Governor designated the Health and Welfare Agency to be the lead agency for the implementation of the Act. On July 17, 1991, this role was transferred to the Office of Environmental Health Hazard Assessment (OEHHA), a department within the California Environmental Protection Agency, by Executive Order W-15-91. OEHHA is directed to implement the Act in a manner that is fair, predictable, and based on a firm foundation of science and to ensure that the implementation is harmonized and coordinated with other chemical regulatory programs in state government.

Appendix 11-2 (continued)

List of Known Carcinogens and Reproductive Toxicants

The Act provides three mechanisms by which a chemical is listed: (1) if in the opinion of the state's qualified experts it has been clearly shown through scientifically valid testing according to generally accepted principles to cause cancer or reproductive toxicity; (2) if a body considered to be authoritative by such experts has formally identified it as causing cancer or reproductive toxicity; or (3) if an agency of the state or federal government has formally required it to be labeled or identified as causing cancer or reproductive toxicity. Title 22, California Code of Regulations, Sections 12306 and 12902, respectively, address the last two listing mechanisms.

The Scientific Advisory Panel (a group of scientists who are contract consultants to the State) represents the "state's qualified experts." The Panel has reviewed chemicals and recommended those to be added to the list of chemicals known to the State to cause cancer or reproductive toxicity. The Panel has also identified as "authoritative bodies" the U. S. Environmental Protection Agency, the U. S. Food and Drug Administration, the International Agency for Research on Cancer, the National Institute for Occupational Safety and Health, and the National Toxicology Program. With regular updates (usually quarterly), the Governor's chemical list has increased in number, and now includes 487 chemicals (371 carcinogens and 116 reproductive toxicants).

Implementing Regulations

The regulations implementing the Act provide guidance and reduce the uncertainties associated with the Act. They are published in Division 2 of Title 22 of the California Code of Regulations, following the list of chemicals, which is contained in Section 12000. The regulations address issues of the operation of the Scientific Advisory Panel, define various terms, and establish no significant risk levels for several dozen chemicals. They also address various aspects of discharge of chemicals into the State's drinking water sources, including waste facilities and pesticides, and track closely on the efforts of the State and regional water boards to protect sources of drinking water.

Additional Sources of Information

The list of chemicals is updated in the California Regulatory Notice Register, which is published by the California Office of Administrative Law ((916) 323-6225) and obtained by subscription.

The list and the implementing regulations are found in Title 22 of the California Code of Regulations, Division 2, beginning with Section 12000. They are also printed in Title 26, Division 21.5, beginning with Section 22-12000. These may be purchased from Barclays Law Publishers((415) 244-6611). Update services are also available.

Appendix 11-3

TITLE 22. OFFICE OF ENVIRONMENTAL HEALTH HAZARD ASSESSMENT

STATE OF CALIFORNIA
ENVIRONMENTAL PROTECTION AGENCY
OFFICE OF ENVIRONMENTAL HEALTH HAZARD ASSESSMENT
SAFE DRINKING WATER AND TOXIC ENFORCEMENT ACT OF 1986

CHEMICALS KNOWN TO THE STATE TO CAUSE CANCER OR REPRODUCTIVE TOXICITY

The Safe Drinking Water and Toxic Enforcement Act of 1986 requires that the Governor revise and republish at least once per year the list of chemicals known to the State to cause cancer or reproductive toxicity. The identification number indicated in the following list is the Chemical Abstracts Service (CAS) Registry Number. No CAS number is given when several substances are presented as a single listing. The date refers to the initial appearance of the chemical on the list

CHEMICALS KNOWN TO THE STATE TO CAUSE CANCER

Chemical	CAS Number	Date
A-alpha-C (2-Amino-9H-pyrido[2,3-b]indole)	26148685	January 1, 1990
Acetaldehyde	75070	April 1, 1988
Acetamide	60355	January 1, 1990
Acetochlor	34256821	January 1, 1989
2-Acetylaminofluorene	53963	July 1, 1987
Acifluorfen	62476599	January 1, 1990
Acrylamide	79061	January 1, 1990
Acrylonitrile	107131	July 1, 1987
Actinomycin D	50760	October 1, 1989
Adriamycin (Doxorubicin hydrochloride)	23214928	July 1, 1987
AF-2; [2-(2-furyl)-3-(5-nitro-2-furyl)]acrylamide	3688537	July 1, 1987
Aflatoxins	---	January 1, 1988
Alachlor	15972608	January 1, 1989
Alcoholic beverages, when associated with alcohol abuse	---	July 1, 1988
Aldrin	309002	July 1, 1988
Allyl chloride	107051	January 1, 1990
2-Aminoanthraquinone	117793	October 1, 1989
p-Aminoazobenzene	60093	January 1, 1990
ortho-Aminoazotoluene	97563	July 1, 1987
4-Aminobiphenyl (4-aminodiphenyl)	92671	February 27, 1987
3-Amino-9-ethylcarbazole hydrochloride	6109973	July 1, 1989
1-Amino-2-methylanthraquinone	82280	October 1, 1989
2-Amino-5-(5-nitro-2 furyl)-1,3,4-thiadiazole	712685	July 1, 1987
Amitrole	61825	July 1, 1987
Analgesic mixtures containing phenacetin	---	February 27, 1987
Aniline	62533	January 1, 1990
ortho-Anisidine	90040	July 1, 1987
ortho-Anisidine hydrochloride	134292	July 1, 1987
Antimony oxide (Antimony trioxide)	1309644	October 1, 1990
Aramite	140578	July 1, 1987
Arsenic (inorganic arsenic compounds)	---	February 27, 1987
Asbestos	1332214	February 27, 1987
Auramine	492808	July 1, 1987
Azaserine	115026	July 1, 1987
Azathioprine	446866	February 27, 1987
Azacitidine	320672	January 1, 1992
Azobenzene	103333	January 1, 1990
Benz[a]anthracene	56553	July 1, 1987
Benzene	71432	February 27, 1987
Benzidine [and its salts]	92875	February 27, 1987
Benzidine-based dyes	---	October 1, 1992
Benzo[b]fluoranthene	205992	July 1, 1987
Benzo[j]fluoranthene	205823	July 1, 1987
Benzo[k]fluoranthene	207089	July 1, 1987
Benzofuran	271896	October 1, 1990
Benzo[a]pyrene	50328	July 1, 1987
Benzotrichloride	98077	July 1, 1987
Benzyl chloride	100447	January 1, 1990
Benzyl violet 4B	1694093	July 1, 1987
Beryllium and beryllium compounds	---	October 1, 1987
Betel quid with tobacco	---	January 1, 1990
Bis(2-chloroethyl)ether	111444	April 1, 1988
N,N-Bis(2-chloroethyl)-2-naphthylamine (Chlornapazine)	494031	February 27, 1987
Bischloroethyl nitrosourea (BCNU)(Carmustine)	154938	July 1, 1987
Bis(chloromethyl)ether	542881	February 27, 1987

Bitumens, extracts of steam-refined and air refined	--	January 1, 1990
Bracken fern	--	January 1, 1990
Bromodichloromethane	75274	January 1, 1990
Bromoform	75252	April 1, 1991
1,3-Butadiene	106990	April 1, 1988
1,4-Butanediol dimethanesulfonate (Busulfan)	55981	February 27, 1987
Butylated hydroxyanisole	25013165	January 1, 1990
beta-Butyrolactone	3068880	July 1, 1987
Cadmium and cadmium compounds	---	October 1, 1987
Captafol	2425061	October 1, 1988
Captan	133062	January 1, 1990
Carbon tetrachloride	56235	October 1, 1987
Carbon-black extracts	---	January 1, 1990
Ceramic fibers (airborne particles of respirable size)	---	July 1, 1990
Certain combined chemotherapy for lymphomas	---	February 27, 1987
Chlorambucil	305033	February 27, 1987
Chloramphenicol	56757	October 1, 1989
Chlordane	57749	July 1, 1988
Chlordecone (Kepone)	143500	January 1, 1988
Chlordimeform	6164983	January 1, 1989
Chlorendic acid	115286	July 1, 1989
Chlorinated paraffins (Average chain length, C12; approximately 60 percent chlorine by weight)	108171262	July 1, 1989
Chlorodibromomethane	124481	January 1, 1990
Chloroethane (Ethyl chloride)	75003	July 1, 1990
1-(2-Chloroethyl)-3-cyclohexyl-1-nitrosourea (CCNU) (Lomustine)	13010474	January 1, 1988
1-(2-Chloroethyl)-3-(4-methylcyclohexyl)-1-nitrosourea (Methyl-CCNU)	13909096	October 1, 1988
Chloroform	67663	October 1, 1987
Chloromethyl methyl ether (technical grade)	107302	February 27, 1987
3-Chloro-2-methylpropene	563473	July 1, 1989
4-Chloro-ortho-phenylenediamine	95830	January 1, 1988
p-Chloro-o-toluidine	95692	January 1, 1990
Chlorothalonil	1897456	January 1, 1989
Chlorozotocin	54749905	January 1, 1992
Chromium (hexavalent compounds)	---	February 27, 1987
Chrysene	218019	January 1, 1990
C. I. Acid Red 114	6459945	July 1, 1992
C. I. Basic Red 9 monohydrochloride	569619	July 1, 1989
Ciclosporin (Cyclosporin A; Cyclosporine)	59865133 79217600	January 1, 1992
Cinnamyl anthranilate	87296	July 1, 1989
Cisplatin	15663271	October 1, 1988
CitrusRed No. 2	6358538	October 1, 1989
Cobalt metal powder	7440484	July 1, 1992
Cobalt [II] oxide	1307966	July 1, 1992
Coke oven emissions	---	February 27, 1987
Conjugated estrogens	---	February 27, 1987
Creosotes	---	October 1, 1988
para-Cresidine	120718	January 1, 1988
Cupferron	135206	January 1, 1988
Cycasin	14901087	January 1, 1988
Cyclophosphamide (anhydrous)	50180	February 27, 1987
Cyclophosphamide (hydrated)	6055192	February 27, 1987
D&C Orange No. 17	3468631	July 1, 1990
D&C Red No. 8	2092560	October 1, 1990
D&C Red No. 9	5160021	July 1, 1990
D&C Red No. 19	81889	July1, 1990
Dacarbazine	4342034	January 1, 1988
Daminozide	1596845	January 1, 1990
Dantron (Chrysazin; 1,8-Dihydroxyanthraquinone)	117102	January 1, 1992
Daunomycin	20830813	January 1, 1988
DDD (Dichlorodiphenyldichloroethane)	72548	January 1, 1989
DDE (Dichlorodiphenyldichloroethylene)	72559	January 1, 1989
DDT (Dichlorodiphenyltrichloroethane)	50293	October 1, 1987
DDVP (Dichlorvos)	62737	January 1, 1989
N,N'-Diacetylbenzidine	613354	October 1, 1989
2,4-Diaminoanisole	615054	October 1, 1990
2,4-Diaminoanisole sulfate	39156417	January 1, 1988
4,4'-Diaminodiphenyl ether (4,4'-Oxydianiline)	101804	January 1, 1988
2,4-Diaminotoluene	95807	January 1, 1988
Diaminotoluene (mixed)	---	January 1, 1990
Dibenz[a,h]acridine	226368	January 1, 1988
Dibenz[a,j]acridine	224420	January 1, 1988

Dibenz[a,h]anthracene	53703	January 1, 1988
7H-Dibenzo[c,g]carbazole	194592	January 1, 1988
Dibenzo[a,e]pyrene	192654	January 1, 1988
Dibenzo[a,h]pyrene	189640	January 1, 1988
Dibenzo[a,i]pyrene	189559	January 1, 1988
Dibenzo[a,l]pyrene	191300	January 1, 1988
1,2-Dibromo-3-chloropropane (DBCP)	96128	July 1, 1987
p-Dichlorobenzene	106467	January 1, 1989
3,3'-Dichlorobenzidine	91941	October 1, 1987
1,4-Dichloro-2-butene	764410	January 1, 1990
3,3'-Dichloro-4,4'-diaminodiphenyl ether	28434868	January 1, 1988
1,1-Dichloroethane	75343	January 1, 1990
Dichloromethane (Methylene chloride)	75092	April 1, 1988
1,2-Dichloropropane	78875	January 1, 1990
1,3-Dichloropropene	542756	January 1, 1989
Dieldrin	60571	July 1, 1988
Dienestrol	84173	January 1, 1990
Diepoxybutane	1464535	January 1, 1988
Diesel engine exhaust	---	October 1, 1990
Di(2-ethylhexyl)phthalate	117817	January 1, 1988
1,2-Diethylhydrazine	1615801	January 1, 1988
Diethyl sulfate	64675	January 1, 1988
Diethylstilbestrol	56531	February 27, 1987
Diglycidyl resorcinol ether (DGRE)	101906	July 1, 1989
Dihydrosafrole	94586	January 1, 1988
3-3'-Dimethoxybenzidine (ortho-Dianisidine)	119904	January 1, 1988
3,3'-Dimethoxybenzidine dihydrochloride (ortho-Dianisidine dihydrochloride)	20325400	October 1, 1990
Dimethylsulfate	77781	January 1, 1988
4-Dimethylaminoazobenzene	60117	January 1, 1988
trans-2-[(Dimethylamino)methylimino]-5-[2-(5-nitro-2-furyl)vinyl]-1,3,4-oxadiazole	55738540	January 1, 1988
7,12-Dimethylbenz(a)anthracene	57976	January 1, 1990
3,3'-Dimethylbenzidine (ortho-Tolidine)	119937	January 1, 1988
3,3'-Dimethylbenzidine dihydrochloride	612828	April 1, 1992
Dimethylcarbamoyl chloride	79447	January 1, 1988
1,1-Dimethylhydrazine (UDMH)	57147	October 1, 1989
1,2-Dimethylhydrazine	540738	January 1, 1988
Dimethylvinylchloride	513371	July 1, 1989
1,6-Dinitropyrene	42397648	October 1, 1990
1,8-Dinitropyrene	42397659	October 1, 1990
2,4-Dinitrotoluene	121142	July 1, 1988
1,4-Dioxane	123911	January 1, 1988
Diphenylhydantoin (Phenytoin)	57410	January 1, 1988
Diphenylhydantoin (Phenytoin), sodium salt	630933	January 1, 1988
Direct Black 38 (technical grade)	1937377	January 1, 1988
Direct Blue 6 (technical grade)	2602462	January 1, 1988
Direct Brown 95 (technical grade)	16071866	October 1, 1988
Disperse Blue 1	2475458	October 1, 1990
Epichlorohydrin	106898	October 1, 1987
Erionite	12510428	October 1, 1988
Estradiol 17β	50282	January 1, 1988
Estrone	53167	January 1, 1988
Ethinylestradiol	57636	January 1, 1988
Ethyl acrylate	140885	July 1, 1989
Ethyl methanesulfonate	62500	January 1, 1988
Ethyl-4,4'-dichlorobenzilate	510156	January 1, 1990
Ethylene dibromide	106934	July 1, 1987
Ethylene dichloride (1,2-Dichloroethane)	107062	October 1, 1987
Ethylene oxide	75218	July 1, 1987
Ethylene thiourea	96457	January 1, 1988
Ethyleneimine	151564	January 1, 1988

Folpet	133073	January 1, 1989
Formaldehyde (gas)	50000	January 1, 1988
2-(2-Formylhydrazino)-4-(5-nitro-2-furyl)thiazole	3570750	January 1, 1988
Furazolidone	67458	January 1, 1990
Furmecyclox	60568050	January 1, 1990
Gasoline engine exhaust (condensates/extracts)	---	October 1, 1990
Glasswool fibers (airborne particles of respirable size)	---	July 1, 1990
Glu-P-1 (2-Amino-6-methyldipyrido[1,2-a:3',2'-d]imidazole)	67730114	January 1, 1990
Glu-P-2 (2-Aminodipyrido[1,2-a:3',2'-d]imidazole)	67730103	January 1, 1990
Glycidaldehyde	765344	January 1, 1988
Glycidol	556525	July 1, 1990
Griseofulvin	126078	January 1, 1990
Gyromitrin (Acetaldehyde methylformylhydrazone)	16568028	January 1, 1988
HC Blue 1	2784943	July 1, 1989
Heptachlor	76448	July 1, 1988
Heptachlor epoxide	1024573	July 1, 1988
Hexachlorobenzene	118741	October1, 1987
Hexachlorocyclohexane (technical grade)	---	October 1, 1987
Hexachlorodibenzodioxin	34465468	April 1, 1988
Hexachloroethane	67721	July1, 1990
Hexamethylphosphoramide	680319	January 1, 1988
Hydrazine	302012	January 1, 1988
Hydrazine sulfate	10034932	January 1, 1988
Hydrazobenzene (1,2-Diphenylhydrazine)	122667	January 1, 1988
Indeno [1,2,3-cd]pyrene	193395	January 1, 1988
IQ (2-Amino-3-methylimidazo[4,5-f]quinoline)	76180966	April 1,1990
Iron dextran complex	9004664	January 1, 1988
Isosafrole	120581	October 1, 1989
Lactofen	77501634	January 1, 1989
Lasiocarpine	303344	April 1, 1988
Lead acetate	301042	January 1, 1988
Lead and lead compounds	---	October 1, 1992
Lead phosphate	7446277	April 1, 1988
Lead subacetate	1335326	October 1, 1989
Lindane and other hexachlorocyclohexane isomers	---	October 1, 1989
Mancozeb	8018017	January 1, 1990
Maneb	12427382	January 1, 1990
Me-A-alpha-C (2-Amino-3-methyl-9H-pyrido[2,3-b]indole)	68006837	January 1, 1990
Medroxyprogesterone acetate	71589	January 1, 1990
Melphalan	148823	February 27, 1987
Merphalan	531760	April 1, 1988
Mestranol	72333	April 1, 1988
8-Methoxypsoralen with ultraviolet A therapy	298817	February 27, 1987
5-Methoxypsoralen with ultravioletA therapy	484208	October 1, 1988
2-Methylaziridine (Propyleneimine)	75558	January 1, 1988
Methylazoxymethanol	590965	April 1, 1988
Methylazoxymethanol acetate	592621	April 1, 1988
3-Methylcholanthrene	56495	January 1, 1990
5-Methylchrysene	3697243	April 1, 1988
4,4'-Methylene bis(2-chloroaniline)	101144	July 1, 1987
4,4'-Methylene bis(N,N-dimethyl)benzenamine	101611	October 1, 1989
4,4'-Methylene bis(2-methylaniline)	838880	April 1, 1988
4,4'-Methylenedianiline	101779	January 1, 1988
4,4'-Methylenedianiline dihydrochloride	13552448	January 1, 1988
Methylhydrazine and its salts	---	July 1, 1992
Methyl iodide	74884	April 1, 1988
Methyl methanesulfonate	66273	April 1, 1988
2-Methyl-1-nitroanthraquinone (of uncertain purity)	129157	April 1, 1988
N-Methyl-N'-nitro-N-nitrosoguanidine	70257	April 1, 1988
N-Methyloacrylamide	924425	July 1, 1990
Methylthiouracil	56042	October 1, 1989
Metiram	9006422	January 1, 1990
Metronidazole	443481	January 1, 1988
Michler's ketone	90948	January 1, 1988
Mirex	2385855	January 1, 1988
Mitomycin C	50077	April 1, 1988
Monocrotaline	315220	April 1, 1988
5-(Morpholinomethyl)-3-[(5-nitro-furfurylidene)-amino]-2-oxalolidinone	139913	April 1, 1988
Mustard Gas	505602	February 27, 1987

Nafenopin	3771195	April 1, 1988
1-Naphthylamine	134327	October 1, 1989
2-Naphthylamine	91598	February 27, 1987
Nickel and certain nickel compounds	---	October 1, 1989
Nickel carbonyl	13463393	October 1, 1987
Nickel refinery dust from the pyrometallurgical process	---	October 1, 1987
Nickel subsulfide	12035722	October 1, 1987
Niridazole	61574	April 1, 1988
Nitrilotriacetic acid	139139	January 1, 1988
Nitrilotriacetic acid, trisodiumsalt monohydrate	18662538	April 1, 1989
5-Nitroacenaphthene	602879	April 1, 1988
5-Nitro-o-anisidine	99592	October 1, 1989
o-Nitroanisole	91236	October 1, 1992
4-Nitrobiphenyl	92933	April 1, 1988
6-Nitrochrysene	7496028	October 1, 1990
Nitrofen (technical grade)	1836755	January 1, 1988
2-Nitrofluorene	607578	October 1, 1990
Nitrofurazone	59870	January 1, 1990
1-[(5-Nitrofurfurylidene)-amino]-2-imidazolidinone	555840	April 1, 1988
N-[4-(5-Nitro-2-furyl)-2-thiazolyl]acetamide	531828	April 1, 1988
Nitrogen mustard (Mechlorethamine)	51752	January 1, 1988
Nitrogen mustard hydrochloride (Mechlorethamine hydrochloride)	55867	April 1, 1988
Nitrogen mustard N-oxide	126852	April 1, 1988
Nitrogen mustard N-oxide hydrochloride	302705	April 1, 1988
2-Nitropropane	79469	January 1, 1988
1-Nitropyrene	5522430	October 1, 1990
4-Nitropyrene	57835924	October 1, 1990
N-Nitrosodi-n-butylamine	924163	October 1, 1987
N-Nitrosodiethanolamine	1116547	January 1, 1988
N-Nitrosodiethylamine	55185	October 1, 1987
N-Nitrosodimethylamine	62759	October 1, 1987
p-Nitrosodiphenylamine	156105	January 1, 1988
N-Nitrosodiphenylamine	86306	April 1, 1988
N-Nitrosodi-n-propylamine	621647	January 1, 1988
N-Nitroso-N-ethylurea	759739	October 1, 1987
3-(N-Nitrosomethylamino)propionitrile	60153493	April 1, 1990
4-(N-Nitrosomethylamino)-1-(3-pyridyl)1-butanone	64091914	April 1, 1990
N-Nitrosomethylethylamine	10595956	October 1, 1989
N-Nitroso-N-methylurea	684935	October 1, 1987
N-Nitroso-N-methylurethane	615532	April 1, 1988
N-Nitrosomethylvinylamine	4549400	January 1, 1988
N-Nitrosomorpholine	59892	January 1, 1988
N-Nitrosonornicotine	16543558	January 1, 1988
N-Nitrosopiperidine	100754	January 1, 1988
N-Nitrosopyrrolidine	930552	October 1, 1987
N-Nitrososarcosine	13256229	January 1, 1988
Norethisterone (Norethindrone)	68224	October 1, 1989
Ochratoxin A	303479	July 1, 1990
Oil Orange SS	2646175	April 1, 1988
Oral contraceptives, combined	---	October 1, 1989
Oral contraceptives, sequential	---	October 1, 1989
Oxadiazon	19666309	July 1, 1991
Oxymetholone	434071	January 1, 1988

Panfuran S	---	January 1, 1988
Pentachlorophenol	87865	January 1, 1990
Phenacetin	62442	October 1, 1989
Phenazopyridine	94780	January 1, 1988
Phenazopyridine hydrochloride	136403	January 1, 1988
Phenesterin	3546109	July 1, 1989
Phenobarbital	50066	January 1, 1990
Phenoxybenzamine	59961	April 1, 1988
Phenoxybenzamine hydrochloride	63923	April 1, 1988
Phenyl glycidyl ether	122601	October 1, 1990
Phenylhydrazine and its salts	---	July 1, 1992
o-Phenylphenate, sodium	132274	January 1, 1990
Polybrominated biphenyls	---	January 1, 1988
Polychlorinated biphenyls	---	October 1, 1989
Polychlorinated biphenyls (containing 60 or more percent chlorine by molecular weight)	---	January 1, 1988
Polychlorinated dibenzo-p- dioxins	---	October 1, 1992
Polychlorinated dibenzofurans	---	October 1, 1992
Polygeenan	53973981	January 1, 1988
Ponceau MX	3761533	April 1, 1988
Ponceau 3R	3564098	April 1, 1988
Potassium bromate	7758012	January 1, 1990
Procarbazine	671169	January 1, 1988
Procarbazine hydrochloride	366701	January 1, 1988
Progesterone	57830	January 1, 1988
1,3-Propane sultone	1120714	January 1, 1988
beta-Propiolactone	57578	January 1, 1988
Propylene oxide	75569	October 1, 1988
Propylthiouracil	51525	January 1, 1988
Radionuclides	---	July 1, 1989
Reserpine	50555	October 1, 1989
Residual (heavy) fuel oils	---	October 1, 1990
Saccharin	81072	October 1, 1989
Saccharin, sodium	128449	January 1, 1988
Safrole	94597	January 1, 1988
Selenium sulfide	7446346	October 1, 1989
Shale-oils	68308349	April 1, 1990
Silica, crystalline (airborne particles of respirable size)	---	October 1, 1988
Soots, tars, and mineral oils (untreated and mildly treated oils) and used engine oils	---	February 27, 1987
Sterigmatocystin	10048132	April 1, 1988
Streptozotocin	18883664	January 1, 1988
Styrene oxide	96093	October 1, 1988
Sulfallate	95067	January 1, 1988
Talc containing asbestiform fibers	---	April 1, 1990
Testosteroneand its esters	58220	April 1, 1988
2,3,7,8-Tetrachlorodibenzo-para-dioxin (TCDD)	1746016	January 1, 1988
1,1,2,2-Tetrachloroethane	79345	July 1, 1990
Tetrachloroethylene (Perchloroethylene)	127184	April 1, 1988
p-α,α,α-Tetrachlorotoluene	5216251	January 1, 1990
Tetranitromethane	509148	July 1, 1990
Thioacetamide	62555	January 1, 1988
4,4'-Thiodianiline	139651	April 1, 1988
Thiourea	62566	January 1, 1988
Thorium dioxide	1314201	February 27, 1987
Tobacco, oral use of smokeless products	---	April 1, 1988
Tobacco smoke	---	April 1, 1988
Toluene diisocyanate	26471625	October 1, 1989
ortho-Toluidine	95534	January 1, 1988
ortho-Toluidine hydrochloride	636215	January 1, 1988
para-Toluidine	106490	January 1, 1990
Toxaphene (Polychorinated camphenes)	8001352	January 1, 1988
Treosulfan	299752	February 27, 1987
Trichlormethine (Trimustine hydrochloride)	817094	January 1, 1992
2,4,6-Trichlorophenol	88062	January 1, 1988
1,2,3-Trichloropropane	96184	October 1, 1992

Triphenyltin hydroxide	76879	July 1, 1992
Trichloroethylene	79016	April 1, 1988
Tris(aziridinyl)-para-benzoquinone (Triaziquone)	68768	October 1, 1989
Tris(1-aziridinyl)phosphine sulfide (Thiotepa)	52244	January 1, 1988
Tris (2,-chloroethyl) phosphate	115968	April 1, 1992
Tris(2,3-dibromopropyl)phosphate	126727	January 1, 1988
Trp-P-1 (Tryptophan-P-1)	62450060	April 1, 1988
Trp-P-2(Tryptophan-P-2)	62450071	April 1, 1988
Trypan blue (commercial grade)	72571	October 1, 1989
Unleaded gasoline (wholly vaporized)	---	April 1, 1988
Uracil mustard	66751	April 1, 1988
Urethane (Ethyl carbamate)	51796	January 1, 1988
Vinyl bromide	593602	October 1, 1988
Vinyl chloride	75014	February 27, 1987
4-Vinyl-1-cyclohexene diepoxide (Vinyl cyclohexene dioxide)	106876	July 1, 1990
Vinyl trichloride (1,1-2-Trichloroethane)	79005	October 1, 1990
2,6-Xylidene (2,6-Dimethylaniline)	87627	January 1, 1991
Zineb	12122677	January 1, 1990

CHEMICALS KNOWN TO THE STATE TO CAUSE REPRODUCTIVE TOXICITY

Developmental toxicity

Acetohydroxamic acid	546883	April 1, 1990
Actinomycin D	50760	October 1, 1992
All-trans retinoic acid	302794	January 1, 1989
Alprazolam	28981977	July 1, 1990
Amikacin sulfate	39831555	July 1, 1990
Aminoglutethimide	125848	July 1, 1990
Aminoglycosides	---	October 1, 1992
Aminopterin	54626	July 1, 1987
Angiotensin converting enzyme (ACE) inhibitors	---	October 1, 1992
Anisindione	117373	October 1, 1992
Aspirin (NOTE: It is especially important not to use aspirin during the last three months of pregnancy, unless specifically directed to do so by a physician because it may cause problems in the unborn child or complications during delivery.)	50782	July 1, 1990
Barbituates	---	October 1, 1992
Benomyl	17804352	July 1, 1991
Benzphetamine hydrochloride	5411223	April 1, 1990
Benzodiazepines	---	October 1, 1992
Bischloroethyl nitrosourea (BCNU) (Carmustine)	154938	July 1, 1990
Bromoxynil	1689845	October 1, 1990
Butabarbital sodium	143817	October 1, 1992
1,4-Butanediol dimethylsulfonate (Busulfan)	55981	January 1, 1989
Carbon disulfide	75150	July 1, 1989
Carbon monoxide	630080	July 1, 1989
Carboplatin	41575944	July 1, 1990
Chenodiol	474259	April 1,1990
Chlorcyclizine hydrochloride	1620219	July 1, 1987
Chlorambucil	305033	January 1, 1989
Chlordecone (Kepone)	143500	January 1, 1989
Chlordiazepoxide	58253	January 1, 1992
Chlordiazepoxide hydrochloride	438415	January 1, 1992
1-(2-Chloroethyl)-3-cyclohexyl-1-nitrosourea (CCNU) (Lomustine)	13010474	July 1, 1990
Clomiphene citrate	50419	April 1, 1990
Clorazepate dipotassium	57109907	October 1, 1992
Cocaine	50362	July 1, 1989
Colchichine	64868	October 1, 1992
Conjugated estrogens	---	April 1, 1990
Cyanazine	21725462	April 1, 1990
Cycloheximide	66819	January 1, 1989
Cyclophosphamide (anhydrous)	50180	January 1, 1989
Cyclophosphamide (hydrated)	6055192	January 1, 1989
Cyhexatin	13121705	January 1, 1989
Cytarabine	147944	January 1, 1989
Danazol	17230885	April 1, 1990
Daunorubicin hydrochloride	23541506	July 1, 1990
Demeclocycline hydrochloride (internal use)	64733	January 1, 1992
Diazepam	439145	January 1, 1992
Dicumarol	66762	October 1, 1992
Diethylstilbestrol (DES)	56531	July 1, 1987
Dinocap	39300453	April 1, 1990
Dinoseb	88857	January 1, 1989
Diphenylhydantoin (Phenytoin)	57410	July 1, 1987
Doxycycline (internal use)	564250	July 1, 1990
Doxycycline calcium (internal use)	94088854	January 1, 1992
Doxycycline hyclate (internal use)	24390145	October 1, 1991
Doxycycline monohydrate (internal use)	17086281	October 1, 1991
Ergotamine tartrate	379793	April 1, 1990
Ethyl alcohol in alcoholic beverages	---	October 1, 1987
Ethylene glycol monoethyl ether	110805	January 1, 1989
Ethylene glycol monomethyl ether	109864	January 1, 1989
Etoposide	33419420	July 1, 1990
Etretinate	54350480	July 1, 1987

Fluorouracil	51218	January 1, 1989
Fluoxymesterone	76437	April 1, 1990
Flurazepam hydrochloride	1172185	October 1, 1992
Flutamide	13311847	July 1, 1990
Halazepam	23092173	July 1, 1990
Hexachlorobenzene	118741	January 1, 1989
Ifosfamide	3778732	July 1, 1990
Iodine-131	24267569	January 1, 1989
Isotretinoin	4759482	July 1, 1987
Lead	---	February 27, 1987
Lithium carbonate	554132	January 1, 1991
Lithium citrate	919164	January 1, 1991
Lorazepam	846491	July 1, 1990
Lovastatin	75330755	October 1, 1992
Medroxyprogesterone acetate	71589	April1, 1990
Megestrol acetate	595335	January 1, 1991
Melphalan	148823	July 1, 1990
Menotropins	9002680	April 1, 1990
Meprobamate	57534	January 1, 1992
Mercaptopurine	6112761	July 1, 1990
Mercury and mercury compounds	---	July 1, 1990
Methacycline hyrdrochloride	3963959	January 1, 1991
Methimazole	60560	July 1, 1990
Methotrexate	59052	January 1, 1989
Methotrexate sodium	15475566	April 1, 1990
Methyl mercury	---	July 1, 1987
Methyltestosterone	58184	April 1, 1990
Midazolam hydrochloride	59467968	July 1, 1990
Minocycline hydrochloride (internal use)	13614987	January 1, 1992
Misoprostol	62015398	April 1, 1990
Mitroxantrone hydrochloride	70476823	July 1, 1990
Nafarelin acetate	86220420	April 1, 1990
Neomycin sulfate (internal use)	1405103	October 1,1992
Netilmicinsulfate	56391572	July 1, 1990
Nicotine	54115	April1, 1990
Nitrogen mustard (Mechlorethamine)	51752	January 1, 1989
Nitrogen mustard hydrochloride (Mechlorethamine hydrochloride)	55867	July 1, 1990
Norethisterone (Norethindrone)	68224	April 1, 1990
Norethisterone acetate (Norethindrone acetate)	51989	October 1, 1991
Norethisterone (Norethindrone)/Ethinyl estradiol	68224/57636	April 1, 1990
Norethisterone (Norethindrone)/Mestranol	68224/72333	April 1, 1990
Norgestrel	6533002	April 1, 1990
Oxazepam	604751	October 1, 1992
Oxytetracycline (internal use)	79572	January 1, 1991
Oxytetracycline hydrochloride (internal use)	2058460	October 1, 1991
Paramethadione	115673	July 1, 1990
Penicillamine	52675	January 1, 1991
Pentobarbital sodium	57330	July 1, 1990
Phenacemide	63989	July 1, 1990
Phenprocoumon	435972	October 1, 1992
Pipobroman	54911	July 1, 1990
Plicamycin	18378897	April 1, 1990
Polychlorinated biphenyls	---	January 1, 1991
Procarbazine hydrochloride	366701	July 1,1990
Propylthiouracil	51525	July 1, 1990
Retinol/retinyl esters, whenin daily dosages in excess of10,000 IU, or 3,000 retinol equivalents. (NOTE: Retinol/retinyl esters are required and essential for maintenance of normal reproductive function. The recommended daily level during pregnancy is 8,000 IU.)	---	July 1, 1989
Ribavirin	36791045	April 1, 1990
Secobarbital sodium	309433	October 1, 1992
Streptomycin sulfate	3810740	January 1, 1991

Tamoxifen citrate	54965241	July 1, 1990
Temazepam	846504	April 1, 1990
Testosterone cypionate	58208	October 1, 1991
Testosterone enanthate	315377	April 1, 1990
2, 3, 7, 8-Tetrachlorodibenzo-para-dioxin (TCDD)	1746016	April 1, 1991
Tetracyclines (internal use)	---	October 1, 1992
Tetracycline (internal use)	60548	October 1, 1991
Tetracycline hydrochloride (internaluse)	64755	January 1, 1991
Thalidomide	50351	July 1, 1987
Thioguanine	154427	July 1, 1990
Tobacco smoke (primary)	---	April 1, 1988
Tobramycin sulfate	49842071	July 1, 1990
Toluene	108883	January 1, 1991
Triazolam	28911015	April 1, 1990
Trilostane	13647353	April 1, 1990
Trimethadione	127480	January 1, 1991
Uracil mustard	66751	January 1, 1992
Urofollitropin	26995915	April 1, 1990
Valproate (Valproic acid)	99661	July 1, 1987
Vinblastine sulfate	143679	July 1, 1990
Vincristine sulfate	2068782	July 1, 1990
Warfarin	81812	July 1, 1987

Female reproductive toxicity

Aminopterin	54626	July 1, 1987
Anabolic steroids	---	April 1, 1990
Aspirin (NOTE: It is especially important not to use aspirin during the last three months of pregnancy, unless specifically directed to do so by a physician becauseit may cause problems in the unborn child or complications during delivery.)	50782	July 1, 1990
	75150	July1, 1989
Carbon disulfide	50362	July 1, 1989
Cocaine	50180	January 1, 1989
Cyclophosphamide (anhydrous)	6055192	January 1, 1989
Cyclophosphamide (hydrated)	75218	February 27, 1987
Ethylene oxide	---	February 27, 1987
Lead	---	April 1, 1988
Tobacco smoke (primary)	66751	January 1, 1992
Uracil mustard		

Male reproductive toxicity

Anabolic steroids	---	April 1, 1990
Benomyl	17804352	July 1, 1991
Carbon disulfide	75150	July 1, 1989
Colchicine	64868	October 1,1992
Cyclophosphamide (anhydrous)	50180	January 1, 1989
Cyclophosphamide (hydrated)	6055192	January 1, 1989
1,2-Dibromo-3-chloropropane (DBCP)	96128	February 27, 1987
m-Dinitrobenzene	99650	July 1, 1990
o-Dinitrobenzene	528290	July 1, 1990
p-Dinitrobenzene	100254	July 1, 1990
Dinoseb	88857	January 1, 1989
Ethylene glycol monoethyl ether	110805	January 1, 1989
Ethylene glycol monomethyl ether	109864	January 1, 1989
Lead	---	February 27, 1987
Nitrofurantoin	67209	April 1, 1991
Tobacco smoke (primary)	---	April 1, 1988
Uracil mustard	66751	January 1, 1992

Date: October 1, 1992

CALIFORNIA ENVIRONMENTAL PROTECTION AGENCY
OFFICE OF ENVIRONMENTAL HEALTH HAZARD ASSESSMENT
SAFE DRINKING WATER AND TOXIC ENFORCEMENT ACT OF 1986
(PROPOSITION 65)
NOTICE TO INTERESTED PARTIES

CHEMICALS TO BE LISTED EFFECTIVE OCTOBER 1, 1992
AS KNOWN TO THE STATE TO CAUSE CANCER OR REPRODUCTIVE TOXICITY

The California Environmental Protection Agency's Office of Environmental Health Hazard Assessment has identified 24 chemicals for listing under the Safe Drinking Water and Toxic Enforcement Act of 1986 (Proposition 65) as known to the State of California to cause cancer or reproductive toxicity. These chemicals will be listed effective October 1, 1992.

The chemicals and their Chemical Abstracts Services Registry (CAS) numbers are listed below. All the chemicals were listed administratively, based on either: (1) a formal requirement by a State or federal agency that the chemical be labeled or identified as causing cancer or reproductive toxicity (chemicals so listed are designated with an "*FR*"); or (2) a formal identification of a chemical as a carcinogen or reproductive toxicant by an "authoritative body" ("*AB*"). These listing mechanisms are addressed in Title 22, California Code of Regulations, Sections 12902 and 12306, respectively.

A complete, updated chemical list is published elsewhere in this issue of the *Register*.

Chemical	*CAS Number*
Carcinogens:	
Benzidine-based dyes (*FR*)	---
Lead and lead compounds (*AB*)	---
o-Nitroanisole (*AB*)	91236
Polychlorinated dibenzo-p-dioxins (*FR*)	---
Polychlorinated dibenzofurans (*FR*)	---
1,2,3-Trichlorophenol (*AB*)	96184
Developmental toxicants:	
Actinomycin D (*FR*)	50760
Aminoglycosides (*FR*)	---
Angiotensin converting enzyme (ACE) inhibitors (*FR*)	---
Anisindione (*FR*)	117373
Barbiturates (*FR*)	---
Benzodiazepines (*FR*)	---
Butabarbital sodium (*FR*)	143817
Clorazepate dipotassium (*FR*)	57109907
Colchicine (*FR*)	64868
Dicumarol (*FR*)	66762
Flurazepam hydrochloride (*FR*)	1172185
Lovastatin (*FR*)	75330755
Neomycin sulfate (internal use) (*FR*)	1405103
Oxazepam (*FR*)	604751
Phenprocoumon (*FR*)	435972
Secobarbital sodium (*FR*)	309433
Tetracyclines (internal use) (*FR*)	---
Male reproductive toxicant:	
Colchicine (*FR*)	64868

Regulated Products, Activities, Professions and Business Practices

Summary and Applicability

This chapter is designed to cover a number of environmental problems that are less significant overall compared to programs described in other chapters of this guide. This is due primarily to the limited number of businesses or facilities that are covered. However, those which are covered will find they are intensively regulated. This chapter includes three major areas:

- Regulatory products/businesses.
- Professions regulated under California environmental law.
- Regulation of business practices.

Within each of these topics are a number of specific programs that will be summarized sufficiently to identify applicability and basic compliance requirements.

Products/Businesses

- Chemical manufacture and importation.
- Chemical product (hazardous substance) information.
- Pesticide manufacturing
- Pesticide distribution, advisors and applicators.
- Fertilizing materials.
- Radiation sources and producing equipment.
- Noise-producing activities and products.

Professions

- Registered environmental assessors and environmental health specialists.
- Underground storage tank integrity testers.
- Underground storage tank removal contractors.
- Asbestos abatement contractors and consultants.
- Registered geologists.
- State-certified laboratories.

Business Practices

- Corporate Criminal Liability act (failure to warn about a serious concealed danger).
- Unfair business practices
- Environmental representations (product advertising claims).

Given the potential liability for fines and even criminal sanctions for violations of the specific regulatory measures described in this chapter, firms engaged in regulated activities or conducting operations or product promotions should determine the requirements that apply and take necessary actions to assure compliance.

Background

The scope of California's environmental laws and regulations extends well beyond the regulation of traditional environmental concerns associated with air, water and toxic substances pollution. It includes a vast array of product regulations, professional and business practice regulations and the relatively new concern over "environmental representations" or advertising or label claims about products. Some of these programs are part of a federal-state coordinated regulatory system, in others they are unique to California. This chapter can present only a brief synopsis of the many varied programs in this area. It is expected that the reader will be able to identify an area of regulation which affects a facility, activity or product, and use the references provided to locate more detailed information.

Given the number of programs presented, each subchapter will be presented as a separate discussion covering the topic, agency responsibility, and penalties for non-compliance. References in the Appendix will provide an outline of specific statutory and regulatory information.

Regulated Products/Activities

◆ Chemical Product Manufacture and Importation

The manufacturer or importer of any chemical substances or chemical-containing product must comply with the federal Toxic Substances Control Act (TSCA) [15 USC 2601-2671]. The chemical regulation provision of this law and the regulatory program established by EPA preempt state and local regulation. Therefore, Federal EPA has sole authority for California facilities subject to TSCA's chemical manufacturing and importation requirements.

TSCA distinguishes between old and new chemicals in its regulatory requirements. Existing chemicals appear on the TSCA inventory of the 64,000 chemicals in commercial use in 1977. Before a chemical is manufactured or imported, EPA must be contacted to determine whether the chemical is on the list. For chemicals not listed, a premanufacture notification (PMN) must be provided to EPA at least 90 days before manufacturing or importing the chemical. Such notices are not required for "existing chemicals" on the inventory unless the activity is a "significant new use." PMNs must include information on the chemical's identity, structure, proposed use, quantities planned, and a description of processing details, persons exposed, disposal methods and any test data available to the submitter. If during the 90-day period and after publication in the *Federal Register,* EPA **does not** take any action, manufacturing or importing may commence. EPA must be notified of the date of commencement. There are narrow exemptions to the PMN rule for research and development, test marketing and small quantity manufacturers. However, compliance with the requirements for these exemptions must be meticulous. [40 CFR §720.]

Finally, a manufacturer or importer of a chemical substance must immediately report to EPA a finding of a significant risk to human health or the environment from a chemical based on reports or test results.

EPA is the enforcing agency for these requirement. The maximum penalty that can be imposed for non-compliance is $25,000 per day for each violation.

◆ Product Hazardous Substances Information

Products containing hazardous substances are regulated under the right-to-know principle based on whether their use is in the workplace or by consumers. With respect to workplace exposures to hazardous substances as broadly defined by the federal and state Hazard Communication Standards [29 CFR §1910.1200 and 8 CCR §5194, respectively], vendors of hazardous substances or products containing hazardous substances must assure that the container meets minimum labeling requirements (chemical name, principal hazards and supplier information) and that Material Safety Data Sheets (MSDSs) are provided to any employer. Under the Hazard Communication Standard, employers have an obligation to convey the relevant information to employees and allow access to MSDSs. MSDSs also are used by other regulatory programs discussed in this handbook to convey regulatory information applicable to the hazardous substance or an ingredient. For example, the following information usually is included on a Material Safety Data Sheet:

- Whether the ingredients are on the TSCA inventory (this chapter).

- Whether the ingredients are subject to EPCRA or other community right-to-know requirements (Chapter 4).

- Whether a chemical component is on the Proposition 65 list of chemicals known to the state of California to cause cancer or reproductive toxicity (Chapter 11).

Manufacturers and distributors are required to assure that MSDSs meet regulatory requirements and are provided to employers. For more information on both manufacturers and distributors, or employers' obligations under the Hazard Communication Standard, see the California Chamber publication *Hazard Communication Handbook.*

Consumer products that are or which contain hazardous substances are subject to the regulation of the federal Consumer Product Safety Commission (CPSC) under authority of the federal Hazardous Substances Act [21 USC §1261, et seq.] and Poison Prevention Packaging Act [15 USC §1471, et seq.]. Regulations of the Commission [16 CFR §1501, et seq.] govern current product safety requirements, including hazardous substance labeling and other safety considerations. There is a potential for conflict with state requirements for Proposition 65 warnings where products subject to both CPSC regulations and state requirements are in question. In addition, there is a large body of laws and regulations that govern products and practices which are potentially harmful to consumers if not regulated. These areas include:

- Foods, food additives, food processing (federal and state).
- Drugs and cosmetics (federal and state).
- Drinking water quality (federal and state).
- Bottled water (federal and state).
- Water conditioning (state).
- Motor vehicle emissions and fuels (federal and state).

Given the volume and complexity of these regulatory programs, further discussion is outside the scope of the handbook.

◆ Pesticide Manufacturing and Distribution

Pesticides are subject to a unique system of duplicative federal and state regulations. Under the federal Insecticide, Fungicide and Rodenticide Act (FIFRA), no person in any state may distribute or sell any pesticide that is not registered by the EPA [7 USC 136(a)]. Pesticides include substances intended for the control of pests or to regulate plant growth, and defoliants or desiccants. This definition also includes under both federal and state law product claims that would lead consumers to believe the product has pesticidal properties.

- **Federal EPA Registration.** A pesticide registration is required for both an active ingredient or an end-use pesticide. New active ingredient registrations require an extensive submission of data on acute, subchronic and chronic effects, including toxicity, reproductive and cancer hazards, as well as environmental concerns. If the product is intended for food crop applications, residue data and establishment of tolerances precede registration for such uses. Through the registration process, the EPA must determine whether the pesticide would pose an unreasonable adverse effect. A product may be registered for general use, restricted use or both. Once active ingredients are registered, end-use products are more expeditiously registered if the registrant has, or can obtain use of, the necessary data to meet registration requirements for the formulated product. There are some limited exceptions to full registration: conditional registrations to expedite product introduction pending complete registration, experimental use permits and local use exemptions. The latter two are very restrictive regulatory approvals short of registration to allow supervised testing or use in emergencies.

  Registration of a pesticide product is evidenced by an EPA-approved label and includes the product name, a list of active and percentage of inert ingredients, the EPA Registration Number, the manufacturing facility number, product application requirements, and various statements about handling precautions, disposal requirements, etc. It is a violation of federal and state law to violate any of the label's requirements during storage, use or disposal of a pesticide.

  EPA also must register establishments that produce, hold or distribute pesticides for sale. [40 CFR § 167.3, et seq.] Reports of significant adverse effects must be made to EPA by registrants based on reports or test results.

  Civil penalties for violation of FIFRA include fines of up to $5,000 per violation for pesticide manufacturers, dealers and commercial applicators, and up to $1,000 for private applicators. The act also specifies criminal penalties for knowing violations by registrants of up to $50,000 and one year of imprisonment. Commercial application of restricted pesticides in violation of FIFRA may result in fines of up to $25,000 and one year of imprisonment.

- **Cal/EPA Registration.** In California, the state has established a regulatory program for pesticides that essentially duplicates the federal system and which manufacturers, distributors and dealers must comply with in addition to meeting federal requirements. This is significantly different than other states, which accept the federal registration process or merely "rubber stamp" federal regulations. California's program is duplicative and more stringent in many respects. The state program is subject to the Food and Agriculture Code and Title 3 regulations of the California Department of Food and Agriculture (CDFA) [Food and Agriculture Code §12500 et seq. and 3 CCR §6000 et seq.]. However, the unit of CDFA responsible for pesticide registrations, enforcement and other functions has been transferred to Cal/EPA in the Department of Pesticide Regulation. Other state agencies also are involved in the state pesticide program, some of which have been integrated into Cal/EPA; for example: Department of Health Services, State Water Resources Control Board and State Air Resources Board. Others, including Department of Fish and Game and Department of Industrial Relations (Cal/-OSHA) have not been reorganized into Cal/EPA. The role of these agencies is primarily advisory during registration application review and program administration. However, if pesticide use affects the regulatory jurisdiction of these agencies, they will be involved in response and enforcement actions. In addition, as discussed later in this chapter, county agricultural commissioners are directly involved in regulation of pesticide applications in the county.

The state pesticide registration process essentially duplicates the federal program, however, the state uses more specific criteria in determining the registrability or to continue a registration. For example, if safer or less destructive alternatives to registration of the proposed pesticide are available, it may not be registered. Similarly, the state reviews efficacy (effectiveness) more intently than EPA and, finally, the state may cancel registrations for failure to conduct required testing specified by the 1984 Birth Defects Prevention Act [Food and Agriculture Code §§13121-130] or the 1985 Pesticide Contamination Prevention Act [Food and Agriculture Code §§13141-152]. These two statutes were enacted to require registrants of older pesticides registered in California to address current "data gaps" as compared to more current pre-registration testing requirements in the area of health effects and potential for groundwater contamination. These two statutes represent an aggressive and accelerated version of EPA's pesticide re-registration and data call-in program.

The state also designates pesticides as restricted materials (a longer list than the federal one) [3 CCR §§6400, et seq.] and environmentally harmful materials [3 CCR §2470]. Restricted pesticides may be used only pursuant to a permit issued by a county agricultural commissioner.

Pesticides are the subject of a groundwater monitoring program conducted by Cal/EPA and, if detected as a result of lawful activities, the registration may be canceled. Pesticides also may be subject to regulation as toxic air contaminants (Chapter 5) in a process in which the pesticide unit of Cal/EPA evaluates the substance in similar fashion as other toxic air contaminants.

Pesticides are subject to annual renewal which is normally routine and requires payment of a fee, but can be the occasion for a regulatory review. State review of pesticide labels is somewhat limited in that the state may not prescribe different labeling than approved by EPA.

- **Enforcement and Penalties.** Violation of the state's pesticide laws are punishable by civil and criminal sanctions. Civil penalties of up to $10,000 per violation may be imposed administratively by Cal/EPA or by the attorney general. If the violation is intentional and

Chapter 12

created a hazard to human health, the environment or crops, or a second or subsequent offense, the maximum penalty is $25,000. If the state does not prosecute, county agriculture commissioners may levy administrative civil penalties not to exceed $500 per violation. Criminal violations may alternatively be prosecuted, which may result upon conviction of a misdemeanor fines of not less than $500, nor more than $5,000 and imprisonment of up to six months in the county jail. Second or subsequent offenses are punishable as misdemeanors with fines of not less than $1,000 nor more than $10,000 and imprisonment of up to six months. If the violation is intentional or negligent and reasonably creates a hazard to human health or the environment, penalties include a fine of not less than $5,000 nor more than $50,000 and imprisonment for up to one year.

◆ Pesticide Businesses and Applicators

California pesticide laws include extensive provisions regulating those in various pesticide-related businesses and applicators of pesticides. The activities not specifically regulated are application of preservatives, household use, or use by industrial sanitation services and seed treatment. Otherwise a person may not be in the business of pest control without a current agricultural pest control license. Demonstration of financial responsibility also must be made. Applications are processed and licenses granted by Cal/EPA. Licensees must register with the county agricultural commissioner and keep records on properties treated and other information required.

- If engaged in **aerial application,** the pilot must hold a pest control aircraft pilot's certificate and register in the county in which applications are made.

- **Agricultural Pest Control Advisors** who recommend pesticides for agricultural or non-agricultural use, and solicit for services or sales related to pesticides must be licensed by the Department of Food and Agriculture based on application and examination. Pest Control Advisors also must register with the county commissioner. Activities of advisors are prescribed in terms of providing written recommendation with copies to the customer and the pesticide dealer, including specified information.

- **Pesticide dealers** are persons who sell pesticides or pest control devices for agricultural use, solicit pesticide sales by making recommendations, and sell restricted materials that require a permit for possession or use. Dealers must hold a license from the Food and Agriculture Department issued upon application and demonstrated familiarity with the pesticide laws and regulations. Pest control advisors do not need to be separately licensed as dealers. Dealers are required to verify that the persons purchasing pesticides are licensed to possess and use the product. This is particularly relevant with respect to use of restricted pesticides.

- **Structural pest control operators** are regulated by the Structural Pest Control Board under authority of the Business and Professions Code §§8505, et seq. An examination is prerequisite to an operator's license.

If a violation of the pesticide law is committed by any person subject to these programs, their license may be suspended by county agricultural commissioners and the department. Each violation is subject to administrative civil liability not exceeding $500; criminal violations can be prosecuted as misdemeanors with a fine of not less than $100 nor more than $1,000 and imprisonment of not less than ten days nor more than six months.

- **Pesticide applications** are subject to the conditions governing the specific product's registration as indicated on the label and other product literature. These include application rates, pests controlled, use or prohibitions on particular crops, fruits and other precautions. It is a violation of state and federal law to use any pesticide in a manner inconsistent with the product's label or to use a restricted pesticide without permit from the county agricultural commissioner. Agricultural field workers and employees who apply pesticides are protected by compliance with requirements which govern field re-entry interval and regulations for worker health and safety [3 CCR §6770, et seq.]. These worker safety measures include:

- Employees who apply pesticides must be trained and wear appropriate protective clothing and equipment.

- Field supervisors must be informed of symptoms of overexposure.

- Employees must be aware of how to obtain emergency medical treatment.

- Employers must provide immediate medical treatment for workers with pesticide illness symptoms.

- Warning signs must be used to warn workers of treated fields.

The penalties which apply to violations of these provision are listed above.

◆ Fertilizing Materials

Fertilizer materials include commercial fertilizers manufactured from mineral or chemical materials, plant or animal by-products, including sewage sludge and naturally occurring minerals. These materials are regulated by the Department of Food and Agriculture to assure the quality, identification and representations made about the fertilizer material to consumers. [Food and Agriculture Code §41501 et seq.]

- **Facility licenses** must be obtained and annually renewed for each facility which manufactures or distributes fertilizer materials unless materials being distributed bear the label of a current licensee.

- **Each fertilizer material must be registered** and annually renewed. The registration application includes the name of the registrants and other information about the analysis of nutrients or ingredients, sources of the fertilizer material and labeling. The department tests fertilizer materials to verify label claims and ingredient, as well as to screen for toxic contaminants.

- **Violations** for failure to register a fertilizer material are penalized with a fine of up to $500 for the first offense and prosecution for a misdemeanor and a fine of not less than $500 and up to $1,000 for subsequent offenses.

◆ Radiation Sources and Producing Equipment

The California Department of Health Services regulates ionizing and non-ionizing sources of radiation to the extent authorized by the federal Nuclear Regulatory Commission. The California Radiation Control Law [Health and Safety Code §§25800, et seq.] and the regulations of the Department [17 CCR §30100, et seq.] govern the regulatory program for any person who is licensed to receive or possesses radioactive materials, as defined, and not exempted. County health departments are authorized to participate in the regulatory process in their jurisdiction based on a memorandum of understanding with the department. The regulatory program includes a licensing requirement, payment of fees, inspections, employee exposure controls and monitoring, and facility and administrative requirements. It is outside of the scope of this handbook to cover in any greater detail the state's regulatory program on radiation sources. If, based on this discussion, a facility may be covered, it is urged to consult the regulations and seek competent professional advice.

◆ Noise

Noise, defined as "excessive and undesirable sound," is considered to be an environmental problem in that it degrades human comfort and enjoyment and may impair ecosystems. Consequently, noise has been the subject of regulation and civil remedies under the general proscription of nuisances and in a more predictable way by statutory programs designed to regulate noise producing activities, equipment and vehicles. In 1972, Congress passed the Noise Control Act [42 USC 4901-4918], which established a model noise regulatory program administered by EPA. The act pre-empts state or local action on a source, which is not identical to the federal standard. However, it allows states and local jurisdictions to use other regulatory measures, including permitting, to enforce stricter noise standards than the federal preemption.

- **The federal act** prohibits the following:

    ✔ Distribution or importation of any new product which does not comply with a noise regulation.

    ✔ Removal or modification of any device which would cause a product to fail to comply with an applicable noise regulation.

    ✔ Use of a product which has been so modified.

    ✔ Distribution of a product not in compliance with a noise labeling requirement.

    ✔ Failure to comply with any order or other noise-related requirement.

- **Noise emission standards** have been issued for a number of types of equipment. Interstate railroad carrier standards for locomotives, rail cars, retarders, car coupling and others are at 40 CFR 201, et seq. Standards for interstate motor carriers are set forth at 40 CFR 202, et seq. Standards for construction equipment are set forth at 40 CFR 204, et seq.; and for Transportation Equipment at 40 CFR 205.

Penalties for violation of federal standards include an administrative civil penalty not to exceed $10,000 per day of violation or criminal penalties of up to $25,000 per day and by imprisonment of up to one year. A private cause of action is available for suits against violators of the federal act who are not being diligently prosecuted by the government in addition to other remedies which are available.

In 1973, the California Noise Control Act was enacted. The act established the Office of Noise Control within the Department of Health Services, which is responsible for coordinating the state's noise control program at the state and local level and interfacing with the federal noise control program. The state act encourages and provides technical assistance to local government noise control programs, which include adoption of noise control ordinances, enforcement programs and inclusion of a noise element in the local government's general plan.

State action to limit noise in some areas involves adoptions of federal standards as state requirements, as in the case of noise limitations for aircraft landings. Any aircraft which entered service after January 1, 1972 in California may not exceed the federal standards. [Health and Safety Code §24181.] In addition, state standards have been set for aircraft operation under a permit from the federal Department of Transportation to encourage cooperative solutions to reduce noise in impacted communities around airports. [21 CCR §§5000, et seq.] **Motor vehicles** are regulated under the Vehicle Code in California which implements the federal noise control standards for motor vehicles as well as additional state provisions designed to address gaps in the federal standards; for example, for off-the-road vehicles. Motor boats and outboard motors are also subject to noise standards set forth in Harbors and Navigation Code §654.05.

Violations of the noise control standards are penalized in accordance with the enforcement provisions of the agency responsible; for example, Department of Motor Vehicles or the local ordinance of the community.

◆ Regulation of Ozone-Depleting Substances

The use of chlorofluorocarbons (CFCs) and other so-called ozone-depleting substances in manufactured products as well as in air conditioners and other refrigeration systems, fire extinguishers and other uses subjects many businesses to federal regulations adopted in response to the Clean Air Act.

In September 1987, the United States signed the *Montreal Protocol on Substances that Deplete the Ozone Layer*. Subsequent amendments to the Clean Air Act promulgated in 1990 authorized EPA to accelerate the initial phase-out date for CFCs and other chemicals listed on the following page. These dates have been accelerated by both amendments to the treaty and regulatory action by the U.S. Environmental Protection Agency.

Further revisions to the CFC phase-out regulations are under consideration at the time of this printing, with a final rule expected by November 1993 effective in 1994.

The phase-out of CFCs and the other substances means that refrigerant manufacturers and distributors, paint manufacturers and other such businesses will need to address the use of alternative substances. Moreover, given its widespread use as a soil fumigant and in commodity quarantine programs, the phase-out of methyl bromide could have far-reaching effects on the agricultural industry in California.

In the interim, however, California businesses also will need to comply with certain other related regulations implemented to meet federal Clean Air Act regulations. These requirements concern product and equipment labeling and equipment maintenance and removal.

Substance	*Phase-out Deadline*
Halon	January 1, 1994
Chlorofluorocarbons (CFCs)	January 1, 1996
Methyl Chloroform (1,1,1-Trichloroethane)	January 1, 1996
Carbon Tetrachloride	January 1, 1996
Hydrofluorocarbons	January 1, 1996
Hydrochlorofluorocarbons (HCFCs)	January 1, 2000
Methyl Bromide	January 1, 2000

- **Labeling.** As part of phase-out regulations for CFCs and other ozone-depleting substances, federal EPA adopted label warning requirements beginning on May 15, 1993. These warnings are required on all containers in which Class I depleters (CFCs, halon, 1,1,1-TCA, carbon tetrachloride) and Class II depleters (hydrochlorofluoro-carbons) are used, stored or transported or if a product was manufactured using such a substance.

  Each container or product must bear the following statement:

  > *Warning: Contains (or manufactured with, if applicable)*
  > *(substance)*
  > *which harms public health and environment*
  > *by destroying ozone in the upper atmosphere.*

  The warning must be placed on the container in a manner considered "legible and conspicuous" according to the following specifications:

  ✔ Statement may appear on the label display plan.

  ✔ If the product or container is normally packaged or otherwise covered, the warning must appear on the outer packaging.

  ✔ Warnings may be placed on a tag, tape, card or sticker attached to the container.

  ✔ When products or containers are not viewed by the purchaser at time of purchase, statements can be placed on display or promotional printed material.

✔ The statement must appear in sharp contrast to any background on which it appears and must be blocked within a square or rectangle.

The mere presence of such labels on products or equipment may *seriously* affect businesses in California, given that many persons may not accept products which have this label (environmentally conscientious consumers, for example). Therefore, the pressure to find alternatives will increase and may accelerate the above schedule.

● Another regulatory area pertaining to ozone-depleters could affect businesses that service, repair and dispose of appliances. By definition appliances include air conditioners, refrigerators or freezers. These rules specify that no person maintaining, servicing, repairing or disposing of appliances may release any CFC or other ozone-depleting substance into the environment.

During maintenance and other covered refrigerant removal operations, all persons performing such tasks *must:*

✔ First evacuate all the refrigerant into a recovery or recycling machine to specific levels set for the type of equipment and substance used.

✔ Ensure the use of a *certified* recovery device in accordance with manufacturer's directions.

✔ Verify the refrigerant has been evacuated from the equipment before disposal. This requires a signed statement from the maintenance person or the person from whom the equipment is obtained that all refrigerant has been removed using a recovery or recycling system.

✔ Refrigerant can be returned to the equipment from which it came or other equipment owned by the same person without being recycled.

This regulation went into effect on July 13, 1993. These regulations can be found at 40 CFR Part 82.

Professions Regulated Under California Environmental Law

California environmental laws and the state's established system for regulating professions to protect consumers and enforce professional standards in certain disciplines have merged to produce a number of regulatory programs that govern the persons who provide professional services in the environmental field. In some cases, these programs are voluntary; in others, mandatory. Covered professionals should be cognizant of the requirements or face possible violations.

◆ Registered Environmental Assessors and Environmental Health Specialists

The voluntary registration of Environmental Assessors was established by the Environmental Quality Assessment Act of 1986 [Health and Safety Code §25570]. The program is administered by the

Secretary of Environmental Affairs (now Cal/EPA). Applicants are screened for the required experience and credentials and placed on a list according to their area of specialty which is disseminated upon request by the state. In 1989, the program was amended to recognize that Registered Environmental Health Specialists who meet the requirements of that profession [Health and Safety Code §514] also are recognized as environmental assessors.

◆ Underground Storage Tank Integrity Testers

Persons who test underground storage tanks after January 1, 1989 (see Chapter 7) for leakage are required to be licensed by the State Water Resources Control Board [Health and Safety Code §25284.4]. Regulations issued by the board [23 CCR §2730] require an application, demonstration of credentials and an examination. Tank tester business practices are also regulated under this regulation. Violations are punishable by administrative penalties of up to $500 or civil liability of up to $2,500 per day.

◆ Underground Storage Tank Contractors Engaged in Hazardous Substance Removal

Following a requirement in the Business and Professions Code [§7058.7], the State Contractors Licensing Board has established a specialty license for hazardous substance removal contractors. The contractors subject to this requirement have been general engineering and excavation contractors engaged in hazardous waste site cleanups. Beginning in January 1992, any person who bids work associated with underground storage tanks also is required to hold this license [Business and Professions Code §7058.7(e)]. Penalties for violations of this requirement are a $3,000 fine for the first offense and $5,000 for subsequent violations.

◆ Asbestos Abatement Contractors and Consultants

The field of asbestos inspections, problem management and abatement or removal is extensively regulated in California. Persons involved in this work must not only meet regulatory requirements that govern the safety and health of the workers and specific procedures of the project, but also professional credentials that must be held by those engaged in asbestos-related work.

- **Asbestos abatement contractors** must hold the specialty license in asbestos abatement from the State Contractors Licensing Board [Business and Professions Code §7058.5]. These contractors and any other employer involved in an asbestos project that disturbs more than 100 square feet of asbestos-containing material also must register with Cal/OSHA [Business and Professions Code §7058.6].

- **Asbestos consultants** are defined as "any person who contracts to provide professional health and safety services relating to asbestos-containing materials." Asbestos consultants must be licensed by Cal/OSHA after January 1, 1991.

The law provides for penalties of $3,000 for first violations and $5,000 for each subsequent violation.

◆ Registered Geologists

In many cases, state or local agencies will require a registered geologist (or professional civil engineer with soil specialty) to perform certain work associated with soil or groundwater contamination. This is due to the Business and Professional Code definition [§7872] of the practice of geology or geophysics, which excludes anyone other than a state-registered geologist from engaging in such work.

To an increasing extent, concern over the quality of technical work, the reliability of data reported in an environmental matter and consumer protection has led to regulation of environmental professionals. This is a trend likely to continue.

◆ Laboratories that Test Hazardous Wastes

Any laboratory engaged in hazardous waste testing must receive certification through the Department of Health Services [22 CCR §§67440.1, et seq.]. The laboratory must demonstrate compliance with specified requirements for test categories; quality assurance; laboratory equipment; analytical procedures; and personnel qualifications. The laboratory also must demonstrate competence in analyzing proficiency/test samples. A certified hazardous waste testing lab must file for certification renewal no later than three months before the certificate expiration date. Facilities that use laboratory services to test for hazardous waste characteristics must be certain the lab used is certified or the results will not be valid in an investigation.

Regulating Business Practices Under Environmental Laws

◆ Corporate Criminal Liability Act

This new law, effective January 1, 1991, established a new section of the Penal Code — Dangerous Business Practices (§387) which imposes personal criminal liability for *actual knowledge of a serious or concealed danger* in a product or business practice, unless, within 15 days or immediately if imminent risk of great bodily harm or death exists, Cal/OSHA is notified and affected employees warned in writing.

The definition of "serious concealed danger" with respect to a product or business practice is when the normal or reasonably foreseeable use of, or the exposure of an individual to, the product or business practice creates a substantial probability of death, great bodily harm, or serious exposure, and the danger is not readily apparent to the individual likely to be exposed.

Penalties for violations are up to three years imprisonment and a $25,000 fine payable upon conviction by the responsible manager; corporate penalties can be as much as $1 million.

Given the relative recent enactment of this statute and the controversy surrounding its interpretation, there is no clear understanding of how it may apply to environmental and chemical regulations described in the guide. However, it reconfirms the general premise that California environmental requirements and enforcement are becoming substantially more stringent.

◆ Unfair Business Practices

Under the state Business and Professions Code §17200, it is illegal to conduct any business in any unfair or unlawful manner. This provision has been successfully employed in prosecutions by the state and local district attorneys for environmental violations on the theory that it is unfair competition when one business complies and another does not. Therefore, the charges filed against a business for an environmental violation can be augmented by violation of this provision of the Business and Professions Code, which carries a maximum penalty of up to $2,500 per violation.

◆ Environmental Representations (misleading advertising prohibition)

One of the most controversial statutes recently enacted by the California Legislature was AB 3994 [Business and Professions Code §§17508.5 and 17580, et seq.] which prohibits "environmental representations" unless the person making such claims can satisfy the fair trade rules of the Federal Trade Commission or the requirements of the statute. Environmental representations include such statements as: "ozone friendly," or any term connoting that stratospheric ozone is not being depleted, "biodegradable," photodegradable," recyclable," or "recycled;" or which connotes that it is not harmful to, or is beneficial to, the natural environment through the use of such terms as "environmental choice," "ecologically friendly," "earth friendly," "environmentally friendly," "ecologically sound," "environmentally sound," "environmentally safe," "ecologically safe," "environmentally lite," "green product," or any other like term. In order to lawfully make these representations, the statute specifies that the person making such statements shall maintain the following information in writing:

- The reasons why the person believes the representation to be true.

- Any significant adverse environmental impacts directly associated with the production, distribution, use and disposal of the product.

- Any measures taken by the person to reduce the environmental impacts directly associated with the production, distribution and disposal of the product.

- Violations of any federal, state or local permits directly associated with the production or distribution of the consumer product.

- If applicable, whether the consumer good meets the definitions of "recycled," "recyclable," "biodegradable," "photodegradable" or "ozone friendly," as defined in the statute.

This information must be furnished to the state or any member of the public upon request.

The penalty for violating this statute, upon conviction, is imprisonment in the county jail not to exceed six months and a fine not to exceed $2,500.

This statute signals the state's intent in policing not only environmental regulatory compliance, but also use of environmental claims and advertising in a manner that cannot be supported or is misleading. Vendors of products in California should maintain a watch on how the state and local prosecutors enforce this statute to curb "green advertising."

Compliance with the environmental and professional regulatory programs and enforcement provisions described in this chapter is not subject to description in the form of a simple checklist. Facilities and vendors of products and services should review the information in this chapter, determine if it may apply to their operations or products and, if so, obtain the needed information to comply. Statutes and regulations can be ordered as indicated in Chapter 2.

Appendix 12-1
Applicable Laws and Regulations
Regulated Products, Activities, Professions
and Business Practices

State Laws

Pesticide Manufacturing and Distribution   Food and Agriculture Code §§11401-15201
- Registration and Regulation of   Food and Agriculture Code §§14281-14390
  Economic Poisons
- Birth Defects Prevention Act   Food and Agriculture Code §§13127-13130
- Pesticide Contamination Prevention   Food and Agriculture Code §§13141-13152
  Act

Pesticide Businesses and Applicators
- Agricultural Pest Control Advisor   Food and Agriculture Code §§12001-12021
  Registration, Fees
- Pesticide Dealer Licensing   Food and Agriculture Code §§12103-12113
- Pesticide Applicator Licensing and   Food and Agriculture Code §§12201-12205 and
  Certifications   §§14151-14155
- Aerial Applicator Regulation   Food and Agriculture Code §§11901-11924

Fertilizing Materials   Food and Agriculture Code §§14501-14622

Radiation Sources & Radiation-Producing Equipment
- California Radiation Control Law   Health and Safety Code §§25800, et seq.

Noise Producing Activities & Products
- Aircraft Noise   Health and Safety Code §24181
- Motor Vehicle Noise   Vehicle Code §27200

Registered Environmental Assessors   Health and Safety Code §25570

Underground Storage Tank Integrity Tester Licensing   Health and Safety Code §25284.4

Underground Storage Tank Contractors   Business and Professions Code §7058.7

Asbestos Abatement Contractors and Consultants   Business and Professions Code §70281,
                                                            §§7058.5-7058.6 and §§7180-7185

Corporate Criminal Liability Act   Penal Code §387

Product Representation as Environmentally Safe   Business and Professions Code §§17508.5 and
                                                            17580-17581

Federal Laws

Chemical Product Manufacture and Importation
- Toxic Substances Control Act   15 USC §§2601-2671

Hazardous Substances Information
- Hazardous Substances Act   21 USC §§1261, et seq.
- Poison Prevention Packaging Act   15 USC §§1471, et seq.

Pesticide Manufacturing and Distribution
- Federal Insecticide, Fungicide and   7 USC §136
  Rodenticide Act (FIFRA)

Noise-Producing Activities and Products
- Federal Noise Control Act   42 USC §§4901-4918

State Regulations

Hazardous Substances Information
- Hazard Communication   8 CCR §5194
- Proposition 65 Warnings   8 CCR §5194(b)

Pesticide Manufacturing and Distribution
- Pesticide Regulatory Program   3 CCR §§6000-6141
- Pesticide Restricted Materials   3 CCR §§6400-6402

Pesticide Businesses and Applicators
- Agricultural Pest Control Advisors   3 CCR §§6550-6556
- Pesticide Applicator Licenses   3 CCR §§6560-6574
- Aerial Applicator Regulation   3 CCR §§ 6540-6544

Fertilizing Materials
- Standards and Labeling   3 CCR §§ 2300-2313
- Classification of Materials   3 CCR §§ 2314-2315

Radiation Sources & Radiation Producing   17 CCR §§30180-30485
Equipment

Noise Producing Activities and Products   8 CCR §5095 and 21 CCR §§5000, et seq.

Underground Storage Tank Integrity Testers   23 CCR §2730

State-Certified Laboratories   22 CCR §§67440.1-67440.7

Federal Regulations

- Chemical Product Manufacture and   40 CFR §§717, 720 and 721
  Importation Reports of Allegations
  that Chemical Substances Cause
  Significant Adverse Reactions to
  Health or the Environment

Hazardous Substances Information
- Hazard Communication   29 CFR §1910.1200
- Noise Producing Activities and   40 CFR §201-205
  Products

Regulation of Ozone-Depleting Substances
- Labeling Requirements   40 CFR §82.102
- Servicing Refrigeration Equipment   40 CFR §82.152

Order Form
Environmental Compliance

Exhibit A

Firm or Company Name _____

Your Name _____ Telephone _____

Street Address_____

City/State/Zip _____

CODE SEGMENT	TYPE	CODE	PRICE	QTY	TOTAL
Title 8, Industrial Relations--Complete Title	Basic Code	08 00 000	$210		
(requires 4 binders)	Amendments	08 00 001	$240		
*Title 8 on diskette	Diskette	08 50031	$ 75		
Title 17, Public Health-Complete Title with Index	Basic Code	17 00 000	$ 78		
	Amendments	17 00 001	$165		
Title 19, Public Safety-Complete Title with Index	Basic Code	19 00 000	$ 30		
	Amendments	19 00 001	$ 55		
Title 22, Social Security- Complete Title with Index	Basic Code	22 00 000	$235		
(requires 5 binders)	Amendments	22 00 001	$325		
Title 23, Waters-Complete Title	Basic Code	23 00 000	$ 40		
	Amendments	23 00 001	$ 56		
Title 26, Toxics with Index	Basic Code	26 00 000	$175		
(requires 3 binders)	Amendments	26 00 001	$240		
*Title 26 0n Diskette	Diskette	26 50 031	$ 75		
Binders for Barclays Official California Code of Regulations	Each	99 90 000	$ 18.50		
Shipping and Handling charges are $4.00 per copy ordered			$ 4.00		

* *Available with purchase of Amendment Service only. Updated 4x a year.*

Sub total _____

(Basic Code only) 8.25% Sales Tax _____

(Basic Code only) Shipping and Handling _____

Binders (if ordered) _____

GRAND TOTAL $ _____

PAYMENT MUST ACCOMPANY ORDER

Mail this form to:
Barclays Law Publishers
P. O. Box 3066
South San Francisco, CA 94083-3066
OR for faster service, call 244-6611

Two ways to Access Barclays Official California Code of Regulations:

1. 900 On-line Service: This unique on-line service lets you search the complete, most up-to-date version of the code using any IBM PC or IBM compatible computer equipped with a modem. There is no membership fee to pay, simply a 900 telephone charge of $2 per minute billed directly through your phone service. Call (415) 244-6611 for free software to access the Code.

2. Electronic Index on CD-ROM: Search the full text of the entire Code for any subject, word, or combination of words in record time. If you would like to preview this powerful tool, call our Client Services Department at (415) 244-6611, and we will send you a sample CD-ROM to preview.

217

California Environmental Protection Agency

Air Resources Board ● Department of Pesticide Regulation ● Department of Toxic Substances Control ● Integrated Waste Management Board
Office of Environmental Health Hazard Assessment ● State Water Resources Control Board ● Regional Water Quality Control Boards

Pete Wilson

James M. Strock

Secretary for Environmental Protection

November 1992

Revised February 1993

CHEMICAL CROSS-INDEX

RECEIVED JUN - 3 1993

The Hazardous Materials Data Management Program is committed to improving the collection, management and dissemination of toxics-related information. The office contracted with the University of California, Davis in 1988 to compile a cross-index of hazardous chemicals regulated by various state and federal agencies. The cross-index (also known as List of Lists) shows, which of the 14 programs is regulating the chemicals. Our current "List of Lists", updated as of November 1992, covers the categories listed on the following page.

Please be aware of new changes on the List of Lists. The List of Lists now shows an (*) asterisk at the beginning of some chemicals. This symbol indicates that a new chemical has been added to the List. The (+) plus signs indicate a chemical on the list has been added to a regulatory program. The (-) minus signs indicate that a particular chemical has been taken off a regulatory program's list.

There is no charge for a hardcopy listing. A floppy disk copy of the list (ASCII Format, 5-1/4, 360K) is available for $20.00.

Send your request with your check to the following address. Checks should be made payable to the **Hazardous Materials Data Management Program**:

> **Cal/EPA**
> **Hazardous Materials Data Management Program**
> **555 Capitol Mall, Suite 235**
> **Sacramento, CA 95814**

This list is updated approximately every six months. Suggestions are welcome regarding additional chemical regulatory programs to incorporate into the list.

If you have questions or comments, contact the Cal/EPA Help Desk at (916) 327-1848.

555 Capitol Mall, Suite 235 ● Sacramento, California 95814 ● 916) 445-3846 ● Fax (916) 445-6401

Printed on recycled paper

CALIFORNIA ENVIRONMENTAL PROTECTION AGENCY
CHEMICAL LIST OF LISTS - BY CHEMICAL NAME

Key to the headings in List of Lists

A: CALIFORNIA OSHA CARCINOGEN USER REGISTER CHEMICALS
     Ref: California Occupational Safety and Health Dept.
     (415) 703-3631 Date of List Jun 1990

B: EPA LIST OF PRIORITY POLLUTANTS
     Ref: Environmental Protection Agency (EPA)
     (415) 744-1911 Date of List Jul 1990

C: AB 1803 - WELL MONITORING CHEMICALS
     Ref: California Department of Health Services
     (916) 323-6111 Date of List Sept 1992

D: SARA SECTION 313 TOXIC CHEMICALS
     Ref: EPA Emergency Planning and Community Right-to-Know Act,
     Section 313 (800) 535-0202 Date of List Jan 1991

E: SARA SECTION 302 EXTREMELY HAZARDOUS SUBSTANCES
     Ref: EPA Emergency Planning and Community Right-to-Know Act,
     Section 302 (800) 535-0202 Date of List Jan 1992

F: MCL (MAXIMUM CONTAMINANTS LEVELS) LIST OF CONTAMINANTS
     Ref: California Department of Health Services
     (510) 540-2177 Date of List Oct 1990

G: AB 2588 - AIR TOXICS "HOT SPOTS" CHEMICALS
     Ref: California Air Resources Board
     (916) 322-8278 Date of List Jan 1992

H: DHS DRINKING WATER ACTION LEVELS
     Ref: California Department of Health Services
     (510) 540-2177 Date of List Oct 1990

I: AB 1807 - TOXIC AIR CONTAMINANTS
     Ref: California Air Resources Board
     (916) 322-8278 Date of List Mar 1991

J: NESHAP (NATIONAL EMISSION STANDARD FOR HAZARDOUS AIR POLLUTANTS)
     SPECIFIC CHEMICALS
     Ref: EPA Office of Air Quality Planning and Standards
     (919) 541-5647 Date of List Mar 1989

K: PROPOSITION 65 CHEMICALS
     Ref: Office of Evironmental Health Hazard Assessment
     (916) 445-6900 Date of List Oct 1992

L: DOT INHALATION HAZARD CHEMICALS
     Ref: Department of Transportation
     (916) 327-3310 Date of List Jul 1991

M: PERMISSIBLE EXPOSURE LIMITS FOR CHEMICAL CONTAMINANTS
     Ref: Department of Industrial Relations
     (415) 703-4050 Date of List June 1991

N: HAZARDOUS SUBSTANCES LIST (AKA "THE DIRECTOR'S LIST)
     Ref: Department of Industrial Relations (CAL/OSHA)
     (415) 703-4050 Date of List May 1990

NEW CHEMICAL (+ *)	CHEMICAL NAME	CAS NUMBER	A	B	C	D	E	F	G	H	I	J	K	L	M	N
	1,1,1,2-TETRACHLORO-2,2-DIFLUOROETHANE	76-11-9													M	N
	1,1,1,2-TETRACHLOROETHANE	630-20-6			C											
	1,1,1-TRICHLOROETHANE	71-55-6		B	C	D		F	G			J			M	N
	1,1,2,2-TETRACHLORO-1,2-DIFLUOROETHANE (FC 112)	76-12-0		B	C	D		F	G						M	N
	1,1,2,2-TETRACHLOROETHANE	79-34-5		B	C	D		F	G			J	K		M	N
	1,1,2-TRICHLORO-1,2,2-TRIFLUOROETHANE	761-31-3	SEE CHLORINATED FLUOROCARBON (FREON 113)													
	1,1,2-TRICHLOROETHANE	79-00-5		B	C	D		F	G			J			M	N
	1,1-DICHLORO-1-NITROETHANE	594-72-9														
	1,1-DICHLOROETHANE	75-34-3		B	C	D		F	G			J	K		M	N
	1,1-DICHLOROETHYLENE	75-35-4		B	C	D		F	G			J			M	N
	1,1-DIMETHYLHYDRAZINE	57-14-7				D	E		G		I	J	K	L	M	N
	1,12-BENZOPERYLENE	191-24-2	SEE BENZO(GHI)PERYLENE													
	1,2,3-TRICHLOROPROPANE	96-18-4		B		D			G			J	+		M	N
	1,2,4-TRICHLOROBENZENE	120-82-1		B	C	D			G			J			M	+
	1,2,4-TRIMETHYL BENZENE	95-63-6														
	1,2,5,6-DIBENZANTHRACENE	53-70-3	SEE DIBENZO(A,H)ANTHRACENE													
	1,2-BENZANTHRACENE	56-55-3	SEE BENZO[A]ANTHRACENE													
	1,2-BUTYLENE OXIDE	106-88-7				D			G			J				
	1,2-DIBROMO-3-CHLOROPROPANE (DBCP)	96-12-8	SEE DIBROMOCHLOROPROPANE													
	1,2-DIBROMOETHANE	106-93-4	SEE EDB													
	1,2-DICHLOROBENZENE	95-50-1		B	C	D			G	H					M	+
	1,2-DICHLOROETHANE	107-06-2		B	C	D		F	G		I		K	L	M	+
	1,2-DICHLOROETHYLENE	540-59-0		B	C	D			G						M	+
	1,2-DICHLOROPROPANE	78-87-5		B	C	+		F	G			J	K		M	N
	1,2-DICHLOROTETRAFLUOROETHANE;FLUOROCARBON 114	76-14-2													M	N
	1,2-DIETHYLHYDRAZINE	1615-80-1							G				K		M	N
	1,2-DIMETHYLHYDRAZINE	540-73-8				D			G				K	L	M	N
	1,2-DIPHENYLHYDRAZINE	122-66-7		B		D			G			J	K		M	+
	1,2-EPOXYBUTANE	106-88-7							G							
	1,2-TRANS-DICHLOROETHYLENE	156-60-5	SEE TRANS-1,2-DICHLOROETHYLENE													
	1,3,5-TRIMETHYLBENZENE	108-67-8													M	+
	1,3-BUTADIENE	106-99-0				D			G				K		M	N
	1,3-DICHLORO-5,5-DIMETHYL-HYDANTOIN	118-52-5				D			G		I				M	N

221

CALIFORNIA ENVIRONMENTAL PROTECTION AGENCY
CHEMICAL LIST OF LISTS - BY CHEMICAL NAME

NEW CHEMICAL	CHEMICAL NAME	CAS NUMBER	A	B	C	D	E	F	G	H	I	J	K	L	M	N
	1,3-DICHLOROBENZENE	541-73-1		B	C	D			G	H						*
	1,3-DICHLOROPROPENE	542-75-6	SEE 1,3-DICHLOROPROPYLENE													N
	1,3-DICHLOROPROPYLENE	542-75-6		B		D		F	G			J	K		M	*
	1,3-DIMETHYLBUTYL ACETATE	108-84-9										J			M	*
	1,3-PROPANE SULTONE	1120-71-4	SEE PROPANE SULTONE													+
	1,4-BUTANEDIOL DIMETHANESUFONATE (MYLERAN)	55-98-1							G				K			+
	1,4-DICHLORO-2-BUTENE	764-41-0		B	C	D			G				K			+
	1,4-DICHLOROBENZENE	106-46-7		B	C	D		F	G		I		K		M	+
	1,4-DIOXANE	123-91-1				D			G				K		M	N
*	1,5-NAPHTHALENEDIAMINE	2243-62-1							G				K			
	1,6-DINITROPYRENE	42397-64-8							G				K			+
	1,8-DINITROPYRENE	42397-65-9							G			J	K			+
	1-(2-CHLOROETHYL)-3-(4-METHYLCYCLOHEXYL)-1-NITROSOUREA (METHYL CCNU)	13909-09-6							G				K			N
	1-(2-CHLOROETHYL)-3-CYCLOHEXYL-1-NITROSOUREA	13010-47-4							G				K			
	1-AMINO-2-METHYLANTHRAQUINONE	82-28-0				D			G				K			+
	1-BUTANETHIOL	109-79-5	SEE BUTYL MERCAPTAN													
	1-BUTANOL	71-36-3	SEE N-BUTYL ALCOHOL													N
	1-CHLORO-1-NITROPROPANE	600-25-9													M	
	1-NAPHTHYLAMINE	134-32-7	SEE ALPHA-NAPHTHYLAMINE													
	1-NITROPROPANE	108-03-2														N
	1-NITROPYRENE	5522-43-0							G							
	1-[(5-NITROFURFURYLIDENE)-AMINO]-2-IMIDAZOLIDINONE	555-84-0							G				K			+
	11,12-BENZOFLUORANTHENE	207-08-9	SEE BENZO(K)FLUORANTHENE													N
	11-AMINOUNDECANOIC ACID	2432-99-7														
	2,2'-AZOBISISOBUTYRONITRILE DECOMPOSITION PRODUCT	3333-52-6	SEE TETRAMETHYL SUCCINONITRILE													N
	2,2'-BIOXIRANE	1464-53-5	SEE DIEPOXYBUTANE													
	2,2,4-TRIMETHYLPENTANE	540-84-1										J				
	2,2-DICHLOROPROPIONIC ACID	75-99-0													M	N
	2,3,7,8-TETRACHLORODIBENZO-P-DIOXIN (TCDD)	1746-01-6		B									K			+
*	2,3-DICHLOROPROPENE	78-88-6				D			G			J				
	2,4 D-ESTERS	94-11-1														N
	2,4,5-T	93-76-5														N
	2,4,5-T AMINES	6369-96-6													M	N

NEW CHEMICAL	CHEMICAL NAME	CAS NUMBER	A	B	C	D	E	F	G	H	I	J	K	L	M	N
	2,4,5-T ESTERS	93-79-8														N
	2,4,5-T ESTERS	1928-47-8														N
	2,4,5-T SALT	13560-99-1														N
	2,4,5-TP ACID (SILVEX)	93-72-1						F								N
*	2,4,5-TRICHLOROPHENOL	95-95-4			C			F	G							N
	2,4,5-TRIMETHYLANILINE	137-17-7				D			G			J				+
	2,4,6-TRICHLOROPHENOL	88-06-2		B	C	D			G			J				+
	2,4,6-TRINITROTOLUENE	118-96-7											K		M	N
	2,4-D [ACETIC ACID (2,4-DICHLOROPHENOXY)-]	94-75-7			C	D		F	G							+
	2,4-DB; 2,4-DICHLORO-PHENOXYBUTYRIC ACID	94-82-6													M	N
	2,4-DIAMINOANISOLE	615-05-4				D			G			J	K			+
	2,4-DIAMINOANISOLE SULFATE	39156-41-7				D			G				K			N
	2,4-DIAMINOTOLUENE	95-80-7				D			G			J	K			N
	2,4-DICHLOROPHENOL	120-83-2		B	C	D			G							+
	2,4-DIMETHYLPHENOL	105-67-9		B	C	D				H						N
	2,4-DINITROPHENOL	51-28-5		B	C	D			G			J				+
	2,4-DINITROTOLUENE	121-14-2		B	C	D			G			J	K			N
*	2,5-BIS(1-AZIRIDINYL)-3,6-BIS(2-METHOXYETHOXY)-1,4-BENZOQUINONE	1072-52-2							G				K			N
	2,6-DI-TERT-BUTYL-P-CRESOL	128-37-0													M	N
	2,6-DIMETHYL-4-HEPTANONE	108-83-8	SEE DIISOBUTYL KETONE													
	2,6-DINITROTOLUENE	606-20-2		B	C	D			G							+
	2,6-XYLIDINE	87-62-7				D			G							+
	2-(2-FORMYLHYDRAZINO)-4-(5-NITRO-2-FURYL)THIAZOLE	3570-75-0	SEE FORMYLHYDRAZINO-4-[5-NITRO-2-FURYL]THIAZOLE										K			N
*	2-(DIETHYLAMINO)ETHANOL	100-37-8													M	N
	2-1-AZIRIDINEETHANOL	1072-52-2														N
*	2-ACETYLAMINOFLUORENE	53-96-3	A			D			G			J	K		M	N
	2-AMINO-3-METHYL-9H-PYRIDO(2,3-B)INDOLE	68006-83-7							G				K			N
	2-AMINO-5-(5-NITRO-2-FURYL)-1,3,4-THIADIAZOLE	712-68-5							G				K			N
	2-AMINO-5-NITROTHIAZOLE	121-66-4											K			N
*	2-AMINO-9H-PYRIDO (2,3-B) INDOLE (A-ALPHA-C)								G				K		M	+
	2-AMINOANTHRAQUINONE	117-79-3				D			G				K		M	N
	2-AMINOETHANOL	141-43-5	SEE ETHANOLAMINE						G						+	
	2-AMINONAPHTHALENE	91-59-8	SEE BETA-NAPHTHYLAMINE												+	

CALIFORNIA ENVIRONMENTAL PROTECTION AGENCY
CHEMICAL LIST OF LISTS - BY CHEMICAL NAME

NEW CHEMICAL	CHEMICAL NAME	CAS NUMBER	A	B	C	D	E	F	G	H	I	J	K	L	M	N	+
	2-AMINOPYRIDINE	504-29-0													M	N	
	2-BUTANONE	78-93-3	SEE METHYL ETHYL KETONE														
	2-BUTOXYETHANOL	111-76-2													M	N	
	2-CHLOROACETOPHENONE	532-27-4				D			G				K		M	N	+
	2-CHLOROETHYL VINYL ETHER	110-75-8		B									K	L			+
	2-CHLORONAPHTHALENE	91-58-7		B													+
	2-CHLOROPHENOL	95-57-8		B	C											N	
	2-CHLOROPHENOL	110-80-5				D			G				K		M	N	
	2-ETHOXYETHYL ACETATE	111-15-9													M	N	
	2-HEXANONE	591-78-6	SEE METHYL N-BUTYL KETONE													N	+
	2-HYDROXYPROPYL ACRYLATE	999-61-1							G				K			N	
	2-METHOXYETHANOL	109-86-4				D			G				K		M	N	
	2-METHYL-1-NITROANTHRAQUINONE (OF UNCERTAIN PURITY)	129-15-7							G				K			N	
	2-METHYLAZIRIDINE	75-55-8	SEE PROPYLENEIMINE														
	2-N-DIBUTYLAMINOETHANOL	102-81-8													M	N	
	2-NAPHTHYLAMINE	91-59-8	SEE BETA-NAPHTHYLAMINE														
*	2-NITROANISOLE	91-23-6							G				K				
	2-NITROFLOURENE	607-57-8							G				K				+
	2-NITROPHENOL	88-75-5		B		D			G				K				+
	2-NITROPROPANE	79-46-9			C	D			G			J	K				
	2-PHENYLPHENOL	90-43-7				D			G			J	K			N	+
	3,3'-DICHLORO-4,4'-DIAMINODIPHENYL ETHER	28434-86-8							G				K			N	
*	3,3'-DICHLOROBENZIDINE AND ITS SALTS	91-94-1	A	B	C	D			G			J	K				
	3,3'-DIMETHOXYBENZIDINE	119-90-4				D			G			J	K				
	3,3'-DIMETHOXYBENZIDINE DIHYDROCHLORIDE	20325-40-0							G				K				
	3,3'-DIMETHOXYBENZIDINE-4,4'-DIISOCYANATE	91-93-0														N	+
	3,3'-DIMETHYLBENZIDINE (O-TOLIDINE)	119-93-7				D			G			J	K				
	3,3'-DIMETHYLBENZIDINE DIHYDROCHLORIDE	612-82-8											K				
	3,4-BENZO-PYRENE	50-32-8	SEE BENZO(A)PYRENE														
	3,4-BENZOFLUORANTHENE	205-99-2	SEE BENZO(B)FLUORANTHENE														
	3,5 DICHLORO-2,4,6 TRIFLUOROPYRIDINE	1737-93-5												L			
	3-(N-NITROSOMETHYLAMINO)PROPIONITRILE	60153-49-3							G				K				
	3-AMINO-9-ETHYLCARBAZOLE HYDROCHLORIDE	6109-97-3							G				K				+

NEW CHEMICAL	CHEMICAL NAME	CAS NUMBER	A	B	C	D	E	F	G	H	I	J	K	L	M	N
	3-CHLORO-2-METHYLPROPENE	563-47-3							G				K			N
*	3-CHLOROPROPIONITRILE	542-76-7	SEE PROPIONITRILE, 3-CHLORO													
	3-METHYLCHLORANTHRENE	56-49-5							G				K			N
	4,4'-DDD	72-54-8		B	C				G				K			+
	4,4'-DDE	72-55-9		B	C				G			J	K		M	N
	4,4'-DDT	50-29-3		B	C				G				K		M	N
	4,4'-DIAMINODIPHENYL ETHER	101-80-4				D			G							N
	4,4'-ISOPROPYLIDENEDIPHENOL	80-05-7				D										
	4,4'-METHYLENE BIS (2 CHLOROANILINE)	101-14-4	A			D			G			J	K		M	N
	4,4'-METHYLENE BIS (2-METHYANILINE)	838-88-0							G				K			N
	4,4'-METHYLENE BIS(N,N-DIMETHYL) BENZENAMINE	101-61-1				D			G				K			
	4,4'-METHYLENE DIANILINE	101-77-9				D			G			J	K		M	+
	4,4'-METHYLENEDIANILINE DIHYDROCHLORIDE	13552-44-8														
	4,4'-OXYDIANILINE	101-80-4	SEE 4,4'-DIAMINODIPHENYL ETHER													
	4,4'-THIOBIS (6-TERT-BUTYL-M-CRESOL)	96-69-5							G							N
	4,4'-THIODIANILINE	139-65-1				D			G				K			N
	4,4'-METHYLENEBIS (2-CHLOROANILINE)	101-14-1														
	4,6-DINITRO-O-CRESOL	534-52-1		B	C	D	E		G			J				+
	4-(N-NITROSOMETHYLAMINO)-1-(3-PYRIDYL)-1-BUTANONE	64091-91-4														
*	4-(NITROSOMETHYLAMINO)-1-(3-PYRIDYL)-1-BUTANONE (NNK)	64091-91-4							G				K			N
	4-AMINOAZOBENZENE	60-09-3				D			G				K			+
	4-AMINOBIPHENYL	92-67-1	SEE 4-AMINODIPHENYL													
	4-AMINODIPHENYL	92-67-1	A			D			G			J	K		M	N
	4-BROMOPHENYL PHENYL ETHER	101-55-3		B	C				G			J	K			N
*	4-CHLOR-M-CRESOL	59-50-7														
	4-CHLORO-3-METHYLPHENOL	35421-08-0			C											
	4-CHLORO-ORTHO-PHENYLENEDIAMINE	95-83-0														
	4-CHLOROPHENYL PHENYL ETHER	7005-72-3		B	C				G			J				
	4-DIMETHYLAMINOAZOBENZENE	60-11-7	A			D			G			J	K		M	+
	4-METHOXYPHENOL	150-76-5				D			G				K		M	N
	4-NITROBIPHENYL	92-93-3	A			D			G			J	K			N
	4-NITROPHENOL	100-02-7		B	C	D			G			J	K		M	N

CALIFORNIA ENVIRONMENTAL PROTECTION AGENCY
CHEMICAL LIST OF LISTS - BY CHEMICAL NAME

NEW CHEMICAL	CHEMICAL NAME	CAS NUMBER	A	B	C	D	E	F	G	H	I	J	K	L	M	N
	4-NITROPYRENE	57835-92-4							G				K		+	+
	4-VINYL-1-CYCLOHEXANE DIEPOXIDE (VINYL CYCLOHEXANE DIOXIDE)	106-87-6							G				K			+
*	5-(AMINOMETHYL)-3-ISOXAZOLOL	2763-96-4	SEE MUSCIMOL													
	5-(MORPHOLINOMETHYL)-3-[(5-NITRO-FURFURYLIDENE)-AMINO]-2-OXALOLIDINONE	139-91-3							G				K		M	+
*	5-AZACYTIDINE	320-67-2													M	N
	5-METHOXYPSORALEN	484-20-8							G				K			+
	5-METHYCHRYSENE	3697-24-3							G				K			+
	5-NITRO-O-ANISIDINE	99-59-2				D			G				K			+
	5-NITROACENAPHTHANE	602-87-9							G				K			+
	6-NITROCHRYSENE	7496-02-8							G				K			+
	7,12-DIMETHYLBENZ(A)ANTHRACENE	57-97-6							G				K		M	N
	7H-DIBENZO[C,G]CARBAZOLE	194-59-2							G				K		M	N
	8-METHOXYPSORALEN WITH ULTRAVIOLET A THERAPY	298-81-7							G				K		M	N
	A-BENZENE HEXOCHLORIDE		SEE ALPHA-BHC													
	A-alpha-C (2-AMINO-9H-PYRIDO[2,3-B]INDOLE)	26148-68-5							G				K			N
	ACENAPHTHENE	83-32-9		B	C											
	ACENAPHTHYLENE	208-96-8		B	C											
	ACEPHATE	30560-19-1			C											
	ACETALDEHYDE	75-07-0				D			G			J	K		M	N
	ACETAMIDE	60-35-5				D			G			J	K		M	N
	ACETIC ACID	64-19-7														
	ACETIC ANHYDRIDE	108-24-7													M	N
	ACETOCHLOR	34256-82-1							G				K		M	N
	ACETOHYDROXAMIC ACID	546-88-3							G				K		M	N
	ACETONE	67-64-1				D			G						M	N
	ACETONE CYANOHYDRIN	75-86-5					E							L		
	ACETONE THIOSEMICARBAZIDE	1752-30-3					E									
	ACETONITRILE	75-05-8				D			G			J			M	N
	ACETOPHENONE	98-86-2							G			J			M	N
	ACETYL BROMIDE	506-96-7														
	ACETYL CHLORIDE	79-36-7													M	
	ACETYLENE	74-86-2													M	N

CALIFORNIA ENVIRONMENTAL PROTECTION AGENCY
CHEMICAL LIST OF LISTS - BY CHEMICAL NAME

NEW CHEMICAL	CHEMICAL NAME	CAS NUMBER	A	B	C	D	E	F	G	H	I	J	K	L	M	N
	ACETYLENE DICHLORIDE	540-59-0	SEE 1,2-DICHLOROETHYLENE													
	ACETYLENE TETRABROMIDE	79-27-6													M	N
	ACETYLENE TETRACHLORIDE	79-34-5	SEE 1,1,2,2-TETRACHLOROETHANE													
	ACIFLUORFEN	62476-59-9							G				K			N
	ACROLEIN	107-02-8		B		D	E		G						M	N
	ACRYLAMIDE	79-06-1				D	E		G		I	J	K	L	M	N
	ACRYLIC ACID	79-10-7				D			G			J			M	N
	ACRYLONITRILE	107-13-1	A	B		D	E		G			J	K	L	M	N
	ACRYLYL CHLORIDE	814-68-6					E									N
	ACTINOMYCIN D	50-76-0					E		G				K			
	ADIPONITRILE	111-69-3														N
*	ADLPIC ACID	124-04-9														
	ADRIAMYCIN	23214-92-8							G				K		M	N
	AF-2; [2-(2-FURYL)-3-(5-NITRO-2-FURYL)]ACRYLAMIDE	3688-53-7							G				K		M	+
	AFLATOXINS								G				K		M	N
	ALACHLOR	15972-60-8			C				G	H			K			
	ALCOHOLIC BEVERAGES, WHEN ASSOCIATED WITH ALCOHOL ABUSE															
	ALDICARB	116-06-3			C		E		G	H						N
	ALDICARB IN DICHLOROMETHANE															
	ALDRIN	309-00-2		B	C		E		G	H			K		M	N
	ALL-TRANS RETINOIC ACID	302-79-4				D	E		G				K	L	M	N
	ALLYL ALCOHOL	107-18-6				D	E		G					L	M	N
	ALLYL AMINE	107-11-9					E									
	ALLYL CHLORIDE	107-05-1				D			G			J	K		M	N
	ALLYL GLYCIDYL ETHER;AGE	106-29-3													M	N
	ALLYL ISOTHIOCYANATE	57-06-7													M	N
	ALLYL ISOVALERATE	2835-39-4														
	ALLYL PROPYL DISULFIDE	2179-59-1													M	N
*	ALPHA-BHC	319-84-6		B	C					H						+
	ALPHA-CHLORINATED TOLUENES								G							
*	ALPHA-ENDOSULFAN	959-98-8		B	C											
	ALPHA-METHYLSTYRENE	98-83-9													M	N
	ALPHA-NAPHTHYLAMINE	134-32-7	A			D			G				K		M	N

227

CALIFORNIA ENVIRONMENTAL PROTECTION AGENCY
CHEMICAL LIST OF LISTS - BY CHEMICAL NAME

NEW CHEMICAL	CHEMICAL NAME	CAS NUMBER	A	B	C	D	E	F	G	H	I	J	K	L	M	N
	ALPRAZOLAM	28981-97-7														N
	ALUMINA	1344-28-1	SEE ALUMINUM OXIDE						G				K			N
	ALUMINUM (FUME OR DUST)	7429-90-5			+				G						M	N
	ALUMINUM OXIDE	1344-28-1				D		F	G						M	N
	ALUMINUM PHOSPHIDE	20859-73-8					E									N
	ALUMINUM SULFATE	10043-01-3														
*	AMIKACIN SULFATE	39831-55-5											K			
	AMINO DIMETHYL BUTYRONITRILE															
	AMINODIMETHYLBENZENE	1300-73-8	SEE XYLIDENE											L		
	AMINOGLUTETHIMIDE	125-84-8														
	AMINOPTERIN	54-62-6					E		G				K			N
	AMITON	78-53-5					E						K			N
	AMITON OXALATE	3734-97-2					E									N
	AMITROLE	61-82-5							G							N
	AMMONIA	7664-41-7				D	E		G				K		M	N
*	AMMONIUM ACETATE	631-61-8													M	N
*	AMMONIUM BENZOATE	3012-65-5														N
*	AMMONIUM BICARBONATE	1066-33-7														N
*	AMMONIUM BICHROMATE	7789-09-5	SEE CHROMIUM COMPOUNDS													
*	AMMONIUM BIFLUORIDE	1341-49-7	SEE FLUORIDE COMPOUNDS													
	AMMONIUM BISULFITE	10192-30-0														N
*	AMMONIUM CARBAMATE	1111-78-0														N
	AMMONIUM CARBONATE	506-87-6														N
*	AMMONIUM CHLORIDE FUME	12125-02-9														+
*	AMMONIUM CHROMATE	7788-98-9	SEE CHROMIUM COMPOUNDS												M	N
	AMMONIUM CITRATE, DIBASIC	3012-65-5														N
	AMMONIUM FLUOBORATE	13826-83-0														N
*	AMMONIUM FLUORIDE	12125-01-8	SEE FLUORIDE COMPOUNDS													
	AMMONIUM HYDROXIDE	1336-21-6														N
	AMMONIUM NITRATE (SOLUTION)	6484-52-2				D			G							N
	AMMONIUM OXALATE	6009-70-7														N
	AMMONIUM SILICOFLUORIDE	16919-19-0														
	AMMONIUM SULFAMATE	7773-06-0													M	
	AMMONIUM SULFATE	7783-20-2				D			G							N

NEW CHEMICAL	CHEMICAL NAME	CAS NUMBER	A	B	C	D	E	F	G	H	I	J	K	L	M	N
	AMMONIUM SULFIDE	12135-76-1														N
	AMMONIUM SULFITE	10196-04-0														N
*	AMMONIUM TARTRATE	3164-29-2														N
	AMMONIUM THIOCYANATE	1762-95-4														N
	AMPHETAMINE	300-62-9					E									
	AMYL ACETATE	628-63-7													M	N
	ANABOLIC STEROIDS												K			
	ANALGESIC MIXTURES CONTAINING PHENACETIN								G				K			
	ANDROGENIC (ANABOLIC) STEROIDS								G							
	ANILINE	62-53-3				D	E		G						M	N
	ANILINE, 2,4,6-TRIMETHYL-	88-05-1					E		G			J				
	ANISIDINE (ORTHO AND PARA ISOMERS) ANTIMONY AND COMPOUNDS, AS SB	29191-52-4													M	
*	ANISINDIONE	117-37-3											K			
*	ANTHANTHRENE	191-26-4														N
	ANTHRACENE	120-12-7		B	C	D			G						M	+
	ANTIMONY	7440-36-0		B		D			G						M	N
	ANTIMONY COMPOUNDS					D			G						M	N
*	ANTIMONY OXIDE (ANTIMONY TRIOXIDE)	1309-64-4	SEE ANTIMONY COMPOUNDS										K			
	ANTIMONY PENTACHLORIDE	7647-18-9	SEE ANTIMONY COMPOUNDS													
	ANTIMONY PENTAFLUORIDE	7783-70-2					E									
*	ANTIMONY POTASSIUM TARTRATE	28300-74-5	SEE ANTIMONY COMPOUNDS													
*	ANTIMONY TRIBROMIDE	7789-61-9	SEE ANTIMONY COMPOUNDS													
*	ANTIMONY TRICHLORIDE	10025-91-9	SEE COMPOUNDS													
*	ANTIMONY TRIFLUORIDE	77883-56-4	SEE ANTIMONY COMPOUNDS													
	ANTIMONY TRIOXIDE	1309-64-4							G							+
	ANTIMYCIN A	1397-94-0					E									
	ANTU	86-88-4					E								M	N
	ARAMITE	140-57-8							G						M	+
	ARGON	7440-37-1														
	AROCLOR 1016	12674-11-2	SEE PCB-1016													
	AROCLOR 1221	11104-28-2	SEE PCB-1221													
	AROCLOR 1232	11141-16-5	SEE PCB-1232													
	AROCLOR 1242	53469-21-9		B											M	+

229

CALIFORNIA ENVIRONMENTAL PROTECTION AGENCY
CHEMICAL LIST OF LISTS - BY CHEMICAL NAME

NEW CHEMICAL	CHEMICAL NAME	CAS NUMBER	A	B	C	D	E	F	G	H	I	J	K	L	M	N
	AROCLOR 1248	12672-29-6	SEE PCB-1248													
	AROCLOR 1254	11097-69-1	SEE PCB-1254													
	AROCLOR 1260	11096-82-5	SEE PCB-1260													
	ARSENIC	7440-38-2	SEE INORGANIC ARSENIC													
	ARSENIC (INORGANIC COMPOUNDS)								G				K			+
*	ARSENIC COMPOUNDS					D			G							N
	ARSENIC DISULFIDE	1303-32-8					E									N
	ARSENIC OXIDE (3)	1327-53-3					E									+
	ARSENIC PENTOXIDE	1303-28-2					E									N
*	ARSENIC TRISULFIDE	1303-33-9														+
	ARSENOUS OXIDE	1327-53-3	SEE ARSENIC OXIDE (3)													
	ARSENOUS TRICHLORIDE	7784-34-1					E							L	M	N
	ARSINE	7784-42-1	A			D	E		G				K		M	N
	ASBESTOS	1332-21-4	A	B		D	E		G		I		K		M	N
	ASPHALT (PETROLEUM) FUMES	8052-42-4													M	N
	ASPIRIN	50-78-2							G				K		M	N
	ATRAZINE	1912-24-9			C			F							M	N
*	ATTAPULGITE	12174-11-7													M	N
*	AURAMINE	492-80-8				D			G				K		M	N
	AUROTHIOGLUCOSE	12192-57-3														+
	AZASERINE	115-02-6					E		G				K			N
	AZATHIOPRINE	446-86-6					E		G				K			+
	AZINPHOS-ETHYL	2642-71-9					E									+
	AZINPHOS-METHYL	86-50-0					E		G						M	+
	AZOBENZENE	103-33-3							G				K		M	+
*	B-BENZENE HEXOCHLORIDE		SEE BETA-BHC													
*	BARBAN	101-27-9														N
	BARBITURATES															
	BARIUM	7440-39-3		+		D		F	G				K		M	N
*	BARIUM CHROMATE	10294-40-3							G						M	N
	BARIUM COMPOUNDS					D			G						M	N
*	BARIUM CYANIDE	542-62-1														+
	BARIUM SULFATE	7727-43-7													M	N
	BAYGON		SEE PROPOXUR													

230

CALIFORNIA ENVIRONMENTAL PROTECTION AGENCY
CHEMICAL LIST OF LISTS - BY CHEMICAL NAME

NEW CHEMICAL	CHEMICAL NAME	CAS NUMBER	A	B	C	D	E	F	G	H	I	J	K	L	M	N
	BENOMYL	17804-35-2	SEE METHYL 2-BENZIMIDAZOLE CARBAMATE													
	BENTAZON	25057-89-0			+			F								+
	BENZAL CHLORIDE	98-87-3				D	E		G							
	BENZAMIDE	55-21-0				D			G							
	BENZENAMINE, 3-(TRIFLUOROMETHYL)-	98-16-8					E									
	BENZENE	71-43-2	A	B	C	D		F	G		I	J	K		M	N
	BENZENE, 1-(CHLOROMETHYL)-4-NITRO-	100-14-1					E									
	BENZENEARSONIC ACID	98-05-5					E									
*	BENZIDINE	92-87-5											K			
	BENZIDINE AND ITS SALTS	92-87-5	A	B	C	D			G			J	K		M	N
	BENZIDINE-BASED DYES								G							
	BENZIMIDAZOL,4,5-DICHLORO-2-(TRIFLUOROMETHYL)-	3615-21-2					E									
	BENZO(B)FLUORANTHENE	205-99-2		B	C				G				K			N
	BENZO(GHI)PERYLENE	191-24-2		B	C											+
	BENZO(K)FLUORANTHENE	207-08-9		B	C				G				K			+
*	BENZODIAZEPINES												K			N
	BENZOFURAN	271-89-6											K			N
	BENZOIC ACID	65-85-0											K			N
	BENZOIC TRICHLORIDE (BENZOTRICHLORIDE)	98-07-7				D	E		G			J	K			N
	BENZOL	71-43-2	SEE BENZENE													
	BENZONITRILE	100-47-0														
	BENZOYL CHLORIDE	98-88-4				D			G							N
	BENZOYL PEROXIDE	94-36-0				D			G							N
	BENZO[A]ANTHRACENE	56-55-3		B	C				G				K			N
	BENZO[A]PYRENE	50-32-8		B	C				G				K			N
	BENZO[J]FLUORANTHENE	205-82-3							G				K			N
	BENZPHETAMINE HYDROCHLORIDE	5411-22-3							G				K			+
	BENZYL BUTYL PHTHALATE		SEE BUTYL BENZYL PHTHALATE													
	BENZYL CHLORIDE	100-44-7				D	E		G			J	K		M	N
	BENZYL CYANIDE	140-29-4					E									
	BENZYL VIOLET 4B	1694-09-3							G				K			N
	BENZ[C]ACRIDINE	225-51-4		B												
*	BERYLLIUM	7440-41-7		B		D			G			J	K		M	N
*	BERYLLIUM CHLORIDE	7787-47-5	SEE BERYLLIUM COMPOUNDS													

CALIFORNIA ENVIRONMENTAL PROTECTION AGENCY
CHEMICAL LIST OF LISTS - BY CHEMICAL NAME

NEW CHEMICAL	CHEMICAL NAME	CAS NUMBER	A	B	C	D	E	F	G	H	I	J	K	L	M	N
	BERYLLIUM COMPOUNDS					D			G				K		M	N
*	BERYLLIUM FLUORIDE	7787-55-5	SEE BERYLLIUM COMPOUNDS													
	BETA-BHC	319-85-7		B											+
	BETA-BUTYROLACTONE	3068-88-0								H						+
	BETA-ENDOSULFAN	33213-65-9		B	C				G				K			N
	BETA-NAPHTHYLAMINE	91-59-8	A			D			G				K		M	+
	BETA-PROPIOLACTONE	57-57-8	A			D	E		G			J	K		M	N
	BETEL QUID WITH TOBACCO								G				K			N
	BICYCLO[2.2.1]HEPTANE-2-CARBONITRILE, 5-CHLORO-6-(((METHYLAMINO)CARBONYL)OXY)IMINO)-,1S-(1-ALPHA	15271-41-7					E									N
	BIPHENYL	92-52-4				D			G			J	K		M	N
	BIS(2-CHLORO-1-METHYLETHYL) ETHER	108-60-1				D			G							+
	BIS(2-CHLOROETHOXY) METHANE	111-91-1		B	C											+
	BIS(2-CHLOROETHYL) ETHER	111-44-4		B	C	D			G				K		M	+
	BIS(2-CHLOROISOPROPYL) ETHER	39638-32-9		B	C		E					J	K	L		+
	BIS(2-ETHYLHEXYL) ADIPATE	103-23-1				D			G							+
	BIS(2-ETHYLHEXYL)PHTHALATE	117-81-7		B	C	D		F	G				K		M	N
	BIS(CHLOROMETHYL) ETHER	542-88-1	A	B		D	E		G		I	J	K		M	N
	BIS(CHLOROMETHYL) KETONE	534-07-6				D	E					J				+
	BIS-(DIMETHYLIOCARBAMOYL) DISULFIDE	137-26-8	SEE THIRAM													
	BISCHLOROETHYL NITROSOUREA (BCNU)	154-93-8							G				K			N
	BISMUTH TEILLURIDE	1304-82-1														N
	BITOSCANATE	4044-65-9					E		G							N
	BITUMENS, EXTRACTS OF STEAM-REFINED AND AIR-REFINED BITUMENS								G				K			N
	BLEOMYCINS	9041-93-4							G							N
*	BLEOMYCINS														M	N
	BOLERO (THIOBENCARB)	28249-77-6			+			F								+
	BORATES,TETRA,SODIUM SALTS															
	BORON OXIDE	1303-86-2														N
	BORON TRIBROMIDE	10294-33-4													M	N
	BORON TRICHLORIDE	10294-34-5					E								M	N
	BORON TRIFLUORIDE	7637-07-2					E									N
	BORON TRIFLUORIDE COMPOUND WITH METHYL ETHER (1:1)	353-42-4					E								M	N

CALIFORNIA ENVIRONMENTAL PROTECTION AGENCY
CHEMICAL LIST OF LISTS - BY CHEMICAL NAME

NEW CHEMICAL	CHEMICAL NAME	CAS NUMBER	A	B	C	D	E	F	G	H	I	J	K	L	M	N
	BRACKEN FERN															
*	BRILLIANT BLUE FCF	3844-45-9											K			N
	BROMACIL	314-40-9			C										M	N
	BROMADIOLONE	28772-56-7					E									
	BROMINE	7726-95-6					E		G						M	N
	BROMINE PENTAFLUORIDE	7789-30-2												L		N
	BROMINE TRIFLUORIDE	7787-71-5												L		N
	BROMINE-CONTAINING INORGANIC COMPOUNDS								G					L		
	BROMOACETONE	598-31-2												L		
	BROMOCHLORODIFLUOROMETHANE (HALON 1211)	421-01-2				D										
	BROMOCHLOROMETHANE	74-97-5													M	N
	BROMODICHLOROMETHANE	75-27-4	SEE DICHLOROBROMOMETHANE						G						M	N
	BROMOFORM	75-25-2		B	C	D			G			J			M	+
	BROMOMETHANE	74-83-9	SEE METHYL BROMIDE													
	BROMOTRIFLUOROMETHANE (HALON 1301)	75-63-8				D										
	BROMOXYNIL	1689-84-5							G				K		M	+
	BUSULFAN	55-98-1	SEE 1,4-BUTANEDIOL DIMETHANESULFONATE													
*	BUTABARBITAL SODIUM	143-81-7											K		M	+
	BUTANE	106-97-8													M	N
	BUTYL ACRYLATE	141-32-2				D			G						M	+
	BUTYL BENZYL PHTHALATE	85-68-7		B	C	D			G						M	N
	BUTYL MERCAPTAN	109-79-5													M	N
	BUTYLAMINE	109-73-9													M	+
	BUTYLATED HYDROXYANISOLE (BHA)	25013-16-5							G				K		M	+
	BUTYRALDEHYDE	123-72-8				D			G							N
	BUTYRIC ACID	107-92-6														N
	C.I. ACID GREEN 3	4680-78-8				D			G							+
*	C.I. ACID RED 114, DISODIUM SALT	6459-94-5							G				K		M	N
	C.I. BASIC GREEN 4	569-64-2				D			G						M	N
	C.I. BASIC RED 1	989-38-8				D			G							+
	C.I. BASIC RED 9 MONOHYDROCHLORIDE	569-61-9				D			G				K			+
	C.I. DIRECT BROWN 95	16071-86-6				D			G				K			+
	C.I. DISPERSE YELLOW 3	2832-40-8				D			G				K			+
	C.I. FOOD RED 15	81-88-9				D			G				K			+

NEW CHEMICAL	CHEMICAL NAME	CAS NUMBER	A	B	C	D	E	F	G	H	I	J	K	L	M	N
	C.I. FOOD RED 5	3761-53-3				D			G				K			N
	C.I. SOLVENT ORANGE 7	3118-97-6				D										+
	C.I. SOLVENT YELLOW 14	842-07-9				D										+
	C.I. SOLVENT YELLOW 3	97-56-3				D			G				K			N
	C.I. SOLVENT YELLOW 34	492-80-8	SEE AURAMINE													
	C.I. VAT YELLOW 4	128-66-5				D										
	CADMIUM	7440-43-9		B	+	D		F	G		I				M	N
*	CADMIUM ACETATE	543-90-8														N
*	CADMIUM BROMIDE	7789-42-6														N
*	CADMIUM CHLORIDE	10108-64-2														N
	CADMIUM COMPOUNDS					D			G		I		K			N
	CADMIUM OXIDE	1306-19-0					E								M	N
	CADMIUM STEARATE	2223-93-0					E								M	+
*	CALCIUM ARSENATE [2ASH3O4.2CA]	7778-44-1					E								M	N
	CALCIUM ARSENITE	52740-16-6														
	CALCIUM CARBONATE	471-34-1													M	N
	CALCIUM CARBIDE	75-20-7														+
	CALCIUM CHROMATE	13765-19-0							G							N
*	CALCIUM CYANAMIDE	156-62-7				D			G			J				N
	CALCIUM CYANIDE	592-01-8														N
	CALCIUM DODECYLBENZENE-SULFONATE	26264-06-2														N
	CALCIUM HYDROXIDE	1305-62-0														N
	CALCIUM HYPOCHLORITE	7778-54-3														N
	CALCIUM METAL	7440-70-2													M	N
*	CALCIUM OXIDE	1305-78-8													M	N
	CALCIUM SILICATE	10101-39-0													M	N
	CALCIUM SULFATE	7778-18-9													M	N
	CAMPHECHLOR	8001-35-2	SEE TOXAPHENE													
	CAMPHENE, OCTACHLORO-	8001-35-7	SEE CAMPHECHLOR													
*	CAMPHOR	76-22-2													M	N
	CANTHARIDIN	56-25-7					E									+
	CAPROLACTAM	105-60-2							G			J				N
	CAPTAFOL	2425-06-1							G			J	K			N
	CAPTAN	133-06-2		C		D			G	H		J	K			N

234

NEW CHEMICAL	CHEMICAL NAME	CAS NUMBER	A	B	C	D	E	F	G	H	I	J	K	L	M	N
	CARBACHOL CHLORIDE	51-83-2					E									N
	CARBAMIC ACID, METHYL-, O-(((2,4-DIMETHYL-1, 3-DITHIOLAN-2-Y-METHYLENE)AMINO)-	26419-73-8					E								M	N
	CARBARYL	63-25-2			C	D			G						M	N
*	CARBAZOLE	86-74-8														N
	CARBOFURAN	1563-66-2			C		E	F	G				K		M	N
	CARBON BLACK EXTRACTS	1333-86-4													M	+
	CARBON DIOXIDE	124-38-9														N
	CARBON DISULFIDE	75-15-0				D	E		G			J	K		M	N
	CARBON MONOXIDE	630-08-0							G						M	N
	CARBON TETRABROMIDE	558-13-4													M	N
	CARBON TETRACHLORIDE	56-23-5		B	C	D		F	G		I	J	K	L	M	N
	CARBONYL CHLORIDE	75-44-5	SEE PHOSGENE													
	CARBONYL FLUOIRDE	353-50-4													M	
	CARBONYL SULFIDE	463-58-1				D			G			J				
	CARBOPHENOTHION	786-19-6	SEE TRITHION													
	CARBOPLATIN	41575-94-4							G				K			
	CARRAGEENAN (DEGRADED)								G							
	CATECHOL	120-80-9				D			G			J	K		M	N
	CELLULOSE (PAPER FIBER)	9004-34-6													M	
	CERAMIC FIBERS (AIRBORNE PARTICLES OF RESPIRABLE SIZE)												K			
	CERAMIC FIBERS (MAN-MADE)								G							
	CERTAIN COMBINED CHEMOTHERAPY FOR LYMPHOMAS												K			
	CESIUM HYDROXIDE	21351-79-1													M	N
	CHEMICAL AMMUNITION													L		
	CHENODIOL	474-25-9							G				K			
	CHLORAMBEN	133-90-4				D			G			J			M	
	CHLORAMBUCIL	305-03-3							G				K			
	CHLORAMPHENICOL	56-75-7							G				K			+
	CHLORCYCLIZINE HYDROCHLORIDE	1620-21-9							G				K			
	CHLORDANE	57-74-9		B	C	D	E	F	G	H		J	K		M	N
	CHLORDECONE (KEPONE)	143-50-0											K		M	
	CHLORDIAZEPOXIDE	58-52-3											K			N

235

CALIFORNIA ENVIRONMENTAL PROTECTION AGENCY
CHEMICAL LIST OF LISTS - BY CHEMICAL NAME

NEW CHEMICAL	CHEMICAL NAME	CAS NUMBER	A	B	C	D	E	F	G	H	I	J	K	L	M	N
	CHLORDIAZEPOXIDE HYDROCHLORIDE	438-41-5											K			N
	CHLORDIMEFORM	6164-98-3							G				K		M	N
	CHLORENDIC ACID	115-28-6							G				K		M	+
	CHLORFENVINFOS	470-90-6					E									N
*	CHLORIDE	68188-88-5			C											
	CHLORINATED DIOXINS AND DIBENZOFURANS (15 SPECIES)										I					
*	CHLORINATED DIPHENYL OXIDE	55720-99-5													M	N
	CHLORINATED FLUOROCARBON (FREON 113)	76-13-1				D		F	G	H						
	CHLORINATED PARAFINS (AVERAGE CHAIN LENGTH, C12; APPROXIMATELY 60 PERCENT CHLORINE BY WEIGHT)	108171-26-2							G				K		M	+
	CHLORINE	7782-50-5				D	E		G						M	N
	CHLORINE DIOXIDE	10049-04-4				D	E		G						M	N
	CHLORINE TRIFLUORIDE	7790-91-2					E							L	M	N
	CHLORNEPHOS	24934-91-6					E									
	CHLORMEQUAT CHLORIDE	999-81-5					E									
	CHLOROACETALDEHYDE	107-20-0					E									
	CHLOROACETIC ACID	79-11-8				D	E		G			J		L	M	
	CHLOROACETOPHENONE, LIQUID	532-27-4	SEE 2-CHLOROACETOPHENONE													
	CHLOROACETONITRILE	107-14-2												L		
	CHLOROACETYL CHLORIDE	79-04-9														
	CHLOROBENZENE	108-90-7		B	C	D		F	G				K		M	+
	CHLOROBENZILATE	510-15-6				D			G			J	K		M	+
	CHLORODIBROMOMETHANE	124-48-1		B	+				G						M	+
	CHLORODIFLUOROMETHANE	75-45-6													M	+
	CHLORODIPHENYL (42% CHLORINE)	53449-21-9	SEE AROCLOR 1242													
	CHLOROETHANE	75-00-3		B	C	D			G				K		M	
	CHLOROETHANOL	107-07-3					E								M	N
	CHLOROETHYL CHLOROFORMATE	627-11-2					E									
	CHLOROFLUOROMETHANE	593-70-4														
	CHLOROFORM	67-66-3		B	C	D	E		G		I		K	L	M	N
*	CHLOROFORMATES, N.O.S.															
	CHLOROMETHANE	74-87-3	SEE METHYL CHLORIDE													
	CHLOROMETHYL ETHER	542-88-1	SEE BIS(CHLOROMETHYL) ETHER													
	CHLOROMETHYL METHYL ETHER	107-30-2	SEE METHYL CHLOROMETHYL ETHER													

CALIFORNIA ENVIRONMENTAL PROTECTION AGENCY
CHEMICAL LIST OF LISTS - BY CHEMICAL NAME

NEW CHEMICAL	CHEMICAL NAME	CAS NUMBER	A	B	C	D	E	F	G	H	I	J	K	L	M	N
	CHLOROPENTAFLUOROETHANE	76-15-3				+										N
	CHLOROPHACINONE	3691-35-8					E								M	N
	CHLOROPHENOLS			B		D			G							
	CHLOROPHENOXY HERBICIDES								G							
	CHLOROPICRIN	76-06-2			C				G	H					M	N
	CHLOROPICRIN AND METHYL CHLORIDE MIXTURE													L		N
	CHLOROPICRIN AND NON-FLAMMABLE GAS MIXTURE													L		N
	CHLOROPIVALOYL CHLORIDE	4300-97-4												L		
	CHLOROPRENE	126-99-8				D			G						M	N
	CHLOROSULFONIC ACID	7790-94-5			C									L		+
	CHLOROTHALONIL	1897-45-6			C	D			G				K			
	CHLOROXURON	1982-47-4			C		E									
	CHLORPYRIFOS	2921-88-2			C		E									
	CHLORTHIOPHOS	21923-23-9														
	CHROMIUM	7440-47-3		B	+	D		F	G		I				M	N
	CHROMIUM (HEXAVALENT COMPOUNDS)	18540-29-9					E		G				K			N
	CHROMIUM (HEXAVALENT)	10025-73-7					E		G							+
	CHROMIUM CHLORIDE (3)					D										
	CHROMIUM COMPOUNDS	1333-82-0							G						M	N
	CHROMIUM TRIOXIDE	10049-05-5														
*	CHROMOUS CHLORIDE	14977-61-8														+
	CHROMYL CHLORIDE	218-01-9		B	C				G				K		M	N
	CHRYSENE	532-82-1														
*	CHRYSOIDINE	59865-13-3											K			
	CICLOSPORIN (CYCLOSPORIN A: CYCLOSPORINE)	87-29-6							G				K			+
	CINNAMYL ANTHRANILATE	101-21-3								H						
	CIPC (ISOPROPYL N-(3-CHLOROPHENYL) CARBAMATE)	156-59-2						F								
	CIS-1,2-DICHLOROETHYLENE	10061-01-5			+											
	CIS-1,3,-DICHLOROPROPENE				C											
*	CISPLATIN	15663-27-1							G				K			+
	CITRININ	518-75-2													M	N
	CITRUS RED NO.2	6358-53-8							G				K		M	N
*	CLOFIBRATE	637-07-0							G				K			+
	CLOMIPHENE CITRATE	50-41-9							G				K			N

CALIFORNIA ENVIRONMENTAL PROTECTION AGENCY
CHEMICAL LIST OF LISTS - BY CHEMICAL NAME

NEW CHEMICAL	CHEMICAL NAME	CAS NUMBER	A	B	C	D	E	F	G	H	I	J	K	L	M	N
	CLONITRALID	1420-04-8														N
	CLOPIDOL	2971-90-6													M	N
*	CLORAZEPATE DIPOTASSIUM	57109-90-7											K			
	COAL TARS	8007-45-2							G				K		M	N
	COBALT AND COMPOUNDS	7440-48-4				D			G				+		M	+
	COBALT CARBONYL	10210-68-1					E									
*	COBALT [II] OXIDE	1307-96-6											K		M	
	COBALT, ((2,2'-(1,2-ETHANEDIYLBIS(NITRILOMETHYLIDY NE))BIS(6-FLUOROPHENOLATO))(2-)-N,N',O,O')-	62207-76-5					E									
	COBALTOUS BROMIDE	7789-43-7														N
	COBALTOUS FORMATE	544-18-3													M	N
	COBALTOUS SULAMATE	14017-41-5														N
	COCAINE	50-36-2											K			
	COKE OVEN EMISSIONS		A						G				K			
	COLCHICINE	64-86-8					E					J	+			
	CONJUGATED ESTROGENS								G				K			
	COPPER	7440-50-8		B	+	D		F	G							
	COPPER COMPOUNDS			B		D			G							
	COUMAPHOS	56-72-4					E									
	COUMATETRALYL	5836-29-3					E									
	CREOSOTE	8001-58-9				D										
	CREOSOTES								G							
	CRESOL (MIXED ISOMERS)	1319-77-3				D			G			J			M	N
	CRIMIDINE	535-89-7					E									
	CRISTOBALITE	14464-46-1												L	M	
	CROTOMALDEHYDE	4170-30-3				D	E		G							
	CROTOMALDEHYDE, (E)-	123-73-9					E									+
	CRUFOMATE	299-86-5														N
	CUMENE	98-82-8				D			G			J			M	N
	CUMENE HYDROPEROXIDE	80-15-9				D			G						M	
	CUPFERRON	135-20-6				D			G				K			
*	CUPRIC ACETOARSENITE	12002-03-8	SEE PARIS GREEN													
	CYANAMIDE	420-04-2													M	N
	CYANAZINE	21725-46-2			C				G				K			

NEW CHEMICAL	CHEMICAL NAME	CAS NUMBER	A	B	C	D	E	F	G	H	I	J	K	L	M	N
	CYANIDE	57-12-5		B											M	N
	CYANIDE COMPOUNDS					D										
	CYANOGEN	460-19-5													M	N
	CYANOGEN BROMIDE	506-68-3					E								M	
	CYANOGEN CHLORIDE	506-77-4												L		
	CYANOGEN IODIDE	506-78-5					E								M	N
	CYANOPHOS	2636-26-2					E									
	CYANURIC FLUORIDE	675-14-9					E									
	CYCASIN	14901-08-7							G				K		M	N
	CYCLOHEXANE	110-82-7				D			G				K		M	N
	CYCLOHEXANOL	108-93-0													M	N
	CYCLOHEXANONE	108-94-1													M	N
	CYCLOHEXENE	110-83-8													M	N
	CYCLOHEXIMIDE	66-81-9					E		G				K		M	N
	CYCLOHEXYL ISOCYANATE	3173-53-3												L		
	CYCLOHEXYLAMINE	108-91-8					E						K		M	N
	CYCLONITE	121-82-4											K		M	N
	CYCLOPENTADIENE	542-92-7											K		M	N
	CYCLOPENTANE	287-92-3											K		M	N
	CYCLOPHOSPHAMIDE	50-18-0							G				K		M	N
	CYCLOPHOSPHAMIDE (HYDRATED)	6055-19-2											K		M	+
	CYHEXATIN	13121-70-5							G				K		M	
	CYTARABINE	147-94-4							G				K			
	D & C ORANGE NO. 17	3468-63-1							G				K			
	D & C RED NO. 8	2092-56-0							G				K			
	D & C RED NO. 9	5160-02-1							G				K			
	D & C RED NUMBER 19	81-88-9	SEE C.I. FOOD RED 15													
	D-D MIX				C											
	DACARBAZINE	4342-03-4							G				K		M	N
	DAMINOZIDE	1596-84-5							G				K		M	
	DANAZOL	17230-88-5							G							
	DANTRON (CHRYSAZIN; 1,8-DIHYDROXYANTHRAQUINONE)	117-10-2														
	DAPSONE	80-08-0							G				K		M	N
*	DAUNOMYCIN	20830-81-3							G				K		M	N

239

CALIFORNIA ENVIRONMENTAL PROTECTION AGENCY
CHEMICAL LIST OF LISTS - BY CHEMICAL NAME

NEW CHEMICAL	CHEMICAL NAME	CAS NUMBER	A	B	C	D	E	F	G	H	I	J	K	L	M	N
	DAUNORUBICIN HYDROCHLORIDE	23541-50-6							G							
	DDD (DICHLORODIPHENYLDICHLOROETHANE)	72-54-8	SEE 4,4'-DDD													
	DDE (DICHLORODIPHENYLDICHLOROETHYLENE)	72-55-9	SEE 4,4'-DDE													
	DDT (DICHLORODIPHENYLTRICHLOROETHANE)	50-29-3	SEE 4,4'-DDT													
	DDVP (DICHLORVOS)	62-73-7	SEE DICHLORVOS													
	DECABORANE(14)	17702-41-9					E							M		N
	DECABROMODIPHENYL OXIDE	1163-19-5				D			G							+
	DELTA-BHC	319-86-8		B										M		N
	DEMETON	8065-48-3					E							M		N
*	DEMETON-O	298-03-3														N
*	DEMETON-S-METHY	919-86-8					E									N
	DI(2-ETHYLHEXYL)PHTHALATE (DEHP)	117-81-7	SEE BIS(2-ETHYLHEXYL)PHTHALATE													
	DI-N-BUTYL PHTHALATE	84-74-2		B	C	D			G			J		M		+
	DI-N-OCTYL PHTHALATE	117-84-0	SEE N-DIOCTYL-PHTHALATE													
	DIACETONE ALCOHOL	123-42-2												M		+
	DIALIFOR	10311-84-9					E									N
	DIALKYLNITROSAMINES								G							
	DIALLATE	2303-16-4				D										+
	DIAMINOTOLUENE (MIXED ISOMERS)	25376-45-8				D										
	DIAMINOTOLUENE (MIXED)								G				K			
	DIAZEPAM	439-14-5											K			
	DIAZINON	333-41-5			C				G	H		J		M		N
	DIAZOMETHANE	334-88-3				D			G					M		N
	DIBENZO(A,H)ANTHRACENE	53-70-3		B	C	D			G			J	K			N
	DIBENZOFURAN	132-64-9				D			G			J	K			N
	DIBENZOFURANS (CHLORINATED)								G				+			+
*	DIBENZO[A,E]FLUORANTHENE	5385-75-1							G							N
	DIBENZO[A,E]PYRENE	192-65-4							G				K			N
	DIBENZO[A,H]PYRENE	189-64-0							G				K			N
	DIBENZO[A,I]PYRENE	189-55-9							G				K			+
	DIBENZO[A,L]PYRENE	191-30-0							G							N
*	DIBENZO[H,RST]PENTAPHENE	192-47-2							G							N
*	DIBENZ[A,C]ANTHRACENE	215-58-7														N
	DIBENZ[A,H]ACRIDINE	226-36-8							G				K			N

240

NEW CHEMICAL	CHEMICAL NAME	CAS NUMBER	A	B	C	D	E	F	G	H	I	J	K	L	M	N
*	DIBENZ[A,I]ANTHRACENE	224-41-9														N
	DIBENZ[A,J]ACRIDINE	224-42-0													M	N
	DIBORANE	19287-45-7					E		G				K			N
	DIBROMOCHLOROMETHANE	124-48-1	SEE CHLORODIBROMOMETHANE													
*	DIBROMOCHLOROPROPANE	96-12-8	A		C	D		F	G	H		J	K		M	N
	DIBROMODIFLUOROMETHANE	75-61-6													M	N
	DIBUTYL PHOSPHATE	107-66-4														N
	DIBUTYL PHTHALATE	84-74-2	SEE DI-N-BUTYL PHTHALATE													
	DICAMBA	1918-00-9														N
	DICHLOBENIL	1194-65-6													M	N
	DICHLONE	117-80-6													M	N
	DICHLORAN	102-30-7														N
*	DICHLOROACETYLENE	7572-29-4							G						M	+
	DICHLOROBENZENE (MIXED ISOMERS)	25321-22-6				D			G							+
	DICHLOROBROMOMETHANE	75-27-4		B	C	D			G				K			N
	DICHLORODIFLUOROMETHANE	75-71-8			C	+									M	N
	DICHLOROETHYL ETHER	111-44-4	SEE BIS(2-CHLOROETHYL) ETHER													
	DICHLOROMETHANE	75-09-2	SEE METHYLENE CHLORIDE													
	DICHLOROMETHYL ETHER	542-88-1	SEE BIS(CHLOROMETHYL) ETHER													
	DICHLOROMETHYLPHENYLSILANE	149-74-6					E									
*	DICHLOROMONOFLUOROMETHANE	75-43-4													M	N
	DICHLOROPHENYLARSINE	696-28-6	SEE PHENYL DICHLOROARSINE													
	DICHLOROSILANE	4109-96-0												L		
*	DICHLORPROP	120-36-5														N
	DICHLORVOS	62-73-7				D	E		G			J	K		M	N
	DICOFOL	115-32-2			C	D			G						M	N
	DICROTOPHOS	141-66-2					E									+
*	DICUMAROL	66-76-2											K			
	DICYCLOHEXYLMETHANE-4,4'-DIISOCYANATE;	5124-30-1	SEE METHYLENE BIS-(4-CYCLOHEXYLISOCYANATE)													
	DICYCLOPENTADIENYL IRON	102-54-5											K		M	N
	DICYCLOPENTADIENE	77-73-6											K		M	N
	DIELDRIN	60-57-1		B	C	D	E		G	M			K		M	N
	DIENESTROL	84-17-3							G				K			
	DIEPOXYBUTANE	1464-53-5				D	E		G				K		M	N

241

NEW CHEMICAL	CHEMICAL NAME	CAS NUMBER	A	B	C	D	E	F	G	H	I	J	K	L	M	N
	DIESEL EXHAUST								G							
	DIETHANOLAMINE	111-42-2							G		I	J	K		M	N
	DIETHYL CHLOROPHOSPHATE	814-49-3				D	E								M	+
	DIETHYL KETONE	96-22-0													M	
	DIETHYL PHTHALATE	84-66-2		B	C	D			G						M	+
	DIETHYL SULFATE	64-67-5				D			G			J	K		M	N
	DIETHYLAMINE	109-89-7														
	DIETHYLCARBAMAZINE CITRATE	1642-54-2					E									N
	DIETHYLENETRIAMINE	111-40-0														
	DIETHYLSTILBESTROL	56-53-1							G				K		M	N
	DIGITOXIN	71-63-6					E									
	DIGLYCIDYL ETHER	2238-07-5					E		G						M	N
	DIGLYCIDYL RESORCINOL ETHER (DGRE)	101-90-6							G				K		M	+
	DIGOXIN	20830-75-5					E									
	DIHYDROSAFROLE	94-58-6							G				K		M	-
	DIISOBUTYL KETONE;2,6-DIMETHYL-4-HEPTONE	108-83-8													M	N
	DIISOPROPYL ETHER	108-20-3	SEE ISOPROPYL ETHER													
	DIISOPROPYLAMINE	108-18-9													M	N
	DIKETENE, INHIBITATED	674-82-8												L		
	DIMEFOX	115-26-4					E									
	DIMETHLYFORMAMIDE	68-12-2							G			J			M	N
	DIMETHOATE	60-51-5			C		E			H					M	N
*	DIMETHOXANE	828-00-2														
	DIMETHOXYMETHANE	109-87-5	SEE METHYLAL				E								M	N
	DIMETHYL PHOSPHOROCHLORIDOTHIOATE	2524-03-0														
	DIMETHYL PHTHALATE	131-11-3		B	C	D			G			J	K	L	M	+
	DIMETHYL SULFATE	77-78-1				D	E		G			J			M	N
	DIMETHYL TETRACHOLORTEREPHTHALATE	1861-32-1			C											
	DIMETHYL THIOPHOSPORYL CHLORIDE	99-98-9					E									
	DIMETHYL-P-PHENYLENEDIAMINE	127-19-5													M	N
	DIMETHYLACETAMIDE	124-40-3													M	N
	DIMETHYLAMINE	79-44-7				D			G			J	K		M	N
	DIMETHYLCARBAMOYL CHLORIDE	79-44-7														
	DIMETHYLCARBAMYL CHLORIDE		SEE DIMETHYLCARBONYL CHLORIDE													

242

CALIFORNIA ENVIRONMENTAL PROTECTION AGENCY
CHEMICAL LIST OF LISTS - BY CHEMICAL NAME

NEW CHEMICAL	CHEMICAL NAME	CAS NUMBER	A	B	C	D	E	F	G	H	I	J	K	L	M	N
	DIMETHYLDICHLOROSILANE	75-78-5					E									
	DIMETHYLHYDRAZINE	57-14-7	SEE 1,1-DIMETHYLHYDRAZINE													
	DIMETHYLHYDRAZINE (SYMETRICAL)	540-73-8	SEE 1,2-DIMETHYLHYDRAZINE													
	DIMETHYLVINYLCHLORIDE	513-37-1							G				K		M	N
	DIMETILAN	644-64-4					E									
	DINITOLMIDE	148-01-6													M	+
	DINITROBENZENE	25154-54-5							G				K		M	N
	DINITROCRESOL	534-52-1	SEE 4,6-DINITRO-O-CRESOL													
	DINITROTOLUENE (MIXED ISOMERS)	25321-14-6				D			G				K		M	N
	DINOCAP	39300-45-3							G							
	DINOSEB	88-85-7	SEE DNBP													
	DINOTERB	1420-07-1					E									
	DIOXATHION	78-34-2					E								M	N
	DIOXINS															
	DIOXINS (CHLORINATED DIBENZODIOXINS)										I					
	DIPHACINONE	82-66-6					E		G				K		M	N
	DIPHENAMIDE	957-51-7			C					H						
	DIPHENYL	92-52-4	SEE BIPHENYL													
	DIPHENYLAMINE	122-39-4														
	DIPHENYLAMINECHLOROARSINE	578-94-9												L		
	DIPHENYLCHLORARSINE													L		
	DIPHENYLHYDANTOIN	57-41-0							G				K			+
	DIPHENYLHYDANTOIN (PHENYTOIN), SODIUM SALT	630-93-3							G				K			+
	DIPHENYLHYDRAZINE	38622-18-3													M	N
	DIPHENYLMETHANE-4,4'DIISOCYANATE	101-68-8	SEE METHYLENE DIPHENYL DIISOCYANATE													
	DIPHOSPHORAMIDE, OCTAMETHYL-	152-16-9					E									
	DIPROPYL KETONE	123-19-3														
	DIPROPYLENE GLYCOL MONOMETHYL ETHER	34590-94-8														
	DIQUAT	85-00-7														
	DIRECT BLACK 38	1937-37-7				D			G				K		M	N
	DIRECT BLUE 6	2602-46-2				D			G				K		M	N
	DISPERSE BLUE 1	2475-45-8							G				K		M	+
	DISULFIRAM	97-77-8													M	N
	DISULFOTON	298-04-4			C		E								M	N

243

CALIFORNIA ENVIRONMENTAL PROTECTION AGENCY
CHEMICAL LIST OF LISTS - BY CHEMICAL NAME

NEW	CHEMICAL NAME	CAS NUMBER	A	B	C	D	E	F	G	H	I	J	K	L	M	N
	DITHIAZANINE IODIDE	514-73-8					E								M	N
	DITHIOBIURET	541-53-7					E								M	N
	DIURON	330-54-1			C										M	N
	DIVINYL BENZENE	1321-74-0													M	N
	DNBP	88-85-7			C		E		G				K			
	DNOC	SEE 4,6-DINITRO-O-CRESOL														
	DODECYLLBENZENESULFONIC ACID	27176-87-0													M	
	DOXYCYCLINE	564-25-0							G				K			
	DOXYCYCLINE CALCIUM (INTERNAL USE)	94088-85-4											K			
	DOXYCYCLINE HYCLATE (INTERNAL USE)	24390-14-5											K			
	DOXYCYCLINE MONOHYDRATE (INTERNAL USE)	17086-28-1											K			
	EDB	106-93-4	A	B	C	D		F	G				K	L	M	N
	EDC	107-06-2	SEE 1,2-DICHLOROETHANE													
	EMERY	12415-34-8													M	
	EMETINE, DIHYDROCHLORIDE	316-42-7					E								M	
	ENDOSULFAN	115-29-7			C		E								M	N
	ENDOSULFAN I	SEE ALPHA ENDOSULFAN														
	ENDOSULFAN II	SEE BETA ENDOSULFAN														
	ENDOSULFAN SULFATE	1031-07-8		B	C											+
	ENDOTHION	2778-04-3					E								M	N
	ENDRIN	72-20-8		B	C		E								M	N
	ENDRIN ALDEHYDE	7421-93-4		B	C			F								
	ENVIRONMENTAL TOBACCO SMOKE								G		I					
	EPICHLOROHYDRIN	106-89-8				D	E		G			J	K		M	N
	EPN	2104-64-5					E								M	N
	EPOXY RESINS								G							
*	ERBON	136-25-4													M	
	ERGOCALCIFEROL	50-14-6					E		G				K			
	ERGOTAMINE TARTRATE	379-79-3					E		G				K			+
	ERIONITE	12510-42-8							G				K			+
*	ESTRADIOL MUSTARD	22966-79-6							G							-
	ESTRADIOL-17B	50-28-2							G				K			-
	ESTROGENS, NONSTEROIDAL								G							+
	ESTROGENS, STEROIDAL								G							+

NEW CHEMICAL	CHEMICAL NAME	CAS NUMBER	A	B	C	D	E	F	G	H	I	J	K	L	M	N
	ESTRONE	53-16-7							G							
	ETHANE	78-84-0							G				K		M	
	ETHANESULFONYL CHLORIDE, 2-CHLORO-	1622-32-8					E									
	ETHANOL	64-17-5	SEE ETHYL ALCOHOL													
	ETHANOL, 1,2-DICHLORO-, ACETATE	10140-87-1					E									
	ETHANOLAMINE	141-43-5					E		G						M	N
	ETHINYLESTRADIOL	57-63-6											K			N
*	ETHION	563-12-2					E		G						M	N
	ETHIONAMIDE	536-33-4					E			H						N
	ETHOPROPHOS	13194-48-4					E								M	N
	ETHYL ACETATE	141-78-6							G						M	N
	ETHYL ACRYLATE	140-88-5				D			G			J			M	N
	ETHYL ALCOHOL	64-17-5			C										M	N
	ETHYL ALCOHOL IN ALCOHOLIC BEVERAGES												K			
	ETHYL BIS(2-CHLOROETHYL)AMINE	538-07-8					E						K			
	ETHYL BROMIDE	74-96-4													M	N
	ETHYL BUTYL KETONE	106-35-4													M	N
	ETHYL CHLORIDE	75-00-3	SEE CHLOROETHANE													
	ETHYL CHLOROFORMATE	541-41-3							G					L		
	ETHYL CHLOROTHIOFORMATE	2941-64-2				D								L		
	ETHYL DICHLOROARSINE	598-14-1												L		
	ETHYL ETHER	60-29-7														
	ETHYL FORMATE	109-94-4														
	ETHYL ISOCYANATE	109-90-0												L		N
	ETHYL MERCAPTAN	75-08-1													M	N
	ETHYL METHANESULFONATE	62-50-0							G				K			
	ETHYL PHOSPHONOTHIOIC DICHLORIDE, ANHYDROUS	993-43-1												L		
	ETHYL SEC-AMYL KETONE	541-85-5													M	N
	ETHYL SILICATE	78-10-4													M	N
	ETHYL THIOCYANATE	542-90-5														
	ETHYL-4,4'-DICHLOROBENZILATE	510-15-6	SEE CHLOROBENZILATE				E									
	ETHYLAMINE	75-04-7														
	ETHYLBENZENE	100-41-4		B	C	D		F	G						M	N
	ETHYLENE	74-85-1				D		F	G			J			M	N

245

NEW CHEMICAL	CHEMICAL NAME	CAS NUMBER	A	B	C	D	E	F	G	H	I	J	K	L	M	N
	ETHYLENE CHLOROHYDRIN													L		
	ETHYLENE DIBROMIDE	106-93-4	SEE EDB													
	ETHYLENE DICHLORIDE	107-06-2	SEE 1,2-DICHLOROETHANE													
	ETHYLENE FLUOROHYDRIN	371-62-0					E									
	ETHYLENE GLYCOL	107-21-1			C	D			G			J			M	N
	ETHYLENE GLYCOL DINITRATE	628-96-6													M	N
	ETHYLENE GLYCOL MONOBUTYL ETHER	111-76-2														
	ETHYLENE GLYCOL MONOETHYL ETHER	110-80-5	SEE 2-ETHOXYETHANOL													
	ETHYLENE GLYCOL MONOETHYL ETHER ACETATE	111-15-9	SEE 2-ETHOXYETHYL ACETATE													
	ETHYLENE GLYCOL MONOMETHYL ETHER	109-86-4	SEE 2-METHOXYETHANOL													
	ETHYLENE GLYCOL MONOMETHYL ETHER ACETATE	110-49-6														
	ETHYLENE OXIDE	75-21-8	A			D			G		I	J	K		M	N
	ETHYLENEDIAMINE	107-15-3				D	E								M	N
	ETHYLENEDIAMINE TETRAACETIC ACID (EDTA)	60-00-4													M	N
	ETHYLENEIMINE	151-56-4	A			D	E		G			J	K	L	M	N
	ETHYLENETHIOUREA	96-45-7			C	D	E		G			J	K		M	N
	ETHYLIDENE NORBORNENE	16219-75-3													M	
	ETOPOSIDE	33419-42-0							G				K			
	ETRETINATE	54350-48-0							G				K			
*	EUGENOL	97-53-0													M	N
*	EVANS BLUE	314-13-6													M	N
*	FAST GREEN FCF	2353-45-9													M	N
	FENAMIPHOS	22224-92-6			C											N
	FENITROTHION	122-14-5					E									
	FENSULFOTHION	115-90-2					E									+
	FENTHION	55-38-9														N
*	FENURON	101-42-8													M	N
*	FENURON-TCA	4482-55-7													M	N
*	FERBAM	14484-64-1														N
*	FERRIC AMMONIUM CITRATE	1185-57-5													M	N
*	FERRIC AMMONIUM OXALATE	2944-67-4													M	N
*	FERRIC CHLORIDE	7705-08-0														N
*	FERRIC FLUORIDE	7783-50-8														N
*	FERRIC NITRATE	10421-48-4														N

246

NEW CHEMICAL	CHEMICAL NAME	CAS NUMBER	A	B	C	D	E	F	G	H	I	J	K	L	M	N
*	FERRIC SULFATE	10028-22-5														N
*	FERROUS AMMONIUM SULFATE	10045-89-3														N
*	FERROUS CHLORIDE	7758-94-3														N
*	FERROUS SULFATE	7720-78-7														N
	FERROVANADIUM	12604-58-9													M	N
	FIBROUS GLASS	1480-60-7													M	
	FLUENETIL	4301-50-2					E									
	FLUOMETURON	2164-17-2				D			G							
	FLUORANTHENE	206-44-0		B												N
	FLUORENE	86-73-7		B	C											
*	FLUORIDE	16984-48-8			C				G							+
	FLUORIDES AND COMPOUNDS															
	FLUORINE	7782-41-4					E		G						M	N
	FLUOROACETAMIDE	640-19-7					E									N
	FLUOROACETIC ACID	144-49-0					E									
*	FLUOROACETIC ACID, SODIUM SALT	62-74-8	SEE SODIUM FLUOROACETATE													
	FLUOROACETYL CHLORIDE	359-06-8					E									
	FLUOROCARBONS (CHLORINATED & BROMINATED)															
	FLUOROURACIL	51-21-8					E		G				K			
	FLUOXYMESTRONE	76-43-7							G				K			
*	FLURAZEPAM HYDROCHLORIDE	1172-18-5											K			
	FLUTAMIDE	13311-84-7							G				K			
	FOLPET	133-07-3							G				K			+
	FONOFOS	944-22-9					E		G				K		M	N
*	FORMALDEHYDE	50-00-0	A			D	E		G	H			K		M	N
	FORMALDEHYDE CYANOHYDRIN	107-16-4					E									
	FORMAMIDE	75-12-7							G						M	N
	FORMETANATE HYDROCHLORIDE	23422-53-9					E									
	FORMIC ACID	64-18-6														
	FORMOTHION	2540-82-1					E									
	FORMPARANATE	17702-57-7					E									
	FORMYLHYDRAZINO-4-(5-NITRO-2-FURYL)THIAZOLE	3570-75-0					E		G				K			N
	FOSTHIETAN	21548-32-3														
	FREON 113	76-13-1	SEE CHLORINATED FLUOROCARBON													

CALIFORNIA ENVIRONMENTAL PROTECTION AGENCY
CHEMICAL LIST OF LISTS - BY CHEMICAL NAME

NEW CHEMICAL	CHEMICAL NAME	CAS NUMBER	A	B	C	D	E	F	G	H	I	J	K	L	M	N
	FUBERIDAZOLE	3878-19-1					E									N
	FUMARIC ACID	110-17-8														N
	FURAN	110-00-9					E									N
	FURAZOLIDONE	67-45-8							G				K		M	N
	FURFURAL	98-01-1													M	N
	FURFURYL ALCOHOL	98-00-0													M	N
	FURMECYCLOX	60568-05-0							G				K		M	N
	GALLIUM TRICHLORIDE	13450-90-3					E									
	GAMMA-BHC	58-89-9		B	C	D	E		G			J	K		M	N
	GASOLINE	8006-61-9							G				K		M	N
	GASOLINE ENGINE EXHAUST								G							
	GASOLINE VAPORS								G							
	GERMANE	7782-65-2							G				K	L	M	N
	GLASSWOOL (MAN-MADE FIBERS)															
	GLASSWOOL FIBERS (AIRBORNE PARTICLES OF RESPIRABLE SIZE)												K			
	GLU-P-1 (2-AMINO-6-METHYLDIPYRIDO [1,2-A:3', 2'-D] IMIDAZOLE)	67730-11-4							G				K			+
	GLU-P-2 (2-AMINODIPYRIDO[1,2-A:3', 2'-D]IMIDAZOLE)	67730-12-5							G							
	GLU-P-2 (2-AMINODIPYRIDO[1,2-A:3',2'-D]IMIDAZOLE)	67730-10-3							G				K			+
	GLUTARALDEHYDE	111-30-8													M	N
	GLYCERIN MIST	56-81-5													M	N
	GLYCIDALDEHYDE	765-34-4							G				K		M	N
	GLYCIDOL	556-52-5							G				K		M	N
	GLYCOL ETHERS					D			G							
	GLYPHOSATE	1071-83-6		+				F								
	GRENADE WITH POISON GAS													L		+
	GRISEOFULVIN	126-07-8							G				K			
*	GUTHION	86-50-0	SEE AZINPHOS-METHYL													
	GYROMITRIN (ACETALDEHYDE METHYLFORMYLHYDRAZONE)	16568-02-8							G				K			+
	HAFNIUM	7440-58-6													M	N
	HALAZEPAM	23092-17-3							G				K			
	HC BLUE 1	2784-94-3							G				K			+
	HELIUM	7440-59-7							G						M	

248

CALIFORNIA ENVIRONMENTAL PROTECTION AGENCY
CHEMICAL LIST OF LISTS - BY CHEMICAL NAME

NEW CHEMICAL	CHEMICAL NAME	CAS NUMBER	A	B	C	D	E	F	G	H	I	J	K	L	M	N
	HEPTACHLOR	76-44-8		B	+	D		F	G			J	K		M	N
	HEPTACHLOR EPOXIDE	1024-57-3		B	C			F	G			J	K		M	+
	HEXACHLORO-1,3-BUTADIENE	87-68-3	SEE HEXACHLOROBUTADIENE													
	HEXACHLOROBENZENE	118-74-1		B	C	D			G			J	K		M	N
	HEXACHLOROBUTADIENE	87-68-3		B	C	D			G			J				N
	HEXACHLOROCYCLOHEXANE	608-73-1														N
	HEXACHLOROCYCLOHEXANES												K			
	HEXACHLOROCYCLOPENTADIENE	77-47-4		B	C	D	E		G			J		L	M	N
	HEXACHLORODIBENZODIOXIN	34465-46-8									I					
	HEXACHLOROETHANE	67-72-1		B	C	D			G			J	K		M	N
	HEXACHLORONAPHTHALENE	1335-87-1				D			G			J	K		M	N
	HEXACHLOROPHENE (HCP)	70-30-4												L		
*	HEXAETHYL TETRAPHOSPHATE AND COMPRESSED GAS MIXTURE															
	HEXAFLUOROACETONE	684-16-2														
	HEXAMETHYLENE-1,6-DIISOCYANATE	822-06-0							G						M	-
	HEXAMETHYLENEDIAMINE, N,N'-DIBUTYL-	4835-11-4					E									N
	HEXAMETHYLPHOSPHORAMIDE	680-31-9				D			G			J	K			N
	HEXANE	110-54-3										J				N
	HEXAVALENT CHROMIUM										I					
	HEXONE	108-10-1	SEE METHYL ISOBUTYL KETONE													
	HEXYLENE GLYCOL	107-41-5														
*	HYDRALAZINE	86-54-4														
	HYDRAZINE	302-01-2				D	E		G			J	K		M	N
	HYDRAZINE SULFATE	10034-93-2				D	E		G			J	K		M	N
*	HYDRAZINECARBOXAMIDE, 2-PHENYL	103-03-7														N
	HYDRAZOBENZENE (1,2-DIPHENYLHYDRAZINE)	122-66-7	SEE 1,2-DIPHENYLHYDRAZINE													
	HYDROBROMIDE ACID	10035-10-6	SEE HYDROGEN BROMIDE													
	HYDROCHLORIC ACID	7647-01-0	SEE HYDROGEN CHLORIDE													
	HYDROCYANIC ACID	74-90-8	SEE HYDROGEN CYANIDE													
	HYDROCYANIC ACID SOLUTION OR LIQUIFIED															
	HYDROFLUORIC ACID	7664-39-3	SEE HYDROGEN FLUORIDE													
	HYDROGEN	1333-74-0												L	M	N
	HYDROGEN BROMIDE	10035-10-6													M	N

NEW CHEMICAL	CHEMICAL NAME	CAS NUMBER	A	B	C	D	E	F	G	H	I	J	K	L	M	N
	HYDROGEN CHLORIDE	7647-01-0				D	E		G						M	N
	HYDROGEN CYANIDE	74-90-8				D	E		G			J			M	N
	HYDROGEN FLOURIDE	7664-39-3				D	E		G			J		L	M	N
	HYDROGEN PEROXIDE (CONC > 52%)	7722-84-1					E							L	M	N
	HYDROGEN SELENIDE	7783-07-5					E								M	N
	HYDROGEN SULFIDE	7783-06-4					E		G						M	N
	HYDROGENATED TERPHENYLS	92-94-4													M	N
	HYDROQUINONE	123-31-9				D	E		G			J			M	+
	IFOSFAMIDE	3778-73-2							G				K		M	+
	INDENE	95-31-6														N
	INDENO(1,2,3-CD)PYRENE	193-39-5		B					G				K		M	+
	INDIUM	7440-74-6											K		M	N
	INORGANIC ARSENIC	7440-38-2	A	B	+	D			G		I	J			M	N
	INSECTICIDE, LIQUIFIED GAS WITH POISON GAS													L		
	IODINE	7553-56-2														
	IODINE-131	24267-56-9							G				K		M	N
	IODOFORM	75-47-8														
	IQ(2-AMINO-3-METHYLIMIDAZO[4,5-F]QUINOLINE)	76180-96-6							G				K		M	N
•	IRON	7439-89-6			C				G							
	IRON DEXTRAN	9004-66-4							G							
	IRON DEXTRAN COMPLEX	9004-66-4	SEE IRON DEXTRAN													
	IRON OXIDE FUME	1309-37-1													M	+
•	IRON, PENTACARBONYL- (IRON CARBONYL)	13463-40-6					E							L	M	N
	ISATIDINE	15503-86-3														
	ISOAMYL ACETATE	123-92-2													M	+
	ISOAMYL ALCOHOL	123-51-3													M	N
	ISOBENZAN	297-78-9					E									
	ISOBUTYL ACETATE	110-19-0													M	+
	ISOBUTYL ALCOHOL	78-83-1													M	N
	ISOBUTYL CHLOROFORMATE	543-27-1												L		
	ISOBUTYLAMINE	78-81-9														N
	ISOBUTYRALDEHYDE	78-84-2				D			G							
	ISOBUTYRONITRILE	78-82-0					E									
•	ISOCYANATES								G							

NEW CHEMICAL	CHEMICAL NAME	CAS NUMBER	A	B	C	D	E	F	G	H	I	J	K	L	M	N
	ISOCYANIC ACID, 3,4-DICHLOROPHENYL ESTER	102-36-3														
	ISODRIN	465-73-6					E									
	ISOFLUORPHATE	55-91-4					E									
*	ISONICOTINIC ACID HYDRAZIDE	54-85-3													M	N
	ISOOCTYL ALCOHOL	26952-21-6													M	N
	ISOPHORONE	78-59-1		B	C		E		G							N
	ISOPHORONE DIISOCYANATE	4098-71-9					E					J			M	N
	ISOPRENE	78-79-5														N
	ISOPROPANOLAMINE DODECYLBENZENESULFONATE	42504-46-1														N
	ISOPROPOXYETHANOL	109-59-1													M	N
	ISOPROPYL ACETATE	108-21-4													M	N
	ISOPROPYL ALCOHOL (MANUFACTURING-STRONG ACID PROCESS ONLY, NO SUPPLIER NOTIFICATION)	67-63-0				D			G							
	ISOPROPYL CHLOROFORMATE	108-23-6					E							L		
	ISOPROPYL GLYCIDYL ETHER	4016-14-2													M	N
	ISOPROPYLAMINE	75-31-0													M	N
	ISOPROPYLMETHYLPYRAZOLYL DIMETHYLCARBAMATE	119-38-0					E									
	ISOPRPYL ETHER	108-20-3														N
	ISOSAFROLE	120-58-1				D			G				K			
	ISOTRETINOIN	4759-48-2							G				K			
	KAOLIN	1332-58-7														N
	KETENE; ETHENONE	463-51-4							G							
	LACTOFEN	77501-63-4							G				K			
	LACTONITRILE	78-97-7					E									
	LASIOCARPINE	303-34-4							G		I		K		M	N
*	LEAD	7439-92-1		B	+	D		F	G				K		M	+
	LEAD ACETATE	301-04-2														N
*	LEAD ARSENATE	7784-40-9														N
*	LEAD CHLORIDE	7758-95-4													M	+
	LEAD CHROMATE	7758-97-6							G							
	LEAD COMPOUNDS					D										
	LEAD COMPOUNDS (INORGANIC)								G				K		M	N
*	LEAD FLUOBORATE	13814-96-5														+
*	LEAD FLUORIDE	7783-46-2													M	N

251

NEW CHEMICAL	CHEMICAL NAME	CAS NUMBER	A	B	C	D	E	F	G	H	I	J	K	L	M	N
*	LEAD IODIDE	10101-63-0														N
*	LEAD NITRATE	10099-74-8														N
	LEAD PHOSPHATE	7446-27-7							G				K			+
*	LEAD STEARATE	7428-48-0														N
	LEAD SUBACETATE	1335-32-6							G				K			+
*	LEAD SULFATE	7446-14-2														N
*	LEAD SULFIDE	1314-87-0														N
	LEAD, INORGANIC	7439-92-1	SEE LEAD													
	LEPTOPHOS	21609-90-5					E									
	LEWISITE	541-25-3					E									
*	LIGHT GREEN SF	5141-20-8														N
	LINDANE	58-89-9	SEE GAMMA-BHC													
	LINDANE AND OTHER HEXACHLOROCYCLOHEXANE ISOMERS												K			N
*	LINURON	330-55-2														N
	LITHIUM CARBONATE	554-13-2							G				K			
*	LITHIUM CHROMATE	14307-35-8							G				K			N
	LITHIUM CITRATE	919-16-4							G				K			
	LITHIUM HYDRIDE	7580-67-8					E		G						M	N
	LORAZEPAM	846-49-1							G				K			
*	LOVASTATIN	75330-75-5							G				K			
	LUBRICANT BASE OILS AND DERIVED PRODUCTS								G							
	M-CRESOL	108-39-4				D			G			J				
	M-DINITROBENZENE	99-65-0				D			G				K		M	N
	M-PHTHALODINITRILE	626-17-5													M	+
	M-TOLUIDINE	108-44-1														
	M-XYLENE	108-38-3			+	D				H		J			M	N
	MAGNESITE; MAGNESIUM CARBONATE	13717-00-5														
*	MAGNESIUM	7439-95-4			C										M	N
	MAGNESIUM OXIDE	1309-48-4													M	N
	MALATHION	121-75-5			C					H		J	K		M	N
	MALEIC ANHYDRIDE	108-31-6				D			G			J				
	MALONONITRILE	109-77-3					E									
	MANCOZEB	8018-01-7			C				G				K			
	MANEB (CARBAMODITHIOIC ACID, 1,2-ETHANEDIYLBIS-, MANGANESE COMPLEX)	12427-38-2			C	D			G				K			

CALIFORNIA ENVIRONMENTAL PROTECTION AGENCY
CHEMICAL LIST OF LISTS - BY CHEMICAL NAME

NEW CHEMICAL	CHEMICAL NAME	CAS NUMBER	A	B	C	D	E	F	G	H	I	J	K	L	M	N
	MANGANESE	7439-96-5														N
	MANGANESE COMPOUNDS				+	D			G						M	N
*	MANGANESE TETROXIDE	1317-35-7				D			G						M	N
	MANGANESE, CYCLOPENTADIENYL-TRICARBONYL	12079-65-1													M	N
	MANGANESE, TRICARBONYL METHYLCYCLOPENTADIENYL	12108-13-3					E								M	N
*	MANNOMUSTINE	551-74-6														N
	MCPA; 2-METHYL-4-CHLOROPHENOXYACETIC ACID	94-74-6														N
	MECHLORETHAMINE	51-75-2	SEE NITROGEN MUSTARD													
	MEDROXYPROGESTERONE ACETATE	71-58-9			+				G				K			
	MEGESTROL ACETATE	595-33-5											K			
	MELPHALAN	148-82-3							G				K			
	MENOTROPINS	9002-68-0							G				K			
	MEPHOSFOLAN	950-10-7					E									
	MEPROBAMATE	57-53-4											K			
	MERCAPTODIMETHUR	2032-65-7	SEE METHIOCARB													
	MERCAPTOPURINE	6112-76-1							G				K			
	MERCURIC ACETATE	1600-27-7	SEE MERCURY ACETATE													
*	MERCURIC CYANIDE	592-04-1														N
*	MERCURIC NITRATE	10045-94-0														N
	MERCURIC OXIDE	21908-53-2					E									
*	MERCURIC SULFATE	7783-35-9														N
*	MERCURIC THIOCYANATE	592-85-8														N
*	MERCUROUS NITRATE	10415-75-5														N
	MERCURY	7439-97-6		B	+	D		F	G			J	K		M	
	MERCURY ACETATE (2)	1600-27-7					E									
	MERCURY CHLORIDE (2)	7487-94-7					E		G							
	MERCURY COMPOUNDS					D			G				K		M	N
	MERPHALAN	531-76-0							G				K			
	MESITYL OXIDE	141-79-7													M	N
	MESITYLENE	108-67-8	SEE 1,3,5-TRIMETHYLBENZENE													N
	MESTRANOL	72-33-3							G				K			
	METHACROLEIN DIACETATE	10476-95-6					E									
	METHACRYLIC ANHYDRIDE	760-93-0					E									
	METHACRYLOYL CHLORIDE	920-46-7					E									

CALIFORNIA ENVIRONMENTAL PROTECTION AGENCY
CHEMICAL LIST OF LISTS - BY CHEMICAL NAME

NEW CHEMICAL	CHEMICAL NAME	CAS NUMBER	A	B	C	D	E	F	G	H	I	J	K	L	M	N
	METHACRYLOYLOXYETHYL ISOCYANATE	30674-80-7					E									N
	METHACYCLINE HYDROCHLORIDE	3963-95-9											K			N
	METHAMIDOPHOS	10265-92-6			C		E									N
	METHANAMINE, N-METHYL-N-NITROSO	62-75-9	SEE N-NITROSODIMETHYLAMINE													
*	METHANE	74-82-8														N
	METHANE SULFONYL CHLORIDE	124-63-0												L		
	METHANESULFONYL FLUORIDE	558-25-8					E									
	METHANETHIOL	74-93-1	SEE METHYL MERCAPTAN													
	METHANOL	67-56-1				D			G			J			M	N
	METHIDATHION	950-37-8					E								M	N
	METHIMAZOLE	60-56-0					E		G				K		M	
	METHIOCARB	2032-65-7					E								M	+
	METHOMYL	16752-77-5			C		E								M	+
	METHOTREXATE	59-05-2							G				K		M	
	METHOTREXATE SODIUM	15475-56-6							G				K		M	
	METHOXYCHLOR	72-43-5			C	D		F	G			J			M	N
	METHOXYETHYLMERCURIC ACETATE	151-38-2					E								M	
	METHOXYMETHYL ISOCYANATE	6427-21-0												L		
	METHYL 2-BENZIMIDAZOLE CARBAMATE	17804-35-2			C				G				K		M	
	METHYL 2-CHLOROACRYLATE	80-63-7					E								M	N
	METHYL 2-CYANOACRYLATE	137-05-3													M	N
	METHYL ACETATE	79-20-9													M	N
	METHYL ACETYLENE; PROPYNE	74-99-7													M	+
	METHYL ACRYLATE	96-33-3				D			G					L	M	N
	METHYL BROMIDE	74-83-9		B	C	D	E		G			J		L	M	N
	METHYL CHLORIDE	74-87-3		B	C	D			G			J		L	M	+
	METHYL CHLOROFORM	71-55-6	SEE 1,1,1-TRICHLOROETHANE													
	METHYL CHLOROFORMATE	79-22-1					E								M	N
	METHYL CHLOROMETHYL ETHER	107-30-2	A			D	E		G					L	M	N
	METHYL CHLOROSILANE															N
	METHYL DEMETON	8022-00-2													M	
	METHYL DICHLOROSILANE	75-54-7													M	N
	METHYL ETHYL KETONE	78-93-3			C	D			G			J			M	N
	METHYL ETHYL KETONE PEROXIDE	1338-23-4													M	N

CALIFORNIA ENVIRONMENTAL PROTECTION AGENCY
CHEMICAL LIST OF LISTS - BY CHEMICAL NAME

NEW CHEMICAL	CHEMICAL NAME	CAS NUMBER	A	B	C	D	E	F	G	H	I	J	K	L	M	N
	METHYL FORMATE	107-31-3													X	N
	METHYL IODIDE	74-88-4				D			G			J	K		X	N
	METHYL ISOAMYL KETONE	110-12-3													X	N
	METHYL ISOBUTYL CARBINOL	108-11-2			C										X	N
	METHYL ISOBUTYL KETONE	108-10-1				D			G						X	N
	METHYL ISOCYANATE	624-83-9				D	E		G			J			X	N
	METHYL ISOPROPYL KETONE	563-80-4				D						J			X	N
	METHYL ISOTHIOCYANATE	556-61-6					E							L	X	N
	METHYL MERCAPTAN	74-93-1					E							L	X	N
	METHYL MERCAPTOPROPIONALDEHYDE	3268-49-3												L	X	
	METHYL MERCURY												K			
	METHYL MERCURY (DIMETHYLMERCURY)	593-74-8							G						X	N
	METHYL METHACRYLATE	80-62-6				D			G			J			X	N
	METHYL METHANESULFONATE	66-27-3							G				K		X	N
	METHYL N-AMYL KETONE	110-43-0													X	N
	METHYL N-BUTYL KETONE	591-78-6												L	X	N
	METHYL ORTHOSILICATE	681-84-5													X	N
	METHYL PARATHION	298-00-0					E								X	N
	METHYL PHENKAPTON	3735-23-7					E			H				L		N
	METHYL PHOSPHONIC DICHLORIDE	676-97-1					E							L		N
	METHYL PHOSPHONOUS DICHLORIDE	676-83-5					E									N
	METHYL PROPYL KETONE	107-87-9													X	
	METHYL TERT-BUTYL ETHER	1634-04-4				D			G			J			X	
	METHYL THIOCYANATE	556-64-9					E									N
	METHYL VINYL KETONE	78-94-4					E									N
	METHYLACRYLONITRILE	126-98-7					E									N
	METHYLAL	109-87-5													X	N
	METHYLAMINE	74-89-5													X	N
	METHYLANILINE	100-61-8													X	N
	METHYLAZOXYMETHANOL	590-96-5							G				K		X	N
	METHYLAZOXYMETHANOL ACETATE	592-62-1							G				K		X	N
	METHYLCYCLOHEXANOL ALL ISOMER	25639-42-3													X	N
	METHYLCYCLOHEXANE	108-87-2													X	N
	METHYLENE BIS(4-CYCLOHEXYLISOCYANATE)	5124-30-1													X	N

CALIFORNIA ENVIRONMENTAL PROTECTION AGENCY
CHEMICAL LIST OF LISTS - BY CHEMICAL NAME

NEW CHEMICAL	CHEMICAL NAME	CAS NUMBER	A	B	C	D	E	F	G	H	I	J	K	L	M	N
	METHYLENE BIS(PHENYLISOCYANATE) (MBI)	101-68-8	SEE METHYLENE DIPHENYL DIISOCYANATE													N
	METHYLENE BROMIDE	74-95-3				D			G						M	N
	METHYLENE CHLORIDE	75-09-2		B	C	D			G	H			K		M	N
	METHYLENE DIPHENYL DIISOCYANATE	101-68-8				D			G		I	J		L	M	N
	METHYLENE ISOCYANATE											J		L		
	METHYLHYDRAZINE	60-34-4				D	E		G			J			M	N
	METHYLMERCURIC DICYANAMIDE	502-39-6					E		G			J	+		M	+
	METHYLTESTOSTERONE	58-18-4							G				K			
	METHYLTHIOURACIL	56-04-2							G				K		M	
	METHYLTRICHLOROSILANE	75-79-6					E		G							
	METIRAM	9006-42-2											K		M	N
	METOLCARB	1129-41-5					E								M	N
	METRIBUZIN	21087-64-9														
	METRONIDAZOLE	443-48-1							G				K		M	N
	MEVINPHOS	7786-34-7					E								M	N
	MEXACARBATE	315-18-4					E								M	N
	MICA	12001-26-2													M	N
	MICHLER'S KETONE	90-94-8				D			G				K		M	N
	MIDAZOLAM HYDROCHLORIDE	59467-96-8							G				K		M	N
	MINERAL FIBERS								G						M	N
	MINERAL OILS (UNTREATED AND MILDLY TREATED OILS)								G						M	
	MIREX	2385-85-5							G				K		M	N
	MISOPROSTOL	62015-39-8							G				K		M	N
	MITOMYCIN C	50-07-7					E		G				K			
	MITOXANTRONE HYDROCHLORIDE	70476-82-3							G				K			
	MOLINATE		SEE ORDRAM													
	MOLYBDENUM	7439-98-7													M	N
	MOLYBDENUM COMPOUNDS														M	N
	MOLYBDENUM TRIOXIDE	1313-27-5				D			G							
	MONOCHLOROACETONE, STABILIZED	78-95-5												L		
	MONOCHLOROBENZENE		SEE CHLOROBENZENE													
	MONOCROTALINE	315-22-0							G				K			N
	MONOCROTOPHOS	6923-22-4					E								M	N
	MONURON	150-68-5													M	N

*

CALIFORNIA ENVIRONMENTAL PROTECTION AGENCY
CHEMICAL LIST OF LISTS - BY CHEMICAL NAME

NEW CHEMICAL	CHEMICAL NAME	CAS NUMBER	A	B	C	D	E	F	G	H	I	J	K	L	M	N
	MORPHOLINE	110-91-8														N
	MUSCIMOL	2763-96-4					E									N
	MUSTARD GAS	505-60-2				D	E		G				K		M	N
	N,N'-DIACETYLBENZIDINE	613-35-4							G				K		M	N
	N,N-BIS(2-CHLOROETHYL)-2-NAPHTHYLAMINE (CHLORNAPAZINE)	494-03-1							G				K		M	N
	N,N-DIMETHYLANILINE	121-69-7				D						J				N
	N-BUTYL ACETATE	123-86-4													M	N
	N-BUTYL ALCOHOL	71-36-3				D			G						M	N
	N-BUTYL GLYCIDYL ETHER	2426-08-6													M	N
	N-BUTYL ISOCYANATE	111-36-4												L		N
	N-BUTYL LACTATE	138-22-7													M	N
	N-BUTYLCHLOROFORMATE													L		+
	N-DIOCTYL-PHTHALATE	117-84-0		B		D			G							N
	N-DIOCTYL-PHTHALATE	117-84-0	SEE DI-N-OCTYL PHTHALATE													
	N-ETHYL-N-NITROSOUREA	759-73-9	SEE N-NITROSO-N-ETHYLUREA													
	N-ETHYLMORPHOLINE	100-74-3														N
	N-HEPTANE	142-82-5														
	N-ISOPROPYLANILINE	643-28-7														
	N-METHYL-N'-NITRO-N-NITROSOGUANIDINE	70-25-7							G				K		M	N
	N-METHYLOACRYLAMIDE	924-42-5							G				K		M	N
	N-NITROSO-N-ETHYLUREA	759-73-9				D			G				K		M	N
	N-NITROSO-N-METHYLUREA	684-93-5				D			G			J	K			N
	N-NITROSO-N-METHYLURETHANE	615-53-2							G				K			N
	N-NITROSODI-N-BUTYLAMINE	924-16-3				D			G				K			N
	N-NITROSODI-N-PROPYLAMINE	621-64-7		B		D			G				K			N
	N-NITROSODIETHANOLAMINE	1116-54-7							G				K			N
	N-NITROSODIETHYLAMINE	55-18-5				D			G				K			N
	N-NITROSODIMETHYLAMINE	62-75-9	A	B	C	D	E		G			J	K		M	+
	N-NITROSODIPHENYLAMINE	86-30-6		B	C	D			G				K			N
	N-NITROSOMETHYLETHYLAMINE	10595-95-6							G				K			N
	N-NITROSOMETHYLVINYLAMINE	4549-40-0				D			G				K			N
	N-NITROSOMORPHOLINE	59-89-2				D			G			J	K			N
	N-NITROSONORNICOTINE	16543-55-8				D			G				K			N

257

CALIFORNIA ENVIRONMENTAL PROTECTION AGENCY
CHEMICAL LIST OF LISTS - BY CHEMICAL NAME

NEW CHEMICAL	CHEMICAL NAME	CAS NUMBER	A	B	C	D	E	F	G	H	I	J	K	L	M	N
	N-NITROSOPIPERIDINE	100-75-4				D			G				K			N
	N-NITROSOPYRROLIDINE	930-55-2							G				K			N
	N-NITROSOSARCOSINE	13256-22-9							G				K			N
*	N-PHENYL-BETA-NAPHTHYLAMINE	135-88-6														N
	N-PROPYL ACETATE	109-60-4													M	N
	N-PROPYL ALCOHOL	71-23-8													M	N
	N-PROPYL NITRATE	627-13-4													M	N
	N-PROPYLCHLOROFORMATE	SEE PROPYL CHLOROFORMATE														
	N-[4-(5-NITRO-2-FURYL)-2-THIAZOLYL]ACETAMIDE	531-82-8							G				K			N
	NAFARELIN ACETATE	86220-42-0							G				K			N
	NAFENOPIN	3771-19-5							G				K			N
	NALED	300-76-5													M	N
	NAPHTHA, COAL TAR	8030-31-7													M	N
	NAPHTHALENE	91-20-3		B	C	D			G			J	K		M	N
	NAPHTHALENE DIISOCYANATE	25551-28-4													M	N
	NAPHTHENIC ACID	1338-24-5														
	NEOMYCIN SULFATE	1405-10-3							G				K			N
	NETILMICIN SULFATE	56391-57-2							G				K			N
	NICKEL	7440-02-0		B		D			G				K		M	N
	NICKEL ACETATE	373-02-4				D			G							N
*	NICKEL AMMONIUM SULFATE	15699-18-0							G							N
	NICKEL CARBONATE	3333-37-3							G							N
	NICKEL CARBONYL	13463-39-3					E		G				K	L	+	N
*	NICKEL CHLORIDE	37211-05-5							G							N
	NICKEL COMPOUNDS					D			G				K		+	N
	NICKEL HYDROXIDE	12054-48-7							G						+	N
	NICKEL NITRATE	14216-75-2							G				K			N
	NICKEL OXIDE	1313-99-1							G							N
	NICKEL REFINERY DUST FROM PYROMETALLURGICAL PROCESSES															
*	NICKEL SUBSULFIDE	12035-72-2							G				K		+	N
	NICKEL SULFATE	778-61-4							G							N
	NICKELOCENE	1271-28-9							G							N
	NICOTINE	54-11-5					E		G				K		M	N

258

CALIFORNIA ENVIRONMENTAL PROTECTION AGENCY
CHEMICAL LIST OF LISTS - BY CHEMICAL NAME

NEW CHEMICAL	CHEMICAL NAME	CAS NUMBER	A	B	C	D	E	F	G	H	I	J	K	L	M	N
	NICOTINE SULFATE	65-30-5					E									N
	NIRIDAZOLE	61-57-4							G							N
	NITHIAZIDE	139-94-6											K			N
*	NITRAPYRIN	1929-82-4													M	+
	NITRATE							F								
	NITRATE (AS NO3)							F								
	NITRIC ACID	7697-37-2			+	D	E		G					L	M	N
	NITRIC OXIDE	10102-43-9	SEE NITROGEN OXIDE (NO)													
	NITRILOTRIACETIC ACID	139-13-9				D			G				K			+
	NITRILOTRIACETIC ACID, TRISODIUM SALT MONOHYDRATE	18662-53-8							G				K			
	NITROBENZENE	98-95-3		B	C	D	E		G			J			M	N
	NITROCYCLOHEXANE	1122-60-7					E									N
	NITROETHANE	79-24-3														+
	NITROFEN	1836-75-5				D			G				K		M	N
	NITROFURANTOIN	67-20-9											K			+
	NITROFURAZONE	59-87-0							G				K			+
	NITROGEN	7727-37-9													M	N
	NITROGEN DIOXIDE	10102-44-0					E								M	N
	NITROGEN MONOXIDE (NO)	10102-43-9	SEE NITROGEN OXIDE													
	NITROGEN MUSTARD	51-75-2				D	E		G				K			N
	NITROGEN MUSTARD HYDROCHLORIDE	55-86-7							G				K			N
	NITROGEN MUSTARD N-OXIDE	126-85-2											K			N
	NITROGEN MUSTARD N-OXIDE HYDROCHLORIDE	302-70-5							G				K			N
	NITROGEN OXIDE (N203)	10544-73-7												L		N
	NITROGEN OXIDE (N204)	10544-72-6	SEE NITROGEN TETROXIDE (N204)				E							L	M	N
	NITROGEN OXIDE (NO)	10102-43-9													M	N
	NITROGEN OXIDE (NO2)	10202-44-0													M	N
	NITROGEN TETROXIDE	10544-72-6													M	N
	NITROGEN TRIFLUORIDE	7783-54-2													M	N
	NITROGLYCERIN	55-63-0				D			G						M	N
	NITROPHENOLS, ALL ISOMERS	25154-55-6														
	NITROPROPANES	25322-01-4														
	NITROSODIMETHYLAMINE	62-75-9	SEE N-NITROSODIMETHYLAMINE												M	N
	NITROTOLUENES	1321-12-6														N

CALIFORNIA ENVIROMENTAL PROTECTION AGENCY
CHEMICAL LIST OF LISTS - BY CHEMICAL NAME

NEW CHEMICAL	CHEMICAL NAME	CAS NUMBER	A	B	C	D	E	F	G	H	I	J	K	L	M	N
	NITROUS OXIDE	10024-97-2														N
	NITTOMETHANE	75-52-5													M	N
	NONANE	111-84-2													M	N
	NORBORMIDE	991-42-4					E									
	NORETHISTERONE	68-22-4							G				K			N
	NORETHISTERONE ACETATE (NORETHINDRONE ACETATE)	51-98-9											K		M	N
	NORGESTREL	6533-00-2							G				K			
*	O,O-DIETHYL O-PYRAZINYL PHOSPHOROTHIOATE	297-97-2	SEE THIONAZIN													
	O-AMINOAZOTOLUENE	97-56-3	SEE C.I. SOLVENT YELLOW 3													
	O-ANISIDINE	90-04-0				D			G				K		M	N
	O-ANISIDINE HYDROCHLORIDE	134-29-2				D			G			J	K		M	N
	O-CHLOROBENZYLIDENE MALONONITRILE	2698-41-1													M	N
	O-CHLOROSTYRENE	1331-28-8														N
	O-CHLOROTOLUENE	95-49-8													M	N
	O-CRESOL(2)	95-48-7				D	E		G						M	N
	O-DINITROBENZENE	528-29-0				D			G			J				N
	O-METHYLCYOHEXANONE	583-60-8				D			G				K		M	N
	O-PHENYLPHENATE, SODIUM		SEE SODIUM O-PHENYLPHENATE													
	O-SEC-BUTYLPHENOL	89-72-5							G				K		M	N
	O-TOLUIDINE	95-53-4				D			G			J			M	+
	O-TOLUIDINE HYDROCHLORIDE	636-21-5				D			G				K		M	N
	O-XYLENE	95-47-6		+		D			G	H		J				+
	OCHRATOXIN A	303-47-9							G				K			+
	OCTACHLORONAPHTHALENE	2234-13-1				D			G						M	N
	OCTANE	111-65-9													M	N
	OIL MIST, MINERAL	8012-95-1											K		M	N
	OIL ORANGE SS	2646-17-5							G				K		M	+
	ORAL CONTRACEPTIVES, COMBINED															
	ORAL CONTRACEPTIVES, SEQUENTIAL															
	ORDRAM (MOLINATE)	2212-67-1		+				F								+
	ORGANIC PHOSPHATE													L		
	ORGANIC PHOSPHATE MIXED WITH COMPRESSED GAS													L		
	ORGANORHODIUM COMPLEX						E									
	OSMIUM TETROXIDE	20816-12-0							G						M	N

260

CALIFORNIA ENVIRONMENTAL PROTECTION AGENCY
CHEMICAL LIST OF LISTS - BY CHEMICAL NAME

NEW CHEMICAL	CHEMICAL NAME	CAS NUMBER	A	B	C	D	E	F	G	H	I	J	K	L	M	N
	OUABAIN	630-60-4					E									N
	OXADIAZON	19666-30-9													M	N
	OXALIC ACID	144-62-7												M	M	N
	OXAMYL	23135-22-0			C		E						K			N
*	OXAZEPAM	604-75-1											K			N
	OXETANE, 3,3-BIS(CHLOROMETHYL)-	78-71-7					E									N
*	OXIRANE	75-21-8	SEE ETHYLENE OXIDE													
	OXYDISULFOTON	2497-07-6					E									N
	OXYGEN DIFLUORIDE	7783-41-7														N
	OXYMETHOLONE	434-07-1							G				K	M	M	
	OXYTETRACYCLINE	79-57-2											K	M	M	
	OXYTETRACYCLINE HYDROCHLORIDE (INTERNAL USE)	2058-46-0											K			
	OZONE	10028-15-6					E		G						M	N
	P-ALPHA,ALPHA,ALPHA-TETRACHLOROTOLUENE	5216-25-1							G				K		M	N
	P-AMINOAZOBENZENE	60-09-3	SEE 4-AMINOAZOBENZENE						G							
	P-ANISIDINE	104-94-9				D			G							N
*	P-BENZOQUINONE DIOXIME	105-11-3		B												N
	P-CHLORO-M-CRESOL	54548-50-4														+
	P-CHLORO-O-TOLUIDINE	95-69-2							G				K			N
	P-CRESIDINE	120-71-8				D			G							
	P-CRESOL	106-44-5				D			G			J	K			N
	P-DICHLOROBENZENE	106-46-7	SEE 1,4-DICHLOROBENZENE													
	P-DIMETHYLAMINOAZOBENZENE	60-11-7	SEE 4-DIMETHYLAMINOAZOBENZENE													
	P-DINITROBENZENE	100-25-4				D			G				K		M	N
	P-NITROANILINE	100-01-6												M	M	N
	P-NITROCHLOROBENZENE	100-00-5												M	M	N
	P-NITROSODIPHENYLAMINE	156-10-5				D			G			J	K			
	P-PHENYLENEDIAMINE	106-50-3				D			G						M	N
	P-TERT-BUTYLTOLUENE	98-51-1														+
	P-TOLUIDINE	106-49-0							G				K	M	M	N
	P-XYLENE	106-42-3				D			G	H					M	N
	P-a,a,a-TETRACHLOROTOLUENE	5216-25-1	SEE P-ALPHA,ALPHA,ALPHA-TETRACHLOROTOLUENE													
	PAHS(POLYCYCLIC AROMATIC HYDROCARBONS)								G	H						
*	PALLADIUM	7440-05-3														N

CALIFORNIA ENVIRONMENTAL PROTECTION AGENCY
CHEMICAL LIST OF LISTS - BY CHEMICAL NAME

NEW CHEMICAL	CHEMICAL NAME	CAS NUMBER	A	B	C	D	E	F	G	H	I	J	K	L	M	N
	PANFURAN S												K			N
	PANFURAN S (DIHYDROXYMETHYLFURATRIZINE)	794-93-4							G						M	+
	PARAFFIN WAX FUME	8002-74-2													M	N
	PARAFORMALDEHYDE	30525-89-4							G				K			N
	PARAMETHADIONE	115-67-3					E								M	N
	PARAQUAT	1910-42-5			C		E									
	PARAQUAT METHOSULFATE	2074-50-2					E								M	
*	PARASORBIC ACID	10048-32-5														N
	PARATHION	56-38-2			C	D	E		G	H		J			M	N
	PARATHION AND COMPRESSED GAS MIXTURE															
	PARATHION-METHYL	298-00-0	SEE METHYL PARATHION											L		
	PARIS GREEN	12002-03-8					E									+
	PCB-1016 (AROCLOR 1016)	12674-11-2		B												+
	PCB-1221 (AROCLOR 1221)	11104-28-2		B												+
	PCB-1232 (AROCLOR 1232)	11141-16-5		B												+
	PCB-1248 (AROCLOR 1248)	12672-29-6		B												+
	PCB-1254 (AROCLOR 1254)	11097-69-1		B											M	N
	PCB-1260 (AROCLOR 1260)	11096-82-5		B												+
	PCBS	1336-36-3	SEE POLYCHLORINATED BIPHENYLS													
	PENICILLAMINE	52-67-5											K			N
*	PENICILLIC ACID	90-65-3														N
	PENTABORANE	19624-22-7					E							L	M	N
*	PENTACHLOROETHANE	76-01-7														N
	PENTACHLOROMONAPHTHALENE	1321-64-8													M	+
	PENTACHLORONITROBENZENE	82-68-8		B	C	D			G	H		J				N
	PENTACHLOROPHENOL	87-86-5		B	C	D	E		G	H		J	K		M	N
	PENTADECYLAMINE	2570-26-5					E									
	PENTAERTYHRITOL	115-77-5														
	PENTANE	109-66-0														N
	PENTOBARBITAL SODIUM	57-33-0							G						M	
	PERACETIC ACID	79-21-0				D	E		G				K		M	N
	PERCHLOROETHYLENE	127-18-4	SEE TETRACHLOROETHYLENE													
	PERCHLOROMETHYLMERCAPTAN	594-42-3					E							L	M	N
	PERCHLORYL FLUORIDE	7616-94-6													M	N

CALIFORNIA ENVIRONMENTAL PROTECTION AGENCY
CHEMICAL LIST OF LISTS - BY CHEMICAL NAME

NEW CHEMICAL	CHEMICAL NAME	CAS NUMBER	A	B	C	D	E	F	G	H	I	J	K	L	M	N
*	PERTHANE	72-56-0														N
	PHENACEMIDE	63-98-9							G				K			N
	PHENACETIN	62-44-2							G				K			+
	PHENANTHRENE	85-01-8		B	C											N
	PHENAZOPYRIDINE	94-78-0							G				K			N
	PHENAZOPYRIDINE HYDROCHLORIDE	136-40-3							G				K			N
	PHENESTERIN	3546-10-9							G				K			
	PHENOBARBITAL	50-06-6							G				K			+
	PHENOL	108-95-2		B	C	D	E		G						M	N
	PHENOL, 2,2'-THIOBIS[4-CHLORO-6-METHYL-	4418-66-0					E			H		J				
	PHENOL, 3-(1-METHYLETHYL)-, METHYLCARBAMATE	64-00-6					E								M	N
	PHENOTHIAZINE	92-84-2													M	
	PHENOXARSINE, 10,10'-OXYDI-	58-36-6					E									
	PHENOXYBENZAMINE	59-96-1							G				K			
	PHENOXYBENZAMINE HYDROCHLORIDE	63-92-3							G				K			N
*	PHENPROCOUMON	435-97-2											K			
	PHENYL DICHLOROARSINE	696-28-6					E									N
	PHENYL ETHER, VAPOR	101-84-8											K	L	M	N
	PHENYL GLYCIDYL ETHER	122-60-1							G				K		M	
	PHENYL ISOCYANATE	103-71-9												L	M	N
	PHENYL MERCAPTAN	108-98-5												L	M	N
	PHENYLCARBYLAMINE CHLORIDE	622-44-6												L		
	PHENYLHYDRAZINE	100-63-0											+		M	N
	PHENYLHYDRAZINE HYDROCHLORIDE	59-88-1					E									
	PHENYLMERCURY ACETATE	62-38-4					E								M	N
	PHENYLPHOSPHINE	638-21-1							G						M	
	PHENYLSILATRANE	2097-19-0					E									
	PHENYLTHIOUREA	103-85-5					E									
	PHENYLTRICHLOROSILENE	57-41-0	SEE TRICHLOROPHENYLSILANE													
	PHENYTOIN AND SODIUM SALT OF PHENYTOIN	298-02-2	SEE DIPHENYLHYDANTOIN		C		E									
	PHORATE						E								M	N
	PHOSACETIM	4104-14-7					E								M	N
	PHOSFOLAN	947-02-4					E									
	PHOSGENE	75-44-5				D	E		G			J		L	M	N

NEW CHEMICAL	CHEMICAL NAME	CAS NUMBER	A	B	C	D	E	F	G	H	I	J	K	L	M	N
	PHOSMET	732-11-6					E									N
	PHOSPHAMIDON	13171-21-6					E									N
	PHOSPHINE	7803-51-2					E		G			J		L	M	N
	PHOSPHONOTHIOIC ACID, METHYL-, S-(2-(BIS(1-METHYLETHYL)AMINO)ETHYL)O-ETHYL ESTER	50782-69-9					E									
	PHOSPHONOTHIOIC ACID, METHYL-, O-ETHYL O-(4-(METHYLTHIO)PHENYL)	2703-13-1					E									
	PHOSPHONOTHIOIC ACID, METHYL-,O-(4-NITROPHENYL) O-PHENYL ESTER	2665-30-7					E									
	PHOSPHORIC ACID	7664-38-2				D	E		G						M	N
	PHOSPHORIC ACID, DIMETHYL 4-(METHYLTHIO) P	3254-63-5					E								M	N
	PHOSPHOROTHIOIC ACID, O,O-DIMETHYL-S-(2-(M	2587-90-8					E								M	N
	PHOSPHORUS (YELLOW OR WHITE)	7723-14-0				D	E		G			J			M	N
	PHOSPHORUS COMPOUNDS								G							
	PHOSPHORUS OXYCHLORIDE	10025-87-3					E		Q					L	M	N
	PHOSPHORUS PENTACHLORIDE	10026-13-8					E		G						M	N
	PHOSPHORUS PENTASULFIDE	1314-80-3					E		G						M	N
	PHOSPHORUS PENTOXIDE	1314-56-3					E		G						M	N
	PHOSPHORUS TRICHLORIDE	7719-12-2					E		G					L	M	N
	PHOSPHORUS TRIFLUORIDE	7783-55-3												L	M	
	PHTHALIC ANHYDRIDE	85-44-9				D	E		G			J			M	N
	PHYSOSTIGMINE	57-47-6					E									
	PHYSOSTIGMINE, SALICYLATE (1:1)	57-64-7					E									
	PICLORAM	1918-02-1													M	N
	PICRIC ACID	88-89-1				D									M	N
	PICROTOXIN	124-87-8					E									
	PIPERAZINE DIHYDROCHLORIDE	142-64-3													M	
	PIPERIDINE	110-89-4					E									
	PIPOBROMAN	54-91-1											K			
	PIRIMIFOS-ETHYL	23505-41-1					E		G						M	N
	PIVAL	83-26-1													M	+
	PLASTER OF PARIS	26499-65-0													M	
	PLATINUM METAL	7440-66-4														
	PLICAMYCIN	18378-89-7							G				K		M	N

264

CALIFORNIA ENVIRONMENTAL PROTECTION AGENCY
CHEMICAL LIST OF LISTS - BY CHEMICAL NAME

NEW CHEMICAL	CHEMICAL NAME	CAS NUMBER	A	B	C	D	E	F	G	H	I	J	K	L	M	N
	POLYBROMINATED BIPHENYLS (PBBS)															N
	POLYCHLORINATED BIPHENYLS	1336-36-3			C	D			G				K		M	N
	POLYCHLORINATED BIPHENYLS (CONTAINING 60 OR MORE PERCENT CHLORINE BY MOLECULAR WEIGHT)					D			G			J	K			N
*	POLYCHLORINATED DIBENZO-P-DIOXINS								G				K			
	POLYGEENAN	53973-98-1							G							
*	POLYVINYL PYRROLIDONE	9003-39-8											K			N
	POM (POLYCYCLIC ORGANIC MATERIAL) (OTHER THAN PAHS)								G							N
	PONCEAU 3R	3564-09-8							G				K			N
	PONCEAU MX	3761-53-3	SEE C.I. FOOD RED 5													
*	POTASSIUM	7440-09-7														N
*	POTASSIUM ARSENATE (ASH3O4.XK)	7784-41-0														N
	POTASSIUM ARSENITE	10124-50-2					E									+
*	POTASSIUM BIS(2-HYDROXYETHYL)DITHIOCARBAMATE	23746-34-1							G				K			N
	POTASSIUM BROMATE	7758-01-2														+
*	POTASSIUM CHROMATE	7789-00-6					E									N
	POTASSIUM CYANIDE	151-50-8														+
*	POTASSIUM DICHROMATE	7778-50-9					E									N
	POTASSIUM HYDROXIDE	1310-58-3													M	N
	POTASSIUM PERMANGANATE	7722-64-7														N
	POTASSIUM SILVER CYANIDE	506-61-6					E						K			N
	PROCARBAZINE	671-16-9														N
	PROCARBAZINE HYDROCHLORIDE	366-70-1							G				K			N
	PROGESTERONE	57-83-0							G				K			N
	PROGESTINS								G							
	PROMECARB	2631-37-0					E									N
	PROMETRYN	7287-19-6			C											N
*	PRONETALOL HYDROCHLORIDE	51-02-5														N
	PROPANE	74-98-6			C				G						M	N
	PROPANE SULTONE	1120-71-4				D						J				N
	PROPANIL	709-98-8														N
	PROPARGITE	2312-35-8											J	K		N
	PROPARGYL ALCOHOL	107-19-7													M	N

NEW CHEMICAL	CHEMICAL NAME	CAS NUMBER	A	B	C	D	E	F	G	H	I	J	K	L	M	N
	PROPARGYL BROMIDE	106-96-7					E									N
*	PROPHAM	122-24-9														N
	PROPIOLACTONE, BETA-	57-57-8	SEE BETA-PROPIOLACTONE													
	PROPIONALDEHYDE	123-38-6				D			G			J				
	PROPIONIC ACID	97-09-4														
	PROPIONIC ANHYDRIDE	123-62-6														
	PROPIONITRILE	107-12-0					E								M	
	PROPIONITRILE, 3-CHLORO-	542-76-7					E									N
	PROPIOPHENONE, 4-AMINO-	70-69-9					E									N
	PROPOXUR	114-26-1				D			G	H		J			M	
	PROPYLENE GLYCOL DINITRATE	6423-43-4														N
	PROPYL CHLOROFORMATE	109-61-5				D	E		G							N
	PROPYLENE (PROPENE)	115-07-1												L		N
	PROPYLENE GLYCOL MONOMETHYL ETHER	107-98-2														N
	PROPYLENE OXIDE	75-56-9				D	E		G		I		K		M	N
	PROPYLENEIMINE	75-55-8				D	E		G			J	K		M	N
	PROPYLTHIOURACIL	51-52-5							G			J	K		M	N
	PROTHOATE	2275-18-5					E									
	PYRENE	129-00-0		B	C		E								M	+
	PYRETHRINS	121-21-1													M	N
	PYRETHRUM	8003-34-7													M	N
	PYRIDINE	110-86-1				D	E		G							
	PYRIDINE, 2-METHYL-5-VINYL-	140-76-1					E									
	PYRIDINE, 4-AMINO-	504-24-5					E									
	PYRIDINE, 4-NITRO-, 1-OXIDE	1124-33-0					E									
	PYRIMETHAMINE	58-14-0														N
	PYRIMINIL	53558-25-1					E									
*	QUARTZ	14808-60-7													M	N
	QUERCETIN	117-39-5										J			M	N
	QUINOLINE	91-22-5				D			G			J				
	QUINONE	106-51-4				D			G			J			M	
	QUINTOZENE	82-68-8	SEE PENTACHLORONITROBENZENE													
	RADIONUCLIDES								G			J				N
*	RADIUM 226	7440-1404			C								K			

CALIFORNIA ENVIRONMENTAL PROTECTION AGENCY
CHEMICAL LIST OF LISTS - BY CHEMICAL NAME

NEW CHEMICAL	CHEMICAL NAME	CAS NUMBER	A	B	C	D	E	F	G	H	I	J	K	L	M	N
*	RADON	10043-92-2														N
	RADON AND ITS DECAY PRODUCTS								G							
	RESERPINE	50-55-5							G				K			+
	RESIDUAL (HEAVY) FUL OILS								G				K			
	RESORCINOL	108-46-3													M	N
	RETINOL / RETINYL ESTERS, WHEN IN DAILY DOSAGE IN								G				K			
	EXCESS OF 10,000 IU,OR 3,000 RETINOL EQUIVALENTS															
*	RETRORSINE	480-54-6														N
	RHODIUM	7440-16-6													M	N
	RIBAVIRIN	36791-04-5							G				K			+
*	RIFAMPICIN	13292-46-1														N
	ROCKWOOL (MAN-MADE FIBERS)								G							
	RONNEL	299-84-3													M	N
	ROTENONE, COMMERCIAL	83-79-4													M	N
*	SACCHARATED IRON OXIDE	8047-67-4														N
	SACCHARIN	81-07-2				D			G				K			
	SACCHARIN, SODIUM	128-44-9							G				K			
	SAFROLE	94-59-7				D			G				K			
	SALCOMINE	14167-18-1					E									N
	SARIN	107-44-8					E									
	SEC-AMYL'ACETRATE (ALL ISOMERS AND MIXTURES)	626-38-0													M	
	SEC-BUTYL ACETATE	105-46-4													M	
	SEC-BUTYL ALCOHOL	78-92-2				D			G						M	
	SEC-BUTYL CHLOROFORMATE	17462-58-7												L		
*	SECOBARBITAL SODIUM	309-43-3					E						K			
	SELENIOUS ACID	7783-00-8					E								M	+
*	SELENIUM	7782-49-2		B	+	D		F	G						M	+
	SELENIUM COMPOUNDS					D			G							N
	SELENIUM HEXAFLUORIDE	7783-79-1													M	
	SELENIUM OXIDE	7446-08-4					E									
	SELENIUM OXYCHLORIDE	7791-23-3							G				K			
	SELENIUM SULFIDE	7446-34-6					E									
	SEMICARBAZIDE HYDROCHLORIDE	563-41-7													M	N
	SESONE	136-78-7														N

CALIFORNIA ENVIRONMENTAL PROTECTION AGENCY
CHEMICAL LIST OF LISTS - BY CHEMICAL NAME

NEW CHEMICAL	CHEMICAL NAME	CAS NUMBER	A	B	C	D	E	F	G	H	I	J	K	L	M	N
	SHALE-OILS	68308-34-9							G				K			+
*	SIDURON	1982-49-6													M	N
	SILANE	7803-62-5														N
	SILANE, (4-AMINOBUTYL)DIETHOXYMETHYL-	3037-72-7					E									
	SILICA	7631-86-9														N
	SILICA, AMORPHOUS	61790-53-2											K		M	
	SILICA, CRYSTALLINE (AIRBORNE PARTICLES OF RESPIRABLE SIZE)															
	SILICA, CRYSTALLINE, TRIPOLI	1317-95-9							G						M	N
	SILICA, FUSED	60676-86-0													M	N
	SILICON	7440-21-3													M	N
	SILICON CARBIDE	409-21-2													M	N
	SILVER	7440-22-4		B		D		F	G						M	N
	SILVER COMPOUNDS			+		D									M	N
*	SILVER NITRATE	7761-88-8														
	SIMAZINE	122-34-9			C			F								
	SLAGWOOD (MAN-MADE FIBERS)								G						M	N
	SODIUM	7440-23-5					E									+
	SODIUM ARSENATE (ASH3O4.XNA)	7631-89-2					E									+
	SODIUM ARSENITE	7784-46-5					E								M	N
	SODIUM AZIDE	26628-22-8					E									N
*	SODIUM BIFLUORIDE	1333-83-1														N
	SODIUM BISULFITE	7631-90-5					E								M	N
	SODIUM CACODYLATE	124-65-2														
*	SODIUM CHROMATE	7775-11-3					E									+
	SODIUM CYANIDE	143-33-9														+
	SODIUM DICHROMATE	10588-01-9							G							+
	SODIUM DODECYLBENZENE SULFONATE	25155-30-0														N
*	SODIUM FLUORIDE	7681-49-4					E								M	N
	SODIUM FLUOROACETATE	62-74-8														N
	SODIUM HYDROSULFIDE	16721-80-5														N
	SODIUM HYDROXIDE	1310-73-2							G						M	N
	SODIUM HYPOCHLORITE	7681-52-9														N
	SODIUM METABISULFITE	7681-57-4													M	N

CALIFORNIA ENVIRONMENTAL PROTECTION AGENCY
CHEMICAL LIST OF LISTS - BY CHEMICAL NAME

NEW CHEMICAL	CHEMICAL NAME	CAS NUMBER	A	B	C	D	E	F	G	H	I	J	K	L	M	N
	SODIUM METHYLATE	124-41-4														N
	SODIUM NITRITE	7632-00-0														N
	SODIUM O-PHENYLPHENATE	132-27-4							G				K			+
*	SODIUM PHOSPHATE, DIBASIC	7558-79-4														N
*	SODIUM PHOSPHATE, TRIBASIC	7785-84-4														N
	SODIUM SELENATE (H2O4SE.2NA)	13410-01-0					E									
	SODIUM SELENITE (H2O3SE.2NA)	10102-18-8					E									
	SODIUM TELLURITE	10102-20-2					E									
	SOOTS								G							
	SOOTS, TARS, AND CERTAIN MINERAL OILS (SEE NOTE 1)															
*	SPIRONOLACTONE	52-01-7											K			N
	STANNANE, ACETOXYTRIPHENYL	900-95-8					E									
	STANNOUS OXIDE	21651-19-4													M	
	STERIGMATOCYSTIN	10048-13-2							G				K		M	N
	STIBINE	7803-52-3														+
	STODDARD SOLVENT	8052-41-3													M	N
	STREPTOMYCIN SULFATE	3810-74-0											K			
	STREPTOZOTOCIN	18883-66-4							G				K			+
	STRONTIUM	7440-24-6			+											+
	STRONTIUM CHROMATE	7789-06-2							G							N
	STRYCHNINE	57-24-9					E								M	+
	STRYCHNINE, SULFATE	60-41-3					E									N
	STYRENE (MONOMER)	100-42-5				D			G				K			N
	STYRENE OXIDE	96-09-3				D			G			J				+
	SUBTILISINS	1395-21-7														N
*	SUCCINIC ANHYDRIDE	108-30-5													M	N
	SULFALLATE	95-06-7							G				K			+
*	SULFAMETHOXAZOLE	723-46-6														N
	SULFOTEP	3689-24-5					E								M	N
*	SULFOXIDE, 3-CHLOROPROPYL OCTYL	3569-57-1					E									N
*	SULFUR	7704-34-9												L		N
	SULFUR ACID	7664-93-9	SEE SULFURIC ACID													
	SULFUR CHLORIDE (MONO)													L		
	SULFUR CHLORIDE/CARBON TETRACHLORIDE MIXTURE															

CALIFORNIA ENVIRONMENTAL PROTECTION AGENCY
CHEMICAL LIST OF LISTS - BY CHEMICAL NAME

NEW CHEMICAL	CHEMICAL NAME	CAS NUMBER	A	B	C	D	E	F	G	H	I	J	K	L	M	N
	SULFUR DIOXIDE	7446-09-5					E								X	N
	SULFUR HEXAFLUORIDE	2551-62-4													X	N
	SULFUR MONOCHLORIDE	10025-67-9													X	N
	SULFUR PENTAFLUORIDE	5714-22-7					E								X	N
	SULFUR TETRAFLUORIDE	7783-60-0					E								X	N
	SULFUR TRIOXIDE	7446-11-9												L	X	
	SULFURIC ACID	7664-93-9				D	E		G						X	N
	SULFURYL CHLORIDE	7791-25-5												L	X	N
	SULFURYL FLUORIDE	2699-79-8													X	N
	SULPHAN BLUE	129-17-9														+
*	SULPROFOS	35400-43-2														
	TABUN	77-81-6					E								X	N
	TALC	14807-96-6														
	TALC CONTAINING ASBESTIFORM FIBERS								G				K			
	TAMOXIFEN CITRATE	54965-24-1							G				K		X	N
	TANTALUM	7440-25-7													X	N
	TANTALUM OXIDE	1314-61-0													X	N
	TELLURIUM	13494-80-9					E								X	N
	TELLURIUM HEXAFLUORIDE	7783-80-4					E								X	+
	TEMAZEPAM	846-50-4							G				K		X	N
	TEMPEPHOS	3383-96-8													X	N
	TEPP	107-49-3					E									
	TERBUFOS	13071-79-9					E									
	TEREPHTHALIC ACID	100-21-0							G							N
*	TERPENE POLYCHLORINATES (STROBANE6)	8001-50-1														
	TERRACHLOR (PENTACHLORONITROBENZENE)		SEE PCNB													
	TERT-BUTYL ACETATE	540-88-5													X	N
	TERT-BUTYL ALCOHOL	75-65-0				D			G						X	N
	TERT-BUTYL CHROMATE	1189-85-1													X	+
	TERT-BUTYL ISOCYANATE	1609-86-5												L		
	TERT-OCTYL MERCAPTAN	141-59-3												L		
	TESTOSTERONE AND ITS ESTERS	58-22-0							G				K		X	
	TESTOSTERONE CYPIONATE	58-20-8											K			
	TESTOSTERONE ENANTHATE	315-37-7							G				K			+

CALIFORNIA ENVIRONMENTAL PROTECTION AGENCY
CHEMICAL LIST OF LISTS - BY CHEMICAL NAME

NEW CHEMICAL	CHEMICAL NAME	CAS NUMBER	A	B	C	D	E	F	G	H	I	J	K	L	M	N
	TETRACHLOROETHYLENE	127-18-4		B	C			F	G						M	N
	TETRACHLORONAPHTHALENE	1335-88-2													M	N +
	TETRACHLORVINPHOS	961-11-5				D			G							+
	TETRACYCLINE (INTERNAL USE)	60-54-8											K			
	TETRACYCLINE HYDROCHLORIDE	64-75-5											K			
*	TETRACYCLINES												K			
	TETRAETHYL PYROPHOSPHATE AND COMPRESSED GAS															
	TETRAETHYL SILICATE	78-10-4	SEE ETHYL SILICATE											L		
*	TETRAETHYLDITHIOPYROPHOSPHATE	3689-24-5	SEE SULFOTEP													
	TETRAETHYLLEAD	78-00-2					E								M	+
	TETRAETHYLTIN	597-64-8					E									N
	TETRAHYDROFURAN	109-99-9													M	N +
	TETRAMETHYL LEAD	75-74-1					E								M	N
	TETRAMETHYL SUCCINONITRILE	3333-52-6													M	N
	TETRANITROMETHANE	509-14-8					E		G				K	L	M	N
	TETRASODIUM PYROPHOSPHATE	7722-88-5													M	N
	TETRYL	479-45-8														N
	THALIDOMIDE	50-35-1							G				K			N
	THALLIUM	7440-28-0		B		D			G							
*	THALLIUM CHLORIDE TLCL	7791-12-0	SEE THALLOUS CHLORIDE	B												
	THALLIUM COMPOUNDS					D										
	THALLIUM SULFATE	10031-59-1					E								M	N +
*	THALLIUM(I) CARBONATE	6533-73-9	SEE THALLOUS CARBONATE													
*	THALLIUM(I) SULFATE	7446-18-6	SEE THALLOUS SULFATE													
	THALLOUS CARBONATE	6533-73-9					E									
	THALLOUS CHLORIDE	7791-12-0					E									
	THALLOUS MALONATE	2757-18-8					E									
	THALLOUS SULFATE	7446-18-6					E									
	THIOACETAMIDE	62-55-5				D			G				K			
	THIOBENCARB		SEE BOLERO													
	THIOCARBAZIDE	2231-57-4					E									
	THIOFANOX	39196-18-4					E									
	THIOGLYCOLIC ACID	68-11-1													M	
	THIOGUANINE	154-42-7							G				K		M	N

NEW CHEMICAL	CHEMICAL NAME	CAS NUMBER	A	B	C	D	E	F	G	H	I	J	K	L	M	N
	THIOMAZIN	297-97-2														N
	THIONYL CHLORIDE	7719-09-7					E							L		+
	THIOPHENOL	108-98-5	SEE PHENYL MERCAPTAN											L		
	THIOPHOSGENE	463-71-8														
	THIOSEMICARBAZIDE	79-19-6					E									N
*	THIOURACIL	141-90-2														N
	THIOUREA	62-56-6				D			G				K			
	THIOUREA, (2-CHLOROPHENYL)-	5344-82-1					E									
	THIOUREA, (2-METHYLPHENYL)-	614-78-8					E									
*	THIOUREA, 1-NAPHTHALENYL	86-88-4	SEE ANTU													
	THIRAM	137-26-8													M	N
	THORIUM DIOXIDE	1314-20-1				D			G				K		M	N
	TIN	7440-31-5													M	N
	TITANIUM DIOXIDE	13463-67-7													M	
*	TITANIUM METAL POWDER	7440-32-6													M	N
	TITANIUM TETRACHLORIDE	7550-45-0				D	E					J		L		
	TOBACCO SMOKE								G				K			
	TOBACCO, ORAL USE OF SMOKELESS PRODUCTS								G				K			
	TOBRAMYCIN SULFATE	49842-07-1											K			
	TOLUENE	108-88-3		B	C	D	E		G	H			K		M	N
	TOLUENE DIISOCYANATE (MIXED ISOMERS)	26471-62-5				D			G				K		M	+
	TOLUENE-2,4-DIISOCYANATE	584-84-9				D	E		G			J	K		M	N
	TOLUENE-2,6-DIISOCYANATE	91-08-7				D	E		G							
	TOXAPHENE (POLYCHLORINATED CAMPHENES)	8001-35-2		B	C	D	E	F	G			J	K		M	N
	TRANS-1,2-DICHLOROETHYLENE	156-60-5		B	+	D	E	F	G							+
	TRANS-1,3-DICHLOROPROPENE	10061-02-6			C			F								
	TRANS-1,4-DICHLOROBUTENE	110-57-6					E									
	TRANS-2-[(DIMETHYLAMINO)METHYLIMINO]-5-[2-5-NITRO-2-FURYL)VINYL]-1,3,4-OXADIAZOLE	55738-54-0							G				K		M	N
	TREMOLITE	14567-73-8														N
	TREOSULFAN	299-75-2							G				K			
	TRIAMIPHOS	1031-47-6					E									
	TRIAZIQUONE	68-76-8				D			G				K			
	TRIAZOFOS	24017-47-8					E									+

CALIFORNIA ENVIRONMENTAL PROTECTION AGENCY
CHEMICAL LIST OF LISTS - BY CHEMICAL NAME

NEW CHEMICAL	CHEMICAL NAME	CAS NUMBER	A	B	C	D	E	F	G	H	I	J	K	L	M	N
	TRIAZOLAM	28911-01-5							G				K		M	N
	TRIBUTYL PHOSPHATE	126-73-8							G						M	N
	TRICHLORFON	52-68-6				D									M	N
	TRICHLORMETHINE (TRIMUSTINE HYDROCHLORIDE)	817-09-4											K			
	TRICHLORO(CHLOROMETHYL)SILANE	1558-25-4					E								M	N
	TRICHLORO(DICHLOROPHENYL)SILANE	27137-85-5					E								M	N
	TRICHLOROACETIC ACID	76-03-9					E								M	N
	TRICHLOROACETYL CHLORIDE	76-02-8					E								M	N
	TRICHLOROETHYLENE	79-01-6		B	C	D	E	F	G		I	J			M	N
	TRICHLOROETHYLSILANE	115-21-9					E								M	N
	TRICHLOROFLUOROMETHANE	75-69-4			C	+	E	F							M	N
*	TRICHLOROMETHANESULFENYL CHLORIDE	594-42-3	SEE PERCHLOROMETHYLMERCAPTAN							H						
	TRICHLORONAPHTHALENE	1321-65-9													M	N
	TRICHLORONATE	327-98-0					E								M	N
	TRICHLOROPHENOLS	25167-82-2														N
	TRICHLOROPHENYLSILANE	98-13-5					E								M	N
	TRIDYMITE	15468-32-3													M	
	TRIETHANOLAMINE DODECYLBENZENESULFONATE	27323-41-7					E									N
	TRIETHOXYSILANE	998-30-1														N
	TRIETHYL PHOSPHINE	78-40-0							G							N
*	TRIETHYLAMINE	121-44-8										J			M	N
*	TRIETHYLENE GLYCOL DIGLYCIDYL ETHER	1954-28-5													M	N
	TRIETHYLENEMELAMINE	51-18-3												L		
	TRIFLOUROMETHYLPHENYLISOCYANATE	1548-13-6														N
	TRIFLURALIN	1582-09-8				D						J			M	+
	TRILOSTANE	13647-35-3							G				K			
	TRILOSTANE	1347-35-3							G				K			
	TRIMELLITIC ANHYDRIDE	552-30-7													M	N
	TRIMETHADIONE	127-48-0							G				K			
	TRIMETHYL PHOSPHATE	512-56-1													M	N
	TRIMETHYL PHOSPHITE	121-45-9													M	N
	TRIMETHYLAMINE	75-50-3													M	N
	TRIMETHYLBENZENE	25551-13-7													M	N
	TRIMETHYLCHLOROSILANE	75-77-4					E							L	M	N

273

CALIFORNIA ENVIRONMENTAL PROTECTION AGENCY
CHEMICAL LIST OF LISTS - BY CHEMICAL NAME

NEW CHEMICAL	CHEMICAL NAME	CAS NUMBER	A	B	C	D	E	F	G	H	I	J	K	L	M	N
	TRIMETHYLOLPROPANE PHOSPHITE	824-11-3														N
	TRIMETHYLTIN CHLORIDE	1066-45-1					E									N
	TRIOTHOCRESYL PHOSPATE	78-30-8							G						M	N
	TRIPHENYL PHOSPHATE	115-86-6							G						M	N
	TRIPHENYL PHOSPHITE	101-02-0							G							
	TRIPHENYLAMINE	603-34-9													M	N
	TRIPHENYLTIN CHLORIDE	639-58-7					E									
*	TRIPHENYLTIN HYDROXIDE	76-87-9											K			
	TRIS(1-AZIRIDINYL) PHOSPHINE SULFIDE (THIOTEPA)	52-24-4							G				K			N
	TRIS(2,3-DIBROMOPROPYL) PHOSPHATE	126-72-7				D			G				K			N
	TRIS(2-CHLOROETHYL) PHOSPHATE	115-96-8											K			
	TRIS(2-CHLOROETHYL)AMINE	555-77-1					E									
	TRIS(AZIRIDINYL)-PARA-BENZOQUINONE (TRIAZIQUONE)	68-76-8	SEE TRIAZIQUONE													
	TRITHION	786-19-6					E			H						N
	TRITIUM	10028-17-8						F								
	TRP-P-1 (TRYPTOPHAN-P-1)	62450-06-0							G				K			+
	TRP-P-2 (TRYPTOPHAN-P-2)	62450-07-1							G				K			+
	TRYPAN BLUE	72-57-1							G				K			N
	TUNGSTEN METAL	7440-33-7													M	N
	TURPENTINE	8006-64-2													M	N
	UNLEADED GASOLINE (WHOLLY VAPORIZED)								G				K			
	URACIL MUSTARD	66-75-1							G				K			
	URANIUM	7440-61-1						F								N
*	URANYL ACETATE	541-09-3														
*	URANYL NITRATE SOLID	10102-06-4														
	URETHANE (ETHYL CARBAMATE) (MONOMER)	51-79-6				D			G			J	K			N
	UROFOLLITROPIN	26995-91-5							G				K			N
	VALERALDEHYDE	110-62-3														N
	VALINOMYCIN	2001-95-8					E								M	
	VALPROATE	99-66-1							G							
	VANADIUM (FUME OR DUST)	7440-62-2				D									M	N
	VANADIUM OXIDE (5)	1314-62-1					E								M	+
	VANADIUM PENTOXIDE		SEE VANADIUM OXIDE (5)													
	VANADYL SULFATE	27774-13-6														N

CALIFORNIA ENVIRONMENTAL PROTECTION AGENCY
CHEMICAL LIST OF LISTS - BY CHEMICAL NAME

NEW CHEMICAL	CHEMICAL NAME	CAS NUMBER	A	B	C	D	E	F	G	H	I	J	K	L	M	N
	VINBLASTINE SULFATE	143-67-9							G				K		M	N
	VINCRISTINE SULFATE	2068-78-2							G				K		M	N
	VINYL ACETATE	108-05-4				D	E		G			J			M	N
	VINYL BROMIDE	593-60-2				D			G			J	K		M	N
	VINYL CHLORIDE	75-01-4	A	B	C	D		F	G		I	J	K		M	N
	VINYL CYCLOHEXENE DIOXIDE	108-87-6														
	VINYLIDENE CHLORIDE	75-35-4	SEE 1,1-DICHLOROETHYLENE													
	VINYLTOLUENE	25013-15-4													M	N
	VM & P (VARISH MAKERS & PAINTERS) NAPHTHA	8030-30-6														N
	WARFARIN	81-81-2					E		G				K		M	N
	WARFARIN SODIUM	129-06-6					E		G							N
	WOOD PRESERVATIVES (CONTAINING ARSENIC & CHROMATE)															
	XYLENE	1330-20-7			C	D	E	F	G			J			M	N
	XYLENES				+											
	XYLENOL	1300-71-6						F	G							N
	XYLIDINE	1300-73-8					E							L	M	N
	XYLYL BROMIDE															
*	XYLYLENE DICHLORIDE	28347-13-9		B			E									N
	ZEARALENONE	17924-92-4														N
*	ZINC	7440-66-6		B	+	D		F	G							N
*	ZINC ACETATE	557-34-6														N
*	ZINC AMMONIUM CHLORIDE	14639-97-5														N
*	ZINC BORATE	1332-07-6														N
*	ZINC BROMIDE	7699-45-8														N
	ZINC CARBONATE	3486-35-9														N
	ZINC CHLORIDE FUME	7646-85-7														N
	ZINC CHROMATE, AS CR	13530-65-9				D										N
	ZINC COMPOUNDS															N
*	ZINC CYANIDE	557-21-1														N
*	ZINC FLUORIDE	7783-49-5														N
*	ZINC FORMATE	557-41-5														N
*	ZINC HYDROSULFITE	7779-86-4														N
*	ZINC NITRATE	7779-88-6														N
*	ZINC OXIDE	1314-13-2							G						M	N

CALIFORNIA ENVIRONMENTAL PROTECTION AGENCY
CHEMICAL LIST OF LISTS - BY CHEMICAL NAME

NEW CHEMICAL	CHEMICAL NAME	CAS NUMBER	A	B	C	D	E	F	G	H	I	J	K	L	M	N
*	ZINC PHENOLSULFONATE	127-82-2														N
	ZINC PHOSPHIDE	1314-84-7					E									+
*	ZINC SILICFLUORIDE	16871-71-9														N
	ZINC STEARATE	557-05-1														N
*	ZINC SULFATE	7733-02-0														N
	ZINC, DICHLORO(4,4-DIMETHYL-5(((METHYLAMINO) CARBONYL)OXY)IMINO)PENTANENITRILE)-	58270-08-9					E									
	ZINEB	12122-67-7				D			G				K			+
	ZIRAM	137-30-4			C											N
*	ZIRCONIUM HYDRIDE	7440-67-7														N
*	ZIRCONIUM NITRATE	13746-89-9														N
*	ZIRCONIUM POTASSIUM FLUORIDE	16923-95-8														N
*	ZIRCONIUM SULFATE	14644-61-2														N
	ZIRCONIUM TETRACHLORIDE	10026-11-6														N

NOTE 1:   Soots, tars and certain mineral oils (mineraloils may vary in composition, particularly in
          relation to their content of carcinogenic polycyclic aromatic hydrocarbons)

Key: * = a new chemical on the List of Lists

       + = a regulatory agency addition for a chemical

       - = a regulatory agency deletion for a chemical

276

California Chamber of Commerce
BUSINESS SURVIVAL GUIDES

Survival Guides to the Labor Law Jungle

California Labor Law Digest

Explains in lay terms how to comply with complex state and federal labor laws. Organized to help the reader find topics quickly. Includes special sections on how to calculate overtime and vacation pay, exempt vs. non-exempt employees, alcohol and drug abuse, employee benefit plans and military return rights. Revised annually to reflect new laws, expanded advice on current problem areas of law. *($65)*

EEO Discrimination in Employment

Clearly explains complex equal employment opportunity discrimination laws and how to avoid discrimination problems. Contains sample employment application and policies. Chapters on Americans with Disabilities Act, sexual harassment, AIDS, pregnancy, employees with disabilities, and statistics you must keep. Discrimination dos and don'ts. *($39)*

Employer Posters

All 12 posters required by the government attractively printed on two 23 x 36-inch posters. Avoid the hassle of contacting seven different state agencies to get them. Available in English and Spanish. One set is free with your purchase of both *Survival Guides to the Labor Law Jungle. ($10)*

Employee Handbook

Employee Handbook: How to Write One for Your Company

Explains why you should have a personnel policy. It then gives step-by-step instructions for writing one for your business. Contains sample policies and a sample handbook, which will enable any company to develop its own written employee handbook with a minimum of time and confusion. Protect your business and avoid unnecessary costly litigation by having your personnel policy in writing. *($45)*

Employee Handbook Software

Makes writing your employee handbook even easier. Select or modify the policies you need, push a button and print your customized, formatted employee handbook. Saves word processing time and makes future updates easy. *Bilingual* software lets you select pre-written policies in English, then print your handbook in both Spanish and English. Purchase of *Employee Handbook* is required so that you will have the legal reasoning and requirements behind the policies you select. (IBM PC-AT compatible — *not* XT; 3.5" or 5.25" diskette) *(English only $60. Bilingual $95)*

Employee Handbook Training Videos

Two-tape set helps you introduce your employee handbook. One video shows managers how to introduce the employee handbook to workers to ensure the least resistance and best results. The second video explains the purpose and benefits of your employee handbook to employees. English and Spanish version on the same tape. *($75)*

Sexual Harassment Prevention

Stopping Sexual Harassment: An Employer's Guide

Written in lay terms and easy to use. Includes policies and methods to prevent sexual harassment; information to train your staff members; a complete investigation procedure; help to prevent lawsuits and defuse explosive situations; critical documentation information in easy-to-understand terms; extensive checklists, forms and a step-by-step guide for investigations. *($39)*

Sexual Harassment Compliance Packet

As of January 1, 1993, all employers must comply with California's new sexual harassment law, AB 2264 (Speier). The packet contains everything you need to comply: a summary of AB 2264; 25 copies of the required Information Sheet to distribute to employees; a sample sexual harassment policy, a complaint and an investigation procedure. Helps employers stop sexual harassment without intervention from a governmental agency and/or attorneys. One packet is free with your purchase of both *Survival Guides to the Labor Law Jungle.* Available in English and Spanish.
(25 sheets to a packet. 1-3 packets: $10/packet; 4-19 packets: $8/packet; 20+ packets: $7.50/packet)

ADA Compliance

ADA: 10 Steps to Compliance

Easy-to-use, comprehensive guide shows you how to determine what you need to do to comply with the Americans with Disabilities Act (ADA), the most complex, sweeping labor law in years. Includes examples, worksheets, checklists, sample forms. Explains key terms, such as "essential functions," "reasonable accommodation," "direct threat," "undue hardship." *($40)*

ADA Software

Job descriptions identifying "essential job functions" are the best way to document your compliance with the ADA. This quality "graphical interface software" helps you write customized ADA-ready job descriptions quickly. Select from 1,300 sample complete job descriptions, then modify, combine, cut 'n' paste or add your own words. (IBM PC, XT, AT, PS/2-compatible with 640K RAM, DOS 2.11 or later. 3MB hard disk capacity. 3.5" or 5.25" disk) *($99)*

ADA Video Set

Two-tape set saves you time and give you the assurance that everyone who oversees or interviews other people will have the knowledge to keep your company out of trouble. One video gives your managers an overview of the ADA. The other shows a manager in action trying to prepare for an interview. *($75)*

Recycling for Business

■ Recycling Handbook for Business

Save time and confusion by starting your recycling and waste reduction program in an organized manner. The business person's guide to a cost-efficient waste reduction program. Follow the logical steps, fill out worksheets and refer to checklists. Model plans to follow for six industries — retail, wholesale, offices, manufacturers, construction and restaurants. *($35)*

■ Employee Training Video

Help build employee enthusiasm, pride and support in every aspect of your business with "Reduce...Reuse...Recycle... The Bottom Line." This video demonstrates techniques that small and large companies are using and which can be adapted readily by smaller and medium-sized firms in nearly every industry. It's an ideal way to launch your recycling program. *($35)*

■ Recycling Organizer

The *Recycling Organizer* will save you time, keep your program on track and document your waste reduction. It's a guide for the recycling novice and has easy-to-follow steps to document your recycling program. This well-planned system is a place to file your initial waste assessment, your waste reduction plan, vendor contracts and records of diverted waste. When the regulator calls, the *Organizer* documents your program and proves you're reducing solid waste. *($25)*

Cal/OSHA Kit

■ Cal/OSHA Handbook

The *Cal/OSHA Handbook* is written for businesspeople who aren't safety experts. It tells how to find the regulations which apply to your firm. Then it gives step-by-step instructions to satisfy the regulations that apply to every firm, and also the most costly rules that apply to most industries. Know what to do when the inspector arrives, your rights, when to appeal a citation and how to do it. *($40)*

■ SB 198 Handbook

SB 198 requires every employer to have a formal, written injury and illness prevention program. The *Handbook* is written with the premise that most employers can comply on a do-it-yourself basis. It contains legal requirements, sample plans to follow for various industries, fill-in-the-blank forms and step-by-step instructions. *($45)*

■ Hazard Communication Handbook

Hazard communication standards apply to every firm where employees may be exposed to chemicals. If you receive an MSDS (Material Safety Data Sheet) from a supplier then you need a hazard communication program. The *Hazard Communication Handbook* gives clear guidelines on how to write your own program. *($35)*

■ Cal/OSHA Organizer

The *Organizer* is a guide for the safety novice to comply with Cal/OSHA. Follow the steps in the *Organizer*. It refers to sections in the three companion handbooks where you'll get clear, detailed instructions on what you need to do, and cookbook-like steps on how to do it. Then file your safety programs and records right in the *Organizer*. *($25)*

Cal/OSHA Tools

■ Cal/OSHA: Beyond the Basics

This new book covers the hottest and newest Cal/OSHA regulations: bloodborne pathogens ● process safety management ● lead ● HAZWOPER ● asbestos ● confined spaces ● cadmium ● formaldehyde ● respiratory protection. Includes overview of the latest trends and developments and what they really mean to employers. A step-by-step guide on how to comply with many new regulations, complete with sample plans and procedures. Get a preview of draft regulations with a major impact on your business: tuberculosis ● ergonomics ● smoking in the workplace ● Federal OSHA reform ● SB 198 changes. *($69)*

■ SB 198 Software

The California Chamber's *SB 198 Software* is made to be used with our *SB 198 Handbook*. It helps you write your SB 198 program and much more. The software is an ongoing recordkeeping system that will save you tremendous amounts of time. Organizes your records of training, accidents and injuries. Allows you to "batch" in updates instead of making single, time-consuming entries. Reminds you to do inspections and training. (IBM PC-AT compatible — *not* XT; 3.5" or 5.25" diskette) *($195)*

■ SB 198 Video Safety Set

Two-tape set makes it easy for you to initially train employees and managers about your injury/illness prevention program then annually review important information. One video lets your employees know safety is their responsibility and very important to your company. It offers common sense instruction about safe work procedures. The second video tells your supervisors and managers how other companies are making their safety programs work and emphasizes the importance of training, hazard identification and inspections. Employee training video also available in Spanish. *(English set $75. Spanish tape $45)*

■ Hazard Communication Training

Comply with Cal/OSHA's second most-cited regulation — hazard communication. This standard requires that the employer have a written hazard communication plan, identify and label all chemicals and train employees by communicating information on Material Safety Data Sheets (MSDSs). This video emphasizes proper procedures to store and handle chemicals, reading an MSDS, and maintaining a workplace free from chemical hazards. (13 minutes) *($45 or $25 if you purchase the Safety Training Series Video set - see below)*

■ Safety Training Video Series

A complete video safety training program at an incredibly low price. You get 12 separate training sessions, each with a quality 8-17 minute video. A quiz at the end of each video keeps employees involved, increases retention and documents your training for Cal/OSHA. Videos will open discussion to unique safety issues at your company. The helpful leader's guide makes your role as safety instructor easy. The program comes on two cassettes, each with six training sessions:

Cassette #1, *Safety for All Employers*, covers the most important safety topics common to every business: reporting to work ● back injury prevention ● office safety ● fire prevention ● ergonomics ● bloodborne pathogens. *($119)* Available in Spanish.

Cassette #2, *Safety for Industrial Employers*, is for the more industrial workplaces with machinery and chemicals: personal protective equipment ● electrical safety ● flammables/combustibles ● machine guarding — lockout/tagout ● material handling equipment ● the environment. *($119)* Available in Spanish.

BONUS! Buy both cassettes for only $199 and get the Hazard Communication Training video for only $25 — Save $59.

Survival Guides to Avoid the Hidden Traps

■ **Guide to Hiring Independent Contractors**

Survive the IRS and state audit war against employers that misclassify workers as independent contractors. A single mistake can cost an employer $15,000 per worker per year. The guide details what factors the IRS looks for, explains special rules for over 300 industries and fatal flaws other companies have made. Contains a sample legal contract, pre-hire worksheet and required government forms. *($40)*

■ **Unemployment Insurance: A Cost You Can Cut**

Unemployment insurance benefit increases of 39 percent started in 1990, meaning wrongful claims and errors by the state and your firm will cost much more. The sweeping reform law that went into effect in 1990 provides protections to employers who know how the system works. Learn how to protest claims and how to audit every unemployment insurance form just like your firm audits any invoice. *($35)*

■ **Employer's Survival Guide to Workers' Compensation**

Explains California's complex workers' compensation system, including how to avoid unnecessary costs and litigation. Explains anti-fraud provisions and limits on stress claims. Chapter on stress teaches you how to avoid and manage stress claims. New information on experience modification and workers' comp and the Americans with Disabilities Act. Includes free Workers' Comp Fraud Kit. *($35)*

■ **Workers' Comp Fraud Kit**

Stop fraudulent workers' comp claims with the help of this kit designed to meet the requirements of the new workers' comp fraud prevention law. Contains: posters warning your employees that filing a phony workers' comp claim is a felony; stickers that you affix to workers' comp claim forms warning that fraud is a felony (meets your legal duty); checklist on how to spot fraud and what to do about it. Available in English and Spanish. One English kit is free with *Employer's Survival Guide to Workers' Compensation. ($5)*

■ **Workers' Comp Videos**

Two-tape video set begins with a strong statement that workers' comp fraud is a felony and that employees don't need a lawyer to get workers' comp benefits. These two videos target a major cause of skyrocketing workers' comp premiums: lawyers. The first video helps educate your employees about how the system works. A second and very similar video is to be shown to your injured workers. It reassures them their medical bills will be paid, they'll get cash benefits while out, and that you want them back on the job. *($39.95)* Available in Spanish.

For the New Small Business

■ **Business Start-Up Kits**

Provides every state, federal and most local government forms and permits necessary to start a business. Tells you what forms are necessary for your business and provides you with the forms, along with lay instructions on how to fill them out. Includes date reminder labels so you don't forget to file forms, and sample letters to government agencies. Three kits are available:

● **Sole Proprietorship/Partnership Kit** (18 forms) *($30)*
● **Corporation Kit** (28 forms) *($39)*
● **Employer Kit** (22 forms) *($34)*

Free with each *Kit:* "Starting and Succeeding in Business," a 40-page booklet covering the 10 biggest pitfalls small business owners encounter.

Environmental Library

■ **California Environmental Compliance Handbook**

Overall guide to California's unique and far-reaching environmental programs. Gives an overview of more than 20 of the most significant environmental programs, along with the essential steps to take for compliance. Provides concise descriptions of numerous additional, but less frequently encountered federal, state and local regulations that have an impact on business and local public facilities. The guide is your checklist and roadmap through California's maze of environmental regulations. *($45)*

■ **Proposition 65 Compliance**

This complex and confusing initiative imposes many requirements on businesses that use or distribute chemicals and products which contain ingredients known to the state to cause cancer or reproductive toxicity. More than 300 substances are subject to the law. The proposition provides for government prosecutions, as well as "bounty hunter" rewards for informants and citizen plaintiffs. The handbook is your best explanation of the law and how to comply. *($40)*

■ **Community Right-to-Know**

For firms that store, sell or use any of thousands of common materials or chemicals that are regulated by local governments under the concept of community right-to-know. Step-by-step instructions explain how to: determine if your firm handles hazardous materials, qualify for business plan exemptions, immediately report releases and develop a business plan in five easy steps. *($40)*

■ **Hazardous Waste Management**

For any business that uses or handles chemicals. Tells how to determine if your business generates hazardous waste, what permits are needed, how to manage hazardous waste, how to ship and dispose of waste and how to determine where permits can be required for certain hazardous waste activities. This handbook explains how to comply with this complicated and stringently enforced area of environmental law. *($49)*

■ **Environmental Organizer**

This tool organizes your many environmental programs and recordkeeping to demonstrate compliance. Divider sections in the *Organizer* provide brief descriptions of each environmental program and how to comply, with references to the companion handbooks for details. *($30)*

■ **California Regwatch**

A monthly newsletter to alert you to new environmental and Cal/OSHA regulations. It's your early warning system with concise news about proposed and enacted regulations. One-year subscription free with purchase of *Environmental Library.* Free to California Chamber members. Cannot be purchased.

International Trade Resources

International Trade Resources Guide

A comprehensive guide to resources available to the California business community for conducting international trade, including domestic and international chambers of commerce; international trade associations; education contacts; local, state and federal government officials; foreign trade zones; foreign government representatives; resources publications; glossaries; world holidays; metric conversion chart; international telephone calling codes; and world monetary units. The *Guide* lists more than 1,600 resources in the public and private sectors. *($17.50)*

Exporting Guide for California

A step-by-step manual to help the California company wishing to become involved in exporting or to expand existing export volumes. Covers organizing for export, identifying markets and distribution avenues, pricing, documentation, shipping and financing. Includes tips on avoiding common pitfalls, plus samples of key documents, including supplier/exporter and distribution agreements. Also highly useful for the person who is new to exporting, but works in a firm that already sells its goods or services in the international market. *($17.50)*

European Community and Europe: A Legal Guide to Business Development

Articles by attorneys and accountants from major international firms summarize important legal and financial considerations for companies doing business in the European Community and Europe. Includes overview of the creation of the European Economic Community, mergers, joint ventures, distribution and franchising agreements, commercial law, tax considerations, finance, employment law, standards, exporting requirements and other business concerns. Also covers major sectors: public procurement, high technology, environment, telecommunications, pharmaceuticals, energy and utilities. Country-specific chapters highlight requirements unique to individual nations in the EC or Europe. *($29.50)*

North American Free Trade Guide

A handbook to help businesses take advantage of opportunities to be created by the North American Free Trade Agreement (NAFTA), linking the United States with Canada and Mexico, its first and third largest trading partners. NAFTA will create the largest and richest market in the world, with 360 million consumers and $6 trillion in annual output. Focuses on what businesses need to know to gain access to the emerging Mexican market, plus good prospects for expansion in Canada. *($19.50)*

To Order Call 1-800-331-8877